Y0-DEV-465

Huan-Ying:
Workers' China

Map: Wu Chao-hsi

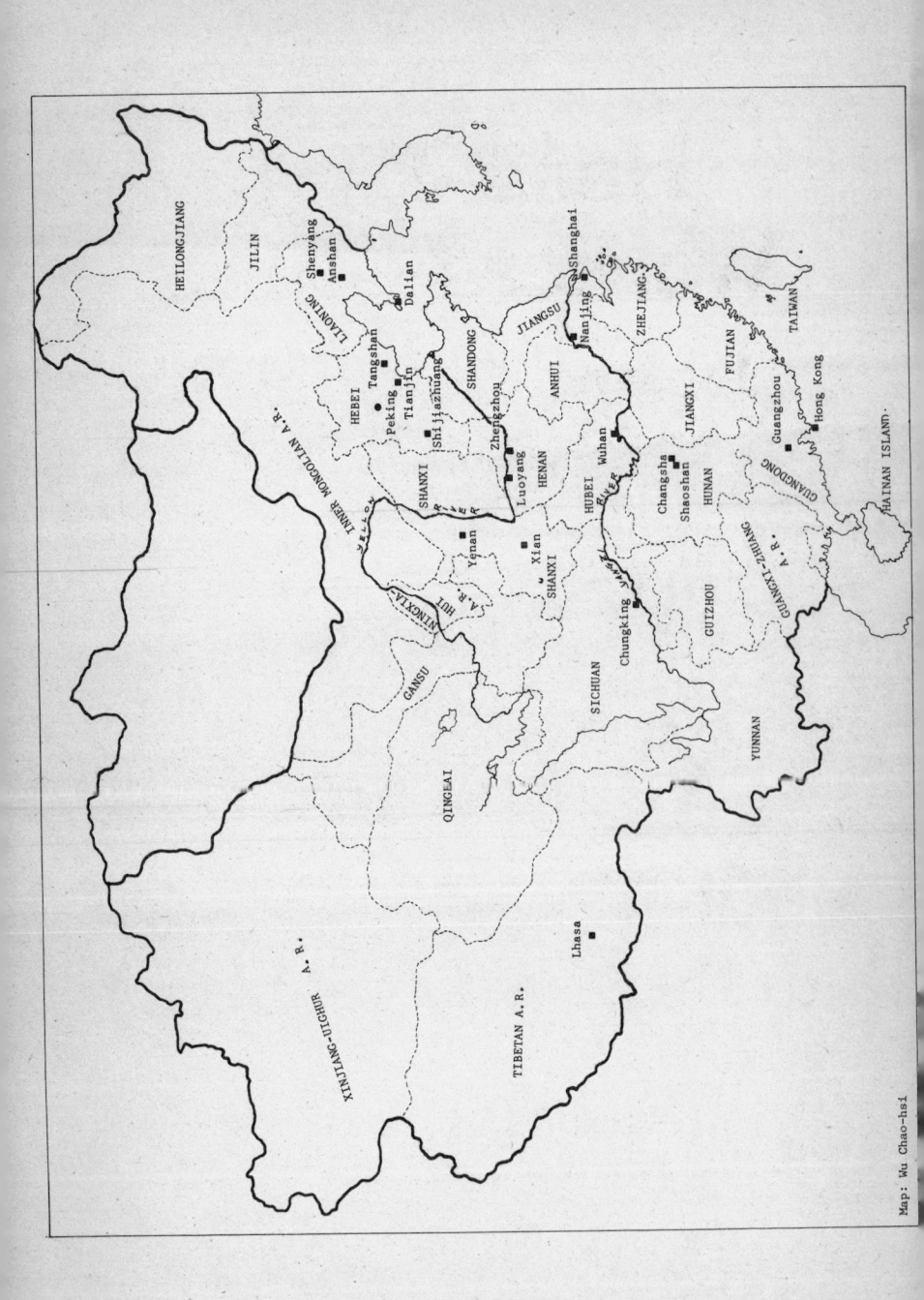

Huan-Ying: Workers' China

by Janet Goldwasser
and Stuart Dowty

Monthly Review Press
New York and London

Copyright © 1975 by Janet Goldwasser and Stuart Dowty
All Rights Reserved

Library of Congress Cataloging in Publication Data
Goldwasser, Janet.
    Huan-ying : worker's China.
    Includes bibliographical references.
    1. China—Description and travel—1949–
I. Dowty, Stuart, joint author. II. Title.
DS711.G623   915.1'03'5   74-7790
ISBN 0-85345-337-7

Monthly Review Press
62 West 14th Street, New York, N.Y. 10011
21 Theobalds Road, London WC1X 8SL

First Printing

Manufactured in the United States of America

Contents

Preface   9
1. Of Chivas Regal and Mao Tse-tung   11
2. Industry: The Leading Factor   41
3. Agriculture: The Foundation   95
4. Women: Half of Heaven   127
5. Leadership: Cadres and Party   190
6. Democracy in China: From the Masses to the Masses   228
7. Philosophy Is No Mystery   255
8. Principles of Chinese Socialism   277
9. National Minorities: Equality, Autonomy, and Unity   316
10. The Struggle Between Two Lines   337
11. Of China and Mao Tse-tung   386

Appendix   395

We wish to acknowledge the help of many friends, both old and new, who read sections of the manuscript during its various stages. The book was certainly improved because of their comments and criticisms. To all we offer our sincere thanks.

To the historic and unquenchable friendship between the people of China and the people of the United States

Preface

"Huan-ying! Huan-ying!" The greeting "Welcome! Welcome!" was something we heard repeatedly during our visit to the People's Republic of China.

We greet you now in the same spirit, passing along the warm welcome the Chinese extend to American friends. We invite you to share, to the extent we can make possible, our exciting experiences journeying through China.

We've written this account for two reasons. First, to provide a practical and useful analysis for those who want to understand modern socialist China but who are not necessarily socialists, and, second, to supply more information about the way Chinese socialism functions.

New China is a socialist country. This is important. To ignore it is akin to looking over a new car without inspecting the motor. To be sure, there are many other eye-catching features that are also important and relevant. But to find out what really makes a car run, one needs to look under the hood—and that's what we tried to do in China. But even after lifting the hood not everyone sees the same things. Individual perception depends to a large extent on previous experiences, education, background, opinions, prejudices, and biases—in short, one's preconditioning. Different people do, literally, see different things.

China is both old and young. During the past twenty years, most of us in the United States have been looking at China from only one perspective, that provided by the commercial, Western media. For the most part this has been a distorted, inaccurate, and incredibly ill-informed viewpoint. Look at its results:

Viewing China solely from a Western bias has ignored basic cultural, social, and economic conditions in China.

Viewing China from the free-enterprise perspective of the commercial media has ignored real, legitimate, and decisive aspects of China's socialist outlook.

We hope that by joining us in our journey through new China you will discover new perspectives and also bring your own into sharper focus. *Huan-ying!*

Quite often in this book we let our Chinese hosts speak for themselves, through direct quotations, which have been taken from our rather extensive notes. We did not use a tape recorder during interviews, but we discovered very quickly the translation process slowed conversations to the point where we could jot down what was being said almost verbatim. We each kept separate notes and cross-checked while preparing our manuscript. We have edited for style and grammar to render off-the-cuff remarks and unpolished translations more readable. This whole process—translation, note-taking, and preparation of our manuscript—may mean that some quotations are not literally, word for word, what was said to us. We are absolutely confident, however, that they accurately represent the gist of the conversations.

During our travels we quickly gained a reputation among our guides and companions for spending almost all our free time behind our invaluable portable typewriter, transcribing our field notes and recording impressions. The time thus spent may have cut into our evening activities, but we feel the result has been well worth it. We now have accurate and detailed records of what we saw, what people said to us, and what we felt about it at the time. This makes it possible for us to share the whole experience, confident that inevitable misunderstandings and shortcomings have been kept to a minimum.

1
Of Chivas Regal and Mao Tse-tung

It was almost obscene. There we were, in soft seats and air-conditioned comfort thirty thousand feet over the Pacific. We were six thousand miles from the United States, but you wouldn't have known it. Smothered by TWA's Ambassador Service, we were surrounded by what we thought we had left behind: familiar brand names like Coke, Kleenex, Sanka, and the rest; movies, a choice of *The Star-Spangled Girl* or a Western in which Kirk Douglas and Johnny Cash gunsling for money; and rock, pop, and CBS news on the six-track stereo. A real Buck Rogers setting. But instead of fighting space criminals, we were served filet mignon and Chivas Regal. And this was economy fare. Imagine what first class was like!

The reason we were doing this—jetting into twenty-hour daylight with steak, booze, and smartly dressed stewardesses to wait on us—was to learn from a people who used to die in the winter for lack of clothing. Who had been illiterate and superstitious. Who had died in floods and droughts, and from starvation and disease. And who, when brought together by ideology and organization, had been able to conquer these problems, to develop a new, socialist society, and to overcome the determined opposition of the super-power whose advanced technology had built this plane.

So our trip to China began, full of contradictions and symbolism. The people who once had starved are now rocking the world. The leader of the super-power had to eat twenty years' worth of crow and join a "march of the defeated" to China's doorstep.* Surely there was something to learn here.

By the time our trip was over we had visited fourteen different Chinese cities in six provinces over a period of seven weeks. We had toured eighteen factories, five people's communes, a coal mine, three colleges or universities, an army hospital, a major harbor, primary and elementary schools, neighborhood organizations, and sites of cultural and historical interest.

It had all started about a year earlier. With perhaps both the luck and daring of the innocent, we walked in off the street and presented the Embassy of the People's Republic of China, in Ottawa, Canada, with an application for a visa. Our application explained who we were; how we had been active in the student and anti-war movements since the early 1960s; how those struggles had educated us about our country; how we had become socialists, Marxist-Leninists; how we had worked full time for a movement group, the Radical Education Project; and how, for the past two years, Janet had worked as a research clerk in an office and Stu had been a spotwelder in an automobile factory. We also explained why we wished to visit China: that as socialists we believed there was much we could learn from seeing Chinese socialism firsthand, and that people-to-people visits were important in building friendship between the peoples of China and the United States. The Embassy staff was very polite; they accepted our application and said they would forward it to Peking.

We didn't hear anything for six months. By then we'd given up hope. But on one of those days when your mind is occupied with the small details of life—getting the car fixed, doing the laundry, paying the rent—a plain dime-store envelope arrived from the Ottawa Embassy. The message inside

* This is how Kim Il Sung, Premier of the Democratic People's Republic of Korea (North Korea), characterized Nixon's 1972 visit to China.

was thunderous: our visa had been approved and we were to get in touch to arrange details. We did.

We arranged to enter China through Hong Kong—where East and West collide. That's where TWA's jet service took us on the first leg of our journey. We awakened early the next morning, knowing that at last *the* day had arrived. A friendly Hong Kong hotel clerk contributed to the excitement, ringing us to make sure we were awake, and then calling back a couple of times to remind us of the train time. Due largely to his eagerness, we arrived at the Kowloon-Guangzhou train station a good hour and a half before our train left for the border.* We spent the time watching boats and commuters at the nearby ferry pier and investigating the sights and smells of snack counters offering pastries, cakes, candies, and roast chicken. Crowds grew and shrank as local trains arrived and departed. Odors from grain and chickens on a nearby siding reminded us that Hong Kong imports most of its food from the People's Republic. Finally, we boarded the train.

The trip to the border took about an hour. During this time we were continually plied by peddlers selling soda pop, candy, cigarettes, gum, newspapers, and just about everything else that could fit into their over-the-shoulder baskets. Across the aisle from us sat three young British women straight out of the nineteenth century. Aristocrats in Asia, they were dressed for horseback riding, country-club style; they carried saddles, narrow-brimmed jockey hats, high boots, and riding crops. We couldn't ignore them: one woman gushed loudly about the difficulties of living in Hong Kong and how her pet dog had recently cornered a rat in the kitchen. She finished the story by telling how her daughter had climbed on top of a table, screaming with fright. They left the train as it neared the border.

We pulled into the Hong Kong border station of Lo Wu. All the people remaining on the train were crossing into China. We were with a group of businessmen headed for the

---

* Guangzhou is the Chinese name for the city Westerners call "Canton."

semi-annual Trade Fair and, somewhat to our surprise, a three-man crew from ABC Television headed by Howard Tuckner, then ABC's Hong Kong bureau chief.

We had read several accounts of this border crossing—of the dramatic steps other travelers had taken across this famous "footbridge." Actually it's a covered railway bridge, and we trudged across on planks laid beside and between the tracks. It was drizzling and we appreciated the roof. On the Chinese side were trains full of poultry, pigs, and foodstuffs, ready to continue their journey to Hong Kong. A crew of men and women, some with broad, black-rimmed Hakka hats, were busily repairing sections of one of the tracks. They talked and joked as they worked.

Others have found this crossing dramatic and symbolic, and have written about it as crossing "from one universe to another," as stepping "off my planet into another world," or as passing "out of one world and into another."* We found the crossing routine. Perhaps this was because we were with a crowd of businessmen who were predictably businesslike. Perhaps it was the manner of the People's Liberation Army border guard to whom we showed our visas and U.S. passports. It was clearly routine to him; thousands of visitors a day were coming through here. But perhaps it was also because we did not consider China, or socialism, "another world," but rather a dynamic and important part of our own.

When our international health certificates were checked, again by courteous army representatives, the routine was broken by our compatriots from ABC. Tuckner, it seemed, had lost his health certificate and was bemoaning his situation. "I'm known, I'm known," he informed the Chinese, citing as proof his visit three months earlier as part of the U.S. press corps trailing Nixon. We were startled by his ar-

---

* This attitude appears in the accounts of several visitors to China. See, for example, the books which these quotes are taken from: Ross Terrill's *800,000,000: The Real China;* Klaus Mehnert's *China Returns;* or Jan Ting's *An American in China.* Their reports also share a perspective which, in spite of some interesting and timely reporting, fails to understand or deal with China's socialist features.

rogance and paternalism, but later, when the Chinese themselves mislaid Stu's health certificate, we developed more sympathy for his problem.

The Chinese side of the border, Shumchun, is a long building—a combination reception house, customs office, and dining facility. We were guided down corridors, past dining rooms crowded with businessmen noisily enjoying lunch before the train for Guangzhou pulled out. Sections of our contingent peeled off as we passed different waiting rooms, and we were finally shown into a pleasant little room with a balcony overlooking a lush green courtyard at the rear of the reception house. A tall bookcase sat in one corner of the room, filled with copies of Chinese periodicals in English and French; *Peking Review, China Reconstructs*, and recent editorials from Chinese newspapers. There were cigarettes and a thermos of hot water resting on an end table. We were served tea and asked to wait a few minutes. Alone, we sank deep into the overstuffed chairs and sipped our tea.

While the crossing had been handled routinely, being in China for the first time was hardly routine for us. We were excited and nervous, not quite sure what was going to happen. We tried to draw in and absorb everything around us; each second, each sight, smell, and sound now seemed important and impossible to preserve.

Shumchun: Into China

The knock on the door produced a smiling—and equally nervous—young man. Zheng Jia-shan introduced himself. He was to be our interpreter, guide, and, as it turned out, close friend and comrade during our stay in China. Zheng was from the North, from Shandong Province. He was thirty-two years old, fairly tall, and his oval face usually held a smile. He had originally worked in a machine shop—running a large planing machine—but during the mid-1960s had been selected to attend a foreign language school. There he learned English and he has since worked as an interpreter for China International Travel Service. Zheng told us something of his family background: his father had worked in the same factory, but he died before Liberation.* The family had been quite poor.

We did not read or speak Chinese. Janet had managed to find time to study a little before we left home, so she knew some common expressions and could read slogans, political billboards, and headlines in the newspapers. But language was important. There was no question that our interpreter would greatly affect what we would learn, and therefore the success of our visit. We were extremely fortunate to be with Zheng because our personalities and our politics meshed. As we grew to know each other well, we developed a deep friendship. Zheng helped us in several ways. First of all, his services as an interpreter were indispensable. His patience with our lack of Chinese never wore thin and he often took time during the few moments when he might have relaxed to pick up a pamphlet or song book and teach us some new Chinese characters. But more important, Zheng played a vital role in arranging details of our visits to factories, communes, and the like. As we arrived in each new city or town, Zheng would consult with local representatives. Familiar with our interests and politics, he was able to let them know our preferences and to give them an idea of the kind of people we were, politically and personally.

We learned much about China from Zheng himself. His experience as a worker came to the fore during our many factory visits. We had many long conversations with him, sometimes about deep theoretical questions and sometimes about the small details of daily life. We soon discovered his love for children and his particular soft spot for little girls. More than once, while walking through a store, down a street, or in a park, we would look up to find Zheng tagging

* After decades of revolutionary struggle, the People's Republic of China was established October 1, 1949. In China that date is universally referred to as "Liberation." People we met commonly spoke of the "old China" and the "new China," or of "before Liberation" and "after Liberation" in reference to 1949.

behind, captured by the smile of a four-year-old. We were not surprised to learn that he had a daughter, aged three; it was clear that her father missed her while traveling with us.

A customs official came to the door, and we went to identify our luggage, which had been checked through from the Hong Kong station. When we pointed out our two knapsacks, the official smiled, marked them with a piece of white chalk, and said that we'd just passed customs inspection. The packs were never opened. Our camera case and typewriter were passed in the same manner.

It was close to noon, and Zheng suggested we have lunch here rather than in Guangzhou, our destination for the day. We went to one of the dining rooms we had passed earlier. It was less crowded now, and the luncheon spread was huge—something we were to find throughout our visit. If our experience was typical, foreign guests in China are fed well, undeniably overfed. But that's clearly the way the Chinese want it, and when we raised criticisms of too lavish and too much food, we received only smiles, chuckles, and sometimes a teasing comment: "What would Americans think of China if you returned home thinner than when you came?"

This was our first meal in China, and it was an unusual one. We were engrossed in conversation with Zheng when we heard a whirring noise and looked up to find one of the ABC cameramen a few feet off, grinding away with a TV camera. "You don't mind, do you?" he mumbled, continuing his work. "Not unless we end up on 'The ABC Evening News,'" we replied loudly, aiming the comment not to the cameraman but to Howard Tuckner, who was dining at a table nearby. Tuckner immediately came to the rescue of his cameraman. He introduced himself, explaining that the Chinese had given him permission to cover the Trade Fair and that, therefore, everything was all right, wasn't it?

It was an unexpected situation, to say the least. Who could imagine that one of the first things to happen to us in China would be a hassle with ABC News? Our backs were up for several reasons. First, we reacted instinctively because of our several years of movement experience in dealing with the commercial mass media. We had found that they consistently distort, take things out of context, or use half-truths. Second, we didn't like the idea of being shown on coast-to-coast TV without knowing what they would say about us—who we were or why we were visiting China. Finally, we were just plain annoyed at being rudely interrupted and treated as objects, as part of the scenery.

While we were talking to Tuckner, the cameraman drifted off, stalking other tables of unsuspecting prey. We let things slide, and everyone returned to lunch. But our reaction to ABC had not gone unnoticed by Zheng or the other Chinese. It became clear that they didn't share Tuckner's idea that he had carte blanche on everything, or everyone, he saw in China. When we boarded the train for Guangzhou, Zheng asked us if we'd prefer seats in a car separate from the ABC crew. We said no, it didn't matter that much, and perhaps we'd reacted a bit hastily and subjectively at lunch. There was no reason to go out of our way to avoid them. Zheng said okay and let us know he understood our feelings.

On the train the ABC crew sat directly across the aisle from us. As the journey to Guangzhou progressed, our relations became more amicable, finally reaching a stage of peaceful coexistence. The two cameramen (actually, a cameraman and a soundman) had staggered aboard buried beneath a mountain of equipment—cameras, lights, tripods, films, microphones, tape recorders, and the like. Tuckner followed, a suave and striking figure in his carefully tailored, modish suit. There was little question who was boss. Tuckner's manner of dressing and carrying himself undoubtedly were signs of his success in his profession, but they stuck out like a sore thumb in the Chinese environment. Zheng took it all in, watching Tuckner adjust his fashionably wide tie or hitch up his bell-bottom, double-knit slacks while the two assistants huffed and puffed under their loads. The expression on Zheng's face gave it all away; there was no question of his disapproval of this strange creature from the land of ABC. We knew then that we were going to get along fine with Zheng.

Of Chivas Regal and Mao Tse-tung 19

We were in a very comfortable coach car, and the train itself was perhaps the quietest and smoothest we've ever ridden. Mild green tea was served by young attendants, who returned to chat with us when they finished their rounds. A woman crew member initiated the conversation, and soon three others joined in, draped over the back of a seat. We asked about their work and daily study. They declared that they wished to improve relations between the Chinese and American people. They were outgoing and friendly, obviously eager to talk to Americans when they had the chance. It was a good talk, an encouraging welcome to China.

We remember little of the countryside the train whisked through, occupied as we were in conversation. There remain only general impressions: green fields, two or three shades of green, set in neat and orderly patterns and broken by light brown ribbons of roads and plain brown patches of village buildings. Nothing seemed casual. The land was well tilled. Clean. Simple.

The Guangzhou train station was crowded and buzzing with activity. We were met by two representatives of China International Travel Service, shown to a car, and driven, our horn honking, through streets where bicycles grudgingly gave way. Our first stop was the Dong Fang Hotel. It, like the train, was crowded with visitors to the Trade Fair.

Guangzhou marked the real beginning of our visit. From there we journeyed to thirteen other cities: Wuhan, Zhengzhou, Luoyang, Xian, Yenan, Shi-jia-zhuang, Peking, Tangshan, Shenyang, Anshan, Tianjin, Changsha, and Shaoshan.* The route took us up the middle of China, as well as to the historic Northwest and the industrial Northeast. We met and talked with workers, peasants, cadres,** army representatives, students, teachers—young and old, men and women.

Our visit was a people-to-people visit. We traveled as indi-

* For an explanation of the romanization of Chinese names, see the Appendix.

** The term *cadre* is used to designate administrators and political leaders in China. For a more complete description of cadres and their role, see Chapter 5.

viduals, not as representatives of any organization or part of any group. We went there to meet Chinese people, and our only credentials were what we had said about our backgrounds in our visa applications. We were not "special" or "important" people; neither were the Chinese workers and peasants we met. Shortly after our return home, someone asked if we'd met anyone important while we were in China. Our first reaction was to think of the various political leaders we'd met at the local, provincial, or national level. Then we realized we'd in fact spent most of our time with the important people of China—the workers and peasants who are the governing classes of the new China.

We had agreed with China International Travel Service (CITS) that our trip was to be for one month and was to be made at our own expense. Travel costs within China were to be paid in one lump sum at the end of the tour. As it turned out, we were to be in China one day less than seven weeks, and the tab for our expenses was picked up by CITS. It happened this way:

About two and a half weeks into our visit, we were called on by Zhao Ri-chen of the head office of CITS. Zhao was an extremely modest and quiet fellow. Young and muscular, he admitted to an athletic history of weightlifting, gymnastics, and cross-country racing. He accompanied us on several of our visits in Peking, and it was probably no coincidence that these included all the sports events we attended and our visit to an amateur athletic school.

Zhao told us that our visa had been extended, and also that we would not be charged for expenses while in China. Our visit was helping to build friendship between the people of China and the United States, he explained, and so our hosts would pick up the costs as a gesture of good will and to help us financially. The visa extension delighted us, but we questioned their paying our expenses.

"We come from a country," we argued, "where it was possible for us to work and save money for the trip. Use the money you'd spend on us to pay for friendship visits by people from poorer countries. Since we can pay our way, we should."

"I understand your feelings," Zhao admitted, "but it's likely to be difficult for you to get jobs when you return, partly because of your visit to China. The money you'd have spent here can be used when you get back." *

That's how it finally was settled. We paid for all travel expenses to and from China, while China International Travel Service provided food, transportation, lodging, guides, and interpreters in China.

The general plans for our trip—which cities we would visit and for how long—were arranged with Zheng in Guangzhou and later adjusted in Peking. Specific details—which factories, schools, communes, etc., we would tour—were worked out in each city with local hosts. We also took walks by ourselves through city streets and shopping centers.

Was our trip stage-managed? Did we see only what the Chinese wanted us to see? We believe not. We can best characterize it as a mutually planned, but not programmed, trip. Prior to arriving in China, we had requested an itinerary of eleven cities, including extensive swings through national minority areas in Inner Mongolia, the Ningxia-Hui Autonomous Region, and the Guangxi-Zhuang Autonomous Region. Of the eleven cities we requested, seven were accepted; the four not approved were all in the distant border areas. We had also asked that our visit emphasize, in addition to specific geographical locations, three facets of Chinese life: workplaces (especially factories), schools, and the national minorities. About 75 percent of these requests were met; it was the part involving national minorities that was only partially fulfilled.

Finally, we made many special written requests during the course of the trip. We asked to visit particular factories or schools, to attend sports and cultural events, to talk with

* In fact, what happened with the money was this book; it allowed us to devote several months of full-time work to the manuscript.

former Red Guards now living in the countryside, etc. Our notes show that fourteen of sixteen such requests were met.

But perhaps most important, we do not feel that efforts were ever made to hide things from us. We visited factories, communes, and schools, all of which had a wide variety of both strong and weak points. To put it most simply, we know we were not given a one-sided tour because what we saw was many sided.

Upon reflection, we think there probably were several reasons why we didn't visit national minority areas. The Chinese maintain a very high standard of accommodations for foreign guests. The national minority areas are some of the least developed and most remote parts of China, and facilities for travelers may not measure up to their standards. Also, these areas are primarily in the border regions, and are militarily and strategically among the most sensitive parts of China. Thus, it's hardly surprising that foreign visitors are seldom taken there. And, finally, our proposed visit to these locations would have created many logistical problems, including the added translation headaches of a third language and the combination of geographical distance with the limited time of our schedule. A visit to these areas would clearly have meant a great deal of extra trouble for our Chinese hosts, and we can understand their decision to use their already overburdened resources in other ways.

Zheng consuled us, saying, "You can't expect to see everything on your first visit!" It was a comforting way to deal with the few requests that weren't met.

A Sheet of Blank Paper

China is now, as it has been for thousands of years, a country of peasants. Four out of five people live in the countryside and work in agriculture; the majority of the population still lives directly off "the good earth." Agriculture supplies about 50 percent of China's national income,

40 percent of the raw materials used in industry, and 70 percent of exports.

Most of the time we traveled by train. We were impressed again and again by the fact that China is still primarily an agricultural country. As we pulled out of city stations the view always changed quickly from densely populated streets and lanes to intensively cultivated farmland. We rolled through mile after mile of rice and wheat fields. Everywhere the polished landscape was tended, terraced, and cared for, with every square inch used. It was hard to comprehend that much of this land had been farmed continuously for centuries, some even for two thousand years.

Clearly, China is not yet an advanced industrial society, but it is definitely no longer a half-starved underdeveloped nation. The Chinese themselves say: "Ours is still a developing country with a relatively backward economy. Decades of hard struggle are still needed to build China into a more prosperous country."*

We saw graphic examples of that hard struggle everywhere. Hand labor was still used extensively; even horse carts seemed a luxury in some places. Factories sometimes housed elaborate modern lathes or other sophisticated equipment in buildings put together from homemade clay bricks and walls of straw and mud. Old-fashioned water wheels, still providing irrigation by centuries-old labor-intensive methods, sat next to new electric water pumps—concrete examples of the Chinese practice of using both the old and the new. They called this "walking on two legs." There was no question about the results; new China was definitely surging ahead.

China has traveled centuries in the past twenty years. To understand the China of today, the China of yesterday must be known. Before 1949 "old China" was described as "semi-

---

* Editorial in *People's Daily*, *Red Flag*, and *Liberation Daily*, in *Peking Review*, August 4, 1972, p. 7. These are probably the three most important nationwide publications in China.

feudal and semicolonial." The Western mind finds it difficult to comprehend living conditions in pre-Liberation China. They resemble nothing within the realm of our experience. We can give here only a brief and superficial indication of those appalling conditions and we recommend that you investigate this question further. One good source is Jack Belden, who lived in old China much of his life. In the late 1940s he wrote:

> Have you ever considered what it means to be a Chinese peasant in the interior of North China? Almost completely outside the influences of modern science and twentieth-century culture, the peasant was a brutal, blundering backwoodsman. He had never seen a movie, never heard a radio, never ridden in a car. He had never owned a pair of leather shoes, nor a toothbrush and seldom a piece of soap. And if he was a mountain man, he perhaps bathed twice in his life—once when he was married and once when he died—not because he so much enjoyed wallowing in the dirt, but because water was scarce and could be spared only for drinking.
>
> Consider the immense implications of such a materially impoverished life. Consider what you as a human being would value most of all in such an environment as this. Is not the answer obvious: food, clothing, shelter, but above all food.*

William Hinton, who was in the Chinese countryside during Liberation, wrote of the peasants at that time:

> People could not speak of the past without weeping. Nor could one listen to their stories dry-eyed. Yet, as the details piled up, horror on horror, one's senses became dulled. The barbarity, the cruelty, the terror of the old life was so overwhelming that in time it ceased to shock. One began to take for granted that worms crawled from dying children, that women and children were bought and sold like cattle, that people were beaten to death, that they fought each other for the leaves on the trees. The impossible took on the aura of the commonplace.**

* Jack Belden, *China Shakes the World* (New York: Monthly Review Press, 1970), p. 129.
** William Hinton, *Fanshen* (New York: Monthly Review Press, 1966), p. 43.

Before Liberation, two-thirds of the land in China was owned by a few landowners or middle and rich peasants. Over two-thirds of the agricultural workers, on the other hand, had little or no land of their own.

Industrial development before Liberation was virtually nil. Here is one summary of the condition of pre-Liberation industry:

> Finally, the industrial economy was an incomplete one; heavy extractive industry or light industry dominated and the output of means of production was negligible (only one percent of the invested capital was in the machine-building industry). Machinery replacements, even for long established industries such as textiles, had thus to be imported, further underlining the dependent character of China's industry.
>
> Before the Second World War, then, the Chinese industrial economy was retarded, geographically highly localized and partially dominated by outside capital. The war against Japan, followed by the Civil War, reduced this flimsy structure to rubble; by 1949, ... the effective capacity of the industrial economy was zero. When the Communists came to power in 1949 Chinese society was, in the words of Mao Tse-tung, "a sheet of blank paper"; as such, it lent itself admirably to receive "the newest and most beautiful words ... the newest and most beautiful pictures."*

In reality, this "sheet of blank paper" sometimes took a good bit of cleaning before any new or beautiful picture could be drawn on it. Nevertheless, industry has grown rapidly, new factories now ring the cities, and small-scale "rural industries" have sprung up all over. The face of the nation has been transformed in the process.

Three Impressions

We returned from China with three general impressions that underpin the rest of our analysis and observations: (1) we were deeply moved by the friendship for the Ameri-

* Keith Buchanan, *The Transformation of the Chinese Earth* (New York: Praeger, 1970), p. 218.

can people expressed by the people of China; (2) we were struck by the possibilities for development opened up by socialism in China;* (3) we became convinced, however, that socialism in itself was not a cure-all—that perhaps the most important feature of Chinese socialism lay in their phrase, "The class struggle continues under socialism."

Each impression has its own importance.

We proclaim to the whole world that what we oppose is exclusively the imperialist system. The Chinese people wish to have friendly cooperation with the people of all countries and to resume and expand international trade in order to develop production and promote economic prosperity.*

—Mao Tse-tung, 1949

Workers and peasants in all parts of China asked us to "please convey our friendship to the American people" and to "convey our support and friendship to the American workers." These greetings were genuine, not spoken out of mere politeness, and they were consistently heard throughout our visit. We told them, and we meant it, that this friendship would be the most important thing that we'd take back to the United States, that it was particularly important in light

---

* What do the Chinese mean by "socialism"? Volumes have been written in an attempt to define socialism—with tremendous variation and disagreement. But perhaps the briefest definition runs something like this: socialism is a system where the economy is owned and the government is controlled by working people. Behind this oversimplified statement lie many concepts, fundamental ideas from Marxist theory. These concepts make up the backbone of China's approach to socialism.

Marxist socialism is based on the view that human society consists of different economic classes that compete for power. This competition, or "class struggle," as Marx called it, has propelled mankind through the various stages of primitive society, slavery, feudalism, and capitalism—to socialism. It will eventually lead to communism, a classless society. The present stage of history is one of worldwide competition between the leading class of the capitalist system (the capitalists, or "bourgeoisie") and the leading class of the emerging socialist system

of the U.S. government policy during the past two decades, which aimed at cutting off friendly relations between the two peoples.

The Chinese made a clear distinction between the American "people" and those whom they call the American "imperialists"—the small handful of top industrialists and politicians who control our country.

One of the leaders of a sewing machine factory in Wuhan told us about their preparations for our visit. He confided that on the day before our arrival one of the factory workers had asked him if they should take down a banner carrying the slogan, "Down With U.S. Imperialism!" He explained how he had said no, believing that we would understand the meaning of the slogan and not take offense. We told him that he was right and added that similar slogans were sometimes used in the progressive movement within the United States.

When Chinese people heard we were from Detroit, they often beamed, "That's the first city our table-tennis team visited in the United States! Did you see them?" We would explain that we'd left Detroit for China only two days before their team arrived; they would then tell us they'd heard the team received a very warm reception in Detroit. "The exchange of ping-pong teams has been a good thing," they

---

(the working class, or "proletariat"). Capitalism is a society run in the interests of private property, free enterprise, and individual profit seeking; socialism means a workers' state—a system where workers (often allied with other classes) create, control, and run the society in their own class interests. Certain principles follow from the effort to accomplish these ends: socialism implies collective ownership of the basic economy by working people (as opposed to private ownership under capitalism); socialism encourages cooperative methods of organization and decision-making (as opposed to the ethics of individualism and entrepreneurship under capitalism); socialist economic production requires rational planning based on societal use (as opposed to production based on the profit motive); and socialism means an equitable distribution of wealth based on one's work, with labor no longer sold as a commodity. Finally, in Marxist theory socialism is regarded as a period of transition between the historical stages of capitalism and communism.

would say. "It has opened up friendly contacts between the Chinese and American peoples."

Nixon's visit, however, was discussed quite differently. It was not mentioned as an example of building friendly relations with the American "people." It was a political event, to be studied and understood politically. Workers, peasants, and cadres everywhere were familiar with the terms of the Shanghai Joint Communique issued by China and the United States at the end of Nixon's visit. They usually noted that China had stated its principled support for the struggles of Third World and all oppressed peoples, and they said it was a good thing that the U.S. government had finally admitted publicly that Taiwan was a part of China. But words were one thing, actions another, they added. The real test would be the actions of the U.S. government, and so far these hadn't changed. Also, Nixon's visit had eased the American-imposed restrictions on travel to China, which the Chinese believed was a good thing and would allow for more people-to-people contacts.

The deep friendship expressed for the American people everywhere we went did not indicate any softening of Chinese hatred for U.S. imperialism; rather, it indicated an understanding that imperialism did not represent the American people.

Socialist revolution aims at liberating the productive forces. The change-over from individual to socialist, collective ownership in agriculture and handicrafts and from capitalist to socialist ownership in private industry and commerce is bound to bring about a tremendous liberation of the productive forces. Thus the social conditions are being created for a tremendous expansion of industrial and agricultural production.

—Mao Tse-tung, 1956

Socialism means the working class is in power, that it is running the economy and the government in its own interests.* This opens up many possibilities for development that were formerly closed but it does not automatically mean development and expansion. A socialist economy, just as any other, can be run with different levels of efficiency and success. But China's tremendous, undisputed economic development since Liberation in 1949, the fundamental changes in the living conditions of the people, and the rapid advances in science, technology, education, and medicine all speak for themselves. They also speak to the potential of socialism, of collective development and planning, and of production based on human motives rather than profit.

In China we saw many things that demonstrated the potential of socialism—but one in particular contrasted favorably with a similar event in the United States. Stu had worked as a spotwelder for one of Detroit's large automobile manufacturers. While he was working there the company installed an automatic spotwelder, a significant technical improvement. But workers in the Detroit plant hated the new machine, and with good reason. It sped up the production line, meaning many had to work even harder. Also, everyone understood that automation took away jobs and meant more unemployment—already quite high in Detroit. The new machine, in a very concrete way, became their enemy. In Peking, on the other hand, we visited the East is Red Auto Factory, where we saw a similar automatic spotwelder. The Peking machine had been built by the workers themselves, with help from technicians and cadres. Many had worked overtime without pay to build it, and all were bursting with pride.

Why the difference? Why was the same machine the workers' friend in Peking and an enemy in Detroit? The an-

* Workers, our hosts asserted, form the leading class in China's socialist society. However, they continued, power is held and shared through a revolutionary alliance with workers *and* peasants as the principal class forces. China is described as "under the leadership of the proletariat and based on the worker-peasant alliance." See "New Year's Message," *People's Daily, Red Flag,* and *Liberation Daily,* January 1, 1973.

swer, we believe, lies in the very nature of the two economic systems. In Peking the new machine meant increased production, but it did not mean speed-up for individuals on the production line. Peking workers could readjust assignments as needed, collectively and equitably. Neither did automation threaten their jobs. There was no danger of unemployment or lay-offs because necessary adjustments could be dealt with rationally within China's planned economic system.

Socialism can open up other possibilities. For example, anyone who has worked in a factory knows that certain production details are understood most clearly by the people who actually do the job. Workers themselves know better than managers, engineers, or foremen where the kinks and problems are, and also how to fix them. In China we were impressed by the system's ability to bring this knowledge and experience into full play—it actually encouraged workers' initiative, resulting in thousands of technical innovations, increased production, and improved quality. Another example of socialism's potential may be seen in China's countryside. There large and expensive undertakings such as water conservation and land reclamation projects became possible only when collective efforts were made. The difference between collective and individual farming has been a crucial factor in China's development.

But we were also convinced by our visit that the possibilities opened up by socialism are not achieved automatically. In China, socialism was the key that unlocked the door of past oppression and misery. How the people crossed that threshold, what path they chose after crossing, was a matter of application, a matter that they call "class struggle."

> *In China, although in the main socialist transformation has been completed with respect to the system of ownership ... the class struggle is by no means over. ... The class struggle between the different political forces, and the class struggle in the ideological field between the proletariat and the bourgeoisie will continue to be long and tortuous and at times will even become very acute. The proletariat seeks to transform the world according to its own world outlook, and so does the bourgeoisie. In this respect, the question of which will win out, socialism or capitalism, is still not really settled.*
>
> —Mao Tse-tung, 1957

Living in the United States, all of us who work are actually quite familiar with class struggle—with the many ways corporations and employers try to control our labor, our lives, and the whole society we live in. We are also familiar with the various means, both spontaneous and organized, that working people use to resist. But class struggle under socialism is something quite different, and this is a point we understood only theoretically before our visit to China.

As socialists, we were of course familiar with the Marxist concept, outlined in the *Communist Manifesto*, that "the whole history of mankind ... has been a history of class struggles, contests between exploiting and exploited, ruling and oppressed classes." Thus we understood that the fundamental combatants in social conflicts are classes—groups of people acting in accordance with their relations to the means of production.

But under socialism, hasn't the exploiting class been overthrown? How does class struggle continue in the new system? During our many visits to factories and communes, the Chinese often talked about the "struggle between the two lines," the "struggle between the socialist road and the capitalist road," or between the "proletarian line and the bourgeois line." We soon learned that what they were talking about struck deep into the heart of their society. It was real; it's what the Cultural Revolution of 1966-1970 was all about. At issue was the whole way the society was to be run.

Liu Shao-chi, several other leaders removed from office

during the Cultural Revolution, and now Lin Piao have been labeled "capitalist roaders" in the Chinese press. Before our visit we had believed it possible that they had made mistakes or become elitist, self-serving bureaucrats. But "capitalist roaders" seemed an exaggeration, an excess of rhetoric. After all, hadn't these men been dedicated Communists for decades? We changed our minds after talking to workers and peasants throughout China. In China the concept of "capitalist roader" was not simply shrill rhetoric. It was an ideological term that aptly describes the direction and ultimate class interests served by the policies advocated by Liu Shao-chi and, later, Lin Piao.

But what were the "two roads"?

On the one hand, there were those who supported Mao Tse-tung's policies. They believed that developing a socialist consciousness was the primary item on China's agenda. Their road to socialism included the following principles:

(1) Collective and group needs should take precedence over individual or personal desires. When the group benefits, the individual benefits also.

(2) The most exemplary incentive in society is to "serve the people."

(3) Manual labor is a basic and respected part of society; manual and intellectual work should be combined.

(4) Differences between the urban and rural environment should be minimized. Agricultural and industrial development should be combined.

(5) Politics should be put in command; that is, once a correct political (class) perspective is achieved, technique can be developed and will follow. Whom the technique serves is the primary question. Hard struggle and self-reliance are important.

(6) Workers and peasants should be directly involved in the management of their factories and communes. The key to development and socialism is to "rely on the masses."

On the other hand, while Liu Shao-chi's supporters—and later Lin Piao's—talked of socialism, they paved their road with quite different materials:

(1) Pursuit of individual careers and seeking status and fame are natural and appropriate occupational motivations.

(2) Material incentives are necessary for economic production, even under socialism.

(3) Separation of intellectual endeavors from manual work is reasonable. It is usually inefficient to combine the two.

(4) Urban industrial development should receive priority over rural development. Economic growth means emphasizing heavy industry.

(5) Technique is most important. What good are correct ideas if you don't have the technique necessary to implement them?

(6) Experts, managers, and technicians should take the lead. Rank-and-file involvement in management has its place, but is basically inefficient.

Both roads claimed to be socialist, to be the direction of China's future. But if we in the United States are not qualified to judge what is true socialism—having never lived in a socialist society—we certainly can judge what are capitalist features on the basis of our daily lives in the most bourgeois of all societies. Using this measuring stick, it becomes obvious that many capitalist features were concealed in the socialist rhetoric of the Liu Shao-chi "road." When workers described the way factories were run under the Liu Shao-chi policies, we realized conditions had resembled what we experienced at home. We understood quickly how universities had functioned under the Liu Shao-chi influence because accounts by students and teachers reminded us of our own university days in the United States.

What all this means is that old ideas die hard. Capitalist ideas, individualist ways of doing things, take on new forms under socialism. They do not quietly slink away. Thus, building a new socialist society is a constant struggle. Postrevolutionary forms are different, the rhetoric employed is different, but the competition between class ideologies continues. The class struggle continues.

We returned from China believing that the theoretical concept of class struggle continuing under socialism is extremely important. In the first place, it provides a basis for understanding how the political struggle for socialism advances, and it prevents backsliding toward capitalist relations of any form. Second, it helps define the political struggles going on within a socialist society. Such struggles are to be expected. Old ideas take on new forms, and they must be exposed to be defeated. And when outdated ideologies rear their heads wearing new masks, people armed with the theory of continuing class struggle can identify them for what they are. Equipped politically and mentally, the people can handle political and ideological struggle without confusing friends and enemies, and without losing sight of their goals.

One final word on this point: we returned from China with the firm belief that understanding this concept (that class struggle continues under socialism) is vital to investigating any socialist society. Finding out what makes China tick has long eluded Western observers, since neither dollar-bill blinders nor rose-colored glasses will help. But this eyepiece surely will. Even with its aid the task of understanding the workings of China's socialism is complex and difficult; without it, the task is almost impossible.

Two Horses

In 1957 Mao Tse-tung said that China is a "big socialist country." As we have noted, socialism depends on a class content: a socialist society is one where the working class holds both political and economic power—where workers own and control the means of production.

Some forms, however, can be used both by socialist and capitalist societies. A common misconception is that socialism means government ownership. But government, or state, ownership by itself does not make a country socialist. Like a horse that can be harnessed to different burdens, government ownership can pull either capitalist or socialist loads. For example, there is a fundamental class difference between government ownership in Britain (where railroads and mines happen to be nationalized) and in China. In Britain, government ownership is simply another form within a privately controlled corporate economy. Corporations and the business elite effectively control the government and the economy; production is still geared toward corporate and individual profits. In China, however, profit motivations have been abandoned in favor of collective, cooperative development, and government institutions are controlled by a political party of workers and peasants.

Forms can also vary within a socialist context. China, for example, has two types of ownership in its socialist economy—"two horses" pulling together down the socialist road. These are the "two horses" of collective ownership and state ownership.

Collective Ownership

Collective ownership in China means that those who work in an enterprise own and control it as a group. People who labor on the land own it jointly; workers in a small factory together own their buildings, machinery, and the products of their labor. Although not isolated from the overall economic planning of the society, collective ownership brings with it more local control and local responsibility than does state ownership. The collective decides how to use its resources—how to divide them between production, capital growth, wages, and benefits. What products are produced, the acquisition of raw materials, and distribution and sales are usually handled through government channels, such as appropriate ministries or bureaus, and are thus coordinated with the overall planned economy. Local responsibility also means investment for growth must come from the collective; it may apply for loans from the government, but the government does not directly invest in its capital growth. Personal income depends upon collective production. In a bad year each individual shares the loss; and a good year brings greater benefits for all.

Collective ownership in China is more common in agriculture than in industry. The primary examples, of course, are the well-known "people's communes" established around 1958. Actually, the communes are many-sided enterprises combining agriculture, industry, trade, education, health, and defense. They are also the local unit of government in the countryside. They are quite large: we visited communes that ranged from twenty thousand members to more than fifty thousand. Collective ownership is subdivided within the commune structure. Here's an example:

It was late April when we visited the Zhao Ling Pu Commune, just north of Shi-jia-zhuang, Hebei Province. With our hosts we sipped tea and munched dry-roasted peanuts—a delicious example of the commune's production. Wang Yu-Shen, a member of the commune's Revolutionary Committee, sketched a picture of commune ownership and organization: "There are three levels of ownership in our commune; each level has collective ownership. First, there is the commune as a whole; second, under that are nine production brigades; and finally there are production teams."

We visited one of their production brigades, which included 2,900 people in 567 households. There were seven production teams within this one brigade. The land—much of it reclaimed from sandy waste and now lush green belts of orchards and winter wheat—was owned collectively at the production team level. The production brigade ran a repair shop for tools, a soybean noodle factory, a brick-making factory, and an oilpress for cooking oil. Some brigades owned tractors, trucks, and farm animals. Larger enterprises, like land reclamation and irrigation projects, were undertaken at the commune level. The commune also operated tractor stations and foundries that turned out plows, hoes, shovels, and other farm tools.

At the present time, our hosts explained, the most basic level of collective ownership within the commune was the production team. Accounting to determine personal income was done at the team level through a system of work points and team productivity. As conditions change, they contended, the basic form of ownership would advance to the brigade level, and then to the commune as a whole. They added that collective commune ownership would, in the distant future, gradually develop into direct state ownership.

A few factories in China are owned collectively, but the overwhelming majority are state owned. Of the more than eighteen factories we visited, two were collectively owned. Both were small, with fewer than four hundred workers each. Both had been established through local initiative, not through state investment or as part of government planning, but were encouraged by the government and represented concrete, local responses to nationwide calls for greater participation in economic development. For example, a collectively owned factory we visited in Peking was started by a group of twenty-two housewives during the Great Leap Forward in 1958. They said they wanted to contribute to "building socialism," and literally had put their factory together with old bricks taken from the city wall, straw and mud, simple tools they had brought from home, and rebuilt machinery they had picked up in junk yards. Today they manufacture a high-precision electronically guided lathe.

Collectively owned factories sometimes change over to state ownership when they grow larger, or when other criteria are met. Liu Xiang-zher, at the Feng Shen Street Committee in Peking, explained that their Street Committee used to have ten collectively owned factories under its wing: "Now we have only six; four of them are state run." Collectively owned factories in the cities usually operated under the jurisdiction of local levels of city administration called Street Committees and Neighborhood Committees. Their production is taken into account in the yearly economic plans for the whole city. Since the government guarantees to purchase their output at fixed prices, collectively owned enterprises do not engage in competition or lack a market. Unlike communes, collectively owned factories distribute personal income through a salary which is not directly tied to changes in productivity.

State Ownership

State ownership—or, as the Chinese put it, "ownership by the people as a whole"—means the enterprise is owned directly by the government: all production is included in the state plan and funds for investment are provided by the state. Wages, although determined within certain boundaries by local discussion, are paid as salaries; they do not fluctuate with production but follow state guidelines. All production is owned by the state and sold through state distribution channels. The government gets most of its revenue directly from this source.

The vast majority of factories are state owned. We visited state-owned factories ranging in size from the one thousand six hundred-worker Dong Feng ("East Wind") Watch Factory in Tianjin to the huge one hundred fifty thousand-worker Anshan Iron and Steel Company in the Northeast. Workers in state-owned factories enjoy fringe benefits guaranteed by general state policy and sometimes subsidized by the state, while these are usually matters of local responsibility in collectively owned enterprises. Child care and maternity leaves are two examples.

There are some state-owned farms, but they occupy a very small percentage of the farmland. In 1964 state farms occupied about 4 percent of the cultivated land in China. Edgar Snow estimates this had grown to about 6 percent by 1970.* Workers on state-owned farms receive wages, like workers in state-owned factories. Money for investment, machinery, and fertilizer comes from the state. One result is that these farms are generally more mechanized than the communes. Since Liberation, some state farms have been carved out of virgin land opened up by the government in the far West, Southwest, and North China regions. Others have a longer history: we briefly visited a state farm at Nanniwan in the Northwest (near Yenan) that had originally been wrested from barren land by a unit of the Eighth Route Army during the war against Japanese aggression.

* Edgar Snow, *The Long Revolution* (New York: Random House, 1971), p. 115.

Personal Property

The "two horses" of socialist ownership in China refer to the means of production: the land, materials, goods, and institutions that make up the society's basic economy. Private property should not be confused with ownership of personal property or of personal possessions. Families, particularly those in the countryside, often own their own homes and everything in them, from radios, bicycles, dishes, clothing, and furniture down to goldfish.

Several older people we met compared conditions today with their miserable lives before Liberation. Individual income has multiplied and with it has come things like wristwatches, books, beds, and bedding. Production of consumer items has soared. Personal property is respected; there is no drive to collectivize personal possessions, and individual items remain with the individual. What is crucial in China's socialist society is that social items—the means of production—are not held in individual hands as private property. These are placed in the hands of the people, collectively.

There are still a few areas of private property remaining in China today, principally in agriculture. Commune members sometimes have small family gardens which are not part of the collectively owned land.* They often have chickens or their own pigs. Private property on this scale is presently encouraged; we were told that privately owned pigs helped raise living standards, provided fertilizer, and made good use of garbage and waste. The peasants can do what they wish with their own animals or produce. For example, members of a production brigade near Peking described a meat exchange they operated: when a family slaughtered a pig, the meat was weighed and sold at the exchange. They received equivalent credit to use whenever they wished—thus avoiding the problem of having to eat all their pork before it spoiled.

---

* Edgar Snow states these private plots made up about 5 to 7 percent of the communes' land in 1971. Productivity was generally equivalent. See *The Long Revolution*, p. 137.

Considered appropriate for the present stage of development, these private plots are nevertheless the tail-ends of private property. Production Brigades publicized as models for others to emulate, like the well-known Tachai Brigade, do not have private plots: all their land is owned collectively. The direction of socialist development is clear, but how, and at what pace, are the questions behind many of the society's political struggles.*

Socialist Goals

Thus the "two horses" of China's socialist ownership—collective ownership and state ownership—are harnessed and pulling together, sharing a common perspective and a common goal. They are striving to build China "into a powerful socialist state with a modern agriculture, modern industry, modern national defense, and modern science and technology."** Workers and peasants eagerly told us of the progress they have made toward that goal. They also soberly but confidently talked of the work that still needs to be done. They said China is now a red country—workers' red. Gao Bai-zhen, a worker in Tangshan, spoke for all when he declared that they're now determined to see that China does not change its color. They're all clearly united in this purpose, although the specific details of how they preserve their hue or deepen its tone vary from place to place.

---

* For example, one of the criticisms now made of the Lin Piao "ultra-left" policies during the Cultural Revolution is that private plots were eliminated prematurely in many places.
** Summary of Chou En-lai's report at the Third National People's Congress, 1964, p. 19.

2
Industry:
The Leading Factor

We found there were always many things happening in Chinese factories. Far from being drab workplaces grinding out products, they were actually social, political, cultural, and educational centers, as well as economic units. Factories were important elements of community life, and they sponsored a wide range of activities not normally part of factory life in the United States. In the United States we think of factories as dull gray places. In China they're colored bright red. Most provided housing for both single and married workers. Nurseries and kindergartens were almost universal. Countless others operated their own primary and middle schools. Dining halls with fantastic quantities and varieties of food lent credence to the assertion that Chinese food is among the tastiest in the world. Health care was implemented through different types of first-aid stations, clinics, and factory-run hospitals and sanitoriums. Workers sometimes broke their routine by short stays on factory-owned farms. Libraries, cultural centers, and sports and recreational activities abounded. But probably the most significant difference between Chinese and American factories was that Chinese workers liked their jobs; they were proud of their factories.

Undoubtedly one reason for this was that Chinese factories had no management as we know it in the West. There were no foremen standing over the workers; no time clocks to punch in and out, no bosses to throw people out of work.

What was produced, how much, and when were decided by the people who actually did the work, in cooperation with government planning agencies. Factories had collective leadership—decisions were made by representative groups of workers, technicians, and cadres—and administration, structured to encourage popular participation, was carried out by the people who actually worked there.

All this sounds good in principle, but what was it like in practice? How could a huge factory like the sixty-seven-thousand-worker Wuhan Iron and Steel Works make decisions collectively?

We discovered the answer lay, ultimately, in the workers. The secret of their workers' control was in the activity of millions. Of course, factories must be structured to allow collective management, but the necessary ingredient for all this to work is human: the political consciousness of the workers themselves.

Self-Reliance and Comradeship

Our visit to the Wuhan Sewing Machine Factory was running behind schedule, so we were invited to stay for lunch. The reason was the success of the visit itself. In the workshops, cadres and workers had grabbed us by the arms, friendly and eager, and explained production details. They continually stopped to pick up pieces, to show us how this or that part was made or how it fit into the finished machine, and how this or that process had been improved through workers' technical innovations. As a result we had lost track of the time, but we'd gained a thorough and lively sense of their work. The mechanical flow of iron and steel, from foundry to small parts to sewing machine, became a human chain, a collective effort propelled by enthusiasm, energy, and innovation.

We sat down for lunch at a large oval table, the center of intense activity. A dozen or so of our hosts sat down with us, occasionally jumping up to bring in more dishes, to make sure our wine glasses were filled, or to see that we were

Industry: The Leading Factor 43

served the latest additions to the growing banquet set before us. Chicken prepared several different ways, ham, cucumbers, fresh vegetables, pork, cooked vegetables, a sweet treat made from sugar and millet, dumplings, steamed bread, soup—all these crowded the table until there wasn't room for the customary rice bowls. Talking and laughing, we all made do with chopsticks and large soupspoons.

We were almost overwhelmed. Janet was beginning to turn a slight shade of green from politely trying to keep pace with the amount of food continuously placed in front of her.

Our hosts giggled proudly about their comrades in the kitchen: "This morning, when we learned you were staying for lunch, we asked the cooks to prepare four dishes. We thought we'd just have a simple lunch. Now they've made more than twelve dishes, saying it's to show their friendship for you and the American people."

We ate and talked in a narrow room, part of the building that housed the factory offices. There were a few pictures on the walls; a plain long wooden table ran down the middle. For lunch an oval table was moved into one end of the room, and we sat on functional straight-back chairs. No padding, no frills. The warmth and hospitality of our Chinese friends filled the room and made for a very relaxed visit.

Dozens of workers from the factory popped in and out, filling several rows of benches at one end of the room. They would sit and listen for a while, perhaps adding a few comments or explanations. A small group of about six stayed with us the whole time, obviously having primary responsibility to host our visit. The others joined us as they wished.

It was a fine Sunday morning. "Friday is our normal day off," the workers explained.* Their factory was fairly simple: about two thousand men and women worked in a cluster of one-story buildings with a basketball court in the center. It had been established in 1958 with seventy-eight workers. Then they produced four hundred sewing machines a year;

* In several cities we were told that factories staggered days off to prevent congestion in markets, parks, and recreation areas.

now they made 624,000 machines a year in two basic foot-pedal models. Sixty-seven percent of the workers were women, and 50 percent of the workforce had been there less than eight years.

"We wondered what we should show you on your visit," one cadre remarked. "We are not as mechanized and we don't have as much electrification as factories in the United States. But we think we have some examples of self-reliance that would be good for you to see with your own eyes."

In fact, the whole factory was an excellent example of self-reliance and hard struggle. We learned their version of self-reliance was collective and came from political roots. It was their local implementation of Mao's call to "be prepared against war, be prepared against natural disasters, and do everything for the people."*

Our Wuhan friends explained, "We think it's important to be self-sufficient in all small parts for our sewing machines. In the past we were called a factory but in reality we were only an assembly shop. For the first few years we only made 28 percent of the parts here, due to the influence of Liu Shao-chi's line. But during the Cultural Revolution we criticized that line and changed our practice. We once depended on Guangzhou for many of our small parts. But if Guangzhou were occupied during a war [as had been the case during World War II], we would not be able to get any parts. We wouldn't be able to produce anything. During the Cultural Revolution we became self-sufficient in all parts. Now we can truly say that we are 'prepared against war and natural disaster.'"

In fact, they were not only self-sufficient in parts; they also made much of their own heavy production equipment. In the casting shop, where they produced heads for the sewing machines, about 90 percent of the equipment was now of their own manufacture. They used local materials as much as possible, sometimes reusing waste from other factories in the area.

Members of a factory cultural group joined us after

* Quoted in *Peking Review*, No. 20, May 16, 1969.

lunch.* They gave a spirited and enthusiastic performance. Most of their brightly colored costumes, which to our eyes looked quite professional, were homemade. They wore stage make-up, in Chinese tradition, and were accompanied by musicians playing traditional Chinese string and wind instruments. Their first number was a song they'd written for the occasion: "Welcome Our American Friends." This was followed by songs from revolutionary Peking operas, like *The Red Lantern*, and dances of national minorities.

We asked what their regular jobs were and learned that the group included three men who worked in the factory repair shop, two women who worked as clerks in the factory office, a woman who worked as a broadcaster, a teacher from the factory-run primary school, a cook, a nurse from the factory-run clinic, three lathe operators (two women and one man), two women from the painting department, and three men who worked in supplies.

Then we found we were to provide the finale! Following Chinese custom, they urged their *mei-guo peng-you* ("American friends") to sing. Janet took the lead in a verse or two of "Solidarity Forever," while Stu stumbled along on the chorus. Actually, it was a good turnabout—a bridge of friendly exchange and informality that everyone could understand despite the language barrier.

Indeed, the Wuhan Sewing Machine Factory was a good example of self-reliance. But the workers and cadres there also exemplified the friendship the Chinese people extend to foreign guests. They saw no contradiction between relying on their own efforts and having friends all over the world. Self-reliance did not mean turning inward and shutting out everything foreign. Rather, it gave them the independence and strength to reach out a comradely hand to friends from far

---

* Cultural groups, common in Chinese factories, communes, schools, and neighborhoods, were sometimes called "propaganda teams." They were spare-time groups, often organized during the Cultural Revolution, which used song and dance to put forth political ideas. "Propaganda" was not a suspect or negative term in China; it simply meant advocating a political point of view.

away. They could now choose to be friends, and therein lay the basis for true friendship.

Factory Organization

"The leading body in our factory is our Party Committee," workers at the Wuhan Sewing Machine Factory declared, "and our Revolutionary Committee implements the decisions of the Party Committee. We make decisions collectively and we oppose one-person decisions."

Other factories we visited followed this same structure: their Party Committee (composed of workers who were members of the Chinese Communist Party) was the basic policy-making body.* The factory Revolutionary Committee was the top administrative body. The Party Committee and the Revolutionary Committee were both representative leadership groups. Equally important, however, were two rank-and-file organizations: the Workers' Representative Congress (or in some places the Trade Union) and the workshop groups, the primary units of factory life.

Together these four organs were the backbone of internal factory organization.** Each deserves description in some detail. Let us begin with the Revolutionary Committees.

---

* See Chapter 5 for a discussion of the general role of the Chinese Communist Party in modern Chinese society.

** We did not investigate the structure of external factory relationships, choosing instead to emphasize more immediate features of daily life. We did learn, however, that all factories were tied into the overall state economy. There were a number of central government ministries responsible for industrial matters; some large enterprises related to them directly. Regional and provincial bureaus of these ministries also coordinated planning and production. There were additional overall economic agencies, such as state trading corporations. It was our understanding that the principal coordination between local factories and higher levels of state economic planning was handled by the factory's Revolutionary Committee and Party Committee leadership. For more on the relationship between local enterprises and the central agencies, see Wheelwright and McFarlane, *The Chinese Road to Socialism* (New York: Monthly Review Press, 1970).

Revolutionary Committees

Revolutionary Committees were new. Born in the midst of the Cultural Revolution, they were children of struggle. Prior to the Cultural Revolution most factories were run by a Party Committee and a manager. The raging struggles of the Cultural Revolution paralyzed the old Party Committees, while factory managers were often targets of mass criticism. New leadership burst forth.

During these struggles Mao called for workers and peasants to establish a "provisional organ of power that is revolutionary and representative and has proletarian authority" in places "where power needs to be seized."* These "Revolutionary Committees," as he called them, were to be composed of a "three-in-one combination" of revolutionary workers, cadres, and representatives from the People's Liberation Army (PLA). In 1967, 1968, and 1969, Revolutionary Committees sprang up all over China in factories, communes, and universities—also in neighborhoods, cities, and eventually even in whole provinces. They literally seized power from entrenched Party bureaucrats. Their legitimacy and authority flowed directly from mass support of workers and peasants rather than from bureaucratic structures.

The Revolutionary Committees became the "provisional organs of power," and provided sole leadership during vital periods of struggle. Then, as the dust settled, Party Committees were reformed. These reconstituted Party Committees reflected the changes brought about by the Cultural Revolution; often they were also "three-in-one combinations."

There usually was a period of one to two years between the establishment of a Revolutionary Committee in a factory and the formation of the new Party Committee. For example, workers at the East Is Red Auto Factory in Peking formed their Revolutionary Committee in February 1969 and their new Party Committee in October of the following year. The Revolutionary Committee of the Shenyang Transformer Fac-

---

* Quoted in an editorial in *Red Flag*, No. 5, 1967. See also *Peking Review*, No. 5, 1967.

tory was set up on June 10, 1968, and the new Party Committee followed in December 1969. The Tianjin No. 1 Machinery Factory had a longer time lag, although it set up its Party Committee earlier than some other factories. Their Revolutionary Committee was founded in December 1967, and their Party Committee followed in April 1970.

However, even with the re-establishment of the new Party Committees, the Revolutionary Committees have not passed out of the picture. Their new revolutionary role of integrating workers, cadres, and army representatives into factory administration has become a permanent feature of China's industrial scene.

"How are new members of the Revolutionary Committee chosen?" we often inquired.

Workers at the Wuhan Sewing Machine Factory answered: "We don't have big election campaigns like in the United States. People are modest and are known among the workers." Then they described an extensive process of nomination and discussion to select worker and cadre representatives for their Revolutionary Committee. We discovered differences in detail from factory to factory, but consistency with the principle of involving rank-and-file workers. Revolutionary Committee representatives included both Chinese Communist Party members and non-Party individuals.

The Wuhan workers first held workshop discussions; small shop groups met and made nominations. These names were then discussed throughout the factory, including the present leading committees. We asked if people ever put their own names in nomination and our hosts replied that people were usually nominated by fellow workers who knew them well. They regarded the kind of electioneering done in the United States as a sign of immodesty and low political consciousness —both undesirable traits for a Chinese leader. After the shop discussions the leading committees gave their opinions on the nominations. Finally, representatives were chosen through a general election.

The process was different at the Tangshan Rolling Stock

Plant, which manufactured locomotives and railroad coaches. These workers called it the "two times up, two times down" process. Wang Guai-yi, vice-chairman of the Revolutionary Committee, explained what happened there: "First, workers in each section of the factory have discussions and put forth names of people for the Revolutionary Committee. The names are sent up to the leading body, which holds its own discussions and sends its opinions back down. This process takes place twice; the names are discussed two times by the masses and two times by the leading body." Hence the phrase "two ups and downs." In some places we were told that this was done three times. "After the final discussion we agree on a group of people for the committee," Wang added. "We do not actually take a vote. We handle everything by discussion." Wang admitted that occasionally some names put forward by the workers were not approved by the leading body: "In such cases we come to agreement through further discussion."

Who was finally selected? Apparently it was those who were respected as active political leaders, as good workers, and who didn't take on bureaucratic airs. Wuhan Sewing Machine workers put it this way:

"We choose our representatives because they are good workers, have close relations with the masses of workers here, and are diligent in studying Marxism-Leninism and the Thought of Chairman Mao."

There were no fixed terms for Revolutionary Committee members, and, as far as we could discern, no regular schedule for elections. Elections were now held to fill vacancies or when conditions made it necessary to expand the committee. The question of term of office, we were told, was something not yet worked out and would be decided through further experience. In addition, the recall of leaders was not a formalized procedure, but could take place at any time. We learned, however, that the typical approach toward a leader stepping out of line was not immediate removal from office. Workers told us they would first confront errant leaders, criticize them, and try to help them understand and correct their mistakes.* Only after this had failed would they remove a cadre or member of a leading committee from office.

We were curious to know if the army representatives on the Revolutionary Committees were chosen in the same way as the workers and cadres, so we questioned workers at the Wuhan Printing and Dyeing Factory. They replied: "The People's Liberation Army (PLA) representatives are sent by a committee of the Army." We found this often to be the case elsewhere. Usually the factory decided the number of PLA representatives and individuals were then selected within the military structure itself. Workers at a few plants told us a list of possible PLA representatives was circulated throughout the factory for discussion. Workers' opinions were considered by the PLA when making its final decision.

We raised another question: Why is the army part of the "three-in-one" combination? What is its role in factories? Zei Zao-huai, our host at the Tianjin No. 1 Machinery Factory, answered us by asserting that this role of the PLA was ideological, not military. "The People's Liberation Army is a great school of Mao Tse-tung Thought," he said. "It was formed and led by Chairman Mao. Army representatives bring a fine tradition with them to the factory." He added that PLA representatives usually came from units stationed nearby and participated in factory production as well as in leadership.

We believe Zei's view to be basically correct. The PLA's inclusion in the revolutionary "three-in-one" combinations clearly reflected political and organizational struggles of the Cultural Revolution. At that time, the PLA was a political stronghold for Mao's supporters. Indeed, since its inception the PLA (or its predecessors, the Eighth Route Army and the New Fourth Army) has functioned close to the people politically. Like "fish in the ocean," soldiers have been integrated into the population. PLA units regularly helped with labor in

---

* See Chapter 5 for example.

the fields and in the shops, provided medical aid, and gave educational assistance. The PLA was also a producer. It was almost totally self-sufficient in terms of food and basic supplies. At the time of the Cultural Revolution the modern PLA was perhaps integrated into society more than any other regular army in the world. Furthermore, during our visit it became obvious to us that the PLA was highly respected by workers and peasants alike all over China. During the Cultural Revolution, the PLA became a reliable and well-organized source of grassroots political organizers and provided ideological and personnel support for those in factories and schools who struggled to implement Mao's policies. Workers, students, and peasants generally welcomed PLA representatives as respected and valuable allies in the common political struggle against Liu Shao-chi's policies.

If our visit was typical, however, today the PLA part of factory "three-in-one" committees keeps a low profile. Though we met scores of men and women from Party Committees and Revolutionary Committees, only once were we introduced to a PLA representative. Our main host at the Foreign Languages Printing House in Peking was an affable middle-aged PLA man who was a leading member of their Revolutionary Committee. Elsewhere we were usually told that there were PLA representatives on the Revolutionary and Party Committees, but we never met the PLA part of the "three-in-one" trio. We can only speculate why. It could possibly indicate PLA representatives were not at the time as closely involved in factory matters as when the Revolutionary Committees were first established. Or it could simply mean PLA representatives did not often have the task of hosting foreign visitors like us.

We found that the size and composition of the Revolutionary Committees varied considerably from place to place, as shown in the chart on the next page.

What did Revolutionary Committees do? What were their powers? These were perhaps the most difficult questions for us to pin down. Revolutionary Committees were part, and only part, of a complex decision-making process. They were in between higher bodies (Party Committees and government agencies) and mass rank-and-file organizations.

Revolutionary Committees were always described to us as the chief administrative bodies in factories, and the Party Committees as the top policy-making bodies. It was usually said that the Revolutionary Committees implemented the general decisions of Party Committees. Of course, the crucial question was what this meant in practice. Were Revolutionary Committees simply rubber stamps for the Party Committees, holding no real power themselves? Or could it be the other extreme: did the Party Committees deal with such broad ideological concerns that the Revolutionary Committees, in effect, ran everything?

Our estimate is that the answer lay somewhere between these extremes. Also, relationships and practice undoubtedly varied considerably from factory to factory.

Size and Composition of the Revolutionary Committees

Factory	Total Employed	Total on Rev. Comm.	Workers on Rev. Comm.	Cadres on Rev. Comm.	PLA on Rev. Comm.
Tangshan Rolling Stock Factory	7,000	25	13	10	2
Wuhan Sewing Machine Factory	2,000	17	9	4	4
Shenyang No. 1 Machinery Factory	6,800	29	16	8	5
Zhengzhou Textile Machinery Manufacturing Factory	5,000	40	23	13	4
Luoyang Tractor Works	23,000	55	36	16	3
Kairan Coal Mine, Tangshan	5,900	33	18	12	3
Red Flag Embroidery Factory, Tianjin (collectively owned)	240	8	5	3	0

Industry: The Leading Factor 53

Our experience indicated that Revolutionary Committees were more visible, more active, in the daily administration of factory matters than Party Committees. Our factory hosts always included members of the local Revolutionary Committee, who were introduced to us as such. Many times we learned that our hosts also included members of the local Party Committee—but that was not a point of introduction.

We can give a few examples of the range of Revolutionary Committee activities. Workers at the Wuhan Sewing Machine Factory told us that their Revolutionary Committee was the factory's ultimate authority over wage decisions.* Workers and cadres at the Shenyang Transformer Factory said their Revolutionary Committee, along with the Party Committee, had responsibility for making basic decisions about overall yearly production. In Tangshan it was the Revolutionary Committee of a local coal mine that made a decision to call a mass meeting of all workers and their families to discuss a suggested change in the mine's yearly output.

Revolutionary Committee subdivisions also gave us a sense of their duties. We learned that officers of Revolutionary Committees typically ran factory bureaus in charge of such things as production, political work, plant logistics, daily affairs, and the militia.

Party Committees

Party Committees were considered the leading policy-making groups in Chinese factories. Members of the new Party Committees were chosen in much the same way as members of the Revolutionary Committees. To become a member of the local Party Committee a worker first had to be a member of the Chinese Communist Party.** Party membership averaged about 15 percent of the total workforce in

---

* See p. 73 below.

** See Chapter 5 for a discussion of the Chinese Communist Party and how workers become members of the Party.

the factories we visited. For example, the Shenyang No. 1 Machinery Manufacturing Factory had a total of 6,800 workers, and 1,100 of these were Chinese Communist Party members. Often everyone in the factory was involved in the extensive discussions about the candidates for the Party Committee, but usually Party members made the final decision. Sometimes all Party members in a factory held a Congress or meeting to make final decisions. Other workers said that discussions among Party members in their factories went through the "two (or three) times up, two times down" process.

New Party Committees were usually "three-in-one" combinations. However, in a few places we were told that the Party Committees were not "three-in-one" combinations in principle. For example, workers and cadres at the Kairan Coal Mine in Tangshan allowed that although they did not have a "three-in-one" principle for their Party Committee, in practice it had worked out that way.

We learned that the term "three-in-one combination" had come to have several meanings. In addition to the basic "worker, cadre, and army" components, people often talked also of "old, middle-aged, and young." Technical innovations were sometimes attributed to combinations of "workers, technicians, and cadres." In schools people spoke about the combination of "students, teachers, and cadres."

Party Committees sometimes stressed the "young, middle-aged, and old" combination. A middle-aged cadre at the Tianjin No. 1 Machinery Factory explained: "The young people participate, and this helps prevent the restoration of capitalism. Our young people have the spirit of 'dare to speak and dare to struggle.' They have less conservative ideas, and they help prevent the leaders from being divorced from the masses. They are quick to raise criticisms.

"The old element is important," he continued, "because veteran workers have gone through the test of war times, and they also have much experience. Sometimes it is hard to say who is old and who is middle-aged," he laughed. He was a person who could fit into either category himself.

Party Committees were usually smaller than Revolutionary Committees. Here are some typical comparisons:

Party Committees

Factory	Total on Party Comm.	Total on Rev. Comm.
Tangshan Rolling Stock Factory	21	25
Wuhan Sewing Machine Factory	10	17
Shenyang No. 1 Machinery Factory	27	29
Zhengzhou Textile Machinery Manufacturing Factory	19	40
Luoyang Tractor Works	36	55
Kairan Coal Mine, Tangshan	25	33
Red Flag Embroidery Factory, Tianjin	3	8

Leading members of the Party Committee often wore two hats, sitting also on the Revolutionary Committee. "We want to have unified leadership," workers in Wuhan explained, "and overlapping on the leading committees helps bring this about." But the extent of overlap varied considerably. For example, the 1,700 workers at the Wuhan Printing and Dyeing Factory had a Revolutionary Committee of seventeen, nine of whom were also on the Party Committee. This percentage seemed to be about average. At the high end of the spectrum was the Shenyang Transformer Factory, five thousand workers strong, where twenty-six of twenty-eight members of the Revolutionary Committee were also on the Party Committee. The smallest overlap we encountered, about 20 percent, was at the Wuhan Iron and Steel Works and the Luoyang Tractor Works. Both were relatively large enterprises, with sixty-seven thousand and twenty-three thousand workers respectively.

Workers' Representative Congresses and Trade Unions

Most factories we visited had a rank-and-file organization called the Workers' Representative Congress. This was a new (and, as it now appears, temporary) group ushered in by the upheavals of the Cultural Revolution.

"Our Workers' Representative Congress was set up by the masses after the Cultural Revolution," a young Shenyang worker told us. "The Workers' Representative Congress mobilizes workers to study, to fulfill the production plan of the factory, to save waste materials, and to join in the movement for technical innovation. It also organizes workers' education, sports, recreation activities, and sets up cultural performances. The Workers' Representative Congress listens to the needs and demands of the workers, collects their opinions, and transmits them to the Party Committee and Revolutionary Committee."

These remarks were typical. The Workers' Representative Congresses were always described as following the leadership of the Party and Revolutionary Committees. Congress branches at the workshop level performed a variety of duties, combining the functions of educator, political conduit, and administrator:

(1) *Educator:* Congresses organized rank-and-file study groups throughout factory workshops. Such study included current political topics, the basic philosophical works of Marxism-Leninism, and technical subjects relevant to the factory's production.

(2) *Conduit:* Congresses served as a link between the rank and file and the leadership by promoting discussions about production plans, eliciting suggestions from the rank and file, and encouraging technical improvements. They were regarded as channels for criticism and feedback from the rank and file to the leadership.

(3) *Administrator:* Congresses organized and operated programs in recreation, sports, and culture, and they also administered what Chinese workers called "workers' welfare." Programs ranged from housing and health to libraries and milk

delivery stations, from retirement funds and subsidy funds for families with special needs to providing sanitary napkins for women workers.

Most, but not all, workers were members of the Congresses. We were told that Workers' Representative Congresses were organizations made up of revolutionary workers. As one Shenyang worker frankly stated, "Since the class struggle still exists, there are some workers who are not qualified." We obtained concrete figures for the Zhengzhou Textile Machinery Manufacturing Factory, where 4,700 of 5,000 workers were in the Workers' Representative Congress.

Workers' Representative Congresses appeared to have superseded the pre-Cultural Revolution trade union structure in many plants.* For example, at the Foreign Languages Printing House in Peking we were specifically told that their Workers' Representative Congress had replaced the former trade union. Workers at the Luoyang Tractor Works, on the other hand, spoke of their union and did not mention a Workers' Representative Congress.

Before the Cultural Revolution the trade union structures had been a stronghold for Liu Shao-chi supporters, and the creation of Workers' Representative Congresses was obviously part of the ensuing political struggle. The new Congresses carried out many functions which had previously been handled by the trade unions.

Workers at the Shenyang Transformer Factory explained

* Trade unions in China have a history that dates back to pre-Liberation times. Prior to 1949 many unions were closely integrated into the general revolutionary struggle; the All-China Federation of Labor was formed in 1925 and functioned underground much of the time between 1927 and 1948. After Liberation, particularly after the socialist transformation of the economy in the late 1950s, the trade unions continued as mass (rank-and-file) organizations of workers but also took on new roles. Their main task, in the socialist context, was considered educational. They were also to function as "transmission belts" (a term Lenin used for trade unions under socialism) between the rank and file and the Party and government organs. In addition, they organized a wide range of programs concerned with workers' welfare, recreation, and culture.

that their old trade unions were criticized because they had been "affected by the Liu Shao-chi line," "neglected ideological work," and "denied class conflict" by bringing capitalists into membership under a slogan, "The Entire Nation Is a Trade Union."*

The Cultural Revolution evidently raised many questions about the role of trade unions in China's socialist system. Workers' Representative Congresses were one answer to those questions—an organizational response itself open to experimentation, change, and development. Chinese workers characterized the Workers' Representative Congresses as new, undeveloped forms that would most likely change when their strong and weak points were sorted and sifted through practice.

Apparently, that sorting and sifting has had some results. The combined 1973 New Year's Editorial of *People's Daily*, *Red Flag*, and *Liberation Daily* urged that "trade unions . . . should be consolidated step by step." In April 1973 Peking and Shanghai held municipal trade union congresses to do just that. It was also announced that other trade union congresses would be held throughout China "when conditions are ripe." We estimate that the reconstituted trade unions are being built by those who had created the Workers' Representative Congresses—that the Workers' Representative Congresses are being directly plugged into the reconstituted unions. A *People's Daily* editorial in April 1973 outlined the duties of the reconstructed trade unions as follows:

> . . . the trade unions must truly be schools for educating the workers . . . workers should be organized to conscientiously study politics, raise their educational and vocational levels, and engage in spare-time recreational and sports activities . . . the trade unions should pay attention to the masses' well being [i.e., the whole range of workers' welfare programs] and see to it that

---

* Quoted in Mitch Meisner, "The Shenyang Transformer Factory: A Profile," *China Quarterly*, November-December 1972. Meisner visited this factory in April 1972, just a few weeks before we did.

work among women workers and workers' families is done well.*

The question of trade unions and Workers' Representative Congresses, their role and forms, is undoubtedly still being widely discussed throughout China. It's likely that these discussions will continue for years. As political conditions change, old forms are discarded and experiments are tried, tested, and developed.

Work Groups

The primary unit of workers' organization in the Chinese factories we visited was at the workshop level. Work groups, composed of workers, cadres, and technicians, were both universal and diverse, varying in size and composition from factory to factory. For example, structures in a large steel plant were apt to be quite different from those in a textile mill or an auto factory. All work groups, however, were integrated into factory-wide structures such as the Workers' Representative Congresses or the trade unions and the Party and Revolutionary Committees.

Work groups were usually composed of twenty to thirty members. Here are some examples: A workshop of about 218 in the Shenyang Transformer Factory was divided into nine work groups. A repairman in the Zhengzhou No. 3 Textile Mill said that his work group numbered thirty. A spinner in the same factory said her group contained twenty-three people, two men and twenty-one women. The largest work group mentioned to us was a group of 120 at the Luoyang Tractor Works.

Such groups met regularly to evaluate their work, to discuss production plans and working conditions, and to study political and technical topics. They also discussed wages,

* The Working Class Must Further Play Its Role as the Main Force," *People's Daily* editorial printed in *Peking Review*, April 27, 1973, p. 13.

nominated and selected factory leaders, settled minor disputes and grievances between members of the group, and coordinated their work with other groups in the factory.

Workshop-level organizations also often included branches of the Chinese Communist Party and its youth group, the Communist Youth League (CYL). Such branches were usually composed of all members of the Party or CYL who worked in each workshop.

Finally, special committees for technical innovation and safety were common workshop units, as was a staff, selected by the work groups, to perform workshop administrative duties.

Workers' control, however, depends upon more than overall forms. True, it is necessary to start with structures that encourage rank-and-file participation. But what about practice, the day-to-day details? How did the rank and file and the leaders relate to each other? What about working conditions? And what real power did workers have in determining safety standards, wages, the pace of work, hours, and the like?

Leaders and Masses Are As One

There was a problem at the Tianjin No. 1 Machinery Factory: Zei Zao-huai had a lot to tell us, but workers in the factory also had a lot to tell him. Zei was a factory cadre, and main spokesman during our visit. He knew production details well, and he also told us about the people who worked there —their special achievements, their problems, their backgrounds, and how long each had been working on a particular job. He eagerly explained all this to us, answering our questions as we walked through huge workshops where gear lathes were constructed. As we went from shop to shop, workers often left their machines to greet us and to talk with Zei. Workers who hadn't seen him for a while would come up and throw an arm around Zei's shoulders as they talked. We didn't mind the interruptions because they revealed the warmth and comradeship so evident throughout this factory. Zei didn't do all the talking. Other workers and cadres often took the initiative in explaining things to us. Among them was young Gao Wei-ming, a tall and slim engineer. He was somewhat shy. Zei mentioned that Gao spoke English, but at first Gao spoke Chinese and deferred to Zheng and to Yu, a local translator from Tianjin. As the afternoon wore on, Gao opened up under Yu's prodding and began using his English. He knew many technical terms and mechanical details that Zheng and Yu did not know, and soon the three of them were trading terms and phrases, filling in each other's weak spots. It wasn't competitive, but was more like a mutual-aid team, in which each learned from the other.

The machinery factory was spread over a large land area to the east of Tianjin. It had grown considerably from the original four hundred workers and staff who started production in 1952. Now over four thousand men and women worked there, and its large brick buildings covered 140,000 square meters. More buildings were being constructed at the time of our visit. Basketball and volleyball courts, ping-pong areas, a nursery, and a kindergarten were spaced among the buildings. In the workshops we noticed many blackboards set aside for adult education that were covered with bright, multicolored chalk displays. Several workshops had also hung banners to welcome us, and we quickly learned to read the Chinese characters: "Warmly Welcome Our American Friends."

Zheng was happy about the visit. Some of the heavy equipment found in this plant had been manufactured at the Shandong machinery factory where he had worked. More than once he paused in front of a huge planing or grinding machine and proudly pointed to the factory name emblazoned across the top in bright red characters.

In one large workshop Zei bounded ahead to open the door of a small enclosed room near the side of the building. Inside was a new, high-precision lathe, delicately carving an enormous gear out of solid bronze. The special room had been constructed to control temperature and humidity, which could affect the metal and might alter its design. Two engineers—a young woman and a man—were running the lathe together with veteran workers who had helped design it. This factory, like several others we visited, had a special kind of "three-in-one" combination for technical innovations. Workers, cadres, and technicians labored together and conducted scientific experiments to develop such things as this special lathe. Engineers were respected for their technical knowledge; they in turn emphasized that they learned a great deal from the workers, who had valuable practical experience.* The results were more technical help at the shop level and technicians who were less removed from the realities of production. Engineers at this factory seemed well integrated into production and factory life. They—and everyone else—were very proud of the new lathe, one more step toward self-sufficiency. Formerly, they told us, precision bronze gears had been imported from the Soviet Union at great expense; now they were manufactured in their own shop.

Time flew by, and all too soon we had to rush off to supper and an evening theatrical performance. Zei, modest to the end, asked us for criticisms and suggestions. "We have many shortcomings," he said. "Our assembly is not always done in a practical way for such a large factory. This is a hangover from when we were small." He clasped our hands and urged us to return, and reluctantly parted, saying, *"Zaijian, zaijian"* ("Good-bye, good-bye"). Gao, the engineer, grinned and bade us good-bye in perfect English. We wished the visit could have been longer. We liked the way the workers and Zei treated each other as close friends and comrades, and we were sorry to leave people whom we had so quickly come to think of as friends.

---

* It had not always been so. Formerly, we were often told, the influence of the Liu Shao-chi line had pushed workers out of the picture. On the other hand, during certain periods of the Cultural Revolution the Lin Piao "ultra-left" line had sometimes completely rejected technical expertise.

The Big and Little Rivers

It was hardly surprising to find that working conditions were reasonable and humane in a society where workers themselves determined such things. Nevertheless, it was deeply impressive. Many factories had production lines similar in design to ones Stu had worked on in the United States. This was particularly true of the Chinese auto and tractor plants we toured. But the resemblance was superficial. The pace of work in Chinese factories was slower; it was not deadening. In very few cases were workers so tied to the speed and flow of the line that they could not step aside and chat with us. They had no problem getting a drink of water, sipping a cup of tea, or using the washroom.

How, then, was production maintained and even increased? Why didn't Chinese workers just slough off? To answer this we thought about the different types of work we ourselves have done. Sometimes we've had large but necessary chores to do at home, such as painting a room or moving boxes and furniture. We wanted to get the job done—and we did—but the work was for ourselves and we didn't have to kill ourselves doing it. Moreover, we set our own timetable and certainly didn't work at the numbing and dangerous pace so common to many American factory production lines. The Chinese factories we saw operated the way we do when working at home. Chinese workers believed they were working for themselves, and they combined a reasonable pace with decent production.

In China, moreover, this sense of working for one's own benefit was not applied individually or selfishly. Workers and peasants repeatedly emphasized the needs of the whole society. "Socialist development depends on a collective consciousness," they would say, seeing no conflict between their own interests and the general needs of society. As one person put it, "When the big river is full, the little river also has more water." Placing priority on personal interests was the way of the capitalist roaders, they argued, and it resulted in selfish conflicts, poor working conditions, and inequalities. If you thought only of the little river, the big river would run dry.

Bread-and-Butter Stuff

Some working conditions in China were guaranteed by the central government. These included, for example, the eight-hour day (lunch period included), a six-day week, fifty-six-day paid maternity leave (seventy days for twins!), six and one-half paid holidays per year, and an eight-level wage scale. The collectively owned factories we visited also generally followed these state practices, each adapting general policies to local conditions. We discovered there was a great deal of flexibility in practice, combining state planning with local options.

The Chinese eight-hour day was different from any we'd ever worked in the United States. It included time for lunch, rest breaks, and in some cases it even included time for study. Lunch breaks were determined by the workers in each factory. The Kairan coal miners had decided on a one-hour lunch break; more typical, however, was the half-hour lunch at the Wuhan Printing and Dyeing Factory. Workers at the Wuhan Sewing Machine Factory included their half-hour lunch period within the eight-hour shift, but they also added an extra hour rest period at midday.

Shifts also varied considerably. The Wuhan Sewing Machine Factory ran only one eight-hour shift. A factory making mine equipment in Luoyang ran three, and the new harbor in Tianjin had a complex three and one-half shift system. At a small factory in Peking, different workshops had different shifts, depending on production requirements. Larger facilities tended to work three shifts, and it was common for workers to rotate shifts each week. We met workers who had arranged shifts to jibe with family needs—some couples worked different shifts so one parent could always be with the children. How many shifts there were, whether workers rotated shifts, which jobs ran one shift and which more—these were all questions decided within each factory and workshop according to specific conditions.

We never saw a time clock in any Chinese factory. Once we encountered a time-sheet system where workers signed in each day. We asked about it, and a young woman lathe operator explained it was used to determine production progress in relation to hours worked. "Before the Cultural Revolution this was used as a club over our heads, but now we use it only for checking production," she proudly told us. "If a person needs a day off, there is usually no problem getting it." Her answer was credible. This was the machinery factory in Tianjin where we had observed extremely warm relations between workers and cadres. We could tell there was a high level of mutual trust from the very way they treated each other.

Overtime

What about overtime, one of the big issues in U.S. factories? Often we inquired, "Are Chinese workers required to work overtime? Do they get paid more for it?"

Workers at the Wuhan Printing and Dyeing Factory told us, "Overtime does sometimes happen, but it's rare." They explained that when it did occur, workers volunteered for political reasons: because they wanted to promote greater production. They didn't receive extra pay for such overtime work.

Wuhan steel workers said that they might work overtime when a big trainload of ore came in. "Everyone works to get it unloaded as quickly as possible, and we stay on the job until it's done. We do this because it's important to get the railway cars back into use. They shouldn't sit around."

Chinese workers also described a type of overtime that is completely foreign to Western factories. Workers at Tianjin No. 1 Machinery Factory reminisced about early days of production in the 1950s: "At first, we could only make simple lathes. During the Great Leap Forward [1958-1959] we decided to produce more complicated gear-shaping lathes. It was an exciting campaign. Many stayed overtime while building the first model. We would bring their food to the workshop. Some became so involved that they even brought bedding from home and slept in the workshop. After eight months we succeeded in producing our first advanced gear lathe." But this kind of round-the-clock campaign was quite exceptional, even in Chinese factories.

Holidays and Vacations

The six-day work week was universal in Chinese factories. Some shut down completely on the seventh day; others, like the Wuhan Iron and Steel Works, alternated days off. While there was some attempt to stagger days off so stores and parks would not be too crowded on any single day of the week, Sunday still seemed to be the most common rest day. Stores, streets, and parks were always buzzing with activity on Sunday mornings.

State policy also guaranteed six and one-half paid holidays per year for workers in state-owned enterprises. These were: (1) Chinese Spring Festival (late January or early February, three days); (2) National Day (October 1, two days); (3) May Day (May 1, International Workers' Holiday, one day); (4) International Women's Day (March 8, one-half day).

Both men and women had a half-day off on International Women's Day in some plants; in others, it seemed to be just the women. If any of these holidays fell on a regularly scheduled rest day, workers received another day off. Additional holidays or differences from the uniform six and one-half holidays were subject to local option and local custom.

In addition to holidays, some factories had provisions for family vacations. Time off for vacations usually related to individual and family needs, and policies were quite flexible. Single workers who lived a distance from their families got about two weeks off with pay each year to visit relatives. Travel expenses were also covered. Workers whose families lived nearby did not get such time off. For example, workers at a district-run factory in Peking reported that they had no special vacations. This happened to be a factory whose workers lived in the neighborhood, many within walking distance, and most families were close by in the city. On the other hand, workers at the Wuhan Printing and Dyeing Factory got fifteen days off each year to visit, or to receive, their families. But this factory had a unique history. It was originally located in Shanghai, but in 1957 moved to Wuhan, lock, stock, and barrel. The majority of the workers moved with it, so most still had relatives in Shanghai.

Four-Wheel-Drive Socialism

The East Is Red Auto Factory was in the eastern section of Peking, and while driving there we passed block after block of small stores—this one selling noodles and rice, that one selling canned goods, another crammed with towering piles of pots and pans. Where two big streets crossed they formed a small square; each usually had its own vegetable vendor surrounded by piles of radishes, cabbages, and cucumbers wet with dew and fresh from the communes that formed a green belt around the city. We turned off an artery street into a smaller lane, and the stores and vegetables gave way to piles of sheet metal and stacks of auto frames. We had reached the factory.

A cluster of large four-story buildings housed the main section of the East Is Red plant. Actually, it could more properly be called a jeep factory, since most of its production came in the shape of an olive-green, canvas-top, four-wheel-drive, 75 horsepower jeep. We watched as they were assembled on a line that moved along steadily. The line was designed very much like that of an auto plant in the United States. Each worker did the same job, over and over again, all day long. This one secured the motor in place, that pair clamped the cab down on the chassis, others tightened several bolts with air-powered tools as the line rolled on.

But this similarity in form belied a drastic difference in content: in China everyone had enough time to do the job well. We asked about quality control and the product rejection rate. "We find 5 percent need repairs when they are fully assembled," one worker told us, adding that they felt they should try to improve. We told him that no apologies were needed. Stu recalled his days in Detroit when the production line ground to a halt because the repair department could not keep up with the backlog of shoddy vehicles being slapped together.

Both workers and cadres were visibly proud of what they had made. Gallantly and trustingly they offered to let Stu take the wheel of one of the newly assembled jeeps. He clambered into the driver's seat, Janet and Zheng scrambled into the back, and a young factory worker hopped in to ride shotgun and give Stu some driving pointers. Stu put the jeep in gear, and off we bounced down a narrow road that led to nearby workers' housing.

We visited Wang Shou-zhen and Zhen Shou-fu, who both worked in the factory. Wang, the wife, served steaming tea as we chatted. Ten-year-old Zhen Xiao-fu, one of their two children, shyly peeked around a corner and was finally coaxed to join us.

Wang and Zhen lived in a small, comfortable apartment of two rooms plus kitchen and bathroom—typical of the city-style housing we visited. They paid about 5 percent of their combined income for rent and utilities. Pictures from revolutionary Peking operas hung on the wall above their beds, where four or five brightly colored quilts were neatly folded.

Both of our hosts were veteran workers. Wang had worked in the factory for thirteen years, operating a milling machine. Zhen, a lathe operator with sixteen years' experience, was also a veteran of the People's Liberation Army. Both originally were from Peking and said that their families and relatives all lived in the Peking area. Zhen was a member of the Chinese Communist Party, having joined in 1964. Like most workers in the factory, he rotated shifts each week—days, afternoons, and then nights. Wang, however, worked days regularly.

After leaving, we took a short, one-block walk to a nursery run by the factory. It was housed in a three-story building, and the age groups grew progressively older the higher we climbed. "The oldest ones manage the stairs best," one of the young teachers explained. We peeked into a room filled with red-cheeked three-year-olds pretending to take their mid-

Industry: The Leading Factor 69

morning nap but who were clearly bursting with curiosity about such strange visitors. We went along with the charade and tip-toed out, passing pools of light from the window and the "sleeping" children on the beds. But one young napper jumped up and ran over to greet us. The teacher laughed and quietly urged him back to his nap while we left before we caused more disruption.

Stu again took the wheel of the jeep. The vice-chairman of the factory's Revolutionary Committee joined us, and we drove to a large brick building that housed offices and meeting rooms. We followed the vice-chairman up a wide stairway, down a whitewashed corridor, and into a large room with windows overlooking factory workshops and fields of neighboring communes. Our group now totaled about a dozen workers and cadres, including a veteran worker from the shops, another who was a member of the Revolutionary Committee, and a young cook from the cafeteria kitchen who was also a newly selected member of the factory's branch of the Communist Party. We all sat down and sipped the ever-present green tea. Color portraits of Marx, Engels, Lenin, and Stalin gazed down from one wall, and opposite was a picture of Chairman Mao. Perched on the edges of overstuffed chairs and couches, we rested our tea cups on long, low tables with intricate lace work covered by glass. Cigarettes, as well as tea, were abundant.

The vice-chairman began by answering questions about production. The factory traced its origin to a small auto repair shop run by the Kuomintang before Liberation. In 1958, workers in the repair shop made an experimental car—and the factory had grown continuously since then. Now there were over eight thousand workers in three plants, four thousand in the main final assembly plant and the remainder in two other plants in Peking. About one-third of the workers were women. Each year they produced ten thousand jeeps and one hundred thousand units for autos, which were sent to the Northeast for assembly. Their production, our host boasted, was actually double the capacity of the original factory design. This was due largely to the six hundred technical innovations that workers, technicians, and cadres had developed in the past few years. Furthermore, he continued, they had manufactured over four hundred of their own production machines. Their jeep sold for about fifteen thousand yuan and was supplied to communes, factories, the army, and other institutions.*

"Our level of production is low compared to U.S. factories," the vice-chairman continued, "and we still have many shortcomings. For example, we have problems at the administrative level and are also backward in technical areas. In some processes we still depend upon hand labor."**

Here, as almost everywhere we visited, our hosts were eager to ask us questions: "What is a U.S. auto factory like?" "Tell us about the workers' movement in the United States." "What are living conditions like for U.S. workers?" "What about the struggles of women, students, and youth in the United States?" We tried our best to answer, always finding their interest genuine and their friendship deep.

We drove out of the factory grounds, past big bicycle corrals and workshops lined by tall green trees. In this factory sheet metal, paint, nuts, and bolts were not the only materials vital to production; workers' control, workers' innovation, and socialist initiative were also built into their jeeps.

---

* 1 yuan equalled U.S. $.42 at the time of our visit, but subsequent dollar devaluation has raised the exchange-rate value of the yuan. A comparison of wages by exchange rates, however, is extremely misleading. The purchasing power of even the lowest wage is adequate for a reasonable standard of living in China. See pp. 75-77 below.

** At a Detroit assembly plant where Stu had worked (a factory of similar size), the annual production was about one hundred thousand vehicles. But direct productivity comparisons are somewhat misleading. To be sure, there is a much higher level of automation in U.S. auto factories. But also, assembly plants in the United States are usually dependent upon outside job shops for many small parts. By contrast, workers at the East Is Red Auto Factory make most of their own small parts—something we saw in large workshops filled with lathes, grinders, and milling machines.

Wages and Living Conditions

Can you imagine workers deciding their own wages? Can you imagine workers declaring that wages are less important than their contribution to production? We found both in China, where wages were determined through a process that combined overall government planning with local options.

Workers' wages were paid by the month, as a salary.* We did not find any hourly pay system, and factory piecework was largely abolished during the Cultural Revolution. (We did encounter one enterprise where piecework was still used—an embroidery production brigade organized by housewives in a Peking Neighborhood Committee. Work in this production brigade was done mostly at home, and the amount of work each person did varied considerably, depending upon other activities and family tasks. It was more of a volunteer, sparetime activity than a full-time job.)

Government policy stipulated an eight-level (-grade) wage scale for state-owned factories. But the precise amount paid, for example, at level eight in one factory usually differed slightly from level eight in another one. Details were determined by local conditions. Wages usually ranged from about 33 yuan per month for level one to over 100 yuan for level eight. Average wages were generally a little more than 50 yuan per month. Monthly wages (in yuan) for several of the factories and workplaces we visited were as follows:

	Low (level one)	High (level eight)	Average
Shenyang Transformer Factory	33	104	60
Xin-Gang Harbor, Tianjin	55	85	70
Wuhan Printing and Dyeing Factory	41	111	63
Wuhan Sewing Machine Factory	32	96	50
Wuhan Iron and Steel Works	37.5	108	57
East Is Red Auto Factory, Peking	34	108	50
Red Flag Embroidery Factory, Tianjin (collectively owned)	32	75	45
District-Run Factory, Peking (collectively owned)	16	70	37

* In the countryside on communes income was quite different. See Ch. 4.

A few individuals, usually veteran technicians or cadres, received wages higher than those listed in the eight grades. Also, separate grading systems for cadres or technicians sometimes had higher upper limits than the workers' levels.* When we inquired about this, workers replied that their eventual goal was to equalize wages. But, they said, the income differences inherited from the old society should be narrowed by raising those in the lower categories, not by lowering a few at the top.** Since the days of Liberation, they explained, the policy of the Chinese Communist Party has been to maintain, not to lower, salaries for technicians and others who stayed on to perform their duties. This brought much technical expertise and ability to the side of the Revolution which otherwise might have been lost. Thus, even today some old-timers still received unusually high salaries; but the new, younger technicians and cadres received normal salaries.

Our hosts also contended that complete economic equality was not yet possible in China. Economic conditions did not yet allow for this, and to push for absolute income leveling at this time would disrupt development. It would be, as they put it, an "ultra-Leftist" error. Present income inequalities, they pointed out, did not prevent anyone from enjoying decent housing, food, health care, and education. They felt the immediate task was to insure that the present wage system provided an adequate standard of living for everyone and that this standard was elevated collectively as the whole country developed.

How were an individual Chinese worker's wages deter-

* See Chapter 5.

** Indeed, this is generally the way changes have taken place. There have been three main nationwide wage increases since Liberation. For example, shortly after our visit many workers in the three lowest grades were raised a grade while the upper five grades remained unchanged. The effect, of course, was a wage increase for those in the lower grades and a reduction in overall income differentials. An interesting sidelight to this event was how it was reported in the Western press. The *London Times* and Hong Kong dailies reported the move as a return to material incentives!

mined? And by whom? The procedure outlined to us by workers at the Wuhan Sewing Machine Factory was typical. Workers first held discussions in their workshop groups and suggested a specific grade for each person. "Do workers suggest what grade they think they should get?" we inquired.

"No, usually fellow workers suggest grades for each other," they replied. Further discussion revealed that except in the case of a new worker's initial grade there was no fixed time or frequency for wage discussions. These were determined, we were told, by production requirements and by government needs. Wage discussions were held when production and political priorities made wage increases possible—all were matters to be coordinated with the overall economic planning of the government agencies.

"Wage recommendations from the workers are taken to the Revolutionary Committee," the Wuhan workers continued. "It either approves them or sends them back for more discussion." They pointed out that since the workers knew each other well and the Revolutionary Committee members were also quite familiar with everyone, any inconsistent grade assignments would be noticed immediately. One worker summed it up. "We all do different jobs, but everyone knows he is working for the Revolution. So we don't argue much about different wages."

Next we asked questions about the criteria workers used to assign wage grades. Who received grade one and who received grade eight? And why?

Answers varied considerably from place to place, but the same combination of factors was always involved. Three criteria were mentioned at almost every factory: skill, political consciousness, and seniority or length of employment. Seniority, we learned, was generally determined by the total length of time a person had worked for any state-owned enterprise, not just for one particular factory. If one moved between state-owned factories, one's seniority was not affected. Seniority appeared to be the single most important criterion, but it was never considered independently of other factors.

When workers at the Luoyang Tractor Works mentioned political consciousness as a criterion, we asked what they meant: who in fact was a person with high political consciousness? They replied that such a person "overfulfills tasks, has good relations with fellow workers, and has a clear understanding of class struggle and the struggle between the two lines." Answers at other factories were similar, emphasizing good work relations and demonstrated initiative and reliability on the job.

High political consciousness, however, never alone resulted in higher wages. Young workers provided a good example. We met many young workers who served on Revolutionary Committees and Party Committees—posts clearly calling for high political consciousness—but who were always in the lower wage grades.

Job classification affected income at only a few of the workplaces we visited. For example, those working underground at the coal face in Tangshan's Kairan Coal Mine averaged 14 yuan per month more than those working aboveground. We were told at the Wuhan Iron and Steel Works that those who worked in high places got an extra 10 yuan a month—a kind of hazardous-duty pay. Workers taking their turn on the night shift at the Luoyang Heavy Equipment Factory received additional money for food. Workers on the night shift at the Luoyang Tractor Works enjoyed a free meal, and there was extra pay if one worked "in a very hot place."

Although another frequently mentioned factor in wage determinations was skill, workers at the Wuhan Sewing Machine Factory placed greater emphasis on putting "politics in command." Their three criteria for assigning wage levels were political consciousness, how well a person worked, and how long the person had worked. "Skill is definitely not a factor," they explained. "Consciousness is the main factor. We do this because a person might have a high level of skill but could also work for the reactionaries. So we put politics in command and use a person's consciousness to determine wages."

In general, Chinese workers discouraged consumer-oriented

Industry: The Leading Factor 75

materialism. Concentration on wages or possessions was considered a sign of low political consciousness. In our discussions most workers stressed the importance of what they were doing with their lives, not how much money they were making. As one woman in Peking put it, "Wages are not a way to measure a person's attitude. We estimate a person according to how he contributes to socialism. Does he unite with other workers? Does he work with enthusiasm? Right now, two-thirds of the world's population has not been liberated and is still suffering. The people in the liberated countries have the duty to support the liberation struggles of people in other countries."

Chinese wages were low by U.S. standards. But in terms of real wages—purchasing power—they were not low. Rent was minimal (usually about 5 percent of a family's income, less for single workers), food very cheap, medical care free or available at nominal cost, education free, pensions guaranteed, and personal income taxes nonexistent.*

Whenever we asked about wages, older workers inevitably compared their present living conditions to pre-Liberation days. Some said the differences "were like comparing night and day." Miners at the Kairan Coal Mine in Tangshan recalled that formerly their daily wage had been less than what management had spent daily to feed a horse. Others often recalled the unstable prices and inflation of pre-Liberation days, saying that prices sometimes jumped so much in a single day that by the afternoon a day's pay became practically worthless.

A cadre at the Shenyang Transformer Factory spoke from

* Taxation in China was mainly through state taxes paid by state-run enterprises and collectively owned units. There were seven state taxes: (1) a unified tax on industrial and commercial enterprises; (2) an income tax on these enterprises; (3) an agricultural tax; (4) a salt tax; (5) a real estate tax in urban areas; (6) a tax on the slaughter of livestock; and (7) licenses for the use of vehicles and vessels. The amount paid by individuals was less than 1 percent of tax revenue, mostly from vehicle and vessel licenses. Moreover, taxation accounted for only about 40 percent of the state's annual income; the main source of state revenue was from sales by state-run enterprises.

his personal experience: "Take me as an example. Before Liberation I was young, but I still remember much. My father was a textile worker. When I was eighteen I began to work with him. There were five persons in my family then, and three of us worked. But three could not feed our family of five. We ate the worst flour. We were very poor. After Liberation there are also now five persons in my family. Two of us work, my wife and myself. Our income is about 100 yuan per month, and we live very well. We pay 3.40 yuan per month for rent. Also, rice and flour are very cheap. We save money every month."

Mu De-xian, a dock worker in Tianjin, summed up his present condition: "As to life now, my family has a happy life. My wages are 79 yuan per month. Four of the seven in my family work, so we have a total income of 250 yuan per month. Actually my wages alone could support the whole family. There are no taxes, flour is cheap—10 fen per catty*— and rent is cheap. We have two rooms and pay 3 yuan per month rent."

By modern U.S. standards, housing in China is crowded. But Mu's family was housed adequately, if not luxuriously. And compared with pre-Liberation times, their housing conditions were tremendously improved. Mu continued: "We also have workers' welfare here. I get two suits in the summer and a padded coat in the winter. As an electrician I get rubber shoes for safety. Also, I have health care and sick leave with pay."

We asked several families to outline their monthly budgets for us. Everyone had plenty to cover the basics: shelter, clothing, transportation, heat, and food. They had money for entertainment, tobacco, and other sundries, and usually purchased items like children's toys, furniture, records, and family photographs. Each family we visited owned larger consumer items, such as bicycles, radios, wristwatches, and sewing machines. Sports equipment, musical instruments, and cameras were common. Consumer items were generally priced

---

* One hundred fen equal 1 yuan. One catty equals 1.1 pounds.

much higher than daily necessities. For example, a bicycle or sewing machine cost about two months' average salary. Most families also saved money each month. Some, with several family members working, put 30 to 40 percent of their total monthly income into state-run savings banks. It was clear that wages in China allowed for an adequate standard of living, simple perhaps compared to the highly industrialized United States, but one that has risen over the years and shows every promise of continuing to rise. Moreover, such basics as food, shelter, medical care, education, old-age care, and pensions were guaranteed to everyone.

"Our Struggle Is Worldwide"

The Shenyang Transformer Factory provided a lesson in international solidarity. We arrived at the main gate and entered a courtyard with sturdy brick factory buildings on three sides. On the walls, bright red-and-white billboards urged, "Workers of the World, Unite!" Traces of multicolored confetti were scattered about, left from a mass welcome given Cambodian Prince Sihanouk the previous day. As banners throughout the city of Shenyang proudly declared, the Chinese support "the just struggles of the three Indochinese peoples"—those of Vietnam, Cambodia, and Laos. Inside the factory we saw numerous blackboards and bulletin board displays detailing Cambodian history and the present stage of the Cambodian struggle against U.S. imperialism.

This transformer factory had international ties of a sort right from its beginning, but not the kind the Chinese want to repeat. The first workshops were built by the Japanese in 1939 during their occupation of Northeast China. Then they produced one small section of a transformer. In 1945 the Japanese were driven out and the Kuomintang took over. The factory was expanded after Shenyang was liberated from the Kuomintang in September 1948. In the 1950s they received aid on an international scale:

"During the period of Stalin we had the support of the

Soviet Union," one cadre explained. "We will never forget this. But Khrushchev pulled out his technicians and tore up the agreements. He wanted China to become revisionist, but he didn't succeed."

After 1960 the factory followed a policy of self-reliance. The Soviet technicians had taken all the plans and blueprints with them, forcing the Chinese workers to learn through experimentation and practice. Our host continued, "In the Cultural Revolution we criticized the Liu Shao-chi line, 'Run the Factory by Experts.' We built new transformers using a three-in-one combination (of workers, cadres, and technicians), and this new equipment is better than the old design. It is lighter, it takes only half as long to make (six months instead of one year or more), and it costs 30 percent less."

The factory produced transformers and current inductors for large electrical systems. We knew almost nothing about the technology involved, and we watched the assembly of several huge transformers, each a couple of stories tall, in open-mouthed amazement. How seldom we give serious thought to the work—the labor involved in making such things in our society. We take electrical power for granted and don't consider what's necessary to build those mysterious complexes behind the high wire fences marked "Danger! High Voltage."

The Shenyang workers described their jobs as labor necessary to provide electricity for millions. And that, they added, was helping the world revolution. Welders, grinders, those who cut and pressed together the miles of paper-based insulation in the transformers—all saw their jobs as a small but direct part of "making revolution." They told us this repeatedly as we toured the workshops; their blackboards and bulletin boards carried the same message.

We saw several different facets of their factory life. We chatted with men and women in the dormitories for single workers. The factory clinic, directly across the street, was a large two-story building where workers received free medical treatment. We walked past basketball courts conveniently located between workshops and dormitories, and we spent a pleasant half-hour or so in the factory-run nursery. The dining hall was clean and simple, featuring colorful wall posters that detailed the different ways to recycle food waste. Small cupboards housing the workers' bowls and chopsticks lined another wall. Outside the kitchen we were surprised to see an old Dodge pick-up truck—undoubtedly as old as we were—which was still used to haul supplies.

The following day we returned to the same factory for a discussion with workers and cadres. Their reception room was furnished with upholstered couches; traditional Chinese paintings shared the wall with portraits of Marx, Engels, Lenin, Stalin, and Mao. Low tables were used to display scale models of the many varieties of transformers and current inductors that the factory produced. The models were fascinating, and we appreciated the practical touch.

A dozen young people, veteran workers, cadres, and technicians gathered for a relaxed discussion, which ranged over a wide variety of topics. They knew each other well, often pointing to one another for an answer to our questions. They, in turn, had many questions about the United States, asking about work conditions, the unemployment rate, and the economy. "What happens when a worker is fired?" "What happens when unemployment insurance runs out?" Others wanted to know about the political and economic position of women. Older workers compared what we told them to the conditions they had known before Liberation, pointing to similarities and differences.

We countered with a barrage of questions about China, from the mundane to the theoretical. "How are shop disputes handled?" "How has political study helped in your work?" "Is surplus value created under socialism?"*

---

* Marxist economics postulates that all value is created by human labor. "Surplus value" under capitalism is the difference between the real value of commodities produced and what the capitalist pays for labor and raw materials. Capitalists get their profits from this surplus value. A simple example might be: a worker makes bricks all day, which his boss sells for their true value of $50.00. The worker is paid $3.00 an hour for eight hours, or $24.00 a day. Raw materials and overhead

Several workers responded to our theoretical question about surplus value. One worker said, "Under socialism, production is for the state, for the country as a whole. The aim of production is to build the country and support peoples' revolution in the world." Another added, "The value created by workers is used for socialist construction and goes to the whole people, not for the profit of a few." Still another said, "Under socialism, we pay attention to the living standards of workers. Individual living standards are increased and basic construction of our society's economic base are both being carried out from the value created by the workers." Finally, a worker summed up, saying, "The aim of the socialist system is fundamentally different. Capitalism aims at getting personal profit from the exploitation of workers' labor, while socialism aims to liberate all workers."

It was clear they had studied such matters. But the overriding impact of this visit came from the internationalism these workers expressed. They stated it best: "We should support the proletarian revolution throughout the world. The class struggle is international. Just because the Chinese people have liberation doesn't mean the rest of the world is free. We Chinese workers can't hold rifles in the front lines in some other country. But we can do our job here—not thinking of ourselves, but helping the oppressed peoples of the whole world, helping to bring an end to the exploitation of man by man. Doing our job well here gives support to the world revolution. Your struggle in the United States is linked to our struggle."

Their internationalism was expressed in practice as well as theory. We saw crated transformers with shipping labels marked in both Russian and Vietnamese, bound for the Democratic Republic of Vietnam. China, the workers emphasized, was a "vast rear area" for the front-line struggles against imperialism in Indochina.

(clay, molds, machinery, etc.) totals $10.00. The owner's total cost is $34.00; the surplus value, added by the labor of the employee, is $50.00 less $34.00, or $16.00.

Differences on the Line

In socialist China work disputes and grievances were handled by the workers themselves. Many grievances common in capitalist countries—complaints about unsafe working conditions and equipment, speed-up, overtime, pay docking, suspension, firing—were simply not points of conflict in Chinese factories. This was a result of placing safety before production in determining working conditions and of using education, not punishment (like docking wages, suspensions, discharge), to solve problems.

But obviously some differences of opinion and conflicts of interest will arise. How were these handled? We raised this question at several factories. Generally, workers told us, disputes were solved through a process of discussion, investigation, and more discussion. Each workshop had a group leader whose duties included investigating and mediating disputes and initiating group discussions when necessary.

A leading cadre at the Shenyang Transformer Factory described how they had handled one particular shop dispute: "We have a drying furnace that is used by two different workshops. Both workshops were trying to overfulfill their production quotas, and each demanded first chance at the furnace. They had a contradiction. Leaders of the two workshops met and discussed the problem. They suggested that all the workers get together and study Chairman Mao's article 'On Contradiction.' Then they used ideas from that article to analyze their situation. They looked at the production of the whole factory and identified the contradictions—when each workshop was key, when each was secondary to the total process of production. Then they worked out a priority in the use of the furnace that satisfied everyone."

That seemed a good long-range approach, we said, but what about immediate conflicts? What about things that can't wait for work groups to study "On Contradiction"? We pushed our point, and then a young woman described a shop conflict about fans. Some workers wanted large fans turned on while they worked, others did not. Everyone affected discussed the question, even when it meant holding up production, until they reached an agreement. Fights among workers nowadays, they said, were pretty much unheard of.

The Backward Few

"We do have a few backward workers, but we consider them brothers in the working class," a spinner at the Zhengzhou No. 3 Textile Mill explained. No one was fired. Wages were not cut. "We have unity with them. We use criticism and self-criticism. We solve problems by mobilizing the masses."

But what does this mean? Take the question of lateness. At the Wuhan Printing and Dyeing Factory we asked what happened if someone arrived late for work. "It doesn't happen often," workers quickly replied, "but if someone is late we first try to find out the reason. For example, if a woman is getting her children ready for school and has problems and is therefore late, we understand. That's not a problem." They added that if a person was often late they investigated thoroughly and tried to solve the concrete cause of the problem.

Absenteeism, although not a large problem, was handled in like fashion. A woman worker at the Zhengzhou No. 3 Textile Mill told us, "Twenty-three of us work together in my group in the spinning department—twenty-one women and two men. The factory operates three shifts, and we rotate shifts each week—one week mornings, the next week afternoons, and the third week nights. One young woman in our group often asked for unpaid personal leave when it was our turn to work nights. She would be off two or three days in the week when we worked at night. We didn't know why she requested leave so often, so we talked to her friends and to other workers who knew her situation. We found out that she simply didn't like working nights. She was young. She and her husband had only one child, and her husband worked. They didn't need much money. She told us that she would rather have the time to herself than have the pay for the work. So we went to one of the older workers and asked him to talk to her about conditions in old times. The young woman was from a poor peasant family, and now she wanted only to enjoy her good life with her family. The old worker told her about conditions before Liberation, about how he had worked twelve to twenty hours a day. We all talked to her to help her change her outlook. We said that her work and ours was all part of the revolution. We don't just work for ourselves, we work to support people in other countries who have not yet made their revolution. Two out of three people in the world today are still oppressed. They are our class brothers and we should work to help them."

The workers reported that this young woman eventually changed her attitude toward work and stopped requesting personal leave every time it was her turn for the night shift.

People Are the Most Precious*

How safe are jobs in China? What is done to prevent accidents? What is done to take care of someone when an accident occurs?

Comrade Ou Hui-tan, a member of the Revolutionary Committee at the Wuhan Iron and Steel Works, talked about safety. "To prevent accidents we educate workers about safety. We tell them to listen to their shop leaders. We also supply safety equipment, like special masks and heavy clothing, and we check to see if it needs to be repaired. For people who work in high places, we try to build fences and rails around their work areas."

In other factories similar measures were taken: heavy clothing, insulated shoes, or other special equipment were issued as a matter of course if the job required it. When a machine needed repair, it was not used until the repair work

* "Of all things in the world, people are the most precious." (Mao Tse-tung, *Bankruptcy of the Idealist Conception of History*, 1949)

was done. Chinese workers didn't have to argue with a foreman to obtain safety equipment or to have defective machinery repaired. Workers themselves saw to it that the repair work got done.

We saw shortcomings in the area of industrial safety, usually resulting from workers themselves taking unnecessary risks. For example, we saw spotwelders and lathe operators working without safety glasses, or workers who treated a punch press more casually than such a dangerous machine deserved. We asked about these things and learned that safety equipment was available but that the individuals involved had not bothered to use it. This, workers and cadres told us, was indeed a shortcoming, but they contended it was one to be solved through more education, not by punishment or restrictive means.

We agreed that education, ultimately, was the answer. A similar situation exists today in the United States with respect to automobile seat belts. Although nobody denies their value, many people just don't use them. Some people have argued for laws that require the use of seat belts and impose stiff fines or penalties. Others say that such laws are impossible to enforce, and push instead for the installation of warning buzzers and lights in newer automobiles. But motorists inevitably find ways to circumvent even these gimmicks and still don't use seat belts. The key, of course, is education—to convince everyone that accidents *can* happen to them and that for safety's sake they should use preventative equipment.

Chinese workers live and work in circumstances that encourage rank-and-file participation. Those who are aware of shortcomings in the use of safety equipment can realistically push for effective educational campaigns. But from what we saw, we felt there were some factories where such campaigns should be placed higher on their list of priorities.

Seldom did we find either factory equipment or production organization at fault in matters of safety. One exception, however, was the Luoyang Heavy Equipment Factory. The

Industry: The Leading Factor 85

work there was arranged less carefully than in most other factories we visited. Red-hot iron from the foundry and sharp metal scraps from lathes were left exposed close to aisles where someone might get a severe burn or cut.

Many accidents in Western factories occur when workers are forced to keep up with a fast-moving line or to maintain a high daily production rate; speed results in taking chances. Not so in today's China. There the pace of work was itself a factor promoting safety. Workers controlled the speed and rate of work, which was reasonable rather than hectic, productive but not back-breaking. A Western time-study expert wouldn't like Chinese factories, where *people* definitely came before *production*.

Accidents do, of course, happen. Our concern about non-use of safety glasses proved justified when we visited a hospital in Shi-jia-zhuang. Among the patients was a young lathe worker requiring an operation who had been hit in the eye by a small piece of flying metal. Accidents and illnesses such as his were covered by an extensive apparatus of workers' medical care which also included dental care. Each factory workshop or section had a worker trained in first aid who could give help on the spot. Small clinics and first-aid stations dotted factory workshops. In one factory we saw a small mobile first-aid wagon that could be rolled from place to place. Many factories had their own hospitals and others had special arrangements with city or district hospitals to provide medical care in case of accident or sickness.

"Before Liberation I had never even seen a hospital run by a factory," mused an older worker in a Zhengzhou factory. "Now we have our own hospital, and the doctors and nurses come to the workshops to see the condition of the workers and to give us treatment." His factory looked after workers' health through a three-level system of medical care: paramedics in each shop, clinics in each section, and a hospital for the factory as a whole.

Medical care for workers was free and usually available at half-cost for family members. By U.S. standards, costs were very low. For example, a hospital bed in a Wuhan factory-run hospital was 5 yuan (about $2.50) per day. An office visit cost about 5 fen ($ .03) and an appendix removal was less than 8 yuan. However, if a family should have any trouble meeting the bill, special arrangements were made. In some cases medical costs were simply waived. The individual situation was always considered. Workers at the Wuhan Printing and Dyeing Factory gave us an example of this. A few years ago the wife of a worker had become very ill. She was hospitalized for two years, and the cost of her medical care totaled 9,000 yuan; half-rate for families cut that down to 4,500 yuan. Her husband earned between 60 and 70 yuan per month, so obviously there was no way they could pay the bill. Leaders at the hospital and the factory discussed the situation. After the circumstances were investigated, they decided simply to waive payment. The woman received all the medical care she needed. Our informants added that in similar cases the government had sometimes picked up the bill.

In some workplaces family members had a cooperative medical insurance plan. For example, the families of workers at the Xin Gang Harbor in Tianjin paid 2 yuan annually and were guaranteed complete treatment for the year. Neighborhood Committees and schools also ran clinics and hospitals. The People's Liberation Army operated hospitals—one we visited offered free treatment to all. Thus, there were numerous ways medical care was provided, and the total picture was that neither workers nor their families lacked medical care for any reason.

The Well-Being of the Masses

"Pay close attention to the well-being of the masses, from the problems of land and labor to those of fuel, rice, cooking oil and salt," Chairman Mao urged in 1934. This has been a guideline ever since, underlying the creation of an extensive network of workers' services and activities run by Chinese factories.

The Wuhan Iron and Steel Works, with its extensive system

of workers' welfare, has been hailed by Mao as a model for factory development. In addition to iron and steel production, this factory organized and supported: a college for workers and their families, housing and apartments for single workers and married families, four middle schools, ten primary schools, three theaters, nurseries, a library, a cultural performance team, a hospital with four hundred beds, several clinics, a rest sanitorium, medical teams, a farm, a militia group, and sports and recreational activities. The factory also subsidized cheap transportation by train, trolley, or bus from the city to the plant, which was located on the outskirts of town.

Workers and cadres at the Foreign Languages Printing House in Peking outlined to us the workers' welfare activities their plant supported: free medical care with half-cost to family members, kindergartens and nurseries, haircuts and a bath house, a retirement system, a library, sports and recreation facilities, cultural performances, films, and a factory-subsidized cafeteria. Also, they said, they had low rents, no taxes, and no unemployment or layoffs. If someone had health needs for special food, he or she could get extra money to cover the cost. Families living in factory-owned housing told us that they got extra money to pay for fuel in the winter. The factory grew apples, rice, and grapes on farms and on the grounds around the workshops. Some of these crops went directly to workers, while others were sold to the state.

Sick leave with pay was standard policy in the factories we visited. For example, the Dong Feng Watch Factory in Tianjin had a policy of six months' sick leave with full pay, after which workers received 60 percent of their salary. Workers at the Zhengzhou Textile Machinery Manufacturing Factory described to us a young woman in their tool department. She had a serious heart condition and was absent from work for four years. The cost of her treatment, which included traveling to Shanghai for special care, amounted to somewhere between 6,000 and 7,000 yuan, and was paid by the state. She still received 70 percent of her wages plus the regular increases given during her period of illness. We were told that she had commented to her fellow workers, "Before Liberation I would have died with such an illness. Then many like me died."

Chinese workers enjoy a retirement and pension system, something which was also unheard of before Liberation. The Zhengzhou Textile Machinery Manufacturing Factory was typical, providing retirement for men at age sixty and for women at age fifty-five with 75 percent of their salary. Health was often a more important factor than age in determining the year of retirement. Poor health might necessitate early retirement, but workers in good health could choose to remain at their jobs. There were also special situations. Workers at the Kairan Coal Mine, for example, could retire at age fifty-five. Our hosts there described one veteran worker who had reached retirement age but had preferred to continue working. His comrades explained that he had heart trouble and couldn't do heavy work, so he had begun to clean up the grounds around the mine buildings and workshops and had mobilized other older workers to do the same thing. He had explained why, saying, "I still want to do something for socialism."

Housing

In China we had many warm and friendly visits with workers and their families who lived in factory-owned apartments. Our small entourage, plus local hosts and curious neighbors, quickly filled a room. People would immediately occupy the few chairs and others would perch on the sides of beds, stools, or on boxes that were hastily scrounged up for the occasion. The apartments were simple, cheerful suites, usually with a small kitchen and bath and two larger rooms doubling as bedrooms at night and living rooms during the day. Bedding typically was folded neatly on wide wooden beds, with bright silk covers adding patches of red, green, orange, or pink to the room. Walls were often covered with dramatic posters and scenes from new revolutionary Peking operas. Many families kept photos of children and other relatives under a piece of glass on a bureau top, or framed on the wall. Wardrobes were sturdy, standup wooden constructions that usually occupied a corner of the room. House plants were popular, and sometimes goldfish swam endlessly in bowls on the window sills.

It always took us several minutes to get settled. There would be a flurry of activity, with our hosts checking to see that everyone had a good seat. Zheng and our other companions would urge our hosts to sit down and not go to too much trouble. Everyone made sure we had plenty of tea or hot water, and those who had not yet learned that we didn't smoke offered us cigarettes. Once settled, we inevitably found our hosts eager to talk about their work, their activities, and their living conditions.

Rent in these apartments usually ran between 4 and 6 yuan per month, depending on size. Utilities were sometimes included in rent, sometimes extra.

Housing for single workers was typically dormitory style. Rent there was also very low, in some places 50 fen per month. At the Kairan Coal Mine it was only 10 fen, and in other places new workers paid nothing at all for dormitory rooms.

We visited Wang Mun-yu, a young man of twenty-seven, who worked at the Shenyang Transformer Factory and lived in a single workers' dorm. Short and trim, with a square face, he hardly looked his age. His good-sized room was filled with late morning sunshine when we entered. Flat wooden beds and simple desks lined the walls, and a white enamel washbasin, holding a toothbrush and brightly colored towels, was stored beneath each bed. The window sills were crowded with potted plants, and Wang explained that one of his four roommates had a green thumb. He had lived in the dorm for the past five years. The men shared quarters on the ground floor, while the second floor was occupied by women. Wang was a middle-school graduate and worked as an electric welder. He told us he and his roommates studied together for one hour each Thursday night. They also studied with their shop groups at other times during the week. He said that he took all three daily meals in the factory dining hall, which was located directly across the street.

We bid Wang *zaijian* (good-bye) and walked upstairs to visit Zen Jiu-lan, who was busy knitting a pair of woolen slacks when we came in. Zen laughed about her knitting, explaining that many layers of clothing were vital during the cold North China winters. On her bed was an *er-hu*, a Chinese fiddle, which she was learning to play under a roommate's tutelage. Her room was similar to Wang's except that bright bedspreads gave it a more homey atmosphere. A clothesline draped with white terry-cloth towels ran the length of the room. Zen said that she paid 90 fen per month rent, while some of her younger roommates paid little or nothing. The difference, she added, was that her eight years' seniority in the factory gave her higher wages and a greater ability to pay. Her family lived in Shenyang, and Zen usually visited them during the week and also on Sunday.

As we left we stopped by the dormitory recreation rooms, which housed ping-pong tables, a TV, and several types of table games. Basketball courts were outside, directly in front of the door.

Both single and married workers chose where they wanted to live. Many city families lived in government-owned apartments and houses. Some people owned their own homes. If two members of a family worked at different factories, they could often choose between housing provided by either one. Some small factories, such as a district-run factory we visited in Peking, did not provide housing. Most workers there were women who lived in city-owned neighborhood housing or in apartments owned by the factory where their husbands worked.

Housing conditions and buildings varied. The newest were usually four- or five-story concrete-and-brick apartment buildings. But not everywhere. Tangshan's Kairan Coal Mine had built one-story stone houses that were similar to the peasant homes we visited in the countryside. They had built these houses in the mid-1950s and sold them to workers, who paid for them in installments without interest. We visited one neighborhood in Tangshan where every family owned its own home. However, housing built more recently was owned by the mine and rented to families. Thirty-five percent of the Kairan miners lived in housing provided by the mine. This percentage was different in other factories. For example, at the Shenyang No. 1 Machinery Factory 60 percent of the workers lived in factory housing.

"Our Children Grow Up Well"

Child care was a characteristic feature of Chinese factory life. Nurseries and kindergartens were as much a part of Chinese factories as the dining halls, workshops, and smokestacks. Working mothers were provided with feeding rooms to nurse their infants, and they usually had forty- to forty-five-minute work-leave in the morning and at midday to attend to the baby's needs. Nurseries we visited typically accepted infants from fifty-six days old—the length of maternity leave for women. Not all parents chose to use the nursery and kindergarten facilities—which were completely voluntary—and children sometimes remained at home with grandparents or even great-grandparents.

The factory-run nurseries did much more than just babysit. They were bright and lively places with lots of activities. Even the littlest ones went on outings. We remember watching one group, barely old enough to walk, toddling around the Peking Zoo. Their teachers pushed large baby-wagons to collect those who got tired; four or five kids could sit in each cart. Preschoolers learned to sing and dance. We'll never forget two five-year-old girls at the Foreign Languages Printing House who performed a scene from the popular Chinese ballet, *The White-Haired Girl.* One sang in a beautiful clear voice while the other danced. They topped off their performance with a very professional joint bow before dropping stage composure and running off to the wings. Education was also important, and in Shenyang we saw another group of five-year-olds learning to write their first characters. Child care always covered the full working day. Some nurseries and kindergartens also offered week-long service, where parents could bring children at the start of the work week and pick them up on the sixth day, enabling the family to spend its holidays together.

There were nominal charges for child care, but costs seemed well within the budget of working couples. Among examples we found: one nursery in Zhengzhou charged 6 yuan per month for all-week care and 1.5 yuan per month for daily care, which did not include food. A nursery run by the East Is Red Auto Factory in Peking charged 11.5 yuan per month for daily care, but this included three hot meals and two snacks a day. The charge for infants in the nursery at the Tianjin No. 1 Machinery Factory and at the Xin Gang Harbor in Tianjin was 50 fen per month. Factories and the government subsidized nurseries and kindergartens since actual operating costs were often higher than the total fees collected. "The state helps make good conditions possible. Our children grow up well," the Party Secretary at the Wuhan Sewing Machine Factory declared proudly.

Rice, Cooking Oil, and Salt

Every factory we visited, large and small, had its dining hall. The small district-run factory in Peking had a kitchen which turned out hot meals and also heated up steamed bread, rice, and other food the workers brought from home. Larger dining halls provided an enormous variety of appetizing dishes at nominal cost. In Wuhan a worker told us, "We've told our cooks to provide a choice of 'three hots' for every meal: hot soup, hot rice, and hot main dish." The cost ranged from a low of 4 fen to a high of 15 fen for a meal, depending on individual choice. The Kairan Coal Mine in Tangshan had a typical dining hall, but during lunch break hot food was also sent below for underground workers.

Just before lunch we walked into a Zhengzhou dining hall, equipped to serve two thousand workers. The room was larger than a basketball court. Tables, sagging under their loads, ran the entire length of one side. Arranged three-deep, there were literally dozens of selections, from cold vegetable dishes and meats, hot noodles and dumplings, chicken, eggs, and pastries of infinite shapes and tastes, to steamed breads, rice, and the staple of all Chinese meals—soups which are so hearty they make a meal in themselves. If the image of old China conjures up starving masses and emaciated peasants, new China is building an image, rightfully deserved, of people who eat well.

Making Life More Lively

Cultural and recreational activities helped make Chinese factories lively and exciting places. The emphasis was on participation, not observation, and workers typically jumped into spare-time pursuits with great zest. Almost every factory we visited had a spare-time group which performed Chinese songs, dances, and scenes from the new revolutionary Peking operas. These groups often created their material from life around them. Sometimes their performances praised the merits of good workers or factory workshops, and urged others to struggle harder. Providing both entertainment and education, they also used songs and dances of China's national minorities. Part of their purpose, as one Peking woman said, was "to make life more lively." The performances we saw certainly did a good job of it! Their artistic level, in our opinion, was quite high. Their enthusiasm was infectious, spreading to all who came into contact with them. This, plus the timeliness and relevancy of their material, made them very popular. Factories usually provided funds for elaborate costumes, instruments, music, and other equipment.

Sports were also very popular. Outdoor basketball courts, ping-pong tables, and volleyball courts were omnipresent. Some larger factories had soccer fields, and even swimming pools and small stadiums. Track meets, tug-of-wars, and other games were often organized. Different factory sections often formed their own teams, but there were also many informal activities and pick-up games after work.

Both men and women were active in sports. At the Tianjin No. 1 Machinery Factory we passed a basketball court just after shift break. Some men had already started an informal game; a group of women stood by, their basketball ready, obviously eager to get onto the court, too. We returned twenty minutes later to see the women playing on one end of the court while a small men's group scrimmaged on the other.

Factories also furnished reading rooms, libraries, TV rooms, and game rooms. Workers at the Red Flag Embroidery Factory in Tianjin were being modest when they told us that they only had a "book corner." "It's too small to really call it a library," they said.

Many cities we visited had a workers' cultural center, which was a combination auditorium and sports and recreation center. Groups from different factories could use the building for performances or sports events. Professional groups also used the facilities for large performances. In Luoyang we spent an enjoyable evening at the workers' club watching the local professional acrobatic troupe. In Guangzhou we visited a cultural park serving the whole city. The activities we observed there were numerous: two outdoor theaters (which took advantage of the mild South China climate), two stages for amateur cultural groups, six industrial and political exhibition halls, a library and reading room, amusements and rides for children, and indoor sports facilities (where we watched a basketball game between teams from a sugar mill and another factory, and also a ping-pong match between a determined shipyard worker and a just-as-determined machinist).

Red is the traditional color of happiness in China. We found that Chinese factories were doubly red—culturally as well as politically.

3
Agriculture: The Foundation

"*Hen hao! Hen hao!*" Janet's work partner encouraged her, saying, "Very good! Very Good!" We were transplanting celery seedlings on the Sino-Hungarian Friendship Commune near Peking.

Actually, our little bit of agricultural work was entirely symbolic. For forty-five minutes we dug up celery seedlings, shook off the dirt, and then replanted them. Stu worked on one side of the path and Janet on the other, each with a different teacher, both surrounded by translators and guides from China International Travel Service, who also participated in the work. Our forty-five minutes were next to nothing, but they were enough to give us the sense that, done all day, this task could be back-breaking. Agricultural labor was surely different from what we'd been doing lately, but it was not entirely new to us. In 1970 we'd both spent two months cutting sugarcane in Cuba and as a youngster Stu had spent several summers in Oregon's commercial strawberry fields; he had also baled hay during his high-school days in Iowa.

There's more to transplanting celery seedlings than meets the eye—at least for the uninitiated. First you have to get the right number of seedlings in a batch, holding them in your hand just so. Then you dig the hole with a small hand trowel to a precise depth—not too shallow, not too deep. Then you place the roots straight down, but not too far, and don't bend them—otherwise they'll never grow. Finally you press earth around the stalks so they'll stand upright—but not too tight—and of course you have to plant the seedlings in even rows. Janet caught on fairly quickly, and after a dozen or so tries the woman teaching her stopped digging up and replanting the ones she had done. The woman with Stu was very polite and didn't replant any, at least while we were there! We were both sobered by the thought that food for the eight hundred million people of China still basically comes from such tedious hand labor as this.

The fields where we worked were bright green, neat, and orderly, and held many varieties of vegetables grown for Peking's markets. As we walked past rows of cabbages, radishes, celery, cucumbers, and eggplants, the head of the local production team explained that they planted vegetables at intervals so the crop does not go to market at the same time.

Our symbolic agricultural work was the result of our request to do productive labor. We had hoped for something which would give us a real sense of what it was like to work in China, but this, of course, was just a token. Lao Liu, from China International Travel Service, teased us good-naturedly and grinned, saying that he realized we had worked only a short time. "If we hadn't given you this opportunity to work," he said, "you would have criticized us." He knew why we wanted to work and made it clear that he understood the political reasons for our request. But he also made it clear that CITS felt—probably for a variety of reasons—that the main emphasis of our visit should be otherwise. Undoubtedly our language difficulties, and the fact that our presence in any work situation would be more a disruption than an aid, were two good reasons why we didn't get more opportunity to work. Nevertheless, token labor or not, our time spent at this commune was hardly wasted.

The Golden Bridge to Communism

Our visit to the Sino-Hungarian Friendship Commune provided a good opportunity to learn how Chinese agriculture developed and collectivized—step by step—since Liberation.

At the time of Liberation the land in this area had been afflicted by drought and windstorms, and to elaborate on this point our hosts recited an old local folk song: *The sandstorm is strong in winter and spring...* They interrupted to add that the wind often blew so hard, and with so much sand, that people couldn't see someone else a few feet away. Before Liberation there were more than one thousand sand dunes in the area. *Drought in the summer... In the autumn frogs cry in the fields.* They explained that in the past there had been no water drainage, and after a rain the fields flooded and water-logged the crops—but gave the frogs a good home! Also, after heavy rains the roads disappeared and even horse carts could not pass.

Liberation came in the autumn of 1948, and immediately there had been land reform. Large land holdings were broken up and distributed to landless and poor peasants. "The land returned to the original masters—the people!" our hosts exclaimed. Formerly 70 percent of the land had been owned by about one hundred landlords. Many local peasants had been landless and homeless, living in huts or pigsties or seeking shelter in the landlords' courtyards. Poor peasants had to eat grain husks to survive while the landlords led an extravagant life. Again, they quoted a folk saying of former times: "We work hard like oxen and horses, but we eat worse than cats and dogs."

The process of change from individual land ownership at the time of Liberation to the present system of collective ownership (the people's communes) had been arduous and difficult. An intense political struggle had taken place over a number of years, with many ups and downs, but with definite stages. Land reform, the cooperative movement, and finally the people's communes destroyed the stagnant social relations of pre-Liberation China and made possible technological change and scientific farming.

Zhou Min-fu, a cadre on the Sino-Hungarian Friendship Commune, told us their story: "We set up mutual-aid teams in the autumn of 1951 and the spring of 1952. They consisted of a few households. Land, draft animals, and farm tools were privately owned. Members helped each other, exchanging work for work. But soon after that we had the problem of dividing the work between rich and poor. This was due to differences in land and to different labor-power needs. The needs of production were not even. About this time Chairman Mao issued a call to get organized and to follow the road of common, rather than individual, prosperity. So in the fall of 1952 we set up two agricultural cooperatives. The present head of our commune Revolutionary Committee, Yang Mei-chun, was a leader of one of these co-ops." (They told us Yang was in Peking at a meeting that day, and also that he had been a delegate to the Ninth Party Congress of the Chinese Communist Party in 1969—indicating that he was a highly respected and important leader.)

Zhou proudly reported that Chairman Mao had written about their co-ops in the mid-1950s,* because they had set up high-level co-ops directly from mutual-aid teams, skipping the stage of semi-socialist co-ops. In most of China's countryside, the cooperative movement typically had passed through two stages of development. The first step (after mutual-aid teams) usually had been a lower cooperative. This co-op, larger than the aid team, was considered semi-socialist; its members pooled land, tools, and animals, which were all used and managed collectively. Income was determined by how much a person had pooled as well as by the amount of work he or she had contributed. Two peasants could labor side by side all year, but one who could contribute an ox or hand cart would earn more than one who couldn't. The second

---

* Probably in *Socialist Upsurge in China's Countryside* (China: 1955), 3 vols. A one-volume English edition was published in 1957. This is a collection of reports about the founding and development of agricultural cooperatives, with introductions to each selection written by Chairman Mao. The volumes played an important role in popularizing the cooperatives and providing guidelines for overcoming problems and political errors.

Agriculture: The Foundation 99

step had been higher, or fully socialist, cooperatives. These were larger, about two hundred households on the average, and previous property ownership did not affect income. Here the land and the means of production were truly collectively owned. Income was determined solely by the amount of work done, or, as our hosts put it, "by the socialist principle, 'from each according to his ability, to each according to his labor.' "*

Zhou continued: "By 1955 all the mutual-aid groups in our area had merged into agricultural cooperatives. But as production developed and expanded, the form of the cooperatives couldn't keep up with it. So several cooperatives merged into a 'big united co-op.' But this was still not a commune. The cooperatives were solely engaged in farming. Communes today organize both the economy and the local government, and they include agriculture, industry, trade, education, health, and the militia.

"For example, at the time we were a cooperative, we had problems with the roads. They were very narrow. Once we asked a tractor station for help in cultivating, but the tractor they sent couldn't get through the roads and had to turn back. In 1956 there was a very heavy rain. We tried to drain the fields, but the ditches went through the fields of other co-ops. We couldn't solve this problem by the force of one co-op alone, so we united co-ops. But the people were still discussing the best form of agricultural production.

"Then Chairman Mao inspected agriculture in Shandong Province and issued the call for people's communes, summed up in his slogan, 'People's Communes are Fine!' We discussed

---

* The Chinese distinguished between the socialist principle ("To each according to his labor") and the communist principle ("From each according to his ability, to each according to his needs"). The latter, they felt, would be possible only at a higher stage of collective development than their present stage of socialism—only when true communism blossoms in a world free from exploitation, imperialism, and capitalism. For those interested in the theoretical origin and background of this distinction, see Karl Marx, *Critique of the Gotha Program* (Sect. I, No. 3); and V. I. Lenin, *State and Revolution* (Ch. V, Sect. III).

the matter here, and in May 1958 we held a rally and decided to set up a people's commune. Four cooperatives merged to form our commune. We now have 36,000 people and 7,600 households in the commune, divided into eleven production brigades and 106 production teams.

"There are many advantages to communes," Zhou declared. "They can develop and expand production and also provide good conditions for farm mechanization. In addition, they solve once and for all the problems of splitting income between the rich and the poor.

"Their first advantage is their big size, and their second advantage is their more socialist nature. People call the communes the 'golden bridge to communism.' Many problems can now be attacked and solved, such as farm capital construction, water conservation, land leveling, soil improvement, well digging, irrigation, and reforestation. In our commune, 95 percent of our land is now irrigated. Before it was 19 percent. We also have over six hundred electric wells and two irrigation canals stretching 95 li.*

"Pig raising and pig breeding have been promoted," Zhou continued. "We raise them for both pork and fertilizer. Pigs have increased from three thousand to forty-one thousand. Also, agricultural production has developed. Our yield per mu of vegetables has grown from 1,000 kilos per mu to 4,500 kilos per mu.** Before Liberation the harvest in grain was sometimes even less than the seeds we used! We now have ninety-three big tractors, sixty trucks, and over six hundred animal-drawn carts. There are seventeen hundred horses and mules. We have four commune-run factories and a farm machine-tool station. We say that the development of production promotes the development of education. We have thirty-three primary schools. In the past there were only 980 students in the area. Now we have 11,000 students. We also have a three-level medical system. On the commune level

---

* One *li* equals 0.31 miles.
** One *mu* equals one-sixth of an acre.

there is a hospital, on the production-brigade level we have clinics and medical centers, and in the production teams we have 'barefoot doctors.'* Before Liberation we had only three doctors—all of traditional medicine. Now we have three hundred medical workers. In 1970 we set up a cooperative medical system. It costs about 2 yuan per year and covers everything."

Zhou concluded with typical modesty: "We have made some improvements, but compared to some advanced units like Tachai we have not improved enough. So we are now carrying out a movement to learn from Tachai."

Learn from Tachai!

"Learn from Tachai!"

This was something we heard throughout China's countryside. In rural areas the most common slogan painted on the sides of buildings or pasted on whitewashed walls—with the characters drawn in thick black strokes on thin pieces of pastel-colored paper—was "In Agriculture, Learn from Tachai!" We soon discovered if we wanted to understand agriculture, we too had to learn from—and about—Tachai. We found that the story of China's agricultural development—its problems, its politics, its future—was the story of Tachai.

The Tachai Production Brigade is part of the Tachai Commune in Xiyang County, Shanxi Province, in Northern China. It's tucked away in the Taihang Mountains, a bit over two hundred miles southwest of Peking, in an area with poor soil, serious erosion, and rock-strewn, mountainous terrain.

---

* "Barefoot doctors" were paramedics trained in first aid, diagnosis, and preventive medicine. In the countryside they were peasants, usually elected by fellow members of their production team, who had undergone short, intensive medical training and who then worked in the fields, continued part-time medical training, and thus served their comrades.

The Tachai Brigade has eighty-three households and 430 people. Ten years ago the village was known only to those who lived in the same county. Today Tachai is a household word in China and is known by additional millions throughout the world.

The question, of course, is *why*? What's so special about Tachai? What is there to learn from Tachai?

We learned that the Tachai Brigade was an advanced unit whose technical and agricultural accomplishments were lessons for all to study. Through hard work, self-reliance and, most important, political struggle, the peasants of Tachai had turned their barren land into some of the most productive in China. Mountains and gulleys were now, literally, terraced fields and orchards. The region was one which throughout history had been plagued by natural disasters—drought, flash floods, and hail storms. But through collective efforts, irrigation and flood-control devices have been built, and even these old enemies have been neutralized. Living standards have risen accordingly, and rows of new stone houses have replaced the earthen cave homes of the olden days.

But the real lesson of Tachai had a deeper meaning than these technical accomplishments. Peasants throughout China told us what they had learned from Tachai, and what they considered its meaning. They always emphasized that the reasons for Tachai's success were political—meaning that the people of Tachai correctly understood class struggle and persisted in that struggle.

Zhen Yong-gui, former Party Secretary of the Tachai Brigade and now a member of the Chinese Communist Party's Central Committee, put it this way: "The fundamental reason [for our success] is that people have changed their thinking. People can change the land, technique, output and village because they have changed their thinking. This change is the result of arming them with Marxism-Leninism-Mao Tse-tung Thought."*

Just so much rhetoric? The people we talked to didn't think so. They pointed to Mao's thought as the guiding force

* *Ta Kung Pao* (English edition), November 11, 1971, p. 6.

behind the development of mutual-aid teams, agricultural cooperatives, and communes. It was Mao's leadership, they argued, that led China's peasants down the road of socialist construction rather than the road of individualistic methods. And they credited their astounding technical and productive achievements to the advantages of collective, socialist efforts.

But there had been a fierce struggle to determine the direction of China's agricultural development. It began soon after land reform in 1949 and 1950, and it has continued up through the Cultural Revolution to the present. Peasants did not idly saunter down one road or another. The battle for direction finally polarized during the Cultural Revolution between what was called Mao's "socialist road" and Liu Shao-chi's "capitalist road." Former hired hands and poor and lower-middle peasants,* the vast majority of the rural population, had been the direct beneficiaries of the mutual-aid teams, cooperatives, and the people's communes. They fought to form them and to make collectivization work. But former rich peasants and ex-landlords opposed collectivization. They preferred the old individualistic system where their money, land, animals, houses, and tools would preserve for them, albeit in new forms, the special privileges and easy life they had formerly enjoyed. They found Liu Shao-chi's policies were the best expression of their interests.

Tachai became a standard-bearer in the struggle for socialism. In 1964 Chairman Mao issued the nationwide call, "In Agriculture, Learn from Tachai!" When people turned to Tachai they saw:

• A brigade which, by following the socialist road, had turned their rocky, barren mountains into green, productive fields. They had transformed some of the poorest, most desolate land in northern China into an agricultural oasis whose

---

* The phrases "poor peasant" and "middle peasant" describe pre-Liberation economic status, specifically how much or little land a person owned and how he or she earned a living. Hired hands, poor peasants, and lower-middle peasants were at the bottom of the economic scale. For a more detailed explanation, see Mao Tse-tung, "How to Differentiate the Classes in Rural Areas" (1933).

production surpassed much of the fertile areas in the southern temperate zones. Tachai's pre-Liberation production had never exceeded 100 jin per mu. Mutual-aid teams had raised this to 120. During the co-op period production grew to 500 jin. Immediately after the founding of the commune it jumped to 700, and by 1967 production of the Tachai Brigade had risen to over 900 jin per mu. Today it is well over 1,000.

• A brigade led by poor and lower-middle peasants, whose leaders and members were close. Zhen Yong-gui, Tachai's best known leader, was a poor peasant who had started working for the landlords at age eight. Tachai's cadres had all along participated regularly in collective, productive work.

• A brigade whose application of self-reliance had been tried and tested in practice—and had worked. In 1963 heavy rains and floods destroyed about 80 percent of their new housing and 90 percent of their crops. The brigade, however, refused government aid, saying, "The state is ours. If we all rely on the state, whom could the state rely on?" Quoting Mao's writings, they said, "Bad things can be turned into good things." They rebuilt with better terraces, better homes, and better flood-control embankments, and they wrested an average grain yield for that year equal to the yield of the previous year.

• A brigade tested in struggle. They had continually fought for socialist and collective development. During the early years, the efforts of Tachai's poor and middle peasants to set up cooperatives had been opposed as "utopian agrarian socialism" by some cadres in their county. These cadres, Liu Shao-chi supporters, alleged that no agricultural cooperative could be established before farming was mechanized. The Tachai peasants stood firm. They opposed profiteering in farm produce, and they confronted the Liu Shao-chi policies of extending private plots, encouraging free markets, setting up small enterprises on a profit basis, and fixing output quotas on a household rather than a collective basis. The Tachai peasants fought against the Liu Shao-chi-promoted "four freedoms": usury, hired labor, sale of land, and private

Agriculture: The Foundation 105

enterprise. Finally, after emerging into the national spotlight, Tachai withstood the efforts of several Liu Shao-chi work teams which descended upon their brigade to overturn its leadership and discredit its achievements.

• A brigade which had done away with private plots and which had pioneered new and more socialist—that is, more collective and political—ways of dealing with the work-point system and the distribution of income. They specifically criticized the use of material incentives.

• A brigade where women played an important role. An "iron girls" work team had been formed to strike out at old taboos and to lead women to an active role in production. Several Tachai leaders were women, such as Song Li-ying, former Secretary of the Tachai Party Branch, and Guo Fenglian, current Secretary of the Party Branch.

• A brigade which consciously followed Mao's thought and believed that following Mao's policies was the key to their development. They saw their struggles as class struggle, and saw Mao's writings guiding their struggle. They openly and earnestly promoted the study of Mao's writings.

Learn from Tao Yuan?

While Mao had urged China's peasants to learn from Tachai, Liu Shao-chi had pointed toward another brigade as a model for agriculture. This was the Tao Yuan Brigade of the Lu Wang Chuang Commune in northeastern Hebei Province. This brigade was situated on a wide strip of fertile land between the mountains and the Bohai Sea.

Comparisons between the two brigades are instructive. While Tachai was nationally publicized as an advanced unit because of its own efforts, at Tao Yuan Liu Shao-chi and his wife, Wang Kuang-mei, consciously set about to construct a model. In the fall of 1963 a work team headed by Wang Kuang-mei was dispatched to Tao Yuan. The results of this effort were then circulated nationally in Wang's book titled *The Tao Yuan Experience*.

But what was the Tao Yuan experience? Reports since the Cultural Revolution, when the peasants of the Tao Yuan Brigade repudiated Wang's work team and its supporters, are quite revealing. Through the work team and subsequent close supervision, the Liu Shao-chi group did the following:

• They overturned the leadership of lower peasants and backed the leadership of Kuan Ching-tong. Kuan had been an upper peasant with a questionable past. In 1953 he had helped set up a lower cooperative whose rules required members to have good land with title, capital, carts, and horses. When higher cooperatives were formed, he slaughtered his bull rather than let it become cooperative property. After the Commune was set up in 1958, he found ways to sell some of the Brigade's high-tension wire, purchased for electrification, at personal profit. In the early 1960s he set up a gambling joint in his house. When the Wang Kuang-mei work team arrived, they found local peasants holding meetings to criticize Kuan. The work team intervened on Kuan's behalf and he became a staunch Liu Shao-chi cadre.

• The work team told the Tao Yuan peasants that an era of prosperity had arrived. They made extravagant promises, such as coal for fuel all winter and white rice all the time.* They then arranged for the Commune to borrow 640,000 yuan from the government, ostensibly for road building and electrification. Previously the Brigade had been putting its own reserves into electrical development and irrigation. New roads had also been planned by the old leadership. Now the Commune took up the burden of heavy debt, throwing overboard the principle of self-reliance and stable economic development.

• They encouraged the use of material incentives to determine income distribution. Their individual favorites received double and triple amounts.

• They established a marriage bureau where bachelors paid as much as 1,000 yuan for wives.

---

* Such things were extravagant in relation to the economic resources and conditions of the brigade at that time.

- Kuan Ching-tong used some of the money from a government loan to erect a monument to Wang Kuang-mei. He also declared that the house where she had lived during the work team's visit be turned into a museum.
- The work team provided a fertile environment for ex-landlords and rich peasants to call for a return to individualist farming. Some ex-landlords even went into the fields and began to reclaim plots which had formerly been theirs but were now collectivized. Ex-landlords and rich peasants opposed the Commune and even attempted to sabotage its development.
- They nursed production up to 619 jin per mu by 1967. This was a respectable figure; the area had pre-Liberation production of about 250 jin per mu. But by comparison, Tachai, in poor land, had less than 100 jin per mu before Liberation and over 900 by 1967.
- Politically, the work team suppressed the study of Mao's writings and circulated only Liu Shao-chi's works.

Two Roads in the Countryside

Thus, two roads existed in China's countryside—one led to Mao's model of Tachai, the other to Liu's model of Tao Yuan. The political struggles between these divergent paths has provided the framework for almost all of China's agricultural development. At the root of the struggle between the two roads lay a fundamental theoretical disagreement: How should China's economic transformation be viewed? Was the struggle for socialism settled?

By the mid-1950s, Mao and Liu had answered this basic question quite differently:

Liu: "Socialist public ownership has now been basically accomplished. The question of who will win the struggle between socialism and capitalism in our country has now been decided."*

* Liu Shao-chi, *The Political Report to the Eighth National Congress of the Party* (1956), p. 27.

Mao: "In China . . . the class struggle between the different political forces, and the class struggle in the ideological field . . . will continue to be long and tortuous. . . . In this respect, the question of which will win out, socialism or capitalism, is still not really settled."*

Thus, the "two roads" in the countryside were quite different, their construction and direction quite distinct. When peasants said they wanted to learn from Tachai, they spoke of more than just high yield, technical development, and hard work and self-reliance—although these were certainly part of the Tachai example. They spoke fundamentally of class struggle and of the divergent paths that can be followed in that struggle. In some of our visits we saw the results of such struggle.

A Visit to the Ma Qi Zhai Commune

Our car stopped, backed up on a wide shoulder of the road, and sought refuge from the stream of horse and mule carts that rumbled past. Xi, a local CITS guide, hopped out and ran back down the road. We were looking for a production brigade of the Ma Qi Zhai People's Commune, several miles west of the ancient city of Xian in Northwest China. Xi returned with information that we had overshot our mark, so we quickly turned around and retraced our path a mile or so.

Xi was well meaning, but getting lost in the countryside was perhaps typical of him. Small and slight, shy and introspective, he was a picture of the young Chinese intellectual in his ruffled cadre suit and round glasses astride a pimpled face. On the second try he found a production team of the brigade we had been seeking.

We turned off the narrow road into a courtyard surrounded by dozens of single-story peasant homes. It was morning,

---

* Mao Tse-tung, "On the Correct Handling of Contradictions Among the People," in *Selected Readings* (1957), p. 464.

and people hurried to and fro on their way to the fields or other work. A group of kids immediately gathered around us to stare at the strange visitors, while chickens scurried everywhere. Xi introduced us to the local production team Party Secretary, a solemn middle-aged man whose work-worn hands and weather-beaten face spoke of years of struggle and labor. The Party Secretary then led us down a dirt lane beside several homes, where we visited a few of the families in his production team.

The first home we entered was built around its own small courtyard, and we had to duck our heads to get through the low gate. A fat, swayback pig grunted from a sty which occupied one corner of the yard—a private pig, we were told, owned by the family. A couple of chickens ran past, also family property. The house at the far end of the yard was a simple, single-story building of whitewashed clay and cement. It was divided into several small rooms, each opening onto the courtyard. A woman, dressed in a black padded jacket and probably in her mid-fifties, greeted us. She was alone, and she explained that the rest of her family of nine had already left for work. She urged us to take seats in one of the rooms—a cozy space which was used for living and sleeping. A large North China kang filled one end of the room.* The house was owned by the family, our hostess explained, as was true for all the families in the team. It had been built after Liberation. The family had paid for materials, but labor had been organized cooperatively. We chatted briefly, and then, at the Party Secretary's urging, we moved on to visit other neighbors.

The homes of other families in the production team were similar. Chairs, boxes, and stools were hastily pushed together for our chats, and we were served hot water in plain glasses or in large colorful tin cups. Older family members typically wore the black padded jackets traditional of China's

---

* A *kang* is a raised brick platform, about two feet high, constructed so that the flue from the cooking fire will run underneath and warm it. Members of the family sleep on the kang, particularly in the cold winter.

peasantry, while the younger people were apt to be wearing more colorful clothing. Homes were cheerful, the walls usually covered with striking posters, pictures of Peking operas, or perhaps family photos.

In one home we noticed a fancy fluorescent desk lamp exactly like one which had caught our eye in a city hotel room. Later we saw the same lamp in a department store, and found out it was rather expensive, selling for 12.76 yuan. Another family had rigged up a simpler but larger fluorescent fixture in one of their rooms.

In one house we were greeted by a widow and her son, who had recently completed middle school and was back in the countryside to work. Although from a peasant background, he was now called an "intellectual" by the others. Several people told us members of their family worked in the nearby city, Xian. One family of eight said that a son worked in a factory; another family of five reported two worked outside the commune. These workers were not considered members of the commune, although they lived with their families in the countryside. Their income was completely separate from commune finances.

Women told us that before Liberation only men had worked in the fields. Now, they said proudly, everyone worked in production. Their brigade did not yet have a permanent nursery. Grandparents usually took care of children, they explained, but they did set up nurseries during the busy season. We were told that an eight-hour work day was the general practice, but in the busy season it was often longer and city people would come to help.

Some commune members said they often went to Xian to see films and live performances, but they quickly added that the commune had a mobile cinema team which regularly visited their brigade.

The last family we visited had ten members, and at this house one daughter, in her early twenties, emerged as the main speaker. Three of her family worked outside the commune—a brother, a sister, and her sister's husband. Speaking of the past—a time which she was obviously too young to

Agriculture: The Foundation 111

remember but with which she was nevertheless familiar—she said that there had been six people in her family. Her father (who occasionally added to her explanation) had worked for the landlord. He, his brothers, and their father had been illiterate. They were very poor and had begged in the streets. Her father, his face beaming with pride, interrupted to point out that now his daughter had graduated from middle school. He also said that after Liberation he had studied in a spare-time school, but that he was too old to remember things well and forgot characters easily.

The daughter went on to tell us there had been a struggle in the family when her older sister married. Her sister and brother-in-law had been given a room in the house, the one where we now were talking, and they had wanted to buy more furniture. The father had disagreed, saying that they should save the money in a state bank where the whole society could use it for socialist construction. He had argued with the young people, telling them about his bitter past and pointing out that many people in the world had not yet been liberated. He believed that furniture was less important—the money should go to build socialism and support other people's liberation struggles. The younger daughter stated that eventually they had agreed with the father, but only after much ideological struggle. She said he had given them "class education."

This young woman made a strong impression on us. We tried to compare her to the picture of women in old China who were tied to the home and shoved to the background. But there was no comparison. We also noticed that her sister's husband had moved in with the family, completely reversing the pattern of the old days of arranged marriages.

It was in this home that the Party Secretary opened up and spoke of his past. A truly rural personality, he never wasted words and spoke only when there was reason.

"Before Liberation there were sixty households here," he began. "Four were landlords or rich peasants. The rest of us were middle or poor peasants. There were 1,200 mu of land, of which 770 were occupied by the landlords and rich peasants. This was also the best land, and we had very poor land. The landlords' rent was very high. They demanded ninety catties per mu for rent. At that time a high yield was about 100 catties per mu. Peasants often worked as laborers for the landlord to get enough to survive. We had a saying then, 'When we eat, we look at our reflection; when we sleep, we look at the stars' [meaning that they had only water or very thin soup to eat and their houses were very poor, made of straw and mud and with many holes in the roof]. Today we say, 'Eating is like eating candy—each dish is sweeter than the last.' Comparing the old days to today is like comparing earth and sky.

"My family had seven members. My father worked for the landlord for forty years. I started to work myself at age twelve, with no pay. My father died and we couldn't pay the rent. We just had food for six months and the other six months we would go hungry. There have been great changes. I can't even measure them. For example, there were no schools before. Only after Liberation was I able to go to a spare-time school and learn to read and write."

He jumped up, pulled out his fountain pen and notebook, and ran across the room to show us lines he had written.

"This is from Chairman Mao!" His eyes were moist. "Without his leadership we would not have had Liberation! I would not know how to read!"

He trembled with emotion and his eyes steeled. "I know what it was like before. I know what it's like to be beaten by the landlords! Look!" He pulled open his shirt to reveal several long, nasty-looking scars running from his chest to below his waist. He sat down, and there was a sudden silence in the room. Our eyes were now moist, and by looking around the room we saw we were not alone. Zheng, our hosts, and the other neighbors there were also deeply moved.

Someone broke the silence by suggesting we take a look around the brigade's fields and small factories. A cadre from the commune office joined us as we walked down the lane to the nearby fields. Light green winter wheat was sprouting in strips, and we were told that vegetables would be planted between the rows, a form of crop management which increased the yields. In one vegetable plot we spotted some of the people we had visited a short time earlier. They waved us over to show us their work, and one of the men explained that his job was to select the best cabbages for seed development and the next crop.

We followed the road to a cluster of small factories—the brigade's industrial side. A simple mud-brick building with a hard-packed dirt floor housed various machines used in food production. Two or three bare light bulbs swung from the rafters. Below, beans were transformed into a local version of glutinous, clear "bean thread," popular in the Chinese diet. Rape seed was also being pressed into vegetable oil. About twelve people labored over simple presses, large crocks, and cooking pots. Across the lane donkeys and horses, hitched to carts, patiently stood outside a brigade foundry, waiting to transport its products to other areas of the commune. We watched as hoes, plows, spades, and shovels were pounded out and repaired—much of the work reminiscent of old blacksmith shops. Red-hot metal was dipped in water, the hiss of rising steam blending with the ringing of hammers and anvils. Next door we visited a third brigade industry which was a direct outgrowth of the foundry. Workers had discovered the foundry waste water contained useful materials. Here, in a combination indoor-outdoor workshop, a group was busily extracting these elements for chemical fertilizer. Indoors, huge pans of a dark-looking material were heated over a low fire; these were treated and brought outside, turning a brilliant turquoise as they dried. The larger pieces were broken up, and all the flakes and scraps were gathered into large baskets and crocks to be carried to the fields.

These enterprises were brigade owned, our hosts explained, and existed only as the result of much ideological struggle. One brigade member recalled, "These small factories were closed during the influence of the Liu Shao-chi line. We reopened them during the Cultural Revolution." Other negative practices were attributed to the influence of the Liu Shao-chi line in agriculture. We were shown two rows of sparkling new brick-and-cement pig sties. They were immaculate, and the brigade members noted that they were washed out each day and the manure was used for fertilizer. We passed someone spraying the new sties, a tank strapped to his back and hose and nozzle in hand. Disinfectant, they explained.

"There are our Liu Shao-chi pigsties!" They pointed to the end of the row. A bit past these sturdy new constructions, over a slight hill, was a fenced-in mud hole; in the middle stood a dilapidated straw-and-mud shack. A couple of pigs wallowed in foot-deep slop.

We're sure Liu Shao-chi and his followers would resent the charge. Obviously, they wouldn't favor run-down, dirty, and backward animal husbandry as opposed to healthy, efficient, and sanitary conditions. But the peasants here dealt with the concrete, not the abstract. To them the result of Liu Shao-chi's line in agriculture—emphasizing the individual, playing down the collective—was the difference between the old pig sties and the new ones, which were built through collective application of self-reliance and hard struggle. Mao's road combined agricultural and industrial development; Liu's emphasized industry, to the detriment, in the end, of both. Mao's socialist road brought the "initiative of the masses" into full play; Liu's road did not. Mao's road tied development to people and politics; Liu's emphasized technique and mechanization. Mao's led people to "do it"; Liu's led people to "wait for the experts." The results of the two roads, our hosts argued, were as different as the pig sties we saw here.

A commune cadre suggested that we see other brigade activities a short drive away. We piled back into the small Shanghai sedan which had brought us there, while the cadre and some others climbed into a second car that had arrived during our visit. Then we did a double-take. It was not another Shanghai sedan, or one of the Polish or Eastern European cars we often saw on the road, but a French Peugeot complete with Esso sticker on the back window.

"Where'd you get that car?" we asked, surprised.

"From the CITS car pool. I knew we'd need it so that the brigade members could show us around," Xi answered, a bit perplexed at our curiosity.

"Yes, but that car—it's French! And that sticker advertises one of the largest imperial oil firms in the world!"

Xi replied: "China trades on a fair and equal basis with countries all over the world. We're still poor, and need to import some things like cars. We can't yet make enough for our needs. I never noticed the sticker before, but I wouldn't have known what it means." He shrugged his shoulders. "Doesn't mean much here, does it, since they don't have any outlets in our country."

We bounced down the road, following the Esso sticker to a large greenhouse used both for experiments and winter vegetable production. From there we went to see brigade stores where hardware, clothing, food, and many children's toys were sold. Prices were the same as in a department store we had previously visited in Xian. Next to the store was a commune clinic staffed by seventeen doctors and nurses. Our tour briefly interrupted the regular Monday meeting of the "barefoot doctors" from the production team, who clapped and welcomed us warmly, crowding near the door to get a better view. These "barefoot doctors" worked regularly in the fields alongside the members of the production team which had selected them for this special responsibility. They had already gone through an initial training period of two to three months, and now they met weekly for additional training and to exchange experiences. After chatting we drove to the commune headquarters, a small cluster of brick buildings, where another cadre served tea and joined our discussion.

"You have visited one of our production brigades and talked to people there," one of the cadres began. "Now we'll try to give you an overall view of our commune. The Ma Qi Zhai People's Commune includes about 4,000 households with over 21,000 people. We have 27,000 mu of land [4,500 acres] and produce mainly grain, cotton, and vegetables. There are twenty-three production brigades and eighty-one production teams in the commune. In the brigade you visited there are 110 households and 578 people."

Another cadre continued. "We have a tractor station and twenty-three supply-and-market departments. The commune owns eight tractors, and four production brigades own their own tractors. Tractors cost up to 10,000 yuan each, depending on size. We also have sixteen primary schools and a middle school with 5,300 students.

"Land was redistributed after Liberation. In 1956 we set up cooperatives and in 1958 established a commune."

"Where are the former landlords now?" we interrupted.

"Now they work as members of the production teams, doing labor," he replied.

"After the commune was established we launched a water conservation movement. Only four hundred mu of our land was irrigated before the commune. Now only four hundred of our twenty-seven thousand mu are not irrigated. We have four pumping stations and 577 electric pumps at wells. Our yield has also increased. Before Liberation we got only between 150 and 200 jin per mu. Now we get 1,000 jin per mu."

"How does your production compare to other communes in the area?" we asked.

"We're third or fourth in the Xian area," one of the cadres replied. "But we're far behind Tachai. Our standard of living has also improved, and last year we averaged cash income of 120 yuan per person, or about 600 yuan per household. Everyone also received 530 jin of grain, and if they had special needs they could get more. The 120 yuan cash is an average—some got more, some got less."

"Is all the income of the commune distributed to the members, either in cash or in grain?" we asked.

"No, the commune as a whole pays a 5 percent tax to the state. Some also goes to public funds to expand and enlarge collective projects. We have a public welfare fund to help families in cases of special need, and we support cultural activities and films. Between 60 and 70 percent of the total income is distributed to members. The members in each brigade make a plan on how to distribute the money and the commune reviews and approves it."

The other cadre interjected, "We follow a priority in distributing goods: first the city, second the commune, then individuals."

"How is your commune organized? Do you have a Revolutionary Committee and a Party Committee?" we continued.

"Yes. Our leading bodies correspond to the three levels of ownership in the commune. On the commune level there is a Revolutionary Committee, set up in January 1968. It has twenty-nine members and is a three-in-one committee. Here the army is represented by our militia. There are two militia, fourteen cadres, and thirteen representatives of the masses on the Revolutionary Committee."

"Are there any women?" we inquired.

"Yes, five."

"How about the Party Committee?"

"The Party Committee was set up in January 1971, and it has ten members. Six are cadres, four from the masses, and two of these are women. Before the Party Committee was set up there was a caucus in the Revolutionary Committee, which did the job the Party Committee does now. Six members of the Party Committee are also on the Revolutionary Committee."

"What about at the brigade and team levels? Is it the same there?"

"Just about. Each brigade or team has its own Revolutionary Committee and Party Branch. They're too small to have Party Committees." (We found this distinction between Party Committee and Party Branch in several places. To the best of our understanding, a Party Committee is a representative, leading body of the Party members in a work unit, while a branch simply consists of all the Party members in a unit.)

We changed the topic again: "Is there a Women's Association in the commune?"

"We have a woman cadre in charge of women's work, under the leadership of the Party. We do education, mobilize the masses, and try to solve the problems women face."

The second cadre added, "Women receive thirty days paid leave when they have a child."

"How often do cadres work?"

"In the busy season cadres work, live, and eat with commune members most of the time. We spend at least one day a week in labor during the slow season."

"Do cadres get workpoints like everyone else?"

"Commune-level cadres are sent by the state and paid by the state. Cadres at the brigade and team level spend most of their time at labor and get workpoints. Cadres sent by the state are chosen from among the masses of workers, peasants, and soldiers, and are not necessarily Party members. We have eighteen commune-level cadres here."

We thanked our hosts for their hospitality and their patience with our many questions. Then we returned to the city. In many respects the Ma Qi Zhai Commune was representative of rural Chinese life. In others it was not. More than once our companions emphasized that communes located near cities were generally richer than those in the remote countryside. Extra labor during busy seasons and the legacy of past development were natural factors responsible for these differences. But the gap, they added, was something all were striving to close.

Production and the "Two Roads"

We wondered if the Cultural Revolution had affected agricultural production. Had it hurt production, as some Western sources had reported, or had it helped? All of the communes we visited reported increased production since the Cultural Revolution. Some attributed the increase to the Cultural Revolution and gave statistics to support their claims.

Ma Qi Zhai Commune, near Xian (primarily grain)

pre-Liberation:	150-200 jin per mu*
1967:	600 jin per mu
1970:	740 jin per mu
1971:	1,000 jin per mu

* One jin = 1.1 lbs.; one mu = one-sixth of an acre.

Zhao Ling Pu Commune, near Shi-jia-zhuang (primarily grain)

pre-Liberation:	200 jin per mu
After Liberation, before the Cultural Revolution:	500 jin per mu
1968:	1,300 jin per mu

Production Brigade, near Tianjin (primarily grain)

pre-Liberation:	100 jin per mu
1958:	300 jin per mu
1966-1971:	"increased every year"
1971:	over 1,000 jin per mu

Lo Kang Commune, near Guangzhou (primarily fruit but also rice)

pre-Liberation:	400 jin per mu (rice)
now:	1,002 jin per mu (rice)
pre-Liberation:	600 jin per mu (fruit)
now:	"great increases," but no figures given

Commune Income and Workpoints

Communes, of course, were owned collectively by their members. Personal income of commune members was determined by two factors: the collective's productivity and the individual's work.

A cadre at the Ma Qi Zhai Commune explained:

"We have a system of work points to distribute income. Those who work more get more points and earn more. Different jobs have different rates, depending on the skill required and how heavy the work is. Skilled and heavy work gets more points. Production teams decide what the work points should be. Since we have three levels of ownership in communes—commune, brigade, and team—this affects income. The cash value of work points, figured out at the end of the year, varies between the teams and brigades. If a team's income is more, its work points are worth more and an individual's income will be more."

The work-point system was a fairly old form. But in many places it had changed, taking on new content as political struggles developed. Zhou Min-fu, a cadre on the Sino-Hungarian Friendship Commune, put it this way: "The principle we use for income distribution is 'everyone does his best, and we pay according to labor.' The work-point system is only a method of distributing income. It has been practiced since the period of cooperatives. But we have come a long way in practice. We have walked the wrong way in practicing this system. The struggle between the two roads was very sharp in regard to the work-point system. Before the Cultural Revolution we were influenced by the Liu Shao-chi theory of 'put work points in command.' Some thought work points were their lifeblood, and commune leaders used them as material incentives. For example, at that time some of the production-team leaders only brought the initiative of the members into play by increasing work points.

"But this line was criticized and repudiated during the Cultural Revolution. Now we use this method: team members have a discussion and set a standard of manpower and work for a certain number of points. Then each member gives an assessment of his or her own work. Then we have a mass discussion. We assign work according to a person's physical condition and abilities, and we carry out the principle of each one doing his best. We encourage each to develop and assess the quality and quantity of work. Now we promote the principle of each doing his best through ideological education. This is part of our campaign to learn from Tachai."

Income in the Countryside

It was not easy to understand income distribution in the communes. One reason was our unfamiliarity with the specifics of agricultural production; another was that income— and the distribution methods of commune income—varied considerably, reflecting the flexibility due to collective ownership and local control.

Some of the communes we visited reported the following income figures:

Ma Qi Zhai Commune, near Xian: average yearly cash income of 120 yuan per person, plus 530 catties of grain.

Production Brigade, near Tianjin: average yearly income of 950 yuan per *member*, including "in kind" goods and services.

Sino-Hungarian Friendship Commune, near Peking: average yearly income of 138 yuan per person.

Lo Kang Commune, near Guangzhou: average yearly income of 125 yuan per person, plus 540 catties of food.

A few points about these figures. First, the production brigade near Tianjin gave us a per member yearly average. Others gave per capita figures which, they observed, included children and old people who couldn't work. The fact remained, however, that this production brigade was clearly richer than the others we visited. They supplied free running water and electricity to members, provided two free tickets a month for haircuts, and ground and processed grain for members at no cost. They had stored enough grain to support their brigade for a year in case of disaster or war, and they reported that 70 percent of the families in the brigade had savings accounts.

Average income varied between brigades within the same commune. Cadres at the Lo Kang Commune reported their average yearly income was 125 yuan per person, but said that the high was about 180 and the low a bit under 100 yuan, depending upon how productive a brigade had been that year and how many work points an individual had accrued. Members of the production brigade near Tianjin told us their work points were worth 28 fen on the average; the lowest brigade had a 21 fen figure, the highest 31 fen. Cadres at the Zhao Ling Pu Commune reported differences between their lowest and highest brigades were only about 5 yuan per year.

The communes we visited were above average. None claimed to be the leading commune in their area (all gave examples of nearby units that were ahead of them), but all were near the top.

Private Income

Many, though not all, communes had set aside a small percentage of their land for family gardens and private plots. Also, peasants often had a source of income from pigs and chickens that they raised. Small, individual handicrafts and side occupations, such as hauling goods by horse- or ox-cart for a fee, were still practiced in some areas. We didn't get statistics about private income, but it obviously represented a very small percentage of total rural income. One published estimate has placed income from private endeavors at about "10 percent of the sum distributed by the collectivity on the average."* We have talked to other recent visitors to China who spent a great deal of time in the countryside, and most thought 10 percent was a high estimate.

Many Western analysts have viewed this private sector as a retreat from socialism, as the break-up of socialist development, or as proof that socialist and collective motivations can't work. Considering the gradual but continuous socialist transformation of China's countryside, this view is, to say the least, rather ahistorical. The fact is that the private plots and animals we saw were remnants of the old, not retreats from the new. No overnight miracles had been performed—we were told that collectivization could not fruitfully proceed at a pace ahead of concrete economic and political conditions. To push for the immediate abolition of all private plots was considered an "ultra-Left" error, an example of the policies pushed by Lin Piao and his supporters during certain periods of the Cultural Revolution. Socialist consciousness, our hosts argued, was built only through a process of struggle, experience, experiment, criticism, self-criticism—and more struggle. As the new forms grew stronger, they said, the old were transformed and eventually replaced.

* Nagels, *Encyclopedia-Guide: China*, p. 274.

We Are Well Provided For!

Wang Yu-shen, a cadre and main spokesman during our visit to the Zhao Ling Pu Commune near Shi-jia-zhuang, led us down narrow dirt lanes between houses and courtyards. The lanes were wide enough for one horse cart—or truck, if one was brave enough to fight the ruts—but somebody would have to back up and give way if two came head on. Faded red characters were scattered on the whitewashed walls, weather-worn but still proclaiming, "In Agriculture, Learn from Tachai!" Occasional chickens ran back and forth across the lane and one or two dogs sat scratching themselves in the sun.

Wang introduced us first to a ten-member family. Their courtyard and house had been built since Liberation, and their income, they said, now provided a good standard of living. Two worked in the nearby city, four worked in the brigade, and all the children were in school. The father's job was tending and feeding the brigade donkeys. Another family member worked in a brigade-run factory, while a third tended chickens and a fourth worked in the fields. The family owned three bicycles, and we were shown bedrooms where each kang held four or five bright red-and-orange quilts stacked in a corner. The family had a sewing machine, a shelf or two of books, and lots of family photos beneath a piece of glass on a table top. Pictures of Chairman Mao decorated the walls. We talked briefly and then moved on to visit other members of their brigade.

Wang popped into a gateway and urged us to follow. We entered a small courtyard where a peasant-style house occupied the rear and one side. On the other side was a stack of firewood and kindling, protected by a lean-to shelter with a thatched top. The family pig sty was next to the firewood. We entered a room in the rear of the courtyard, a type of living room bounded on each side by larger bedrooms half-filled by kangs. The fires in the kangs were fed from openings in the room where we sat.

Dun Xiu-zyen, the grandmother of the family, eagerly greeted us. She was caring for some grandchildren while most of the rest of the family was at work. There was the usual scramble to get stools and chairs, to give us a cup of tea, and to tell us about their new life. Dun's was a large family with eighteen members, although not all lived on the premises. Two sons, Dun said proudly, worked on the railroad; one lived in Xian and the other in Shi-jia-zhuang. Another grandson was an artist, a painter, and lived elsewhere. Five members of the family worked in the production brigade, Dun added, and two were students in school. "And two are infants," she laughed, gently pushing forward the toddlers, who peeked at us from between her legs.

We were joined by the oldest member of the four-generation family, Liu Le-lei, Dun's father-in-law. At least three of the family—Dun, old Liu, and Liu's wife—did not work because they were too old or retired.

Dun explained that the family had two courtyards with a total of seventeen rooms. They owned the houses, which were built with cooperative labor and materials they themselves had purchased. Both houses had been built after Liberation, the second in 1965.

"Before Liberation we had only four shabby rooms," Dun continued. "My husband worked as a laborer for the landlords and we were very poor."

"We had nothing to eat," old Liu added. "After Liberation, under Chairman Mao's leadership, life got much better. Before we had to eat waste vegetables and the seeds we found in the streets."

Dun interrupted, a tinge of anger in her voice. "When I got married we had no grain for the wedding. We asked the landlord if he would lend us some but he refused, so we had to do without it. Now the children go to school. Before this did not happen. My husband and his brother went to spare-time school after Liberation and learned to read. Now we have food, clothes, and houses!"

Bursting with enthusiasm, she jumped up and took Janet by the arm, gesturing for her to stand up. Then Dun raised the top of the large trunk Janet had been sitting on to reveal its contents—bushels of dried kernels of corn! She hurried across the room and uncovered a huge earthen crock to show us a supply of wheat. Another crock sitting next to it contained ground flour.

Dun literally pulled us into the bedroom and opened up a dresser and closets, displaying the blankets and comforters the family now owned, and their supply of winter wool clothing. There was a desk which, as in other homes, was covered with family photos crowded together under a glass.

Dun pointed to the paintings hanging on the wall. They had been done by her grandson, the artist. One depicted a rural harvest scene full of ripe fruits and vegetables arrayed in colorful autumn fields. Another was a portrait of a determined-looking militia woman, ready to defend the revolution against any enemies. A map of the world also was tacked to the wall. It was divided down the Atlantic and gave the center projection to Asia and China instead of to North America, as we were so accustomed to.

Dun hurried to other rooms in the courtyard, showing us a sewing machine, other household items, and furniture. She pulled us into the two small kitchens used for family cooking, one for general use and one built specifically for steaming rice and *man-tou* (steamed bread). The stoves were wood-burning, built from bricks and clay. Pots, bowls, and simple kitchen utensils were stacked to one side. Then she led us to the second family courtyard, right next door, showing us still more. "I'm happy to show you these things," she bubbled, "because it shows what a difference Liberation has brought. We're well provided for!"

In the second courtyard we met old Liu's wife, a small elderly woman. She was friendly and quiet, smiling and nodding, but saying almost nothing. Her tiny bound feet, however, spoke of the oppression she had suffered in the old society.

The family gathered around as we left, urging us to please, please come back to see them again. And also to please take their friendship to the American people. Old Liu picked up one of his great-grandsons, who clutched a fading but still colorful rag doll, and helped the infant wave good-bye.

Life in the Countryside

The standard of living and the quality of life which we saw in the countryside compared favorably to life in the cities. There were, of course, differences which made life more comfortable for the factory worker and city dweller. Income in the city appeared in general to be higher than in the countryside. The urban setting included many services—day-care facilities, dining halls at work—less commonly found in rural areas. City stores stocked a wider variety of goods than were available in commune stores, although prices were the same.

There were also differences that we didn't see. For example, all the communes and brigades we visited had electricity, but we were told there were still rural areas which did not.

From our urbanized point of view, city housing, with its central heating and indoor plumbing, seemed more desirable. However, the homes we visited in the countryside were generally roomier and brighter than many of the city apartments. Some of the most pleasant homes we visited were on the production brigade near Tianjin.

Hospitals, clinics, "barefoot doctors," primary and secondary schools, ping-pong tables, basketball courts, cultural performances, and mobile film teams were all part of commune and brigade activities. They're all collective endeavors. Their availability and quality undoubtedly varied, according to the different priorities and consciousness of the various collectives. But nowhere were these aspects of life ignored. Progress in the standard and quality of life in the countryside has accompanied progress in agricultural production and technology. And everywhere the peasants declared their determination to continue this progress by traveling the "socialist road" in agriculture.

4
Women: Half of Heaven

Women we met in China identified first as members of the whole society—as workers, peasants, or cadres. Sexual definitions, like wife, mother, or daughter, usually came second. This in itself reflected an enormous change in the status of Chinese women since Liberation. We were, of course, very curious how China's socialist revolution had affected women's place in society. We asked a lot of questions about women, keeping in mind two comparisons.

First, we knew the status of women in modern China must be judged in contrast to the conditions of old China.

Second, we also made comparisons with our own experiences in the United States.

The first comparison, new versus old, was obviously more important in understanding the specific character of Chinese women's struggles. Old customs, attitudes, and economic conditions—each had contributed to the present level of equality in education and employment and to contemporary Chinese attitudes toward sex, marriage, and the family.

The second comparison, China and the United States, was severely limited by the two nations' vast cultural, political, and economic differences. Nevertheless, some contrasts here proved quite useful. Our own personal experiences in dealing with men and women in both societies taught us a great deal.

Chinese women—and men—considered the struggle for women's equality an integral part of the overall revolutionary struggle for socialism. For them, women's liberation was not separated from other aspects of the class struggle. Time and again Chinese women reminded us: "Women carry half of heaven upon their shoulders" (a quote from Mao Tse-tung, meaning half the world is theirs). Their "half of heaven," they acknowledged, would be fully realized only by continued and protracted struggles—struggles which we found to be complex but also concrete, exhilarating but also at times intense.

The Three Terraces

We had one of our best and frankest discussions about women at the Sino-Hungarian Friendship Commune near Peking. Lu Pei-zhou, vice-chairman of the commune's Revolutionary Committee and a female cadre in charge of women's work in the commune, explained, "Before Liberation women were despised. Since Liberation women are not despised."

"In the old society we had a saying about women," Zhou Min-fu, a man on the Revolutionary Committee, recalled. "All day long a woman moves between three terraces: the kang, the kitchen stove, and the millstone."

"Chairman Mao has recently said," Lu Pei-zhou continued, "that times have changed, and today men and women are equal. Whatever men comrades can accomplish, women comrades can, too."

"But are men and women completely equal now?" we asked.

Zhou Min-fu answered, "Not completely. For example, we try to have equal pay for equal work, but we haven't really reached that in our commune. This is a shortcoming, a remnant of the feudal past that we will try to sweep away."*

* The semi-feudal conditions of old China meant that working outside the home was itself a significant liberating step for Chinese women. But this step was also important for the economic development of the whole society, since everyone's welfare depended upon economic im-

Then Lu Pei-zhou described their struggle to bring about equality for women. "First, we had an education movement on the significance of women working in production. We spread Chairman Mao's teaching, 'When women all over the country rise up, that will be the day of victory for the Chinese Revolution.' Women had to have the determination to leave their homes, to abandon the feudal conventions, and to take part in work. But when we mobilized women into production, we also tried to solve their concrete problems. For example, take the jobs of sewing, mending, and grain husking. We set up a grain processing factory; five women can now do the husking for all seven thousand households. We also have a group to do sewing and mending. We set up nurseries and kindergartens so the children can go to day-care centers. We try to have equal pay for equal work. The number of women taking part in agriculture has increased. The old people who stay at home also help. They say they will do a good job there so that their sons and daughters won't have to worry about things at home and can concentrate on agricultural production."

Lao Liu, from China International Travel Service, joined in. "Women now have equal political standing with men and they have the same rights as men. It's crucial for the liberation of women that they be independent economically. But we can't say that women are 100 percent liberated; that will take time. After all, for thousands of years China followed the doctrines of Confucius, who said that a woman at home must obey her husband and parents-in-law. If her husband died, she had to obey her son. So even a young boy had power over an older woman. Another fallacy of the Confucian doctrine was that the virtue of a woman lay in her being untalented. The less skill and knowledge she had, the more

---

provement. Thus, a discussion of women's liberation in China often emphasized their role in production. However, most of the Chinese people we talked to were aware that simply bringing women into the workforce did not solve all the problems. They were also aware that work outside the home should not become (as it has so frequently in the United States) a "second job" for a housewife.

virtuous she was. Before Liberation, women were regarded as evil. If a woman came by when a well was being dug, people believed the well would never have water. Some thought that if a woman plowed the ground no crops would grow. Women were kept at home, never going outside. So in the past the feudal society took man as the focus, as the center. It takes time to change all this."

Lu Pei-zhou added, "Before, in family matters the husband decided everything. Now we women have equal footing with men."

Lu, Liu, and Zhou talked a lot about the past—about what the position of women had been in the old society and about the decades-long battle to break with the old and build the new. It had been a protracted struggle, not isolated but rather part and parcel of the profound revolutionary process that has been transforming China for the past fifty years. They did not claim this battle was over, nor that it had been won. But they pointed proudly to its progress and urged us to investigate its history. We did, and we learned a lot. It's both a sobering and an exciting story. It took much effort to advance from the "three terraces" of the past to the present battlelines of struggle. We'd like to take a brief look at that history.

". . . Like a Pony Bought"

For thousands of years feudal oppression had been the lot of Chinese women, and the old Chinese folk sayings, popular for centuries, offer us hints of women's burden down through history. One goes, "Officials depend on seals, tigers depend on mountains, and women depend on their husbands." Another tells us, "If I buy a horse I can beat it; if I marry a wife I can do as I like." Still another goes, "A wife married is like a pony bought—I'll ride her and whip her as I like." Or, "When a woman is angry her husband beats her. When he is angry he also beats her." And finally, "Flour is ground, a woman is beaten."

Perhaps the most dramatic and the best known example of this feudal oppression was the practice of footbinding. At a young age a girl's feet were tightly bound with cloth, the toes bent under, either broken or crushed. This incredibly painful process usually started around age five and continued for several years. "For every pair of bound feet, a bucket of tears," the peasants said. The result of this agony was a pair of maimed stumps, euphemistically called "pepper feet" or "golden lillies," which were regarded as erotic in feudal mores and which insured the dependence, physical and economic, of women. During our visit we met older women who still hobbled about on tiny bound feet. For them, Liberation had come too late to undo the damage of childhood.

In old China, women had no choice in marriage. Matches were arranged by parents, often when the couple was still in infancy or childhood. Women had no legal or property rights. They themselves were property. A woman could not get a divorce. If her husband divorced her, she was disgraced and left with nothing. If he chose to bring home concubines or a second wife, she had no grounds for complaint. Her job was to produce sons, and she was to obey men—first father, then husband, then son. With no chance to earn money on her own, she was totally dependent on them for support. When a daughter married, she became a part of her husband's family. "A daughter married is like water poured out the door," peasants lamented. This reinforced the desire to have sons, for a widow with no sons had no one to turn to for help in her old age.

The centuries-old feudal status of Chinese women began crumbling during the early decades of the 1900s, but some of the immediate changes were hardly for the better. Semifeudal and semi-colonial, China underwent convulsions of change that brought women into the workforce. Industry, mostly foreign owned, began employing women in cotton and silk mills, but this amounted to simply another form of slavery. Women trudged to mills in predawn darkness and worked straight through until 8:00 or 9:00 at night. Lunch breaks did not exist. A woman who married faced a cut in her already desperately low pay, and pregnancy was grounds for immediate dismissal. But babies need to be fed, food required money, and money meant working. So a working woman in the city, spared the cruelties of footbinding, would now tightly bind her stomach with cloth to hide pregnancy. There is no record of the number of miscarriages, deformed babies, or crippled mothers that resulted. A working mother faced a cruel dilemma. She could leave her infant at home with no food while she spent twelve to fourteen hours a day at the mill. Or she could bring the baby to work, hide it from the foreman in a pile of cotton, risk the chance that her child might suffocate or be crushed, and feed it when she could sneak a spare moment.

Four Thick Ropes

Slave of the slave—such was the position of most women in old China. But women's status was hardly one blot on an otherwise clean page; the crumbling feudal order was incredibly oppressive for everyone—both men and women. In the century preceding Liberation China was torn between its moribund feudal past and the new ravages of aggressive Western penetration. Foreign interests, beginning with the British-imposed Opium Wars of the 1840s, interjected new contradictions. Women, to be sure, still remained at the bottom of the pile, since a change in their position required—and indeed would itself precipitate—a wholesale social and political upheaval.

Jack Belden, who witnessed these contradictions in the raw during the struggle for Liberation, believed that women's struggles were profoundly related to the overall struggle:

> Not only Chinese society in general, but even the structure of the state, from the village at the bottom to the throne at the top, was definitely influenced by the status of women as slaves, private property, labor powers, and producers of sons for the ruling classes. The family was a training ground for loyalty to state

authority. The father was the supreme autocrat in the family. Submission of female to male, of son to father, found its natural reflection in the submission of peasant to gentry, tenant to landlord, and landlord to state ruler. From the foregoing it should be obvious that any all-out attempt to free women could only result in the upheaval of the whole social pyramid and a tremendous change in the correlation of forces struggling for power.*

The liberation of Chinese women meant the liberation of the whole society. The two were tied together. Belden's view was not new; others had made the same point and acted upon it. In 1927, Mao Tse-tung made this analysis of Chinese women's oppression:

> A man in China is usually subjected to the domination of three systems of authority: (1) the state system (political authority) ... (2) the clan system (clan authority) ... and (3) the supernatural system (religious authority).... As for women, in addition to being dominated by these three systems of authority, they are also dominated by the men (the authority of the husband). These four authorities—political, clan, religious, and masculine—are the embodiment of the whole feudal-patriarchal system and ideology, and are the four thick ropes binding the Chinese people, particularly the peasants.**

Everyone's freedom—both women's and men's—depended on breaking all four ropes. One rope alone was not enough; nor was breaking only the first three sufficient.

The fight against male supremacy was part of the Chinese Communist Party's program and activities from its founding in 1921. They saw the struggle to free women as integral to, not separate from, the struggle to free all of China. The four thick ropes were intertwined, often in complex and snarled tangles. Patriots, progressives, Communists; intellectuals, peasants, workers; men and women—all set about undoing these tangles, attacking all four ropes.

* Jack Belden, *China Shakes the World* (New York: Monthly Review Press, 1970), pp. 310-311.

** Mao Tse-tung, "Report on an Investigation of the Peasant Movement in Hunan," in *Selected Works of Mao Tse-tung* (Peking: Foreign Languages Press, 1967), Vol. I, p. 44.

Early Women's Organizations

From 1924 to early 1927 the Chinese Communist Party and the Kuomintang (Nationalist, or KMT) Party cooperated in a joint fight against reactionary warlords and foreign imperialists. The Chinese Communist Party was only a few years old. The KMT's history dated back to the revolutionary struggle, led by Dr. Sun Yat-sen, which had overthrown the Manchu Dynasty in 1911. Sun Yat-sen strongly supported the United Front between the two parties, and for three years Communists worked openly within the more politically diverse KMT. Several seats on the Kuomintang's Central Committee were held by Communists. Sun Yat-sen died in March 1925, and almost exactly two years later the United Front was shattered when the KMT's right wing, led by Chiang Kai-shek, turned on Communists and on non-Communist progressives. Thousands, particularly in Shanghai and Guangzhou, were murdered in a cold and calculated massacre. Revolutionaries became victims of executions in the streets. Progressives were driven underground; many fled to the countryside.

The three years of cooperation had seen the rise of a Women's Section of the Kuomintang Party and also a uniformed women's political division in the United Front armies. Local Women's Unions, separate from the Kuomintang, had been set up, organizing women to struggle against their special oppression while also mobilizing them to fight feudal and reactionary warlords.

Some of these courageous women described their activities in 1927:

> We travel behind the Army, but we take no part in fighting.... We are attached to the political department of the Army which organizes the first provisional civil government in the new territory. Our work is to organize the women. For this we go into the homes and markets, wherever women are to be found and talk with them. When we have talked enough, we organize a local women's union and leave it to handle affairs in that district. Then we move to another district.... We explain that men and women are now equal. Even though you are a woman, you are still a

person. We say they have a duty to society, and not only to husbands. It is a good thing to ask the advice of parents about your marriage but not to let the parents decide everything concerning it. We explain the new doctrine of free choice in marriage. That young folks have the right to select their own life partners. We also explain that, by the new law, women may inherit property. And we say that the feet of young girls must not be bound.*

These were revolutionary demands. Women activists faced stiff opposition. Warlords and reactionaries often resorted to what they believed was the simplest way to crush new ideas: summary execution.

After the break-up of the 1924-1927 United Front, the Chinese Communist Party set up Soviets—liberated districts— in several parts of South China. One of the earliest liberated areas, organized in 1927-1928, was in the Hailufeng District of Guangdong Province. Mass organizations were set up, including a General Women's Union. Cai Ting-li, a Communist leader in that district, described their Women's Union:

> There was also a General Women's Union [in addition to a Peasant Union] made up of peasants, students, teachers, and industrial workers. It had over a thousand members. All were young, and they were enthusiastic because of their recent release from suppression. Some of the men hated this organization because it defended the rights of women and took care of the divorce problem. A women would come to the union to complain against her husband's or family's treatment, and the union would investigate the case and see to it that the woman either received better treatment or was given a divorce. It was teasingly called the "Bureau for Divorce and Remarriage." ... This organization was active and effective.**

The whole Hailufeng District, however, was brutally suppressed by Chiang Kai-shek's Kuomintang in 1928. Its Women's Union, Peasant Union, and other progressive mass organizations were smashed.

* Quoted in Anna Louise Strong, *China's Millions—Revolution in Central China, 1927* (Peking: New World Press, 1965), pp. 104-105.
** Quoted in Nym Wales, *Red Dust* (Stanford, California: Stanford University Press, 1952), p. 202.

In 1934-1935 other South China liberated areas were abandoned, the famous six-thousand-mile Long March to the Northwest was made, and a decade of resistance against Japanese aggression, led by the Communists, began in earnest. Throughout these years women's unions and women's associations were formed:

> To educate and organize women for struggle against their double oppression, the Communists first helped them to set up Women's Associations. These associations aimed at safeguarding women from oppression and drawing them into both revolutionary activity and production. On the one hand they took up cases of maltreatment of wives; on the other they organized women for spinning and weaving, making quilts, uniforms and cloth shoes for the 8th Route Army and for working in the fields.... Their contributions to the struggle against the Japanese invaders both strengthened the economy and raised their own status.*

During the War of Resistance—which included another, very shaky, United Front with the Kuomintang—work among women was coordinated by a Women's Department in the Communist-led border region government in Yenan. A Yenan Women's University was also established in 1937. During our visit to Xian, the city which served as a gateway to Yenan in those years, we were told that 30 to 40 percent of those passing through Xian on their way to Yenan had been women.

The Japanese were defeated in 1945 and there followed over three years of civil war between the Kuomintang and the Communists. During this period an Organizing Committee of Women's Organizations in the Liberated Areas was formed to coordinate women's work.

The Women's Federation

The First National Congress of Chinese women was held March 24 through April 3, 1949, in Peking, just two months

---

* Isabel and David Crook, *The First Years of Yangyi Commune* (London: Routledge and Kegan Paul, 1966), p. 241.

after the city was liberated. This Congress founded the All-China Democratic Women's Federation, which boasted a membership of over 20 million women in the Liberated Areas. The People's Republic of China was founded six months later, on October 1, 1949.

On May 1, 1950, a new Marriage Law was enacted. The law abolished the old feudal marriage system and proclaimed equality between husband and wife in the home as well as in society generally. It established the right to divorce for both parties; equal rights to property; and equal responsibility for care of children. It called for families based on a new kind of marriage, one founded on free will, with mutual respect between man and woman. The old practices of "bigamy, concubinage, child betrothal, interference with the remarriage of widows, and the exaction of money or gifts in connection with marriages" were prohibited by law.*

No longer could it be said: "Married to a chicken, a woman must fly; married to a dog, a woman must walk." Women no longer had to marry husbands chosen by their parents and accept their lot as determined by fate.

During the first few years after Liberation the number of divorces skyrocketed. Women who had been trapped in forced matches now used their new rights to get their freedom.

The All-China Democratic Women's Federation took on two immense jobs: first, informing women of their new legal rights and, second, encouraging them to demand and use those rights. The Federation organized groups of women to read and discuss the new law with friends and neighbors. Plays and theatrical performances outlining the law's provisions were staged. In April 1953, the Federation formed a special committee to "thoroughly implement" the provisions of the Marriage Law, to ensure that all women throughout the country were protected.

The work of the Federation extended beyond educational

---

* *The Marriage Law of the People's Republic of China*, 1950, Chapter 1, Article 2.

activity. They also tackled the job of rehabilitating and caring for thousands of prostitutes, particularly in the large cities where young girls had been stolen, kidnapped, or sold into brothels. The Federation provided medical care and trained these women in productive work. They carried out educational campaigns to help people understand that these women were not corrupt, but rather were cruelly exploited and oppressed victims of the old, decadent system. The Federation opened schools for former prostitutes; some of their students, freed from the brothels, were only thirteen years old. The Federation recorded women's life stories to help women understand that their oppression came from the influence of foreign capitalists, the corruption of the old society, and the class base of the old system. These histories were sometimes dramatized, illustrating for people throughout China the indignities forced upon women.

The Federation then shouldered what was perhaps a more important and more difficult task: encouraging all women to change their social and economic identity by leaving the confines of their homes to work in productive labor alongside men. It set up day-care centers for children and even organized factories to produce the toys needed by these centers.

The Federation also ran courses on home management for housewives: how to cook economically, how to budget expenses. On the one hand, they encouraged women to come out of the home into society; on the other, they tried to make life more productive and easier for those older women who remained at home.

The All-China Democratic Women's Federation held Congresses in 1949, 1953, and 1957. At the 1957 Congress the name was changed to the National Women's Federation.

The National Women's Federation still exists. Like everything else in China it had been deeply affected by the political struggles of the Cultural Revolution, and at the time of our visit its direction and future were still being discussed and thoroughly evaluated. When we asked to meet with leaders of the Federation, we were told it was still in the process of "struggle-criticism-transformation," and thus they preferred not to discuss unsettled details with us.

Since our visit some of those details have obviously been settled. More recent visitors to China have had extensive interviews with leaders of the Women's Federation. And in September 1973, congresses of municipal Women's Federations were held in Peking and Shanghai, each attended by well over one thousand delegates representing local units. Top Party and government leaders addressed both gatherings.

In many localities we were told about local women's associations. Sometimes workers or peasants talked of regional and provincial organizations of women in their area; they often had special women's representatives within trade unions, Workers' Representative Congresses, and leading committees. Here, as in most aspects of life in China, there was significant variety at the local level. The goal was equality for women; the means differed somewhat from place to place and time to time.

The Three Fronts

Zhou Min-fu, a cadre at the Sino-Hungarian Friendship Commune, gave us a useful framework to view the contemporary struggle:

"We try to solve the problems of women in three ways—on three fronts," he said.

"The first is the ideological front. We give education to women and also to men. We fight against the old idea that women should not be in production; we fight against the feudal mentality.

"The second front is solving concrete problems. For example, we try to solve the practical problems of housework which women face.

"And third, we try to make sure women take part in leadership. We make sure they are on leading bodies. This is important so that women can be respected, can be looked up to as leaders. This promotes an equal standing. Also, women should be on these bodies because they know the problems of women better than we men do."

We kept these "three fronts" in mind throughout our visits, asking and probing to find out what was being done on each front.

Ideology. Practical Problems. Leadership.

Were fierce battles still being waged? Where were old ideas most deeply entrenched—and who was on the offensive or defensive?

We will try to describe what we found on each front. In each there were large and significant battlefields where Chinese women justifiably hailed tremendous victories. But we also found that occasionally some operations appeared to have bogged down or to be in need of reinforcements.

We also soon learned our investigations were not to remain that of detached observers. We, too, were inevitably affected by, and eventually drawn into, the fray; and it was probably these personal experiences that were, in the end, the most instructive.

Old ideas had to be challenged. Men's ideas about women had to be changed; women's ideas about themselves needed overhauling. Feudal and traditional ideas about marriage, woman's place in society, sex roles, and sex objectification were all targets of the struggle on the ideological front.

The first step for women was not easy. As one woman described it: "It was as though not only their feet but their minds had been bound."* Once these mental bonds had been broken, women faced the opposition of many men, parents, and parents-in-law. But their struggles were closely intertwined with the revolutionary struggles of the whole society. New ideas of socialist equality challenged the traditional views of women's inferior status.

---

* A Hubei woman cadre who had spent years organizing women to enter production, as quoted in Dymphna Cusack, *Chinese Women Speak* (Sydney: Angus and Robertson, 1958), p. 54.

Women: Half of Heaven 141

Perhaps the biggest battle on the ideological front was against the notion that a "woman's place is in the home." One weapon in this battle was Article 9 of the 1950 Marriage Law, which declared: "Both husband and wife have the right to free choice of occupation and free participation in work or in social activities." We encountered several examples of how this battle had been fought.

One Pair of Scissors, One Piece of Cloth

To reach the Red Flag Embroidery Factory our car wound through the crowded streets of Tianjin. Buildings here were taller than in most of the cities we visited, with pillars and huge ornamental fronts in Western style. Yu, a local guide, explained that the face of the city showed its past. Before Liberation, Tianjin, like Shanghai, had been partitioned into "foreign concessions": Britain, France, Germany, Japan, and other countries physically held and ruled sections of the city. The imposing Victorian-style bank structures and the multi-storied hotels and commercial buildings were products of foreign, not Chinese, culture. Yu explained that formerly the Chinese had to pay a toll to enter or pass through the concessions. Even a rickshaw picking up or delivering a European passenger was taxed. Our car crossed a bridge which, he said, had been off-limits to all Chinese before Liberation.

We competed for space on the narrow streets with other autos, tandem buses, Tianjin-manufactured "mini-buses," and bicycles.

We pulled up in the middle of a block lined with small shops, the sidewalk buzzing with activity. Yu jumped out and led us to a narrow door squeezed in between two shops. A small welcoming committee greeted us, shook hands, urged us to follow them, and disappeared into the dimness of the doorway. We followed, climbed a steep flight of stairs, walked toward the back of the building (which looked over rooftops and the activity of neighboring one-story shops), and then breezed up four more steep, narrow flights. We emerged into a recreation and meeting room where the factory ping-pong table had been converted, by the simple addition of a white tablecloth, into a guest table appropriately fitted out with cups of tea and cigarettes. Once settled, we listened as our hosts gave a brief introduction.

Some veteran workers spoke of their factory's development—how the Red Flag Embroidery Factory had grown from a women's production team established in 1953 and how they had fought to take part in productive labor outside the home.

"There was a struggle when I went out into society," Pan Xue-yin began. "In the old society women had no position. We had to attend to our husbands, to our parents-in-law, and to our houses. We were also weighed down by the two big mountains.* In the old days we had no say at all. If a husband said something was one, we dared not say it was two. If a visitor came, we were not allowed to speak. If we didn't attend to our parents-in-law or husbands, we were beaten and cursed.

"[After Liberation] the All-China Women's Federation in the district where I lived mobilized us; they said times were different and we should go out and work. We went to meetings of the Federation but when we came home our husbands would not agree to let us work. They said if we went to work, then who would look after them, who would care for our parents-in-law? But we persisted and argued with them. We said, 'If we work, we'll earn money, and that will help our family.'

"At the beginning [1953], seven of us organized ourselves into a self-help production team. We had only one knife, one pair of scissors, and one bolt of cloth when we started. We got materials and did the work in our homes and also tended to our families. By 1956 we had grown to 80, and we got one

---

* The "two big mountains" refers to a passage in "The Foolish Old Man Who Removed the Mountains," an article by Mao Tse-tung. The passage reads: "Two big mountains lie like a dead weight on the Chinese people: one is imperialism, the other is feudalism."

room for an office. During the Great Leap Forward [1958] the factory grew to 170 and gathered workers together in one place. But it was not easy for women to leave home.

"Over the years our parents-in-law, who had feudal ideas, came to like the idea that we were working. They were convinced when they saw the money we earned. But in my family we still had struggles. We fought ideologically and I held to my position. At first my husband tried economic suppression. At one point we were on the verge of getting a divorce.

"My husband did change his attitude, but only after struggle. At first he tried to stop me from working. But the leaders where he worked did education with him, to teach him he was wrong to try to stop me. His attitude began to change. But I still had problems. How was I to work and still care for my children? I decided to take the children from the house to a nursery run by the Neighborhood Committee. I would take the children there in the morning and then go and work. In the evening I would bring the children home and then do the cooking and all the other work in the house. My husband was finally moved by my actions, and he started to help with work in the house. Now things are much easier."

Sun Gui-fan, vice-chairman of the factory's Revolutionary Committee, added her comments: "Women insisted on going out because we wanted to be independent economically. We knew that only when we have economic independence can we have real equality. Changes in the family followed the changes in production. Our husbands' consciousness has been raised; now they help with the washing, they take care of the children, they cook. The children help, too. Before Liberation we had no rights in the home; now we are equal. Things are different financially—we women have our own wages."

The factory had over 240 workers, about 90 percent women, and had grown from "one pair of scissors, one bolt of cloth" to electric sewing machines, many embroidery machines for fancy work, and motor-powered scissors. Their products were exquisite, colorful embroidered pillowcases, tablecloths, towels, aprons, and shawls; most were for export.

Changes had been political as well as technical and material. Yan Gou-zhen, another veteran worker, talked about their political development: "When we first started work, our ideological level was not very high. Most of us were working just to get more money. During the Great Leap Forward [1958] we came to understand that our jobs were an important part of building socialism. But we didn't really have a thorough understanding of this. During the Cultural Revolution we all studied together. We read the 'Three Constantly Read Articles,'* especially 'Serve the People.' We learned that all our jobs serve the people, whether they are high or low. Also, in the Cultural Revolution we learned a lot about class struggle and the struggle between the two lines.

"After the Cultural Revolution we linked up our present work with the world revolution. We produce to meet the needs of the world's people. We women have high aspirations and say: 'Working in embroidery we have the whole world in view so that we will never leave the revolutionary road.'"

Yan concluded, "We should try to do our job well. We have liberation, but the world's women do not have liberation yet. We should work to help them get liberation."

The factory workshops were small rooms stacked one above another, four stories in all, and tied together by the narrow metal staircase we had ascended. Work was divided into cutting, sewing, embroidery, ironing, pressing, and packing. We poked our heads into rooms where the clatter from double rows of twenty or thirty sewing machines rose in rhythmic and almost musical crescendo. Here and there we noticed young men who, like the women alongside them, were busily stitching flowers, birds, and delicate border designs. The cutting rooms were quieter, with only the buzz of the electric scissors. Ironing was done with heavy, old-fashioned flatirons. Packing meant securing heavy wooden crates suitable for trans-ocean shipping, and that work, we noticed, was done almost entirely by men.

Tabletops and work benches throughout the factory were

* The "Three Constantly Read Articles" are "Serve the People," "In Memory of Norman Bethune," and "The Foolish Old Man Who Removed the Mountains," all by Mao Tse-tung.

blanketed with colorful cloth, a smorgasbord of prints, patterns, and designs. Some were traditional Chinese embroidery; others were done specifically for export, like some bright red and green table decorations with Christmas trees, candy canes, and sleigh bells. "These were ordered by Scandinavian countries," they told us when we expressed surprise at finding Christmas themes in a Chinese embroidery factory.

We learned that their factory was collectively owned by the workers and cadres. A Tianjin District Administration, they added, "gives guidance and leadership but it can't take any of the money in the factory's reserves." Neither could anyone use the funds individually. They had an eight-grade wage system similar to that of the state-owned factories. Money from sales was held by the collective for construction and expansion. They did not receive government investment funds.

"What if you need money for expansion and don't have enough yourself?" we asked. "If we have a financial problem and our savings are not enough, then we can get a loan from the state bank. We repay it as we are able."

The factory was led by a Revolutionary Committee of eight members (five women and three men) and a local Party branch of three members (two women and one man). In this factory of 90 percent women the chairman of the Revolutionary Committee was a man; the vice-chairman was a woman.

These women were proud and confident in their work. We also found this the case in another "housewives' factory" we visited in Peking—a factory which had started producing simple metal buckets and stove pokers twelve years ago and now manufactured a high-precision, electronically guided lathe. In both factories we were especially impressed by the older women, the ones who before Liberation had been expected to live out their lives traveling "around the stove." They now had radically different ideas about "women's work." Women, as well as men, should work "to put in one brick for socialism," one of them aptly commented.

Women at Work Everywhere

Chinese women were not working only in factories they had organized and developed themselves. We saw women at work in all areas. Every factory and commune we visited had women workers, though the percentage varied. In the countryside women took full part in agricultural labor, many times doing jobs that had formerly been reserved for men. There were, however, some jobs that seemed to be the women's domain. The staffs in all the nurseries we visited were entirely women; teachers at the primary schools we visited were overwhelmingly women.

Some work often reserved for women in the West was done by both men and women in China. For example, the Dong Feng (East Wind) Watch Factory workforce was half men and half women; there tedious hand work of small parts production was shared equally. At the Norman Bethune International Peace Hospital in Shi-jia-zhuang, we visited laboratories where both men and women spent the day doing blood counts, combining the old and new in dramatic fashion by use of modern microscopes to examine and an abacus to count.

There was little noticeable division of jobs along sex lines in the factories we visited. Men and women worked in the same workshops and often the group operating a particular machine would include both men and women. We saw women working in skilled and semi-skilled jobs: operating cranes on the Tianjin docks, driving fork-lift trucks, running overhead cranes in large workshops, driving buses, operating lathes, doing welding.

At the Shenyang No. 1 Machinery Factory we stopped to talk with a young woman electrician who was wiring the controls for large lathes. Other workers teasingly called her a "veteran worker"; she had worked in the factory for eight years and the term was usually reserved for those with several decades of experience. She was teaching a young man who had just graduated from middle school the complexities of wiring the panel. Outside, we chatted with another young woman who was busy with acetylene torch welding. She had learned her skill since she had come to the factory one year before. Many engineers we talked with were women, including one at the Tianjin No. 1 Machinery Factory who was helping develop a new gear-shaping lathe. About half the doctors at the army hospital we visited were women; the same was true for a health sanitorium near Anshan in the Northeast. In both places most of the nurses were women, but nursing was not exclusively a woman's job.

At two workplaces we were told that certain jobs were not filled by women. Workers at the Xin Gang Harbor near Tianjin said 10 percent of their workforce was women—the women operated cranes, hi-lo fork lifts, and trucks—but no women did heavy physical labor in the holds of ships or directly loaded or unloaded slings. This policy had been set, they said, by the workers themselves.*

At the Kairan Coal Mine in Tangshan only about 7 percent of the workers were women. "In the beginning," one mine cadre explained, "we tried having women work alongside men in the mine itself. But it was not good for women's health, so now no women work underground. Women work in the repair shops and in our headquarters building."

This sexual division of labor seemed inconsistent with the principle of "whatever men can accomplish, women can, too," and the reasons given were not convincing. After all, was work in the mines any better for men's health? The excuse at the harbor, that the policy had been set by the workers themselves, also begged the question of equality. Old ideas, it appeared, sometimes stuck around in new forms; the battle against them progressed unevenly.

A "Housewife" in China

Although most women in China worked outside the home, there were some, mostly older women, who did not. We met

* Friends who visited the Shanghai docks in 1973, however, reported that they observed young women there loading and unloading trucks.

Mo Ze-lian in Tangshan, Hebei Province, northeast of Peking. We liked her immediately; she was warm and friendly, the sort of person you feel at home with right away. Mo was a "housewife"; she had never worked outside the home and, since she was in her fifties, probably never would.

Mo and her husband had five children, four sons and one daughter. The eldest son was a steel worker; the second worked in another city; and the third and fourth sons were working on a commune in the countryside. Mo's daughter worked in a machine factory in Tangshan and lived with her parents.

Mo greeted us outside their family home and hustled us into the pleasant one-story house built of rocks and mortar. The house, like the others in the neighborhood, had been built by the Kairan Coal Mine in 1956 and 1957. Before Liberation, Mo recalled, almost half the families in the neighborhood had lived in slum housing: "We had no thought then of having new houses; all we hoped for was enough to eat. Some of us had to sell our sons and daughters, we were so poor."

She then proudly showed us her wristwatch, a gift from one of her sons who worked in the countryside. "Look at this watch! Just think—that a son can now send his mother a wristwatch! Before Liberation we hardly had money for food and none for things like watches."

Mo Ze-lian's husband had worked at the Kairan Coal Mine for many years. He was now retired and enjoyed a regular monthly pension of 70 yuan. They both received free medical care provided by the mine. The changes brought about by Liberation had certainly improved life for Mo and her family. But she and the other housewives in her neighborhood had not sat back, minded the house, and merely kept to themselves. They were deeply involved in neighborhood and community political work.

Mo Ze-lian was active in the local Neighborhood Committee, a local organization common in China's cities. Above it, she explained, was a structure of local government Street Committees and a District Committee.

Mo's Neighborhood Committee had many different functions. They organized women to go and help at the mines and factories when there was a special need or, in the busy season, to help with agricultural work in the countryside. They helped single workers clean their cotton quilts and padded clothing, a tremendously time-consuming task. They did health work in the mines and in the neighborhoods. They organized study among housewives and retired workers in the area, and worked with children to give them "class education."

"We try to teach the children to be revolutionary successors," Mo told us. "Since the young people have only lived in this 'Red Flag Period,' they don't know about the past. We give them education about what it was like before Liberation."

Mo Ze-lian was also a member of a cultural group in the Neighborhood Committee. Mo's group performed in the neighborhood, especially for young people. They also went to the mines, where they put on performances to help raise the political consciousness of the workers.

"Before Liberation, women couldn't even touch the gate of the mine. Now we go and perform there; we have direct contact with the leading workers," one of Mo's neighbors told us.

Mo apologized for having "something wrong with my throat," and then sang a popular aria from *The Red Lantern*, one of the new revolutionary Peking operas. It was especially appropriate for her, because the song was about a grandmother telling her granddaughter to carry on the revolutionary struggle.

Mo Ze-lian and the other housewives in her neighborhood had clearly moved a long way from their isolation and confinement in the old society. While that isolation had been broken directly by women who left the home and worked in productive labor, those who remained as housewives had also changed. Like the women in factories we visited, Mo was, in her own way, "adding one brick for socialism."

Education for Equality

Weapons of all sorts were brought into play on the ideological front. Informational and educational campaigns about equality for women were common in newspapers and magazines. Wall newspapers, blackboards, signs, posters, and billboards were used to root out, identify, and destroy old ideas, old practices. Battlelines were drawn wherever remnants of the old, feudal-patriarchal ideology cropped up.

Westerners can find examples of this kind of mass education in *China Reconstructs*, a monthly Chinese periodical published in several languages. Recent articles give an idea of the strides women are taking, as well as the extent to which old, male chauvinist concepts still remain. One article, for example, chronicled the struggle of women in a People's Liberation Army artillery corps. Some people had objected when women demanded an active role in defense work, saying: "Girls from fishermen's families can only weave nets. How can they fire artillery guns?" Or: "Women learn to fire guns? It's like using the sky for a hat—too bold!" But the women overcame both the chauvinist attitudes and technical difficulties, learning to handle even the heaviest guns.*

Another article, in March 1972, described women who ran a fleet of "March 8th" fishing boats. They also had faced opposition, represented by such gems of feudal wisdom as: "No one ever heard of women going deep-sea fishing. It can't be done." And: "A woman wants to go to sea to show her strength? That's like a baby chick trying to eat a soyabean—she'll choke on it!"

The women learned all the tasks involved in deep-sea fishing and soon operated boats with all-women crews, including captains. Their new thinking was summed up by one of the first women captains: "Paths are made by people walking. Someone has to carry the heavy load."**

---

* "Women Gunners on the South China Sea Front," *China Reconstructs*, Vol. XVIII, No. 6, June 1969, p. 32.

** "The 'March 8th' Fishing Boats," *China Reconstructs*, Vol. XXI, No. 3, March 1972, p. 12. March 8 is International Women's Day.

We saw other forms of mass education about women's equality. At the Wuhan Printing and Dyeing Factory we noticed a huge billboard and wall newspaper celebrating the March 8th International Working Women's Day. It was still up six weeks after the holiday. A drawing of a strong and determined-looking textile worker, leading her fellow workers on, filled the center of the billboard, commanding attention and overshadowing related news items and short articles on either side. We learned this was typical of displays put up on International Women's Day.

The celebration of International Women's Day as a holiday was itself significant. It honors working women, and women in struggle, everywhere. Its origin also helps illustrate the worldwide perspective of Chinese women. International Women's Day originated in two strikes of women garment workers in the United States. The first was on March 8, 1857, in New York City and the second was fifty-one years later on March 8, 1908. In 1910 Clara Zetkin, a German socialist, proposed that March 8 be proclaimed International Women's Day in commemoration of the U.S. demonstrations and to honor working women the world over. It is currently celebrated widely around the world.

Cultural and artistic forms have also been used in battles on the ideological front. *The Women's Representative* was a play popular in the early 1950s. Its plot revolved around the struggles of Chang Kuei-yung, a young woman chosen leader of her village Women's Association. Chang had to fight the opposition of both her mother-in-law and her husband in order to take part in agricultural labor and to continue her work for women's rights. The play spoke to the reality many Chinese women faced. A few years after it was first produced, one woman told about difficulties encountered in staging it in the first place:

> It wasn't easy going at the beginning. Old people objected to women going on stage. The mother-in-law of one girl who played the heroine in *The Women's Representative*—a play that mirrored many of our own problems—used to carry on frightfully about it, nagging her and sometimes even refusing to give her anything to

eat. In fact, she was just like the mother-in-law in the play. But the girl continued and the play was a great success. And the mother-in-law was quite changed after it, for she thought the author was showing her up in the play!*

Modern drama, such as the new revolutionary Peking opera, also reflected women's struggles. Products of the Cultural Revolution, these new operas and ballets portrayed women prominently, in strong roles. This was a great change from female roles in traditional Peking opera. Even after Liberation, in the early 1960s, Peking opera portrayed women in feudal terms:

> The female leads are usually demure, modest creatures, though sometimes they may be quite alluring coquettes.... Their eyes are elongated [by make-up], giving them a particularly exquisite and delicate look.**

We saw several new operas while in China and although they did not deal specifically with women's oppression, as had *The Women's Representative*, their characterization of women as activists, militants, and leaders provided positive and unmistakable models of liberated women.

While in Peking we also enjoyed an evening at the ballet, seeing a new adaptation of *The White-Haired Girl*. Lao Liu, from China International Travel Service, and Jia Ai-mei, a lively and friendly interpreter, accompanied us. As usual, we were full of questions and intermission provided an opportunity to raise them.

"When was this ballet written?" It had first been performed as a ballet, they explained, about 1960. But the ballet came from a much older play and opera, originally written in the 1940s. An earlier movie version had also been made.

"But," Liu emphasized, "the earlier versions had their shortcomings. The version you're seeing is improved."

---

* Wang Wang-jing, quoted by Dymphna Cusack in *Chinese Women Speak*.

** Philip Bonosky, *Dragon Pink on Old White* (New York: Marzani and Munsell, 1963), p. 20.

"What were the shortcomings? How is it improved?" We were curious.

Liu and Jia recalled that the original version had portrayed peasants as docile and downtrodden, not fighting back.

Liu and Jia's comments prompted us to do a bit of research and we discovered several versions of the play. It was originally written collectively, by about six writers, and was probably the most popular play performed in the Liberated Areas during the late 1940s. It has changed with the times, reflecting different stages of political development.

In one early version Xi-er, daughter of a poor peasant, is surrendered by her father to a landlord to honor a debt. Xi-er becomes a kitchen slave and is also made pregnant by the landlord, who takes advantage of her powerless situation. The landlord, however, refuses to marry her and arranges to marry the daughter of another wealthy landlord. When the wedding takes place Xi-er runs away in despair; her baby is born in the wilderness and dies of starvation. Xi-er's hair turns white from this experience. The ending is happy, however, as the Eighth Route Army arrives, including her childhood fiancé, and accounts are settled with the landlord.*

Other versions, dating from about 1949, portrayed Xi-er waylaid by the landlord's agents, raped by the son of the landlord, and then narrowly escaping murder because the landlord's son wants to conceal his crime. Xi-er gives birth to a child who dies in the wilderness; her hair turns white, and then she joins the guerrillas, who eventually liberate her village.**

The version we saw was still different. The landlord, on the pretext of demanding repayment of a debt, tries to abduct Xi-er. Xi-er's father fights back but is killed in the struggle. Xi-er is then carried off by the landlord's henchmen. Her fiancé and other villagers immediately went to fight the land-

---

* Reported by William Hinton in *Turning Point in China* (New York: Monthly Review Press, 1972), p. 50.

** See Jack Belden, *China Shakes the World*, p. 210, and Robert Payne, *Mao Tse-tung* (New York: Henry Schuman, Inc., 1950), p. 231.

lord and rescue her, but realizing they are weak and unorganized and would be defeated, they go off to join the Eighth Route Army. In the landlord's house Xi-er fights off his lustful advances and escapes to the mountains with the help of another woman servant. Her hair turns white from the difficulties of living in the mountains, not from childbirth. There is a happy ending, including a tender and moving scene when Xi-er and her fiancé meet again. The village is liberated, all join together, and the landlord receives his due punishment. In the finale, everyone resolves to continue the struggle because millions the world over are still suffering oppression.

Women, strong and independent, leaders in revolutionary struggle; such were the models we saw projected through popular culture and the media. Change the material base for women's oppression and change the way both men and women think about women; such were some of the battles being waged on the ideological front.

The Three Rs—and More

The primary school at the Luoyang Tractor Works buzzed with activity. Children recited lessons in shrill, excited voices, their eyes flashing back and forth between lesson, teacher, and American visitors. Buttons almost popped from their shirt fronts as they swelled with enthusiasm.

We entered a classroom where a group of sixth-graders was busy with arithmetic problems. The lesson came to an abrupt halt as students and teachers jumped up to welcome us. We visited a while and then strolled across the school courtyard to watch some younger children learn to write characters. A small nursery filled with toddlers was attached to the school and tended by a group of nurses and teachers. A student song-and-dance group put on a spirited performance for our benefit, with dozens of other kids crowding the doorway to watch us, not the performance.

Regular education was another important component of

the battle on the ideological front. What boys and girls were taught in school about the role of women, whether there were differences in education for boys and girls, and whether education was equally open to women and to men—these were some questions we kept in mind during our visits.

The primary school at the Luoyang Tractor Works was typical of those we visited. Built in the late 1950s, it had about one thousand students and seventy-four teachers. It stood in sharp contrast to education in pre-Liberation China. Education before Liberation had been reserved primarily for boys. There had been little public education and what few public schools existed often lost students when the devil's claw of poverty forced them to go to work. Thus, families who were not rich had little chance to give even their sons an education; their daughters had virtually no opportunity to study. Now all children went to school; neither economics nor feudal attitudes held them back.

The new generation was being taught values that challenged old notions of women's inferiority. The simple practice of universal, co-educational primary education was itself a bold step forward. But more impressive was the absence of any difference in educational content along sex lines, at least in the places we visited. Boys and girls were together in classes and took the same courses. We did not encounter classes which project sex roles in later life, such as special homemaking classes for girls or boys-only shop and mechanics courses. Sports activities and gym classes were also coeducational.

An important part of education in China, particularly since the Cultural Revolution, was combining study with manual labor. Education in a workers' society, they believed, should not separate people from labor nor create what they termed "spiritual aristocrats." The educational system was geared to teach respect for manual labor, to prepare students for a life where intellectual and physical work were combined. We found no differences in the application of these goals to boys or girls. Every student at the No. 26 Middle School in Peking, for instance, took a turn doing productive labor, about one full month each year, in one of the school's workshops. We watched a young girl in the carpentry workshop tack together wood-and-canvas chairs, while a male classmate planed the legs for a table. In their transistor factory a group of junior-middle school students were testing parts manufactured by classmates; there was no noticeable division of jobs by sex.

Labor and study were also combined outside the schools. We visited the Wuhan Sewing Machine Factory on a Sunday. There we met a group of middle school students who had volunteered to help build a road on their day off. Boys and girls had divided up into separate teams, but all were busy at the same tasks; shoveling earth and leveling gravel between the workshops.

Another factor about education was impressive. Young people were taught to think of society first. Collective consciousness was emphasized, socialist values of equality were promoted. This was itself in direct contradiction to the old notion that women should only concern themselves with the affairs of the home. Today boys and girls studied side by side and learned to think of the affairs of the whole society.

Families

The family was still strong in China. We visited several three- and four-generation households. But it was a new family, not the feudal, patriarchal family of the old society. To be sure, old ideas still persisted, but they appeared to be on the retreat against the onslaught of new ideas and new ways of doing things. Throughout our journey we witnessed small examples of such change:

- Lu Fen-zhen, a grandmother, was the host during our visit with her family, and her husband stayed outside and did the cooking for lunch.

- The young woman, a daughter, on the Ma Qi Zhai Commune who acted as spokeswoman for her family. Her brother-in-law had reversed tradition and moved into their home instead of her sister leaving to live with his family.
- Zhen Shou-fu and Wang Shou-zhen, husband and wife, who both worked at the East Is Red Auto Factory, both passed around cigarettes, got hot water for tea, and participated in the discussion when we visited in their home.
- Sun Gu-shan and Zhan Jian-lan who similarly shared tasks of hosts. Sun, the husband, worked at Foreign Languages Printing House. It was here that Zhan Miao-yu, a factory cadre and member of the People's Liberation Army, asked us who was the "head" of our family. When we told him our two-member family didn't have a "head," that we made joint decisions, he smiled and remarked, "A revolutionary family must have equality between man and woman."
- A four-generation family in Peking whose financial decisions for all nine members were made jointly and then implemented by the grandmother, Song Guan-zhen. She told us they planned what they bought and that presently they were saving money for a twenty-six-year-old son's marriage. Song said the six who worked turned their money over to her and she did the buying after decisions were made collectively.
- Comrade Ge, who had moved to Changsha because of her job with China International Travel Service. While their children had come with her, Ge's husband had remained behind in their nearby hometown of Shaoshan, where he worked.

We also visited a few homes where older patterns of family life seemed to survive. Near Tianjin we visited Wang Zhou-pin and his wife Zhan Zhe-fen; both were of the older generation. Wang had been a poor peasant before Liberation and had received land only after land reform. They greeted us at the doorway of their modest home and Zhan immediately retired to heat water for tea. She sat in an adjoining room, listening to our conversation but not taking part. She reappeared as we left, her face revealing an enthusiasm at having foreign friends visit her home. Instead of shaking hands as we parted, she pressed her hands together and bowed slightly in the traditional manner.

New ideas about the Chinese family were evident in a conversation between Chou En-lai and Nixon during the latter's visit to China in February 1972. The comments revealed not only Chou's favorable attitudes toward changing family patterns, but also his refusal to string along with clumsy attempts at male humor. During a tour of the Shanghai Industrial Exhibition, Nixon saw a number of women technicians. He asked Chou if women were more intelligent than men. Chou replied dryly that whatever men can do, women can do also. The conversation then went on:

> *Nixon:* But in the home the woman is always more intelligent than the husband.
>
> *Chou:* Not necessarily! For instance there was an interpreter that was interpreting for Mr. Rogers [visiting U.S. Secretary of State]. In her family her husband takes more of the share of the domestic work than the wife. And that's the same in her house [pointing to another woman in the Chinese group]. In her family her husband does more of the home chores than she does because she has more work now that she is Party Secretary. She works outside of the home more and she does more political work and therefore her husband takes charge of the family. That's something that's not quite the same in the situation in our families of our generation. That's something different from our generation.
>
> *Nixon* (laughing): Just be sure that your husband doesn't stay home and just look at television.*

Chou En-lai evidently did not find the emerging role of women in Chinese society, and the resulting changes in family life, a laughing matter.

The Chinese women we met all used their own family names. In the past a woman married to a man named Wang would have been called "Wang tai-tai" (Mrs. Wang) or "Wang

---

* Recorded by CBS News and broadcast on their program "Sixty Minutes" on February 27, 1972. This conversation was also reported by Max Frankel of the *New York Times* in his February 28, 1972, dispatch in the "A Reporter's Notebook" series on President Nixon's visit.

fu-ren" (Madame Wang or literally "Wang-woman"). "Tai-tai" in particular was considered a form of pre-Liberation China. We did not meet anyone who used those terms today. The Marriage Law stated: "Both husband and wife shall have the right to use his or her own family name." Nor were we ever introduced to Chinese couples who used the term "fu-fu"; "Wang fu-fu" would roughly be the equivalent of saying "Mr. and Mrs. Wang," or "Wang, husband and wife."

Which name children took varied from family to family. Zheng, our guide and translator, mentioned that his daughter's family name was the same as her mother's. But the daughter of Zhen Shou-fu and Wang Shou-zhen, workers at the East Is Red Auto Factory, had taken her father's family name, Zhen. Families were free to decide for themselves how to handle this question.

A Bosom Line Is Hard to Find

In recent years several Western male journalists have returned from China disappointed that women were no longer sex objects. A good example is J. Edward Murray, who spent three weeks in China in the fall of 1972 with a twenty-two-member all-male delegation from the American Society of Newspaper Editors. Murray bemoaned:

"Romance and Sex Muted... in China."
"Signs of sex are hard to find in China."
"... men and women look almost the same in their drab, shapeless, blue and gray cotton clothes. All women wear long pants."
"In twenty-three days in China I didn't see a single grown woman in a skirt. And a bosom line is almost as hard to find."*

Poor Mr. Murray. We think he displays unfortunate hang-ups. We'd guess he found Hong Kong more to his liking,

* All quotes from the *Detroit Free Press*, October 30, 1972. Murray is associate editor of that paper and was President of the American Society of Newspaper Editors at the time.

where Chinese women in mini-skirts, tight sweaters, and sexy, provocative fashions are common. Hong Kong society, we might add, is also well known for its logical extension of this type of sex in its Suzy Wong bars, topless go-go joints, and world-famous brothels.

We do agree with Mr. Murray that a grown woman in a skirt was difficult to find. During our seven weeks in China the only women in skirts we saw were in stage costumes for various dances and performances. The same was true for make-up—and stage make-up was worn by both men and women.

We saw no public displays of affection; romance and sex were regarded as personal matters. We chose to respect individual feelings on this subject so we do not claim to know the inside story of sex life and romantic love in China. We question, however, whether they are "muted," as Mr. Murray declares. Warm, deep, and meaningful personal relationships obviously existed between men and women and within families.

And if sex has been muted in China, their continued population growth has yet to reflect this change of events.

Perhaps it is Mr. Murray's type of "romance" and Mr. Murray's type of "sex" that were muted. We believe that more to the point. There are differences between what he considers "sex and romance" and how many people the world over, not just in China, view sex, romance, and sexual equality. These differences, we believe, hold deep implications regarding the role of women in the society.

In today's China men dealt with women as people, as comrades, as fellow workers—not as possible conquests or a good-looking eyeful. We're sure some men still dealt with women as sex objects, but the entire social setting was one that promoted women as people, not as objects.

Sex was not used to sell soap powder, toothpaste, beer, or anything else. There were no skin-flicks, raunchy magazines, peek-a-boo shows, or girly houses. Young girls were not taught that to get a man they must dress sexily and be pleasing in bed. In fact, girls were not taught that the most important thing in their life was to get a man. Gone forever were the painted ladies with lily feet of the feudal era. Gone too were the made-up and smartly fashioned ladies of Western influence. "Girl-watching" was not a pastime or method to boost a male ego, and was not socially acceptable.

Mr. Murray complained that men and women looked alike in their "drab, shapeless" fashions. We discovered that since flashy, provocative garments were absent, we remembered people by their faces. Murray's kind often complain that China's lack of showcase fashions takes away a person's individuality; we discovered that without distracting wardrobes and strutting peacocks we tended to see individuals as people, not objects.

We also had our own individual reactions to China's sexual atmosphere.

From Janet's point of view it was the first time in her life she had been in a society where she was not given the "once-over" by men. She did not have to worry about her friendly remarks or common gestures being wildly interpreted as sexual come-ons. Sitting and talking with a man, as in going over a language lesson or learning verses of a new song with Zheng, was not an occasion for raised eyebrows or the worry that it would be misinterpreted by passers-by, or by Zheng. She could dress comfortably and practically and not be looked down on as "unfeminine" or "looking like a man."

Stu's perspective was different, but really the other side of the coin. Twenty-nine years of being trained to look at women as sex objects, living in a society which continually reinforced that practice, was difficult to leave behind. But China's social setting did remarkable things: it encouraged viewing women as people, as workers, teachers, peasants, soldiers, or students, rather than as physical specimens. This was a tremendous aid in the struggle to get rid of old ideas, of male chauvinist ways of thinking. How much of a difference it made really became evident when we returned through Hong Kong. There the provocative fashions and sex-laden culture immediately triggered old ways of thinking and looking at women that simply hadn't been a problem in China.

The public role of women in China was as full citizens in a socialist society. This meant the society had lost some things; for example, it had lost the practice of treating women as sex objects. Those who cry over this loss, we believe, say more about their own problems than about China's.

The Second Front: Practical Problems

Battles on the ideological front have been crucial in the assault on old ideas, to free women from the confines of the home and bring them into productive labor. But there are other fronts, important in the overall struggle to liberate women and guarantee socialist equality for all, men and women, in China's developing socialist society.

Practical problems were being tackled head on, although our general impression was that greater strides have been made in solving these problems in the cities than in the countryside. But in both places the second front was active.

Child care was an important part of the struggle on the second front. Perhaps typical of nurseries we saw was one at the Shenyang Transformer Factory, housed in a solid, functional two-story brick building. The halls rang with voices of children singing songs; a three-year-old boy popped out into the hallway, bouncing a small basketball, and then dashed back into his classroom. The center cared for almost 500 children each day, 170 of whom stayed overnight during the work week. Use of the nursery was completely voluntary and parents chose whether they wanted day care or week-long care. The facilities were simple, clean, well-staffed, and lively.

There were also one hundred nursing mothers at the factory. They had a special feeding room with nurses in attendance to care for their infants. Mothers received two half-hour periods for feeding, one in the morning and one in the afternoon. Here they also had a special local option: if infants were left at home to be cared for by grandparents or even great-grandparents, the mother could take a lunch-time "mothers' bus" provided by the factory. Her two half-hour feeding breaks were then combined with her regular lunch period, giving her one long break at the middle of the day. The "mothers' bus" was also used to provide transportation to and from work for the mothers and infants who opted to use the feeding room facilities at the factory.

Every factory we visited, large or small, state-owned or collectively owned, had a nursery. Some also ran their own kindergarten for older age groups; others told us that neighborhood kindergarten facilities were readily available.

Day-care facilities were used by a significant percentage of workers. The Dong Feng Watch Factory in Tianjin had a nursery with 160 children, from fifty-six days to two years old. Estimating one child per family, this meant at least 10 percent of the sixteen hundred workers had children that age and made use of the nursery. The percentage was probably higher, since the workforce undoubtedly included married couples. The nursery at the East is Red Auto Factory, with four thousand workers, had a total of 500 toddlers. The section of the nursery we visited had two hundred children and a staff of fifty.

In the countryside child care was generally, but not always, available for working women. Steps were definitely being taken on the communes we visited to deal with this practical problem through collective means.

While we were walking through a production brigade near Tianjin we heard a baby crying, the wails coming from a room in the midst of the brigade's headquarters. Curious, we stopped, looked inside, and discovered the brigade's small and rudimentary nursery. Four or five elderly women, some of whom still had bound feet, smiled and greeted us. They were in charge of a group of about twenty "little people." A huge wooden bed with rails on the sides half filled the room. It was covered with soft quilts and babies crawled about on top. Some of the women sat in the middle, cuddling and comforting those that needed attention. The infant we had heard crying now sat happily in the arms of a substitute grandmother and gazed at us in amazement. The women explained their nursery was free. Working mothers came back at lunch time to feed the children themselves.

By comparison, the Sino-Hungarian Friendship Commune near Peking had both nurseries and kindergartens on a regular basis. The Ma Qi Zhai Commune near Xian, however, had a nursery only during the busy season; the rest of the year working women made their own arrangements, usually with grandparents.

Nurseries we visited in factory and city districts were often subsidized by the government. On the communes they were paid for entirely from brigade or commune funds, reflecting one difference between the basis of collective ownership in the communes and state ownership of the factories.

Family Planning

The question of having children, and how many, was something Chinese women could now control themselves. Family planning was encouraged by the government, and contraceptives and birth control operations, including abortions, were free and readily available. When operations were performed, time off from work, with pay, was a common practice depending upon medical needs and health conditions. Abortions were available on request and, we were told, were most often practiced when pregnancy occurred in a family which already had the number of children they desired.

It was also interesting to learn that medical treatment was available upon request in cases of infertility.

Birth control programs were conducted through social and collective educational campaigns, accompanied by voluntary compliance. The programs, understandably, were not carried out conspicuously where foreign visitors could readily observe them. We saw no street signs, banners, or parades proclaiming the merits of family planning and birth control. We learned, however, that family planning programs were matters of priority in grassroots workplace and neighborhood

Women: Half of Heaven   165

organizations, with Party leaders playing important roles. Smaller families were encouraged—two children the ideal. Late marriage was also viewed as part of family planning.

It is worth noting China's overall view of population control. While obviously trying to reduce population growth rates, the Chinese did not view their large population as a problem or, as some Western theorists have argued, as the reason for China's pre-Liberation backwardness and poverty. Chi Lung, the Chinese representative at a recent United Nations-sponsored conference, made this clear:

> We hold that, of all things in the world, people are the most precious. They are first of all producers and then consumers. As producers, they ceaselessly concentrate on production in breadth and depth and can produce more products than they consume. Under certain socio-historical conditions, some problems may arise as the population increases. This is caused by various obstacles blocking the development of the social productive forces. ... Those views which regard people as a negative factor, that people are purely consumers and that growth in population means an obstacle to economic development do not correspond to the historical facts in the development of mankind.*

To back this up, the Chinese pointed to the fact that their population had increased by more than 50 percent since Liberation, but that grain production had more than doubled, there was adequate food, living standards had improved, unemployment had been eliminated, and the country was developing at a rapid rate.

They also argued that China's population increases should take place in a planned way, coordinated with the development of social production. This was why they have sought to reduce the population growth rate and have encouraged family planning.** Their state guideline for an overall annual

* Chi Lung, Deputy Representative of the Chinese delegation to the 29th Session of the United Nations Economic Commission for Asia and the Far East, April 16, 1973. The full text of his speech was printed in *Peking Review*, April 27, 1973.

** The national minorities of China were an exception. In fact, because of their severe past oppression, national minorities were encouraged to seek population increases if they so desired.

growth rate was 1.5 percent; the actual growth rate recently has averaged something near 2 percent. In 1972 the Peking and Shanghai municipalities reported increases of 1.17 percent and .6 percent respectively. But recent figures from the countryside indicate growth rates from 2.7 percent to 1.7 percent.*

The Chinese clearly understood that the question of population control, and how it was handled, had a great effect upon women's lives. Chi Lung summed it up: "It is also necessary to have a planned population increase in order to promote the thorough emancipation of women. . . ."

The Millstone and the Stove

In old China women spent hours each day tending the stove or doing the tedious work of grinding grain at the millstone. Almost everywhere we saw collective efforts to free women from these chores. Factories usually ran canteens and dining halls that served three hot meals a day. Food was plentiful, prepared well, and reasonably priced. There was usually a wide variety. How often one ate there was entirely a matter of choice, and the cost was not significantly higher than cooking at home. Most families we visited had opted for cooking at least one meal a day at home, while single workers usually took all three meals in cafeterias and canteens. In cities, restaurants were abundant, inexpensive, and, judging from the crowds, popular.

The situation was somewhat different in the countryside. We did not visit any commune or production brigade dining halls. Most cooking, apparently, was done in the home. In some rural areas public canteens were set up soon after the communes were formed (late 1950s), but later were dropped because they put too much of an economic strain on collec-

* Figures from Han Suyin, "Population Growth and Birth Control in China," *Eastern Horizon*, Vol. XII, No. 5, and Binneg Y. Lao and Ping Sheng, "China—Impressions," 1973, unpublished manuscript.

tive resources and were not yet practical.* We learned that some communes planned to establish (or re-establish, as the case may be) canteens in future years when they developed a greater economic base.

Though cooking in the countryside was usually done at home, we did witness efforts to collectivize the tedious work of food processing. Peasants at the Sino-Hungarian Friendship Commune had organized collective grain grinding. We talked with two women who worked full time running a small grinding mill. They showed us the different machines they used: one was a handsome, efficient-looking blue electric grinder, probably purchased from the state. They also "walked on two legs," for next to the new machine was an old-fashioned millstone, now rigged up to an electric motor instead of the traditional donkey, ox, or human power. The women said that five of them working full time did the grinding for the more than seven thousand households of the commune. Done in the home by hand, this work had formerly demanded thousands of hours of women's labor.

On communes we saw general stores, well-stocked with hardware, dry goods, meats, canned fruits and vegetables, fresh produce, eggs, and baked goods. Such stores made available convenient prepared and processed foods which had seldom before reached a peasant's home.

A Woman's Work Is Changing

"Who does the cooking in your family?" we once asked Zheng.

"One night I cook the main dish and my wife cooks the rice; the next night she will cook and I will make rice," he replied. Since he was from North China and she was a southerner, this arrangement did more than even out the chores. It also made sure each one's culinary tastes were satisfied: Zheng got his favorite sweet dishes, and his wife prepared her more spicy, southern-style food.

* See Isabel and David Crook, *The First Years of Yangyi Commune.*

But what struck us as extremely important in the long run were the social and collective means being developed to deal with the old burdens of "women's work." A Neighborhood Committee we visited in Peking provided some good examples.

Liu Xiang-zher was chairwoman of the Da Cheng Neighborhood Committee. A bright, cheerful woman, she impressed us as being an energetic, no-nonsense type of person. Her neighbors clearly thought highly of her and made sure we understood that Liu could have gone to work in a factory instead of devoting all her energies to the Neighborhood Committee. At the factory she would have been paid; in the Neighborhood Committee all her work was volunteer. Liu smiled, a bit embarrassed at their open compliment, and quickly changed the subject:

"We have organized a service center with eight substations in the neighborhood. We provide over one hundred kinds of services to families in this area. For example, we do sewing, mending, tailoring, repairing shoes and radios, making bamboo curtains, washing laundry, and many other such things. The substations are scattered through the neighborhood to make them convenient for everyone."

Other neighborhood residents added to the conversation:

"We have organized study groups; the housewives and retired people have learned from the spirit of Norman Bethune.* We should help others."

"For couples where both the husband and wife are working, we mobilize neighbors to take in their laundry. We buy charcoal for them and keep their stoves going if they are away, so they can cook easily when they come home. We buy food for

---

* Norman Bethune was a Canadian surgeon who worked in China from 1938 until his death in 1939. Mao Tse-tung's eulogy, "In Memory of Norman Bethune," reads in part: "Comrade Bethune's spirit, his utter devotion to others without any thought of self, was shown in his boundless sense of responsibility in his work and his boundless warm-heartedness towards all comrades and the people." This essay was popularized during the Cultural Revolution and was used to promote ideas of unselfishness and service to others.

them if this is needed, and watch after their children when they come home from school."

"The Neighborhood Committee organizes to build the spirit of mutual help."

Liu explained that the Neighborhood Committee, and the larger Street Committee of which it was a part, operated nurseries, kindergartens, primary schools, medical centers, and a housing department whose responsibilities included home maintenance and repair.

Neighborhood and Street Committees like these existed throughout China. They organized a myriad of services and activities and made collective contributions toward solving the practical problems of liberating women.

Conditions of Work

We were discussing work conditions in the United States with workers and cadres at the Tianjin No. 1 Machinery Factory. Zei Zao-huai, a middle-aged cadre, suddenly looked up, startled. "What?" he interrupted us. "You mean a woman in the United States might lose her job if she leaves to have a baby? But that's ridiculous!"

We repeated our comment that while it was not universal, it was common, particularly in low-paying and non-union jobs.

Zei then proudly reviewed provisions for women workers similar to those we had already encountered in other Chinese factories: fifty-six days maternity leave, with pay, and seventy days for twins. Nursing mothers received two periods, included in the eight-hour day, to feed infants. There was no cut in their pay and special "feeding rooms" were provided. The factory also provided low-cost nurseries and kindergartens. Zei added that upon reaching the sixth or seventh month of pregnancy a woman was given work "suitable to her condition." This sometimes meant lighter work or shorter hours; sometimes it meant transfer to sunny places or outside in good weather, or to spots with better ventilation, etc.

In the countryside, similar guidelines had been drawn up for working women:

> When pregnant they must be given light work, not heavy. When nursing they must be given work close by, not far away. During monthly periods they must be given dry work, not wet.*

These provisions were not regarded as a kind of privilege given to women. They did not come from a masculine gallantry which graciously bent the principle of equality between men and women. Rather, they were viewed as simple, sensible steps necessary to achieve equality. They were considered a necessary basis for equality, for women to take their full place in society, insuring good health, safe conditions, and equal participation.

Leadership: The Third Front

Ideology. Practical problems. The third front was leadership. Of the three, involving women in leadership probably depended more upon advances on the other two fronts than vice-versa. From our observations, progress on the leadership front has been varied, and contained some of the most obvious territory yet to be conquered.

We raised a lot of questions about this front, everywhere asking how many women were on local leadership bodies, how many members of Revolutionary Committees and Party Committees were women. We asked this so frequently that Zheng soon came to anticipate it, and if we happened to forget he reminded us!

We soon learned that any meaningful analysis had to go deeper than simply counting the number of women leaders. Chinese revolutionaries have successfully employed guerrilla warfare for decades, pointing out that superior troops are more important than superior numbers. Politics are more important than structure, and content more important than

---

* Isabel and David Crook, *The First Years of Yangyi Commune*, p. 126. Quotation is from a Party directive used during the period of formation of the people's communes.

	Work-force	Party Committee		Revolutionary Committee	
	Women (%)	Women (%)	Total Members	Women (%)	Total Members
East Is Red Auto Factory	33	10	3 of 29	12	5 of 43
Tangshan Rolling Stock Factory	16	5	1 of 21	4	1 of 25
Zhengzhou Textile Machinery Manufacturing Factory	18	5	1 of 19	7	3 of 40
Wuhan Sewing Machine Factory	67	10	1 of 10	12	2 of 17
Foreign Languages Printing House	33	16	3 of 19	18	3 of 17
Shenyang No. 1 Machinery Factory	12	11	3 of 27	10	3 of 29
Kairan Coal Mine	7	8	2 of 25	6	2 of 33
Luoyang Tractor Works	26	14	5 of 36	9	5 of 55
Tianjin No. 1 Machinery Factory	25	7	1 of 15	7	2 of 27
Doug Feng Watch Factory	50	12	2 of 17	18	3 of 17
Red Flag Embroidery Factory	90	67	2 of 3	63	5 of 8

In agriculture, the workforce is approximately 50% women, maybe a little less

Ma Chi Zhai Commune		20	2 of 10	17	5 of 29
Tianjin Production Brigade		14	1 of 7	22	2 of 9
Lo Kang Commune		16	3 of 19	15	5 of 33
Peking No. 26 Middle School					
Teachers and Staff	23				
Student body (approx.)	50	0	0 of 7	7	1 of 15

form. We found that in most places there was a conscious effort to involve women in leadership. There was usually at least one woman leader with special responsibility for women's work. But at the workplaces we visited the percentage of women on leading bodies was significantly lower than their percentage in the workforce as a whole. Some examples appear in the table on the preceding page.

Workers and cadres at some places conceded that women were under-represented and regarded it as a problem. For example, workers at Foreign Languages Printing House dealt with the question frankly. Without making excuses, they declared there were not enough women on their leading bodies. But they pointed out that women were taking a steadily increasing role in leadership, particularly compared to the past. Workers and cadres at the Wuhan Sewing Machine Factory were also honest and direct. They said there was only one woman on their ten-member Party Committee, although 67 percent of the workers were women. They explained they had plans to add three more people to their Party Committee and since women were under-represented, they were placing special emphasis on recruiting women for the posts.

Our hosts at the No. 26 Middle School in Peking were not so frank. Twenty-three percent of the teachers there were women, and their fifteen-member Revolutionary Committee included only one woman member. There were no women in the local Party Branch, the "leading core" of the school. We asked why. They gave embarrassed, evasive answers.

"Each grade has a leading body; many of those leaders are women," one teacher pointed out, squirming nervously in his chair.

"Not many of the leading comrades at this school are women, but No. 49 Middle School has a woman vice-chairman," another offered rather limply.

Why were women generally under-represented in local level leadership? We raised the question during our visit to Tangshan, and kicked off a lengthy discussion covering several aspects of leadership. Zheng and a young CITS cadre from

Tangshan—whom we'll call Bai since we didn't get his full name—were with us.

Bai's appearance suggested an intellectual background: wire-rimmed glasses, a smooth face, always very neatly dressed. But he had done an excellent job of "putting politics in command," and while we were in Tangshan he arranged three days filled with visits to factories, a coal mine, and a workers' history exhibition.

"From what we've seen, women have entered into leadership in different degrees," Janet commented, "but generally they seem to be under-represented. In the United States today many oppressed groups, like Blacks and women, are demanding a proportion in leadership equal to their size. In some cases they've raised demands for quotas or ratios to protect their interests. Have such demands been raised in China?"

Both Bai and Zheng found the concept of quotas in leadership bodies a strange idea. "Simply having a certain number of women in leadership does not mean that women's interests will be looked after," Bai asserted. "Having a specific person as a watchdog to do that is more important."

Zheng joined in, and both he and Bai agreed that leadership was a political quality, to be judged on the basis of political consciousness and individual qualities, not because a person was a man or woman. They felt strides forward would be made only by choosing leaders with good politics, not by choosing women simply because they were women.

"I agree leaders should be chosen on a political basis," Janet responded, "but that doesn't explain why there are so many more men in leadership than women. Shouldn't as many politically sound individuals come from women as men?"

"You're right," Bai replied, "there should be. In China the reason for fewer women in leadership is the severe oppression women had in the old society. Women have not been engaged in production as long as men and have less experience. The number of women who are entering into leadership is much higher now than it was before Liberation. As the process of production continues more women will develop into leaders."

Zheng added that he thought the low percentage of women in leadership showed old ways of thinking were still holding on, that hangovers from the feudal past remained. "It takes time to sweep away old ideas," he remarked. "The more women take part in production, the easier that job will become."

Leaders at the Zhao Ling Pu Commune near Shi-jia-zhuang voiced a similar opinion when we asked the same question: "The number of women on a production team's leading committee depends on individual leadership abilities, not on the number of women in the team. Of course all leaders are chosen democratically, so all women participate in deciding who are leaders."

Were these simply lame excuses for the reality of women's under-representation? We'd heard similar arguments in the United States, and they were generally used to resist change, to resist efforts to bring women into full and equal participation.

But the situation was different in China. To be sure, there were some men in China who used such arguments to camouflage their real opposition to including women in leadership. But most men and women we met were honestly working to tear down the remaining barriers that kept women out of leadership. Those barriers were remnants of the past oppression of Chinese women. Feudal holdovers sometimes popped up in new forms, and their impact should not be underrated. But they could now be identified and attacked precisely because the base of women's oppression, the semi-feudal, semi-colonial social and economic system of pre-Liberation China, had largely been destroyed.

We believe another point should be emphasized regarding the Chinese perspective on the question of women in leadership. Bai and Zheng's reluctance to view women's roles in political leadership simply as a question of proportional, constituent representation was not unique. Most people in China we talked to, men and women, shared this perspective. There were some solid historical and political reasons for this. There was never a significant separate feminist movement in China. From the beginning the women's struggle was an integral part of the over-all Communist-led revolutionary struggle. It was not just a fight for women's equality. It was a fight for women's equality while resisting Japanese aggression; a fight for women's equality while expelling Kuomintang reactionaries. The special interests and special needs of women were met through women's bureaus and women's associations which were politically and organizationally part of the overall revolutionary struggle.

Local Leadership

Often a woman cadre or leader was introduced to us as being "in charge of women's work." Workers at the Zhengzhou No. 3 Textile Mill told us: "We have women in charge of women's work in all our leading bodies. They help older women solve problems in housework; they increase the consciousness of the young workers; they organize young workers to help the old at home. The old teach the young to increase their skill. Old and young learn from each other."

The only woman (of twenty-one members) on the Party Committee at the Tangshan Rolling Stock Plant explained: "A women's organization was set up here even before Liberation. During the Cultural Revolution it went through criticism-struggle-transformation. In October 1971 we reorganized. Now each workshop has one representative for women and we have a standing committee of forty-two women. Every level of the factory has a special leading member in charge of women's work. They organize women to study and mobilize women to meet the production plans. Now our plant is reorganizing regulations and administrative work, discussing questions of safety and quality. Women are mobilized, as is everyone else, to discuss this."

Workers and cadres at the Luoyang Tractor Works told us they had a special women's group within their union.

But cadres at the Dong Feng Watch Factory said: "We have no special women's federation in the factory now. We had one in the past. Now we have women's representatives on leading bodies in charge of women's work. They organize women to participate in the three great revolutionary struggles [the struggle for production, class struggle, scientific experiment], and also look after women's health, and children."

The Tangshan Pottery Research Institute had a Revolutionary Committee of five; one was a woman, Zhan Li-ling. Zhan was clearly a strong leader: others in the group called her the "representative of the women comrades." Thirty-seven percent of the workers there were women, and Zhan was both a representative of women's interests and a factory-wide political leader, an exemplary worker with high political consciousness.

Hosts at a couple of places we visited gave what they felt was a minimum desired percentage for women on leading bodies. Peasants on the Sino-Hungarian Friendship Commune believed at least one-third of the members of their leading bodies should be women; 30 percent of their Revolutionary Committee were women at that point. Workers at the Wuhan Sewing Machine Factory, where 67 percent of the workforce was women, said their immediate goal was to increase the number of women on their leading committees to at least 20 or 30 percent.

All the people we talked to clearly understood it was essential that women take a direct part in leadership. But political leaders, they also firmly believed, should be the most advanced and politically conscious representatives of the masses, whether they be men or women. Thus the goal was to construct social and economic conditions which produced an equal number of women and men leaders. In the meantime, special interests, special needs, and special efforts necessary to reach this goal were guarded through women's associations, women's bureaus, and by women cadres with specific responsibilities to look after women's interests.

Higher Leadership

As with local leadership, Chinese women are proportionally under-represented on higher leadership bodies. The trend over the years, however, has been toward greater percentages of women in top leadership positions. A good example is the percentage of women on the Central Committee of the Chinese Communist Party, the Party's top leadership group. Here are figures for the three most recent Party Central Committees:

	Full Members	Women No.	%	Alternates	Women No.	%
Eighth Party Congress (1956) C.C.	96	4	4.2	94	4	4.3
Ninth Party Congress (1969) C.C.	170	13	7.6	109	10	9.2
Tenth Party Congress (1973) C.C.	195	20	10.3	124	20	16.1

The Tenth National Congress in 1973 was attended by 1,249 delegates; over 20 percent were women.

Women have also headed ministries in the national government and have served as deputies to the National People's Congress, the highest governmental body in the country.

Another indication of increased women's participation in higher leadership was their representation at the recent municipal trade union congresses in Peking and Shanghai. In April 1973 the Sixth Congress of Peking Trade Unions was attended by 2,396 delegates; 36 percent were women. This trade union congress elected a 120-member leading committee which was 35 percent women. A similar congress was held in Shanghai the same month. Shanghai's gathering had 1,598 delegates; 39 percent were women. Shanghai's delegates selected a 158-member leading committee which was 31 percent women.

"Mischievous Things"

The battle for women's equality on all three fronts (ideology, practical problems, and leadership) has put old ideas and old customs on the run. But male chauvinism is not completely routed; some still lingers on, sniping at the new society and refusing to die quietly. The old feudal-patriarchal ideology, in Soong Ching-ling's words, "still does yield mischievous things" in China today.* As she recently observed in an article about the liberation of women in China:

> In certain villages patriarchal ideas still have their effect.... As farmers want to add to the labour force in their families, the birth of a son is expected while that of a daughter is considered a disappointment. This repeated desire to have at least one son has an adverse effect on birth control and planned births.**

We saw this ourselves. For example, we asked staff members at a health clinic in the Da Cheng Neighborhood Committee about their voluntary birth control program. One woman told us there were fifty-five women of child-bearing age in the area. "All but one have decided to take measures so they will not have more children. In the past three years, only one child has been born among these fifty-five women." She then added, "This was because the one woman had old ideas; she still wanted a son even though she has two daughters."

Old ideas also influenced the distribution of workpoints in the countryside. When we were in Changsha, Comrade Ge described a campaign in the Chinese press against rural wage inequalities: "Chairman Mao has said women should be equal. This means political equality because physical conditions are different and women aren't equal physically. But some old attitudes remain. For example, we still have problems in some places with equal pay for equal work. I've re-

---

* Soong Ching-ling, "Women's Liberation in China," *Peking Review*, Vol. 15, No. 6 (February 11, 1972), p. 7. Soong Ching-ling is Vice-Chairman of the People's Republic of China and widow of Sun Yat-sen.

** Ibid.

cently read in the newspapers about Party Committees that criticized men for looking down on women. The articles gave an example of one commune where there were big differences in work points. The men got ten work points while women got only five for doing the same work. They also mentioned that there was some work on this commune that the women had done better than the men, like feeding the pigs. The women were more careful than men and therefore raised bigger pigs. We must organize education for the men and teach them not to look down on women."

Peasants and cadres at the Ma Qi Zhai Commune near Xian explained they assigned work points on the basis of the type of work done. Heavy work got a greater number of points than light; skilled got more than unskilled. They also explained:

"Heavy labor is generally men's work; light labor, like work in vegetables, is generally done by women." The result was that women got fewer work points.

Even at Tachai, where type of work was not such a factor in determining work points, most women were generally rated lower than men since physical strength and amount of work were still included in the criteria used.

The problems of equalizing workpoints came not only from male chauvinism, but also from objective conditions in the countryside. Production was still largely tied to hand labor, to physical strength, and income was dependent upon production. Thus collective income was affected not only by how hard one worked and how dedicated one was, but also by how much one actually produced. For example, two people might work with equal enthusiasm carrying baskets of millet from the fields to a storehouse. The income of the collective, however, rested on the amount each had actually brought in, something dependent upon physical strength, not just spirit or dedication. Income distribution on communes followed the socialist principle of "from each according to his ability, to each according to his work," and commune members interpreted this to mean more work points to those who actually performed more work. Since men generally were stronger than women (this is not to deny there were women who could, and did, outwork men), the realities of extensive hand labor in the countryside tended to favor men over women.

Dividing work on the basis of sex (heavy work for men and light work for women) certainly smacked of old ideas about "men's work" and "women's work." But even if tasks were not directly divided by sex, any tabulation of work points that included physical strength as a criterion also harbored inequalities which favored men. The overall fact was that as long as agricultural production required such dependence on physical labor, inequalities would undoubtedly continue to exist. As agricultural production becomes mechanized, depending more on skill, dedication, and technique than sheer physical strength, then an economic base for real equality of income will exist in the countryside. The more equitable situation in China's industry indicated to us that as an economic base for equality was established the struggles against male prejudice blossomed, taking great strides forward.

Sour Notes

In many ways our visit was like a performance of a good symphony, exciting, uplifting, rising in crescendo. But it was not without sour notes. When old practices or old ideas raised their heads they became discordant notes in a new composition. They did not by any means ruin the whole symphony; but to pretend they were not struck would be turning a deaf ear to harsh chords that were out of tune with the rest of society.

China has made great strides in fighting what Mao called the "authority of the husband," but male prejudice was still there, still kicking. Janet, in particular, felt this firsthand. In our case this problem was probably complicated by cultural differences and by our own rejection of some of the more traditional aspects of male privilege in our society.

We had applied for visas as two people, Janet Goldwasser

Dowty and Stuart Dowty, not "Mr. and Mrs. Dowty." We used our own names; we included individual, separate biographies, and described the political work each of us had done. We always used our own names when introducing ourselves. Thus we were somewhat taken aback when guides and hosts called us the Chinese equivalent of "Mr. Dowty and wife," or simply called Janet "Mrs. Dowty" ("Dowty fu-fu" or "Dowty fu-ren").

This was more than a matter of form, of names or words. Sometimes along with it came this practice: men spoke to Stu and ignored Janet; hosts greeted Stu and disregarded Janet; translators made sure Stu could hear, not caring that Janet couldn't. These were not common instances, but occurred often enough during the first few weeks of our visit to make us realize that among the old ideas still kicking was the assumption that the man was the center of a family and the wife was acquired and subservient property.

Perhaps we should make a few side comments here. We don't want to blow these types of incidents out of proportion to their meaning, and we don't want to be petty. Nor do we want to give the impression that our objections were simply on the grounds that such conduct toward Janet was rude and impolite. It was, but that's not the point. These types of practices are some of the most common manifestations of male chauvinism or male prejudice. Men, often without realizing it, interrupt women, cut them off, leave them out of conversations, or simply ignore their comments. This is particularly true in situations where the discussion is on topics outside the "woman's role," such as politics, science, history, etc. The problem comes from the attitude that women have nothing of value to say and allows such conduct while being totally unaware of it. Very few men openly argue that women should shut up and keep in their "place"; quite a few, however, act that way consciously or unconsciously. The effect is the same.

Thus, these incidents caused problems for us because they made it difficult for Janet to participate politically in conversations and discussions. It is extremely difficult to raise political points, and have them answered, when you cannot get the floor in the first place. It is hard to hold a political discussion when people simply do not "hear" comments you make; when people are "tuning out" the content of your remarks. It is difficult to get people to take your comments seriously when they regard you simply as someone else's satellite. These were the problems; they were matters of political content and maintaining in practice the socialist principle of equality. They were not simply matters of personal effrontery.

The afternoon we spent at the Guangdong Teachers College was a case in point. Li, a guide from China International Travel Service in Guangzhou, was doing the translating, giving Zheng a breather. In many respects Li was a good guide and translator; he was friendly, eager to explain his country to visitors, and quite competent technically. But he also clearly felt his job was to translate for Stu, as if Janet were along for purely ceremonial or decorative purposes. Both of us had lots of questions, but Janet's were seldom answered. It wasn't that our hosts at the college were reticent or ignored them. The problem was that Li had inordinate difficulty in realizing that Janet had something to say, and either ignored her or cut her off. Many questions simply were never translated. On this occasion, and several others, Janet had to grit her teeth and swallow hard until we found a way to change what was happening.

About two weeks into our trip we visited a People's Liberation Army hospital in Shi-jia-zhuang; we remember the visit for both positive and negative reasons. It was run by the army unit that Dr. Norman Bethune had worked with in 1938-1939. The hospital programs and services were exciting examples of Chinese medicine. Here we saw operations using acupuncture anaesthesia alongside other creative applications of both traditional and modern medicine. And here we saw a hospital providing free treatment for all who needed it, not only army personnel but also workers and peasants.

But this was also a difficult and depressing visit for Janet.

The hospital staff had put up colorful signs to welcome us. Several places we had previously visited had also done this, warmly welcoming "two American friends." Here the signs welcomed "Stuart N. Dowty and wife." It was an ominous indication of things to come.

We toured the hospital, walking from one department to another. Doctors and technicians stood waiting to greet the visiting American friend "and wife." At almost every ward the responsible person eagerly grabbed Stu's hand, welcomed him with many loud and friendly "*huan-ying*s" and then immediately turned his (or her) back without giving Janet even a nod. More than once Janet found herself putting out a hand for a friendly greeting only to have it ignored. Tactical maneuvering on our part helped little. Stu tried to stay behind Janet so people would meet her first, but then they simply walked right past and began talking to Stu.

By the end of the day Janet was seething. However, an explosion or confrontation then and there would have accomplished little; and although the experience was depressing, we both had learned a good deal about the hospital. But something had to be done.

We had suggested to Zheng that when we got to Peking, halfway through the trip, we should sit down and jointly evaluate what had happened up to that point. This would give all of us a chance to raise criticisms, point out weaknesses and misunderstandings, and hopefully improve the second part of the trip. The visit to Shi-jia-zhuang and the PLA hospital was the last stop before we arrived in Peking. Thus, two days after the hospital visit we raised some of these problems directly with our China International Travel Service hosts.

We sat down with Zheng, Lao Liu from the Peking office of CITS, and Jia Ai-mei. Jia translated much of the time we were in Peking; Liu accompanied us on many of our visits in the city. We had several long political discussions with both of them, as well as with Zheng.

We summarized the trip to date as we saw it, making both

self-criticisms and criticisms. We pointed out that strengths far outweighed weaknesses, but that weaknesses were there and were quite real. These shortcomings hampered our ability to get the most out of visits and successfully meet the objectives of our journey, such as building friendship through people-to-people contact. We described the problems Janet had faced, and explained how they hampered good, productive visits. We also put forward our opinion regarding the root of the problem, why such incidents occurred.

"We wondered what could be the cause of this," Janet said, "and we thought of three possibilities. First, perhaps people are trying to respect Western customs and formalities, using the 'Mr. and Mrs. Dowty.' However, this is a Western custom which we reject and which we've never used during our visit. In this respect we may be different from other Western couples who have visited China. But the problem has been more than form, more than the use of names. People have ignored me while warmly greeting Stu, pushed me out of conversations, cut me off when I try to ask questions, and dealt with us as if Stu were the only one who could speak for us and our activities in the United States."

"These kinds of things," Stu continued, "bring us to the second possible cause. It appears that the old custom, which is both Chinese and Western, of taking the man as the head or center of the family still survives among some people. They assumed I was the person to talk to and ignored Janet. This was true only for a small percentage of all the people we've met, but it was nevertheless true of enough to become a problem."

Janet added: "The third factor has to do with the way China International Travel Service is introducing us to the factories, communes, and other places we visit. What seems to have happened is that you've arranged visits on the basis of telling our hosts only about Stu and describing him only in terms of what he's been doing for the past two years, working in an automobile factory. So when we arrive at a place our hosts are expecting 'auto worker and wife.' This causes problems because, as you know, our backgrounds involve much more than that, and your introduction leaves me out of the picture as a person completely."

We suggested that for the rest of our visit they describe both of us to people at places we were to visit, giving something of both backgrounds. Also, we asked Zheng to continue, as he had been, using both our names in introductions. This would not, of course, solve the individual manifestations of male chauvinism we would encounter, but it would help structure situations to discourage it and allow Janet to participate equitably.

Liu, Zheng, and Jia all responded to our criticisms and suggestions. Liu said that he felt there were some cultural differences between the United States and China in how names were used and perhaps that had contributed to the problem. For the sake of example Liu pointed to Jia and said she would be insulted if he, or anyone else, referred to her by her husband's name or used the old terms "tai-tai" or "fu-ren." However, he said, they rarely met foreign couples who didn't follow the usual custom of "Mr. and Mrs." But, Liu concluded, this was no excuse for what had happened, and they would try to be better prepared and see that it didn't happen again.

Zheng said he should take a lot of the responsibility for the problems and agreed to use both our names in introductions and in arranging visits. He was overcritical of himself, for he had always used both names in direct introductions and had never ignored Janet or treated her as if she were Stu's appendage. Having spent the previous two weeks on the road with us, sharing all these experiences, Zheng had clearly been aware of the problem. He also was able to compare the different places we had visited and had a sense of the proportion of the problem in relation to the whole trip.

It was Jia, perhaps, who most quickly understood our perspective. She had previously accompanied groups of young Americans with similar attitudes, including both delegations of the Committee of Concerned Asian Scholars (CCAS). She recalled how the women on the first CCAS delegation had insisted that every individual's name be mentioned in public statements. Otherwise, they had explained to her, the delegation would be described in the Western press as visiting American scholars "and their wives."

It was a good discussion. We went on to evaluate other aspects of our trip, talking about some of the strong points of the visits and then mentioning some areas where we thought we had made mistakes. The evaluation brought us and our Chinese hosts closer together. Raising the criticisms this way strengthened our mutual friendship and understanding. Zheng and other China International Travel Service representatives did what they could to follow through on the discussion, and it helped tremendously. From then on places we visited expected "two American friends" instead of "Dowty and wife." Zheng took extra care, in personal introductions, to give a short account of both our backgrounds. Individual cases of chauvinism and male prejudice became much easier to handle now that the current flowed with us rather than against us. A good example came up during our visit to Peking University.

When we arrived a brief introduction was given by a silver-haired professor who as a young man had studied and taught at the college level in the United States. He spoke of the history of Peking University: how Mao had once worked there as a librarian's assistant, about the revolutionary activity of students in the May 4th Movement of 1919, and about their more recent struggles during the Cultural Revolution. The professor knew perfect English but spoke in Chinese (which was then translated into English), so everyone in the room could understand. Nearing the end of his talk, he indulged in some pleasantries and got a bit flowery; Chinese phrases of "warmly welcome," "great honor," and *"Dowty fu-fu"* (Mr. and Mrs. Dowty) cropped up. At the third reference to *"Dowty fu-fu"* one of the young workers in the group threw down his pen and interrupted: *"Bu shi fu-fu! Shi tong-zhi!"* ("It's not Mr. and Mrs! It's comrades!"), he exclaimed, adding something we could not catch with our smattering of Chinese, but which sounded quite ripe! The rest of the day we were called *"Dao-ti tong-zhi"* and *"Zha-*

ni-te tong-zhi," as we were at most other places we visited.

A final comment on these events: One reason we were so sensitive to manifestations of male prejudice was that in the United States they are usually indications of greater, much deeper types of discrimination. In the U.S. they are the tip of an immense iceberg; beneath lies an intact base of economic discrimination, sexual exploitation, and complex social stratification. In China, however, that iceberg had for the most part been shattered. But it was not completely destroyed. Several pieces still floated about, dangerous to all passers-by. It was some of these scattered pieces, flotsam of the past, which we scraped against. The experience confirmed two things in our minds: first, it had been absolutely necessary to shatter that economic and social base before progress could really be made, and second, even after the base had been shattered the remnants would not melt away by themselves. They were still dangerous and there was the possibility of several coming together again, forming a new hazard. Women and men needed to mount continuous and direct attacks against such holdovers.

Strengths and Weaknesses in One

Our visit to the Lo Kang People's Commune near Guangzhou provided a graphic example of the struggle against old ideas and how it continued, albeit unevenly.

The Lo Kang Commune concentrated on fruit production. At lunch we tasted fresh lichee for the first time, and must confess to stuffing ourselves with what has to be one of the extraordinary taste delights of the world. We then visited one of their food processing plants where olives were dried, sweetened with orange flavoring, and wrapped for shipment. Most were exported to South Asian countries. Outside, beneath South China's bright sun, a group of men dried olives in huge flat baskets. We noticed that only men did this job; no women were in sight. Then we went inside a workshop where the olives were wrapped. First one, two, then three olives were placed on a piece of colored cellophane, several quick twists, and they were tossed into a basket. Reach for three more. Tedious hand labor. And here only women worked. This was the only place on our whole trip where we saw such a clear-cut sexual division of labor. Old ideas about some things being "men's work" and others being "women's work" had been carried over into the new society.

At this same commune, however, we saw women directly challenging superstitions, taboos, and old ways of thinking. At the commune's water conservation project eight work teams had volunteered to dig a water tunnel through a small mountain. The tunnel was 670 meters long and would carry water from a nearby stream to the commune reservoir, providing irrigation for over twenty-six thousand mu of previously drought-stricken land. Two of the teams were women, whose average age was twenty-two. The work was extremely arduous: the women swung sledgehammers at foot-long steel chisels, chipping holes for dynamite in the solid rock wall. After the blasting they carried the rubble out of the tunnel piece by piece, using hand carts and shoulder poles and baskets. We recalled the old superstition, "If a woman comes by when a well is dug, it will never have water." This was more than hard work; the women were breaking old taboos.

Thus, on the same commune conditions representing the old and new existed side by side. It was like the whole country in microcosm: weaknesses and strengths intertwined. Both existed, and the Chinese themselves were the first to point that out. But they would also usually emphasize, as we would, too, that old ideas unsuitable to the new society were retreating as the whole country marched down the road to socialism.

Direction of Struggle

It's difficult to sum up succinctly something as complex as the role and position of women in China today. There was not complete equality. Women were not "100 percent liberated." But it was also clear that the road to equality was now open.

Chinese women did not see men, per se, as the enemy. They did not consider their struggle as one between the sexes. Their enemies were the feudal ways of thinking and acting, the capitalist and bourgeois ways of doing things. Their battle was part of the battle of the new (socialism) against the old (feudalism and capitalism).

Women in China had advanced an incredibly long distance along the road to equality in a very short time. Within one generation the most glaring aspects of inequality had been wiped out. Now women were freed from the confines of the home; women received pay directly for the work they did. Women had free choice in marriage; no longer were little girls forced through the agony of "lily feet." Prostitution, child-selling, and infanticide had been abolished. Women received education on a basis equal with men. Admittedly, problems of inequality remained and consciousness about these problems was uneven. But the whole social context favored and encouraged future battles to destroy the tag-ends.

When discussing their situation, Chinese women often quoted Chairman Mao, reminding us again and again of the statement: "When women all over the country rise up, that will be the day of victory for the Chinese Revolution."*

They were standing up. Not merely for themselves, but as part of the whole struggle to push their country, and the world, forward.

---

* Quoted in *Peking Review*, No. 11, 1968, p. 23.

5
Leadership: Cadres and Party

"Before the Cultural Revolution no workers took part in administration; now there are workers in the leading bodies."

The man speaking was Zui Jian-guo, Vice-Chairman of the Revolutionary Committee at Foreign Languages Printing House in Peking. We learned that he had been Vice-Director of that printing plant prior to the Cultural Revolution.

"Before, our administrative offices were very big and swollen," he went on. "There were too many office workers who did not directly take part in production. I myself was divorced from workers and labor; other cadres were also divorced from practice. Formerly we had a Party Secretary here who followed the Liu Shao-chi line. He pushed the 'one-leader system' and said, 'Don't rely on the masses.' During the Cultural Revolution the workers rebelled against his revisionist system."

Zui concluded: "The principle of leadership in our Party is collective leadership. The 'one-leader system' violated this principle and divorced leaders from the masses."

Leadership in China, we found, was a complex and dynamic political process. Among Westerners it has been one of the least understood aspects of socialist China, perhaps because tucked beneath its wings are several unfamiliar concepts. For example, take the concept of "the mass line," an approach to leadership tidily expressed in the Chinese slogan, "From the masses, to the masses." Many Westerners have

Leadership: Cadres and Party 191

trouble understanding this because to us the term "masses" has negative connotations.

Masses? We tend to think of unruly mobs, ignorant peasants, gullible and malleable workers, mindless slobs all.

What about the term "political line"? We generally think of subterfuge, a concocted camouflage, opportunistically designed to win support regardless of conviction or principle. To "run a line" means, in our colloquial talk, to jive, to con, to deceive.

In China these terms were different both in language and import. "Masses" (*qun-zhong*) was used as we use "rank and file" or "general public." It was a positive term. The masses were important, respected.

"The masses are the real heroes."

"The masses have boundless creative power."

"We should go to the masses and learn from them."*

The Chinese "line" was what we would call a "principle" or a "policy," but without the cynicism toward political rhetoric we accept as customary. For Chinese leaders the "mass line" meant:

> All correct leadership is necessarily 'from the masses to the masses.' This means: take the ideas of the masses (scattered and unsystematic ideas) and concentrate them (through study turn them into concentrated and systematic ideas), then go to the masses and propagate and explain these ideas until the masses embrace them as their own, hold fast to them and translate them into action and test the correctness of these ideas in such action.... And so on, over and over again in an endless spiral, with the ideas becoming more correct, more vital and richer each time.**

In the West we have come to think of leadership in other ways. Public office "Western style" often means power over others at their expense, and leaders are normally expected to acquire fame, fortune, and other material rewards. Becoming

* Mao Tse-tung, *Quotations*, pp. 118 and 129.

** Mao Tse-tung, "Some Questions Concerning Methods of Leadership," in *Selected Works*, Vol. III, p. 119.

a leader is a highly individualized process where ambition and personal empire-building are openly accepted motivations for "public service." "Back scratching," "log rolling," "horse trading," "machines," and "bosses" are all terms we associate with the political process in our society.

To be sure, none of us idealize these things. Rather, we tend to shrug our shoulders with fatalistic pragmatism. "Power corrupts," we philosophize, and heave more sighs of resignation than cries of indignation.

The Chinese attitude toward leadership was fundamentally different. They were not cynical about their system; they fully expected it to work, to live up to its principles. They fought to change things when it didn't, as the Cultural Revolution demonstrated.

They believed leadership should not involve personal gain, fame, or material reward. They expected leadership to be a collective, not an individual, process. They believed leadership rested on the "mass line," the collective summing up of the desires and needs of laboring people. They expected leaders to follow and integrate themselves with the masses. The worst thing that could happen to a leader was to become divorced from the masses. And, in principle, they believed power came directly from the masses: "Who is it that gives us [the Communist Party] our power? It is the working class, the poor and lower-middle peasants, the laboring masses comprising over 90 percent of the population."*

The crucial question, of course, was how close reality came to these principles and expectations. Was the "mass line" really implemented? Or was it simply a shroud covering up a bureaucratic elite? Did power really come from the support of the people? Or did leaders manipulate and intimidate the "masses"?

We sought answers to these questions, and immediately found ourselves probing two institutional features of Chinese leadership which culturally and politically are unfamiliar to

---

* Mao Tse-tung, quoted in "Absorb Fresh Blood from the Proletariat," *Peking Review*, October 1968.

most Westerners. First were the "cadres" (*ganbu*), and second was the Chinese Communist Party itself.

What Is a Cadre?

Cadre: Neither the term nor the role is common in the United States. Perhaps the easiest way to describe Chinese cadres is to call them "administrators," but that's just part of what they do. Foreign observers have sometimes called them "managers," but that connotes a superior-subordinate, boss-worker type of relationship which just doesn't accurately portray reality, particularly since the Cultural Revolution. You could call cadres "civil servants," since most are directly paid by the government and assigned to jobs by government agencies, but that's rather misleading too. Cadres aren't simply bureaucrats who make sure the trains run on time. They are also political leaders and their administrative and political tasks are closely integrated. Cadres are sometimes called "officials," but that tends to obscure the fact that most cadres are workers and peasants, often serving in factories and communes where they have worked for a long time. Finally, cadres have sometimes been labelled "party functionaries," but that implies all cadres are members of the Chinese Communist Party, and not all are. Besides, "functionary" sounds very stuffy, and the cadres we met seldom fit such an image.

To add to the confusion, the Chinese themselves tended to use the term loosely, or so it seemed to us. We seized the opportunity to clarify the elusive concept during our visit to a May 7th Cadre School,* and fired off a series of questions:

"How do you tell who is a cadre, and who isn't? Can you define 'cadre' exactly? And who becomes a cadre?"

Two leading members of the Cadre School, together with Zheng and Xi, a China International Travel Service cadre from Xian, responded. They were sympathetic and a bit

---

* See pp. 203-211 below.

amused, the latter because their own comments didn't jibe with each other. It was Xi who finally admitted what we suspected: "There really are two meanings of the term. First, it's used informally to refer to someone in charge of special work, to those who are leaders, including people who stay at normal production jobs. For example, yesterday we met the Party Secretary of a production team on the Ma Qi Zhai Commune. He works in the fields regularly, like other members of his team, but he's also a leader and has some political duties. Therefore, we called him a cadre.

"But there's also a more formal definition of the term. Cadres are people in responsible positions doing special work for the government. Their wages are paid by the government and they have been assigned to their jobs by the government. Cadres on the three-in-one Revolutionary Committees and the Party Committees are all cadres in this formal sense."

Cadres were people who, in Xi's words, had "some special skill" to carry out administrative and political tasks. In years past, cadres from intellectual and managerial backgrounds were often predominant. The Cultural Revolution, however, accelerated the rate of cadre recruitment from worker and peasant backgrounds. Public reports in early 1973 for Peking, Shanghai, and Wuhan indicated that more than 64,000 workers in those cities had been promoted to cadre positions during the previous few years. The new cadres were described as "veteran workers with many years of experience, as well as young workers who have distinguished themselves in revolution and production." One Peking construction company was cited as now having 59.2 percent of its cadres of worker origin, as compared to 31.6 percent before the Cultural Revolution.*

There was no one "type" of cadre. They were as heterogeneous as any other large group of people. Young, old, women, men, outgoing, reserved; arrogant, modest, efficient, inept. We met all kinds of cadres.

---

* *Ta Kung Pao*, English edition, No. 363, May 3, 1973. The Chinese use the word "company" for publicly owned enterprises.

Cadres: Young and Old

Let us tell you about some of the cadres we met.

One cadre we got to know very well was Liu Yu-kun who worked for China International Travel Service's head office in Peking. We called him "Lao" Liu affectionately, borrowing a Chinese custom of using Lao (old) as a nickname for friends older than oneself.

Lao Liu was a resilient, friendly man, middle-aged and beginning to show a little gray in his tousled hair. He accompanied us on most of our travels around Peking; part of his job had been to contact factories, schools, etc., to arrange our visits. Like us, Lao Liu was always full of questions. We had many long discussions with him about China, the United States, the history of revolutionary movements, and Marxist-Leninist theory.

We passed through the Peking railway station several times, and it was Lao Liu who came to greet us and see us off. He always joined in the press of people scrambling to help us with our luggage, and Stu's knapsack became his favorite. Once, after he had shouldered the pack like an old veteran, we asked if he had been in the army. "Yes," he answered quietly, "I joined up in the late 1930s and served through the 1940s." He didn't elaborate. He probably could have given many first-hand accounts of the resistance to Japan and then of the Civil War. But he characteristically turned the conversation away from himself to broader political topics.

Lao Liu had a great sense of humor, which we enjoyed immensely. He also did his job well. He was no stuffy bureaucrat by any stretch of the imagination. A veteran army man, now an urban cadre, Lao Liu continued to serve the revolution wherever he was needed.

We met two cadres in Zhengzhou, in central China, who were quite different from Lao Liu in both style and personality. They came closer to the stereotype of functionaries or bureaucrats than any other cadres we met. Both were middle-aged and worked for China International Travel Service in Zhengzhou. Snappily dressed in well-pressed wool suits, they roared about town in a huge black Russian limousine with drawn curtains. The auto, the size of a small tank, had built-in fold-down seats, making it three-deep riding. With them we plowed through city streets in the curtained car, zooming from hotel to restaurant, from factory to school, from museum to theater. They treated us to a lavish lunch in the private room of a local restaurant. At other such gatherings during our journey, people were usually hopping up and down, serving food, clearing the table, giving the waiters and waitresses a hand. Here our hosts sat back and waved their cigarettes in the air, expecting a waiter to run over with a light.

They also took us to a performance of local opera. Again we roared right up to the door in our black bomb, and much to our surprise we marched in an entrance at the *front* of the auditorium. The place was packed with hundreds of local opera lovers, who greeted us with a loud round of applause, and as soon as we had taken our seats the lights went out and the show began. At intermission we were ushered to a private room at the rear and served tea; again the curtain waited until we returned to our seats. Previously arranged? Of course. But even though curtain time was tied to our movements, and the crowd undoubtedly had been told that "American friends" were attending the performance, the friendship expressed was clearly genuine, not contrived. The special treatment was an honest attempt to be polite, to show friendship, not to put on any sort of false front. But whatever their intentions, the style of work these two cadres dished up was certainly flavored with bureaucratic spices.

Lest we be too harsh on our Zhengzhou hosts, however, we should add that they had fairly successfully "put politics in command" in arranging our visits. We asked to see factories, talk to workers, and visit with workers in their homes. All these things they arranged.

We labeled the China International Travel Service cadres who hosted and arranged our visits in Shenyang the *gan-bei* crowd. *Gan-bei* is the Chinese term for "bottoms-up," and of all cadres we met our young hosts in Shenyang earned the title. We fondly remember them for the "informal" dinner they threw for us, and the many excuses they found, all in good spirit and enthusiasm, to *gan-bei* glass after glass of *mao-tai*. *Mao-tai*, being over 120 proof, is something you don't fool around with. Its high proof is perhaps one reason why it tastes like aviation fuel, and if you aren't careful it's likely to get you off the ground before you know it. The evening soon glowed as our hosts urged us to finish glasses "to the end" with toast after toast and then a little more "because it's good for your colds." We were, it was true, getting over head colds at the time, but the *mao-tai* probably did little more than help us forget our ailments for the evening. It was all very pleasant, and the warmth and depth of friendship exchanged was moving, but we were glad that nothing else was scheduled following the meal, particularly when we wobbled back to our room!

The next day it was one of the *gan-bei* crowd who noticed Janet's love for flowers. While walking through the grounds of a sanitorium Janet had half-consciously picked up a small sprig of lilac from the ground. She carried it around for a bit, leaving it outside a building when we entered and picking it up again when we came out. As we got ready to leave the sanitorium one of the *gan-bei* cadres cut a large bunch of lilac branches, rooted around in the trunk of the car and found something akin to a red ribbon, and tied a red bow around them. Then, giggling and grinning, he presented the impromptu bouquet to Janet with exaggerated ceremony. The gesture was both humorous and beautiful; unfortunately the lilacs didn't survive the heat of our two-and-one-half hour drive back to the hotel.

We met scores of local cadres during our visit. Many, like the leading cadres at the Wuhan Sewing Machine Factory and the Tianjin No. 1 Machinery Factory, literally grabbed us by the arms and eagerly guided us through their plants, continually talking, pointing out new aspects of production, introducing us to workers. They were obviously excited about building a new socialist society. A few, like the leading cadre at the Dong Feng Watch Factory, breezed through workshops in a perfunctory manner, monopolized the conversation, and avoided political discussion. But the overwhelming majority were highly motivated, capable, dedicated to their tasks and, it seemed, well-respected by the people they worked with.

Perquisites of Power?

We saw few institutionalized privileges for cadres. There were no stores with better, cheaper, and a wider variety of goods reserved for cadres, as we understand exist for leaders in the Soviet Union. We did not see or hear of special housing, resorts, mountain villas, or similar pleasures established for their benefit. Theaters and stadiums had no obvious sections with better seats reserved for them.

We ate in a couple of very old and quite posh restaurants: one of the famous Peking Duck restaurants (in Peking, of course), and the North Garden Restaurant in Guangzhou. They were open to all and obviously popular. We asked about prices at the Peking Duck Restaurant. Jia Ai-mei, one of our translators, mentioned that her family had recently celebrated a special event over a meal of Peking Duck there. The meal cost about 2 or 3 yuan per person, well within the range of the average Chinese working family. The North Garden Restaurant in Guangzhou was crowded when we were there, and judging from comments that was normal. It was a very large restaurant, serving the best of luxurious Cantonese cuisine to thousands daily. Its many rooms were packed with families. People wore everyday work clothes and several men relaxed in undershirts in the warm evening air.

We did notice that cadres were generally more snappily dressed than most workers and peasants, and we sometimes wondered if they had spruced up a bit to meet us. While the Chinese were far from fashion conscious, there were distinguishable styles of dress. We learned the general differences between peasant garb, factory clothing, and a cadre style. But pressed pants and sturdy wool suits, the mark of many cadres, were still simple, practical, and priced within the range of all. Differences were more a matter of choice and practicality than of privilege.

Wage scales for factory cadres were sometimes higher than production workers, but it was the older, veteran cadres who generally received the higher wages. Some comparison of workers' and cadres' wages we found were as follows (in yuan per month):

Factory	Workers Low	Workers High	Cadres Low	Cadres High
Zhengzhou No. 3 Textile Mill	33	92	?	145
Zhengzhou Textile Machinery Manufacturing Factory	33	108	33	167
Luoyang Heavy Equipment Factory	32½	105	?	170
Luoyang Tractor Works	32½	102	36	259
East Is Red Auto Factory	34	108	35	170
Shenyang No. 1 Machinery Manufacturing Factory	33	104	32	120
Foreign Languages Printing House	40	100	40	100*
Shenyang Transformer Factory	33	104		**

We asked our hosts at the Luoyang Tractor Works why some cadres received higher wages, and were told: "Cadres' wages are higher because of their long history of service to the revolution. Some date back to the Japanese war, and have made more contributions to the revolution. Thus they deserve something more. Young cadres will not get the high wages."

Workers and cadres both recognized that administrative work by its nature often led to separation from the day-to-day world of labor and production. In order to carry out their responsibilities cadres had to develop special knowledge,

* We were told cadres received the "same as workers."
** We were told cadres received "a little less than average," but here they also had two old intellectual cadres who still received over 200 yuan per month, something they wished to change. Average workers' wages were about 60 yuan a month; cadres averaged a little less.

expertise, and skill of coordination in order to run large enterprises successfully. Thus differences between cadres and rank and file tended to develop, and in China's socialist society these differences were of particular concern. Unlike capitalist societies, where status differences and privileges are considered normal or even necessary, China's socialist ethic called for closing the gap between leaders and rank and file. We learned that several steps had been taken in China to combat privilege and bureaucratic tendencies and to insure that cadres did not become "divorced from the masses."

The "Two Joins"

"The administrative work in our factory is large," commented Ou Hui-tan, a cadre at the 67,000-worker Wuhan Iron and Steel Works. "Thus we try to do three things. First, we have Party leadership. Second we 'put politics in command.' And third, we have the 'Two Joins.' The 'Two Joins' means that workers join in leadership and cadres join in labor."

China's system of cadre participation in productive labor has been around for quite a while. Its roots lie in the Communist Party's several decades of revolutionary struggle. Since Liberation, and particularly since 1958, cadres have often gone to the countryside or factories to do labor, but it was not until the Cultural Revolution that cadre participation in labor really blossomed forth.

The cadres we met were enthusiastic about joining in productive labor and felt it helped them to do their jobs better. They were not embarrassed or ashamed at getting their hands dirty; manual labor was not considered degrading. On the contrary, they had a feeling of pride, a sense of purpose in their work. Cadres told us that capitalist relations, owner vs. employee, automatically divided workers from management. In a socialist system, they argued, those structural barriers had been torn down. But, they said, there was still a constant struggle to close the gap between leaders and workers, a struggle to do away with old ideas, old concepts of status and self-importance. Participation in production was one part of this struggle. They felt it did little good in a socialist society to train administrators and technicians who did not share the needs, attitudes, and interests of working people. Those with special skills should not harbor attitudes of superiority over others. Many referred us to a widely circulated comment by Mao Tse-tung:

> It is necessary to maintain the system of cadre participation in collective productive labour. The cadres of our Party and state are ordinary workers and not overlords sitting on the backs of the people. By taking part in collective productive labour, the cadres maintain extensive, constant and close ties with the working people. This is a major measure of fundamental importance for a socialist system; it helps to overcome bureaucracy and to prevent revisionism and dogmatism.*

There were many different ways *lao dong* ("labor") was scheduled. For example, workers at the Foreign Languages Printing House had adopted a rule that cadres must spend at least one day a week in the workshops. During the Cultural Revolution they also required cadres who had never before participated in labor to spend one year working full time in the shops.

One day of manual work a week was typical for factory cadres. In some places cadres did a full week each month, as their schedules permitted.

Commune cadres told us they were required to spend at least sixty work-days a year in the fields, and that they spent most of the busy season in manual labor. Cadres at brigade and team levels within communes sometimes split their time, half and half, between administration and production.

Day-to-day contact in the fields and workshops greatly facilitated evaluation and criticism of cadres by workers and peasants. Our hosts at Foreign Languages Printing House ex-

---

* Quoted in "On Khrushchev's Phoney Communism and Its Historical Lessons for the World," in *Quotations from Chairman Mao Tse-tung*, pp. 282-283.

plained: "Every six months we sum up our cadres' work. We mobilize the masses to criticize our cadres. Since we began this practice, the relationship between cadres and workers has changed greatly."

We caught, perhaps, a small glimpse of such changes. During lunch Zhan Miao-yu, a cadre and Chairman of the printing house's Revolutionary Committee, pointed his chopsticks at a woman worker who was talking to Janet. He chuckled, telling us she was the factory "watchdog," always bringing up criticisms. It was a friendly comment and actually an indirect compliment. Zhan made it clear he had been the target of some of her criticisms, and we wouldn't be surprised if a fair amount of struggle had been involved. But the experience appeared to have brought them together in a healthy way.

We met Gao Bai-zhen in Tangshan. Gao was a cadre with a personal account of how rank-and-file criticisms had affected him and helped him maintain touch with shop work. Gao was Vice-Chairman of the Revolutionary Committee at the Tangshan Pottery Research Institute. A tall, middle-aged man with a thin face, he had worked there for many years as an artist, creating and testing new designs for pottery. During the Cultural Revolution he was chosen by other workers to be a leader on their new Revolutionary Committee.

"But I had a contradiction between the need to do a lot of administrative work," Gao remarked, "and the need to do productive labor. I only did work in the office and I never went into the workshop. The workers came and told me: 'You were a worker, but now you're a bureaucrat!' I learned from them, and now I spend two days a week in the workshop, four days in administrative work." He added, "We say that a person can change his position, but he shouldn't change his color!"

Cadres generally did their labor at regular production jobs within their own factories. Some factories employed a system of quarterly rotations for cadre work sites so that cadres became well acquainted with specific conditions in many parts of their factories. A few plants we visited—the Foreign Languages Printing House in Peking and the Wuhan Iron and

Steel Works—operated farms in the nearby countryside where cadres did agricultural work. We occasionally saw small lots around and between factory buildings planted with vegetables, while workshops were sometimes lined with fruit trees and walls or gateways covered with grape vines. Such arrangements had dual benefits: factory cadres gained the experience of farm work, politically desirable in a nation with over 70 percent of its people in the countryside, and the harvests supplemented local food supplies.

Not all cadres, however, could do productive work within their own factories or communes. Many worked in state and governmental agencies which had no directly related workshops or farms. To meet these and other political needs a new institution was born in China during the Cultural Revolution, the May 7th Cadre Schools. The May 7th Cadre Schools were possibly one of the most important and innovative creations of the whole Chinese Revolution.

Plain Living and Hard Struggle

We visited a May 7th Cadre School during our stay in Yenan in the historic Northwest. It was a bright, crisp April morning when we climbed into one of the practical Shanghai sedans, accompanied by An Wei, a guide and interpreter from Yenan, and headed for Nanniwan, about twenty-five miles to the southeast. It took over two hours, for we soon turned off the paved valley highway onto a steep and winding gravel road which cut through the mountains. Spring had not yet arrived with determination in this rugged country and the sharp, jagged slopes looked barren and brown; here and there splotches of evergreens lent a bit of color. Production teams were busy plowing and planting, often working terraces built during winter months. Children ran out from their cave-homes, a traditional and practical style of housing in the region because of the loess clay-type soil, and waved friendly greetings as our car labored past.

The Nanniwan May 7th Cadre School was located in an

area with strong revolutionary traditions. In the early 1940s the Nanniwan valley had been transformed from a remote and unpopulated area into fertile, productive fields with accompanying handicrafts and small industries. The army unit responsible for this change, the 359 Brigade of the Eighth Route Army, has won a place in modern Chinese history for their exemplary combination of productive, military, and political tasks. Today the Nanniwan May 7th Cadre School occupied the site of a former artillery school, while a state farm prospered nearby.

We turned off the gravel road and navigated a bumpy and narrow lane leading to the school's headquarters, a group of buildings nestled against the side of some low hills. Many were in the Yenan cave-dwelling style, and several were still in the process of construction. Even the free-standing structures, built away from the hills, followed the style of caves, with high arched roofs and lattice-work over the fronts. They were easy to heat in winter, pleasantly cool in summer, but a bit too chilly for our comfort in April. A welcoming committee of a half dozen or so greeted us with loud and enthusiastic *huan-ying*s and led us to a small meeting room in one of the cave-style houses. There some of the cadres from the school outlined the history and purpose of their unique institution.

"Our school was established in October 1968," a leading cadre began, "following Chairman Mao's directive for cadres to do manual labor.* In three years we have trained 1,700 students at this school.** The school has had two stages of development. The initial group of 476 students were cadres from several bureaus and departments of the Xian municipal

---

* During the Cultural Revolution, Mao Tse-tung issued the following call in October 1968: "Going down to do manual labour gives vast numbers of cadres an excellent opportunity to study once again; this should be done by all cadres except those who are old, weak, ill or disabled. Cadres at their posts should also go down in turn to do manual labour." Quoted in *Peking Review*, May 12, 1972, p. 7.

** All cadres at May 7th Cadre Schools were referred to as students, regardless of age, experience, or how high a post they held.

government.* In February 1970 we started to train cadres. Our students come from municipal, district, and commune levels. Many are leaders of Revolutionary Committees and other leadership bodies. They are cadres from many fronts: communication, agriculture, industry, commerce, political work, law, and culture.

"Our school is now in its fourth term and has 680 students. This term we began a new short term of six months. Formerly it was a year, but we have shortened it so we can train cadres more quickly. After the term most go back to their original jobs."

The Nanniwan school was one of two operated by the Xian municipal government. Our hosts estimated that it would take about five years for all ten thousand cadres in Xian to spend a term at one of the schools. Then they planned to have people come for a second time, and perhaps more.

They talked about the school's purpose and program:

"Chairman Mao issued a directive on May 7, 1966, which pointed out that cadres and staff should engage in agricultural work and industrial production, and also in mass work and criticism. Our school is run according to the May 7th directive. While students are engaged in study they also take part in physical work. While making criticism of the bourgeoisie, they engage in mass work.**

"We are a new type of school, different from the old Party schools. This school is run in light of the three great strug-

---

* Xian, the largest city in the area, was about 200 miles southwest of Yenan and had a population of between 1 and 2 million.

** The May 7, 1966, directive urged those working in Party and government organizations to "learn other things" while engaging mainly in their own work. The "other things" to be learned included "industrial production, agricultural production and military affairs . . . also [to] criticize and repudiate the bourgeoisie." (*Peking Review*, May 12, 1972, p. 7) Thus, the May 7th Cadre Schools took their name from this general political directive. They were first established, however, only after the more specific October 1968 call from Mao to "go down in turn to do manual labour."

gles: the class struggle, the struggle for production, and the struggle for scientific experiment. Practical activities raise the political consciousness of the students and their consciousness of the struggle between the two lines."

The Nanniwan school took advantage of their special historic location, as the cadres pointed out: "We follow the Yenan spirit of self-reliance and hard struggle. Once enrolled the students visit revolutionary sites here. They talk to veterans of the border region struggle.* We also organize hikes to Yenan to visit the exhibits and museums there. It's 80 kilometers over some very rugged mountains. These trips provide valuable lessons to the students. Some are themselves veteran cadres of the old period and can be reminded of past struggle. New cadres can be profoundly educated by the experience of these visits. They come to understand that victory was not easy. They understand the importance of maintaining Red political power, and of making good use of it.

"Manual labor is an important aspect of educating the students. All students are the same in school, regardless of their length of service or where they have served. Each person must take on a concrete job, such as pig raising, machine repairing, carpentry, grain raising, brick-making, and so forth. This strengthens their feeling for laboring people; it helps them push aside the airs of a bureaucrat. It strengthens their class stand. By taking part in manual labor they also try to follow Chairman Mao's teaching: 'Provide our food and clothing by our own labor.'

"We want to develop a new kind of cadre who can 'go down and up,' who is both official and common person, who can do both mental and manual labor. Our school is a fundamental measure to prevent the country from going revisionist, from 'changing its color.'

"We have also produced some wealth for the state. In three years we have delivered 430,000 catties of grain and 310,000 catties of vegetables. We have built a grain processing mill, a

---

* The area, with Yenan as the capital, was known as the Shanxi-Jiangsu-Ningxia Border Region during the late 1930s.

brick-making factory, an animal breeding station [pigs], and a farm tool repair station. We also make lime. We've renovated about seventy-eight cave dwellings and are building several new buildings and caves.

"Another method of learning is to receive education from poor and lower-middle peasants. We use two methods. Small detachments of students go to the countryside to live and work with peasants for periods of time. We also invite peasants to come to the school and tell of their bitter past. Veterans tell of the sufferings of the old society and compare it with the new. Also, some peasants are invited as teachers. They help in sheep herding, brick-making, and farm tool repair. When problems of production in agriculture arise, we turn to the peasants for help and they give us guidance."

They ended their introduction with typical modesty:

"In the past three years some work has been done, but we have some shortcomings. Our grain output is high, but we are still not self-sufficient. We are far behind Tachai and other communes in capital construction and water conservation.* Also not enough work has been done on the school living quarters.

"But come, you must have a chance to see things for yourselves."

First we visited their grain processing mill. Simple but mechanized, it ground millet, maize, and rice. One of the students, busy loading hoppers with unground kernels of corn and then sacking the rather crudely ground grain, was a veteran woman cadre, over fifty years old. She had fought in guerrilla struggles during the border region period. Normally, she said with a smile, her job was as a cadre in communications work in Xian.

Men in the carpentry workshop were using an electric table saw to make shelves. Others were turning out forms for poured concrete, used in building. We found out that none of them had had any carpentry skills before coming to the

---

* Capital construction in rural areas usually meant such large projects as terracing, irrigation, etc.

school. Their brick-making factory was actually an outdoor workshop with a roof and no walls. It literally hummed with activity; production, they told us, was two thousand bricks an hour. The high clay content of the loess soil of the region was natural brick-making material. After shaping and cutting, the wet bricks were stacked to dry for a week and then fired for several days in one of three huge kilns.

Next to the brick factory was another outdoor work area, a yard for masonry. Squatting on their haunches, several men carefully and skillfully chipped away at large stones with hand chisels. Under their patient attention the shapeless stones were almost miraculously transformed into solid square building blocks. That particular job, our cadre hosts told us, demanded years of experience and skill, so most of the people doing it were local peasants. Some students labored in the yard carrying stones to and fro, and a mechanical winch pulling heavy loads up the hillside was operated by a middle-aged woman who normally was an actress and a cadre in cultural and theatrical work.

The school pigsty was under the charge of an accountant from Xian. Far from being ashamed or embarrassed by his job, he was actually quite proud and eager to show us what was being done to improve pork production. He was experimenting with special fodder made from ground chaff mixed with yeast and fermented for a few days. They were also cross-breeding the rather runty local breed of pigs with some larger, sturdy-looking Danish porkers. We'd guess that when he returns to his regular city job and sits down to a meal of sweet-and-sour pork or pork-filled dumplings, he'll have a real understanding of the work involved in making such food available.

The school medical clinic was staffed by people who were regularly doctors and nurses. Their services were not limited to students but were available to local residents. The school sent medical teams out into the countryside on a regular basis.

Shortly before lunch we stuck our heads into the kitchen

of the school's dining hall. Here a team of student cooks was busy chopping and trimming vegetables, pounding and rolling out dough for dumplings and steamed bread. A stocky middle-aged man wielding an enormous cleaver transformed a head of cabbage into bite-sized shreds in seconds. He told us he was normally a cadre in a foodstuffs factory. "But none of us were ever cooks before we came here," he warned us with a chuckle. "After lunch you'll have to give us criticisms so we can improve." "During the first week or so of the term," another new cook chimed in, "we got a lot of complaints from the students. They were right. We really weren't very good. We've learned a lot, but we still have a lot of room for improvement."

If our lunch was any indication, they'd learned their new skills well. Over a table laden with specialties, most notably a platter of humble white potatoes dressed in a delightful sweet sauce, we pressed our hosts with questions: "What are most students like? How old are they, and do they get to see their families? Are most of them members of the Communist Party?"

Several people responded. Of the 680 students, 80 percent were Party members. Some were over fifty, a few below thirty, and the average age was about thirty-nine. There were twenty-seven women in the group.* All students continued to receive their regular pay during their term at the school. Students could visit their families if they wished, and families could also spend their holidays at the school.

"How is study organized?" we asked.

They replied that the schedule for a week was five work days and one day of study, which included a good deal of self-study as well as group discussions. Local residents who worked at the school had their own study groups. The free day, they added, was usually spent in personal pursuits, like

* This was a low percentage of women compared to published reports about other May 7th Cadre Schools. Edgar Snow happened to visit this same school a year before we were there, and he reported the class at that time was 25 percent women. See *The Long Revolution*, p. 121.

doing laundry and recreation, but students also often used some of this time for study.

"What do you study?"

Students mostly read the classics of Marxism-Leninism and Chairman Mao's writings. The *Communist Manifesto* and Marx's *The Civil War in France* were mentioned specifically.*

"Who runs the school, how is it administered?" we continued.

They answered that it was run by the Xian municipality, under its Revolutionary Committee. There were thirty permanent staff cadres at the school and from this a school Revolutionary Committee provided day-to-day leadership. Groups dealing with political direction, production, and administrative tasks functioned under the Revolutionary Committee.

After lunch we were treated to a performance by the school cultural group. We saw the actress who had been running the winch, now singing bold and brilliant arias from Peking operas. One of the cooks we had joked with earlier smiled at us from a women's quartet which sang popular folk songs. The performance was enlivened by a hundred or more local peasants who had come to enjoy the music, by songs from a group of visiting overseas Chinese (from Japan), and, last but not least, by our own contribution of "Union Maid," sung by Janet with Stu stumbling along on the chorus.

May 7th Cadre Schools have received some attention in the Western press, but most often as places of punishment, as farms where errant cadres and intellectuals are forced to do demeaning, degrading work. This was not the case; the

---

* An article about May 7th Cadre Schools in *Peking Review* (May 12, 1972) sheds some additional light on the orientation of study at these institutions. Noting that students take part in "criticizing the bourgeoisie" (a term used during our visit also), the article states that criticism is made of "the theory of the dying out of class struggle, the bourgeois theory of human nature, the theory of productive forces, idealist apriorism, the theory that doing manual labour is a punishment and the theory of going to school in order to get an official post."

schools were not set up to punish aberrant intellectuals. True, some cadres were removed from positions during the Cultural Revolution due to their bureaucratic and elitist practices, and many were sent to May 7th Cadre Schools. But the purpose was not to exact penance; the hope was that such cadres would develop better attitudes toward work, workers, and peasants.

Moreover, all cadres, not just those who had made bureaucratic mistakes, were expected to do labor. The May 7th Cadre Schools were thus a type of preventative medicine to ward off the ailments of bureaucracy and elitism.

The Core of Leadership

> *If there is to be revolution, there must be a revolutionary Party. The Chinese Communist Party is the core of leadership of the whole Chinese people.*
>
> —Mao Tse-tung

There was a second piece in the composite picture of leadership in China: the Chinese Communist Party. Most members of the Chinese Communist Party were not cadres; they were ordinary workers and peasants, and the Party was the basic institution they used to run their society. It was the thread tying it together and providing basic political leadership. Founded in 1921, the Communist Party mobilized and organized peasants, workers, and Chinese patriots of all classes during the decades of revolutionary struggle. It was, indeed, the "core of leadership." The Party itself has frankly declared:

> State organs, the People's Liberation Army and the militia, labour unions, poor and lower-middle peasant associations, women's federations, the Communist Youth League, the Red Guards, the Little Red Guards and other revolutionary mass organizations must all accept the centralized leadership of the Party.*

---

* The Constitution of the Communist Party of China, adopted by the Tenth National Congress of the Communist Party of China, August

The Party's power and leading position was fundamental to the new society. It cannot be separated from China's transformation. If credit is due for advances made, that credit is due the Communist Party. If criticism is due for failures, that too is the Party's responsibility.

These frank assertions raise many questions: Are all other organizations merely sham? Are government organizations only bureaucratic structures, simply used by the Party? What about the Revolutionary Committees in provincial and city governments, communes, and factories? What about "workers' control"?

We tried to get at some of these questions by finding out who was in the Communist Party. What types of people joined and how did they become members? We also tried to get a sense of how the Party functioned in relation to the larger society, how it put the "mass line" into practice. We weren't able to come home with answers to everything, but we did talk to many rank-and-file Party members, ordinary workers and peasants, and we did return with a human content for that abstraction, "the Party."

Like Seeds and Soil

> We Communists are like seeds and the people are like the soil. Wherever we go, we must unite with the people, take root and blossom among them.
>
> —Mao Tse-tung, 1945

Like the seed, the Chinese Communist Party owes its origin to the soil, the people. Chinese Communists were not some foreign force burrowing into their society. They were a local product, growing from the local population and nurtured by them. Chinese Communists were workers, peasants, cadres, intellectuals, and soldiers. They banded together, determined to transform not just the face, but the very structure of their society.

28, 1973 (*Peking Review*, September 7, 1973). The Constitution adopted at the Ninth Party Congress in 1969 had a similar clause.

The Western mass media often pictures Communist parties as insidious, impersonal, and unprincipled bureaucracies, ruled from the top by a handful of men intent on world domination. Such a picture hardly corresponds to the reality we saw. The Communists we met in China were warm, live people; they were the most active, the most responsible, and the most respected members of their communities. Neighbors, fellow workers, peasants, local cadres; the Party had millions of members.

In 1973 Party membership was announced as being 28 million. This represented a steady growth: in 1966 membership was estimated at about 20 million, while official 1956 figures reported 17 or 18 million.* Information on the Central Committee of the Chinese Communist Party also shows a steady growth. The Eighth Party Congress (1956) elected a Central Committee of 96 full members and 94 alternates, a total of 190. The Ninth Party Congress (1969) elected a Central Committee of 170 full members and 109 alternates, a total of 279 and an increase of almost 47 percent. In 1973 the Tenth National Party Congress elected a Central Committee of 195 members and 124 alternates, a total of 319 and a 14 percent increase over 1969.

During the Cultural Revolution a widely circulated quote from Chairman Mao emphasized the need for the Party to absorb "fresh blood." This had been done in many places. Workers at the Foreign Languages Printing House, a factory of 1,600, told us they had added more than fifty new Party members in the six years since the start of the Cultural Revolution. We met young workers in several factories who had joined the Party during the past year or two. In 1969 the Peking Woolen Mill reported that they brought sixty-four new workers into the Party from their workforce of 2,000.**

Usually one of every six or seven workers was a Party member so that Party membership constituted about 15 percent of a factory's total workforce. The Shenyang No. 1 Ma-

---

* Snow, *The Long Revolution*, p. 13.
** See *China Reconstructs*, August 1969, pp. 20-25.

chinery Factory, for example, had 1,100 Party members among 6,860 workers, or about 16 percent. The Kairan Coal Mine in Tangshan reported 900 Party members out of a total of 5,900 miners, about 15 percent. The Tangshan Rolling Stock Plant had 7,000 workers and 1,600 Party members, or about 23 percent. Workers at the East Is Red Auto Factory in Peking put their figure at 13 percent, and those at the Foreign Languages Printing House said they had about 15 percent Party membership, and that this was average.

We have no information on the percentage of Party membership on communes, but it was probably lower than 15 percent. A higher Party concentration in factories was hardly surprising politically. The Chinese Communist Party has always described itself as "the political party of the proletariat," following the theoretical perspective of Marx and Lenin. Since its inception, the Chinese Communist Party has consistently held to this political perspective. But it has applied proletarian politics in a society whose population was well over 70 percent peasantry. Thus, without discarding their basic working-class perspective, the Chinese Communist Party has forged alliances with other classes, particularly the poor and lower peasantry, and welcomed into the Party revolutionaries from diverse class backgrounds. In 1956 the Communist Party reported that 14 percent of their membership came from the ranks of workers, 69 percent from the peasantry, and 12 percent from the intellectuals (students, teachers, engineers, technicians, and professional people).* In 1960 Edgar Snow reported Party make-up as 66 percent peasantry, 15 percent workers, 15 percent intellectuals, and 4 percent national minorities.** More recent figures are not available. However, delegates to the Party's Ninth National Congress (1969) were described as follows:

> As compared with any of the previous congresses of our Party, there have never been such great numbers of delegates of Party

* "Political Report to the Eighth National Party Congress," Peking, 1956. The remaining 5 percent were not accounted for.
** Edgar Snow, *The Other Side of the River* (New York: Random House, 1961), p. 344.

members from among industrial workers in factories, mines, and other enterprises, and from among the poor and lower-middle peasants in people's communes, and delegates of women Party members on all fronts.*

Party Structure

The basic unit of the Chinese Communist Party is the Party Branch. Branches are formed in factories, communes, schools, offices, in companies of the People's Liberation Army, and in neighborhoods, "in accordance with the requirements of the revolutionary struggle and the size of the Party membership."** Most factories we visited had several Party Branches, sometimes corresponding to subdivisions of departments and workshops. Party Branches on communes were usually formed on the production brigade level. At the time of our visit there were probably well over 1 million Party Branches throughout China. Their size undoubtedly varied but was usually less than twenty.† We were given membership figures for three Branches and all had under ten members.

As the basic unit of the Party, the Branch recruited and took in new members. It could also expel members. Branches were given the responsibility for ultimate implementation of Party decisions, and were expected to organize ideological study for both Party and non-Party people. The Party Constitution instructed Branches to maintain close ties with people outside the Party and to listen to their opinions.

---

* Press Communiqué of the Secretariat of the Presidium of the Ninth National Congress of the Communist Party of China. April 1, 1969 (distributed by *Peking Review*).

** *Constitution of the Chinese Communist Party*, Chapter VI, Article 11.

† See estimates by Franz Schurmann in *Ideology and Organization in Communist China* (Berkeley: University of California Press, 1966), p. 134.

Party Committees were "leading bodies" of Party members at various levels in government, factory, commune, and Party structures. Almost every factory we visited had a Party Committee which was their "leading body"; it ran the plant in conjunction with a Revolutionary Committee. A parallel system existed on communes in the countryside. Party Committees also functioned at higher levels, such as city, county, and province. They were elected by a congress or general membership meeting of all Party members in the corresponding unit.

Central leadership is provided by the highest body in the Chinese Communist Party, the National Party Congress. Only ten Congresses have been held since the founding of the Chinese Communist Party in 1921. The most recent was in 1973 and it was attended by over 1,200 delegates; undoubtedly many others came as alternates and observers. A glance at Party history shows Congresses have generally been called at major political crossroads in the Party's development. The Congresses have been: First: 1921; Second: 1922; Third: 1923; Fourth: 1925; Fifth: 1927; Sixth: 1928 (held in Moscow); Seventh: 1945; Eighth: 1956; Ninth: 1969; and Tenth: 1973.

The National Party Congress elects a Central Committee which acts in its place between sessions. Historically, the Central Committee has been the seat of many political struggles as, for example, the conflict between the "two roads" which culminated in the Cultural Revolution. There is a smaller Political Bureau of the Central Committee which in turn has its own Standing Committee. The Political Bureau of the Tenth Central Committee had twenty-one full members and four alternates; its Standing Committee had nine members. Several administrative bureaus and organs function under the Central Committee, and with the Political Bureau carry out day-to-day tasks.

The Party: People

Zhen Lin-di worked in the Zhengzhou No. 3 Textile Mill and was a member of the Chinese Communist Party. We visited her in the compact but comfortable apartment her family rented from the factory. Both she and her husband worked in the spinning department of the mill, but on different shifts to allow one to be home with their three children.

"I usually get up around six o'clock," Zhen said, "and the children play for a while and then go to school. Two are in middle school and one is in primary school. I study Chairman Mao's works and also study international affairs and the affairs of the country."

She had joined the Communist Party in 1954, when she lived and worked in Shanghai. Her husband was not a member. Zhen added that her Party responsibilities included a weekly meeting.

"What does it mean to be a Party member?" we inquired.

"A Party member," Zhen Lin-di said after a few moments' thought, "should serve the people well, both the Chinese people and the people of the world. Second, Party members should study to increase their consciousness.* Third, Party members should have a high consciousness."

"How do you tell if someone has high consciousness?" we asked.

"People with high consciousness," she replied, "are those who are tempered in the three great struggles: the class struggle, the struggle for production, and the struggle for scientific experiment."

Two weeks later in Peking we met Zhen Shou-fu. Both he and his wife, Wang Shou-zhen, worked in the East Is Red Auto Factory. Both were rather quiet, talking softly and a bit shyly. Zhen Shou-fu was a veteran of the People's Liberation Army, a lathe operator with sixteen years' experience in the factory, and a member of the Chinese Communist Party.

* The Chinese often talked of increasing "consciousness," or more specifically "class consciousness." They meant studying historical and current affairs to improve one's understanding of what is going on in the world, and specifically doing this from the class viewpoint of working people.

"To be a member of the Communist Party," Zhen Shou-fu explained, "a person should give his or her life for the Revolution, not just in China but the Revolution of the whole world. To meet the needs of the Revolution you must be willing to sacrifice your life if necessary. A Party member must also promote production and grasp revolution."*

We asked Zhen how long he had been a Party member, and how he had joined the Party.

"I joined in 1964," he recalled. "I put in an application to be a member and was approved by the members of the Party Branch in my workshop. They asked the advice of the masses I worked with [i.e., the non-Party workers in the workshop] before approving my application. The general procedure is to make an application, have two Party members recommend you, and then the Party Branch must give its approval. About 10 percent of the people in my workshop are Party members; 13 percent of the workers in the whole factory are in the Party."

Zhen told us he had "Party activities" for two hours each week. But as we talked we learned Party membership involved more than just occasional meetings. Zhen's activities indicated some of the responsibilities local Party members shouldered: he was a leader in his production group; he organized study in the workshop; and he was in charge of militia training.

In Shenyang we talked to Wang Mun-yu and Zen Jiu-lan. Both were young workers at the Shenyang Transformer Factory. Wang, twenty-seven, was a cadre in the Communist Youth League. He told us: "To be a member of the Youth League a member must study Marxism–Leninism–Mao Tse-tung Thought, serve the people wholeheartedly—the people of China and of the whole world—and also must be linked with the broad masses of the people.

"I applied to join, was discussed by Youth League mem-

---

* The slogan "Grasp Revolution, Promote Production" was used during the Cultural Revolution. Its aim was to encourage workers to overturn "capitalist roaders" while simultaneously maintaining and even increasing production.

bers, and then approved by the leading body. In the Youth League we study; we have educational and cultural activities like song and dance; and we do exercises. We also make technical innovations and mobilize the people to collect waste materials. Youth League members can be up to twenty-five years old; cadres in the Youth League can be older. I'm twenty-seven and a cadre in the Youth League. You can join the Communist Party at eighteen and some people are members of both."

Zen Jiu-lan was twenty-eight; she was a Communist Party member and told us why she had wanted to join: "I looked at the nature of the Communist Party and considered it a glorious organization. I applied, with this consciousness, in 1966. The Party paid more attention to my growth and education after I put in my personal application. Party members helped me, and with such help and education my consciousness was raised. My fellow workers who weren't in the Party also discussed my application; but the vote and decision of membership was made by the Party members. In 1969 I was approved for membership.

"I should continue to make revolution and re-mold my world outlook," she concluded with typical modesty.

The Communist Party members we met impressed us in many respects. In the United States you would describe them as being "honest," "hard working," and "just plain folks." In China they were Communists, and it was considered a compliment to call them that. It became obvious to us that being a Communist in China was not easy. It took a lot of effort, hard work, and sacrifice without material or personal reward.

The Advanced Elements of the Proletariat

The Chinese Communist Party "should be composed of the advanced elements of the proletariat . . . a vigorous and vital organization of vanguards. . . ."* But what are "van-

* Mao Tse-tung, quoted in "New Year's Editorial," *Peking Review*, January 1968.

guards" and "advanced elements"? Does this rhetoric simply disguise and justify a new elite?

We think not.

Most Party members we met, living examples of "vanguards" and "advanced elements," were also rank-and-file workers. They took their Party membership seriously, knowing and accepting the standards set before them. Their comments reflected their personal commitment and echoed public standards defined, for example, in the writings of Mao Tse-tung. Over the years Mao has said a lot on the subject, and his "composite Communist" emerges as a person who:

> [is] more concerned about others than about himself.

> Must be ready at all times to stand up for the truth.

> Must be ready at all times to correct . . . mistakes.

> Use their own heads and carefully think over [things] . . . on no account should they follow blindly and encourage slavishness.

> Should set an example.

> Should be the most far-sighted, the most self-sacrificing, the most resolute, and the least prejudiced . . . and should rely on the majority of the masses.

> Should be pupils of the masses as well as their teachers.

> Should be a friend of the masses and not a boss over them, an indefatigable teacher and not a bureaucratic politician.

> Must never be opinionated or domineering.

> Must listen attentively to the views of people outside the Party.*

Living up to these standards was a big order and of course not everyone in the Party did. But in China people took these guidelines seriously and fully expected Communists to measure up. Party members who slacked off were apt to be criticized by fellow workers and, if they didn't mend their ways,

---

* All quotes taken from *Quotations from Chairman Mao Tse-tung*, Chapter XXVIII; original sources are mostly from Mao's essays written during the 1938-1945 period.

might be removed from leadership positions and possibly even expelled from the Party.

If such high demands were made of Communist Party members, with no promise of material or personal reward, then why did anyone bother to join? Obviously there was no single answer to this question. Some people have apparently joined the Party seeking careers and personal advancement. We heard a fair amount of criticism of careerists, an indication that such problems did exist. The Party Constitution warned specifically that "special vigilance must be maintained against careerists."

But if the people we met were typical, most Party members did not join for self-centered reasons. Most joined the Communist Party because they felt it their duty, their "civic responsibility." They believed strongly in socialism; and their satisfaction arose from working toward that goal in an organization they respected and trusted.

People supported the Communist Party because it was composed of their neighbors, their fellow workers, or their fellow commune members. It was not an outside force, directing their lives from offices in Peking; it was made up of people they lived with and worked with, people who were highly respected and whose membership in the Party they had themselves discussed.

This was our fundamental impression: people believed in the Party, trusted its leadership, and wanted to do their small part in implementing its programs. Whether members or not, the workers, peasants, cadres, and intellectuals we met regarded the Chinese Communist Party as *their* Party, and felt it represented *their* interests. This attitude was genuine, not a sham or hollow rhetoric. And not only did they feel it was their Party, but as the Cultural Revolution showed, they fought to cleanse its ranks and put it back on course when they felt it had strayed from its principles.

Both Democracy and Centralism

"The organizational principle of the Party is democratic centralism."*

Democratic centralism? We in the West tend to scoff. What kind of confused concept is that? Democracy and centralism are opposites; how can they be combined? Isn't "democratic centralism" Communist rhetoric, Communist propaganda, used to cover up a lack of democracy and an authoritarian regime?

Perhaps. Perhaps not. To answer these questions we need to understand the way the Chinese look at these things.

Chinese Communists believe that combining opposites is normal. They believe it can be done, that it can have good results, and that the "unity and struggle of opposites" is in fact the natural order of things in the world. Everything has a contradictory nature. Consider two light-hearted examples: A mixture of sugar and vinegar probably doesn't sound very appetizing, but a well-prepared dish of sweet-and-sour pork does wonders with the "unity" of these "opposites." Night and day are opposites but the combination of both, in the right proportion, is essential for any green plant to grow.

The concept of democratic centralism seeks to combine such opposites as freedom and authority, spontaneity and discipline, to combine democracy and centralism and retain the benefits of both. Democracy: because that is the essence of communism, because it brings out the initiative, talents, and opinions of the people, and because it is needed for the people to control their own destiny. Centralism: because united action is needed to achieve these goals, and organization with leadership, direction, and discipline are weapons in the hands of the population when pursuing such collective goals. The point is to maintain a proper balance between the two, to keep a proper mix. Communists argue that no set of written rules can guarantee this; rules alone cannot prevent lapses into authoritarianism or ultra-democracy. In reality, they assert, the two are constantly in a state of flux, of

* *Constitution of the Chinese Communist Party,* Article 5.

struggle. Thus at different times their Party has emphasized one or the other to correct the imbalance.*

The new 1969 Constitution of the Communist Party of China, and its 1973 revisions, are themselves examples of the constant struggle between democracy and centralism. Politically the 1969 document represented the consolidation and victory of the fight against the Liu Shao-chi forces. The 1973 revisions represented the victory of the political struggle against forces represented by Lin Piao. One of the major criticisms of both groups was that they were authoritarian, elitist, and "did not rely on the masses." Inside the Party this was considered "commandism"—that is, too much centralism and not enough democracy.

Both the 1969 Constitution and the 1973 revised version reiterated previously stated principles about centralism:

> The whole Party must observe unified discipline: The individual is subordinate to the organization, the minority is subordinate to the majority, the lower level is subordinate to the higher level, and the entire Party is subordinate to the Central Committee.**

But regarding democracy, both versions listed new formulations:

- Leading bodies of the Party at all levels shall regularly report on their work to congresses or general membership meetings, constantly listen to the opinions of the masses both inside and outside the Party, and accept their supervision.
- Party members have the right to criticize Party organizations and leading members at all levels and make proposals to them.
- If a Party member holds different views with regard to the decisions or directives of the Party organizations, he is allowed to reserve his views and has the right to bypass the

---

* Ultra-democracy is not a term common in our country. How can there be too much democracy? The Chinese use the term to indicate selfishness or individualism at the expense of others, and to describe what we call "anarchy," "anarchist tendencies," or disorder and chaos.

** "The Constitution of the Communist Party of China," *Peking Review*, September 7, 1973.

immediate leadership and report directly to higher levels, up to and including the Central Committee and the Chairman of the Central Committee.

The 1973 revision added this sentence: "It is absolutely impermissible to suppress criticism and to retaliate."

Both versions summed up the goal of the Party's democratic centralism:

> It is essential to create a political situation in which there are both centralism and democracy, both discipline and freedom, both unity of will and personal ease of mind and liveliness.

One key element in the Chinese practice of democratic centralism was the "ups and downs" procedure. The 1969 Constitution and the 1973 revisions at the Tenth National Party Congress were formulated through this process. In response to a proposal by Chairman Mao in November 1967, local Party branches throughout China sent thousands of drafts of constitution revisions to the Party's Central Committee. After sorting and sifting, the Central Committee returned a composite draft to the local units for evaluation. The draft was discussed both inside and outside the Party. More feedback followed and a final document was approved at the Ninth National Party Congress in April 1969.

The "ups and downs" procedure was employed in much the same manner in 1973. Revisions were initiated at a working conference of the Party's Central Committee in May 1973. Party Committees at lower levels then set up groups to discuss the revisions and forty-one drafts were formally sent back to the Central Committee. Discussions held inside and outside the Party at the lower levels resulted in a number of suggestions that were sent directly to the Central Committee. The Central Committee then went over all suggestions and drew up a list of proposed revisions which was submitted to the Tenth National Party Congress.

Delegates to the Congresses were also selected through an "ups and downs" procedure. Nominations and discussion involved Party organizations at various levels and the final selection was made by provincial level Party Congresses.

Thus, centralism was exercised and democracy encouraged. Higher bodies were expected to issue directives, to lead. But local members were expected to participate, to put forth their opinions, help make decisions, and choose leadership from among their own ranks.

The history of the Chinese Communist Party has been a history of political struggles. Democracy has been slighted during certain periods; ultra-democracy became disruptive at other times. Centralism was lost on occasion but turned into rigidity and bureaucracy on other occasions. But the principle, the successful combination of democracy and centralism, has remained consistent. It has been and is the way most people in China want their Communist Party to function.

Higher Leadership

We did not meet any members of the Party's Central Committee. We did, however, meet and talk with a worker who was involved in national-level leadership, a man who had been a delegate to the Ninth National Party Congress.

Mu De-xian was an electrician who worked at Xin Gang Harbor, near Tianjin. Quiet and slight of build, he talked about himself only after other workers had urged him to do so. They first described some of the work he had done: he had taken the lead in the construction of a new magnetic crane now used in the harbor and was an activist and leader in study.

"After studying," Mu explained, "I loved the motherland more and realized I should contribute to socialist construction. We should create wealth and liberate manpower for socialism.

"Strength for my study," Mu continued in a strong but soft voice, "comes from my comparison with the old days. I became a dock worker at the age of twelve. I pushed a small wheelbarrow and was paid only when I could get a job with a ship. I often went hungry. In the old days we were exploited economically and suppressed politically. We suffered especially during the Japanese occupation and many people died of hunger and beatings.* Life for the worker was not sure. Many people had to separate from their families to get by; some had to sell their children. People could not buy grain and ate leaves and wild grasses. Our income for one day could not support one person. Workers also resisted and waged struggles during this period. Sometimes we slacked down in work in waging struggles for better wages.

"After Liberation, we were emancipated and now we work for the people. After Liberation, spare-time schools were run for the illiterate, to teach us how to read and write, and to study why we suffered in the old days. I joined the Communist Youth League in 1954 and in 1956 I joined the Communist Party. I am now Secretary of the Party Branch in my workshop and on the Standing Committee of the Party Committee [for the harbor]. And I participated in the Ninth Party Congress personally, but that honor belongs to the workers and staff of the whole harbor."

Mu De-xian was only one of many veteran revolutionaries who held leadership positions in China. In 1961 Edgar Snow estimated that there were about eight hundred top revolutionary leaders who traced their involvement back to the late 1920s. These eight hundred, Snow reported, held the leading positions in the Party and government structures.**

Today many, if not most, of the top leaders in China are still of that generation, including Mao Tse-tung and Chou En-lai. Over half the seats on the Tenth Central Committee (1973) were held by veterans who had spent practically their whole adult lives in service to the Party, army, and government.

Mao Tse-tung (chairman of the Party's Central Committee) and Chou En-lai (a vice-chairman of the Central Committee and Premier of the State Council) are, of course, the best

* Gruesome evidence of this remained. When we arrived at the harbor our hosts told us we had driven past a nearby spot where over ten thousand people were buried in a mass grave, victims of the oppression of the old days.

** Snow, *The Other Side of the River*, p. 331.

Leadership: Cadres and Party 227

known of China's leaders. What about the other 317 people who sit on the Tenth Central Committee, the pinnacle of power and leadership?

Statistically the group has these features:

Composition. It has 195 full members and 124 alternate members.

Experience. Sixty-eight percent had joined the Chinese Communist Party before 1934. (Such veterans had made up 80 percent of the Ninth Central Committee.)

Continuity. 140 (72 percent) of the 195 full members had been on the Ninth Central Committee as either full or alternate members. 52 (27 percent) of these full members had been either full or alternate members on the Eighth Central Committee (1956). At least three were on the Eighth and Tenth Central Committees, but not the Ninth.

Fresh Blood. 52 (27 percent) of the 195 full members were new to that position. 57 (46 percent) of the 124 alternates were new to their positions.*

The Party Central Committee has within it: old Party veterans who can look back over forty or fifty years of struggle, Party cadres who stuck to their socialist principles before the Cultural Revolution and fought back regardless of hardships and personal sufferings, cadres who were criticized for making mistakes during the Cultural Revolution, rank-and-file workers and peasants who rose to leadership during the struggles to build socialism, intellectuals, technicians, diplomats, and young people who sparked the initial battles of the Cultural Revolution.

---

* For a look at some of the faces behind these statistics, see the Appendix, below.

6
Democracy in China: From the Masses to the Masses

"From the masses, to the masses." The mass line. Cadres. The two joins. The May 7th Cadre Schools. The Communist Party of China. Democratic centralism. Revolutionary Committees. Party Committees.

How do all these add up? What do they mean to the average person? Is there democracy in China? Freedom?

The Chinese say that their socialist system is a "dictatorship of the proletariat." Isn't this an open admission of totalitarianism, of an authoritarian and undemocratic society? People may eat in new China, but what can they say, what can they think?

Good questions—in fact, some of the most common ones raised in our country. We returned from China with impressions which perhaps can help people draw their own conclusions. But first, we should clarify what we mean by democracy and freedom, and second, we should clarify what the Chinese mean when they talk about the "dictatorship of the proletariat." The Chinese also talk about democracy a lot, often referring to what they call the "people's democratic dictatorship," and see no contradiction in these terms.

Democracy for Whom?

Democracy is a question of content, not form. It is *how*, and *for whom*, a government functions, not what form or structure it takes. This would seem an obvious truism, but unfortunately *democracy* in our country has come to mean "our form of government." We speak glibly of the United States as a democracy and label socialist countries "totalitarian." The fact is that everyone (except out-and-out fascists) says they're in favor of democracy. Capitalists and socialists both claim their systems are democratic. Both agree democracy means equality, equal rights, and public involvement in running society. Democracy, both assert, places power in public hands through representative forms of decision-making and accountability; it also protects the freedoms necessary to guarantee these public powers.

But we know capitalists and socialists hardly see eye to eye. The difference comes from the whole way one looks at the world.

The Chinese, as socialists, analyze society from a class perspective. To understand the way they look at things, we suggest a brief theoretical digression.

Class and State

Let's imagine we can attend the Chinese equivalent of a 4th of July celebration. National Day in the People's Republic of China is October 1st, and throughout the land there are public celebrations. It's a good time to find a park in a South China city and stroll through the crowds, enjoying the music, dancing, games for kids, and other festivities. If we inquire we're certain to find a group of friendly people eager and willing to sit down and talk to us.

"What's this about the 'dictatorship of the proletariat' and 'democracy'?" we might ask as an opener.

A buzz and then a flurry of answers is apt to come from the group celebrating the anniversary of their government. Noting that we are Americans, one young worker starts off by explaining the Marxist concept of the term "state." "State, in the Marxist sense, does not mean New York or California," he begins. "It is what you in the United States would call government, or public authority. Understanding the nature of the state is crucial to the questions of democracy and freedom."

A young woman interjects, suggesting we need to look at the whole historical development of mankind to understand the Marxist concept of state. "After all," she says, "Marxism comes from an analysis of social conditions as they developed over the centuries. Thousands of years ago mankind lived in primitive society where there was no state or public authority. This is what Marx called 'primitive communism.' In primitive society people lived mostly by hunting and fishing, and ownership of land was not defined. Then agriculture developed and people started dividing up the land for private ownership. There had to be some way of regulating conflicting economic interests. This is when the modern state arose. It arose at the same time that different economic classes appeared. Antagonisms between these classes developed, such as nobility against serfs, landlords against tenants, and in the modern era, capitalists against workers. It became necessary to have a public authority which could preserve order in the midst of this competition for power among the different classes."

The young woman might modestly add that she remembers this because her study group at work has recently read Engels' *The Origin of the Family, Private Property, and the State*.

A third person, a middle-aged peasant visiting relatives in the city during the holiday, joins the discussion. "You're right," he responds to the young woman, "but don't leave our American friends with the impression that the state is neutral, like a referee at a ping-pong match. You have to go further."

He explains: "History has shown that because the state arose out of class conflicts it has generally been captured by one class or another and become its tool to control society. That way the economically dominant class is usually also the politically dominant class. Classes maintain their power by the authority of the state. Slave-owners in ancient times did that. Feudal lords in medieval times did that. And today in much of the world big capitalists do that, too."

He recalls something from Lenin which he recently read, quoting: "The state is a machine for maintaining the rule of one class over another."

"That's what we mean when we talk about 'dictatorship,'" another young man ventures. "The state is the dictatorship of one class over another. All states, regardless of form, are class dictatorships. You Americans often have trouble understanding this because of the nature of the state you live in. Your form of government, a democratic republic, is simply the means by which the monopoly capitalists rule. They control the state as a whole. Every four years you get to choose between two different representatives of the capitalists to be your president. The capitalist class maintains control regardless. So while a state may be a democratic republic in form, it is still controlled by a dominant class. Thus, it is still a class dictatorship."

The historically minded young woman speaks up again: "These ideas may be new to you because one of the characteristics of the capitalist state is to deny it is a class state. It claims to be a state of all the classes. Its ideology claims class struggle has ended.

"Although the capitalist state today proclaims liberty for all, it is actually set up to give more power and influence to the rich. Private property and private enterprise are protected. This means freedom for a few to economically exploit the many."

By now our conversation has undoubtedly attracted quite a crowd of curious on-lookers.

An older worker steps forward and says that a revolution is when one class overturns the rule of another. "After a revolution," he declares, "there is a different class ruling the state. In China the old dictatorship was a dictatorship of the landlord class and big capitalists. But the majority of the people were peasants and workers. The triumph of the revolution in

1949 brought a new class dictatorship. Now the workers and peasants run the state. We call this our people's democratic dictatorship."

If we look puzzled by the idea of a "democratic dictatorship," he might explain further: "In 1949, in China," he says, "the working class, the peasantry, the urban petty bourgeoisie, and the national bourgeoisie came together and formed a new state. Led by the working class, this coalition of classes ruled over the old landlord class and big capitalists. Chairman Mao called this 'New Democracy.' We practiced democracy within the ranks of the people, but we denied reactionaries their 'rights' to continue exploiting people.

"Chairman Mao said," he quotes, "that the combination of these two aspects, democracy for the people and dictatorship over the reactionaries, is the people's democratic dictatorship."

A young student, waiting to talk, interrupts to make sure we understand. "Foreigners who accuse us of practicing 'totalitarianism' or 'dictatorship,' " he argues adamantly, "are usually the very people who practice it themselves. They practice the class dictatorship of the capitalists over the majority of the people, the workers. But here in China our state is a class dictatorship where the majority of the people rule in their own class interests. The people enjoy democratic rights of freedom of speech, assembly, association, religious belief and so on. We believe that our socialist democracy is democracy broader than any that can be found in capitalist countries."

The student turns and gestures to a dozen or so of his friends. "Our study group has just been reading some materials on this question," he says, "and we have something here Chairman Mao wrote in response to United States charges that China was 'totalitarian.' " One of his friends passes up a book and the young man reads:

> ... A government led by the Communist Party is a government that exercises dictatorship over domestic and foreign reactionaries and does not give them any freedom to carry on their counter-revolutionary activities. ... Like food and clothing, this power is

something a victorious people cannot do without even for a moment.... The more the reactionaries rail 'totalitarian government' the more obviously it is a treasure.... For the masses of the people, a government of the people's democratic dictatorship led by the Communist Party is not dictatorial or autocratic but democratic.*

"It all boils down to this," the student says, putting the book aside. "Capitalist rulers claim that their democracy applies to everyone, regardless of wealth, belief, religion, or so forth. We Chinese look at the reality and say: capitalist democracy is really a democracy for a few, for the rich. Here in China we don't make the impossible claim of having democracy for everyone, 100 percent. In order to have democracy for the vast majority of our people, we know we have to control the old ruling class. We do so with no qualms.

"Look at what giving the reactionaries their freedoms meant to us in the old society!" he exclaims. "What good is a right to vote if you're starving? What good is an election if all candidates represent your oppressors? What good is freedom of the press if you're illiterate? We think the people's livelihood first needs to be guaranteed, and then these democratic rights really mean something."

A soldier joins the discussion. "The working class is now the most important class in China. Thus our original 'people's democratic dictatorship' changed during the 1950s to become a 'dictatorship of the proletariat.' This happened as we created a more socialist society and moved from the stage of New Democracy to socialism. But still, the poor and lower-middle peasants are close allies of the working class in running our socialist state.

"As we became more socialist," he continues, "we really became more democratic. We limited the so-called freedoms of private property and free enterprise of the capitalist and landlord class. Our history has shown us if we allow capitalists and landlords the freedoms of private property or usury

---

* Mao Tse-tung, "Why It Is Necessary to Discuss the White Paper," 1949, in *Selected Works*, Vol. IV, p. 444.

the majority of people end up with the 'freedom' to go hungry, to be unemployed, to starve, and to sell their labor only on the capitalists' and landlords' terms.

"With socialist democracy we now have both political and economic rights," he concludes.

The middle-aged peasant speaks again: "We now have a state which is a class dictatorship of the vast majority over those few who had formerly oppressed us. All states are class dictatorships of one sort or another. In old China most people were oppressed and exploited. Now, under the dictatorship of the proletariat, it is more democratic for more people. Someday in the future, when capitalism and oppression do not exist anywhere, the state itself will gradually disappear. But that's a long time away."

We thank our imaginary friends and move on, strolling through the holiday activities, wondering about this dictatorship of the proletariat. Is it as they say, is there actually more democracy?

This discussion is a composite of the way our Chinese hosts approached the question of democracy. We found that workers and peasants were quite willing to discuss such topics. They proudly stated that their ideology was Marxism-Leninism; they took its perspective seriously, and they analyzed their society accordingly.

Decisions that Affect Your Life

During the mid-1960s, student activists in the United States popularized a slogan which perhaps captures the essence of democratic goals: "People should be able to make those decisions that affect their lives."

Have you ever helped decide what wages your co-workers should get? What about deciding production speed, safety measures, and shop conditions? Have you ever participated in the decision of how much and what your factory should produce?

If you're an office worker, have you ever helped decide

how your office should be organized or what is bureaucratic and unnecessary paperwork? Have you ever held regular sessions to evaluate and criticize your boss and your fellow workers?

If you're a small farmer, how do you decide what to grow, when to market it, and how to use your profits? Are market fluctuations, which affect your income, more important than the needs and desires of consumers for certain products?

We found that people in China participated in many of these "decisions that affect their lives," and often over a much broader area than we know in the West. This was particularly true at the point of production, and it was no accident: emphasis on the workplace is an understandable application of socialist ideology.

Rank-and-file workers and ordinary peasants we talked to felt very much a part of China's decision-making system. They also openly admitted problems, raised criticisms, and explained shortcomings to us. Weak points, however, were regarded as failures to apply socialist principles fully, not as problems of the system itself. Only occasionally did we meet workers or cadres who made embarrassed attempts to cover up defects.

Workers and cadres at the Shenyang Transformer Factory gave us one example of this decision-making process. A leading cadre explained how production goals were determined: "The general task of our factory is set by the state [economic planning agencies in the industrial ministry] according to state plan. The capacity and needs of our factory are also considered. Cadres first take the state plan, consider our factory and the number of workers, and make a proposal. The workers in each workshop then discuss the figures.

"For example, last year the leadership of our factory felt that twelve thousand units a year was a good production figure. This suggestion was taken to the various workshops for discussion. It was broken down in terms of their particular tasks and what this meant for each job. During the discussions the workers did not agree. They said the potential of the factory was greater, that production should be stepped up. Finally the Party Committee and the Revolutionary Committee agreed with the workers and settled on a figure of fourteen thousand. This year [1971] we produced fourteen thousand units and finished five days ahead of schedule."

He added, "Many decisions are made this way. There are other examples, such as deciding the workers' study plan and the percentage of our funds that go for welfare purposes [medical care, housing, recreation programs, etc., run by the factory]. The Workers' Representative Congress is very involved in these discussions."

A parallel example of decision-making in the countryside has been related by Felix Greene. His anecdote, although ten years old, illustrates dramatically reasons why communes had developed so far by the time of our visit. We believe his story provides a good example of "making decisions that affect your life," Chinese style.

Greene described a commune he visited in Henan which had developed a good-sized fish-raising enterprise. He discovered, however, that the commune members ate mostly noodles and steamed bread, reserving fish for special holidays about three times a year. He asked why. His hosts explained that whether to eat fish or not had been a matter of considerable controversy in the commune. There had been several mass meetings, discussions, and special sessions of the commune's leading committee. Some wanted to eat the fish. But others had argued the fish should be sold for money to use in constructing a hospital, new schools, and a library, and for new film projectors and new homes for old people. They argued that eating fish could come later, when they were more developed. This viewpoint won out and commune members, by their own choice, were eating simple buns and noodles so they could build hospitals, schools, and homes for the elderly.*

The communes and factories we visited all had collectively supported health, recreation, education, and welfare facilities, perhaps the results of similar decisions. And by 1972 they appeared to be eating their fish, too.

* Felix Greene, *The Wall Has Two Sides* (London: Jonathan Cape, 1972), pp. 154-199.

The First Freedoms

Americans firmly believe, at least in principle, that our First Amendment freedoms—of the press, religion, speech, and assembly—are vital to democracy. What about these freedoms in China? Are they abrogated under the dictatorship of the proletariat?

No, and yes. The Chinese Communist Party, under Mao's leadership, has always said it was fighting for the following freedoms:

> Freedom of speech, press, assembly, association, political conviction and religious belief and freedom of the person are the people's most important freedoms. In China only the Liberated Areas have given full effect to these freedoms.*

Freedom of expression was totally unknown in old China.** To the vast majority of the Chinese people these freedoms became part of their lives only after Liberation. Wall posters (*dazibao*), public criticism of leaders, work group evaluations, and participation in such rank-and-file organizations as the trade unions, Workers' Representative Congresses, and the Women's Federation, became realities only in new China.

The China we visited was not an intimidated society. People were not afraid to talk with us, whether we met them through prearranged visits or in chance encounters on city streets, in stores, and in public parks. People did not hesitate to express opinions.

But freedom of expression for a few people had been curtailed. The Chinese made no apologies for this. Indeed, they argued that the very existence of democracy for well over 90 percent of the people was contingent on suppressing certain

---

* Mao Tse-tung, "On Coalition Government," 1945, in *Selected Works*, Vol. III, p. 243.

** See almost any account of Kuomintang China. For example: Han Suyin, *Birdless Summer* and *The Morning Deluge;* or the Schurmann and Schell reader, Vol. II: *Republican China;* or *China! Inside the People's Republic* by the Committee of Concerned Asian Scholars.

—not all—of the privileges of their former oppressors. The former landlords, big capitalists, and foreign imperialists were considered "class enemies" of the socialist state. They still had economic rights to a means of livelihood, as did everyone else. For example, peasants on the communes we visited told us their former landlords were now regular production team members. These former landlords, we also learned, regained political rights only when the peasants became convinced they had truly reformed and understood the new collective society.

The Media

Capitalists, landlords, and representatives of foreign imperialists did not have access to the mass media in China, i.e., to the daily press, radio, and television. The media reflected the interests of the dominant class, the peasants and workers, and was therefore pro-socialist. But within this context different views, opinions, and public criticisms could be found.

Newspapers were popular, available by subscription or sold on the street at a few fen a copy.* Daily papers were about four to six pages long, with small type and few pictures. We saw many papers posted on bulletin boards along sidewalks and in front of department stores and public buildings. They were usually surrounded by groups of all ages, carefully reading articles that caught their attention.

Our inability to read Chinese was of course a handicap and prevented us from making any systematic survey of the content of the daily papers. We did occasionally corral Zheng or another translator in free moments and sit down with a copy of *Renmin Ribao (People's Daily)*. It is the most widely circulated paper in the country and the official daily paper of the Chinese Communist Party. It usually had a mix of international and national news. There were articles written by ordinary workers or peasants on such things as a local work-

---

* 1 fen is about half a U.S. cent.

ers' study group's analysis of recent theoretical readings, or the experiences of a production brigade in agricultural development. There were articles which described failures as well as accomplishments. International news emphasized the war in Indochina, foreign dignitaries currently visiting China, and the establishment of diplomatic relations and trade with other countries. There was no advertising.

Each province had a major newspaper and principal cities had one or two dailies of their own. Peking had three in addition to the *People's Daily:* the *Liberation Army Daily*, aimed at PLA members; the *Kwangming Daily*, which emphasized cultural and intellectual topics; and the *Peking Daily*, which ran more local news.*

Another popular mass media we saw was a type of syndicated photo display system. Collections of large glossy prints showing current events, international affairs, cultural happenings, and national news were put up on bulletin boards. A short, descriptive caption accompanied each photo. They were often glass enclosed for protection from the weather and lit up at night. The displays amounted to a kind of public photo news magazine. There was obviously a coordinated and centralized service which provided graphics for these displays to many parts of China. We saw the same photo essay on achievements of a particular commune in several locations, as well as coverage of foreign dignitaries who attended May Day festivities in Peking. We also saw many local homemade bulletin board and photo displays.

Are the Chinese limited to only the socialist viewpoint? And doesn't such overt control of the mass media by the government and Communist Party amount to "thought control"?

We would say no to both questions.

The socialist viewpoint was not the only perspective avail-

---

* For a brief account of these papers, and some examples of debates and articles in the Chinese press (e.g., workers criticizing their leaders for being too bureaucratic), see Julian Schuman, "Serving the Revolution with Words," in *Far Eastern Economic Review*, January 22, 1972, pp. 18-19.

able. While we were in Peking two news packets in English were delivered regularly to our hotel room. One was a daily compilation of Chinese Press Agency (Xinhua) dispatches covering domestic and international affairs. The second rather surprised us: it was "News from Foreign Agencies and Press." This packet of about twenty-five pages contained news dispatches and editorials from the United States (Associated Press, United Press International, United States Information Service, and The New York Times service), Britain (Reuters), France (Agence France Presse), and occasionally the Soviet Union (Tass). They were printed without comment. The packet was heavy on international affairs but included some coverage of domestic United States and European events. It was, of course, for the convenience of foreign guests. We asked Zheng if similar information was distributed to the average Chinese. He said yes, anyone in China could subscribe to a four-page daily tabloid, *Reference News*, consisting solely of reprints, translated into Chinese, from the foreign press.* Subscriptions were cheap (about 50 fen, or 25¢, a month) and the tabloid was often circulated at places of work and schools. Recent reports have put circulation at more than 6 million. A comparable service in the United States might be if Washington published, in English, a cheap and readily available daily paper full of news dispatches from Xinhua, Tass, Prensa Latina (Havana), and North Korea or North Vietnam.

We also discovered that radio receivers brought into China such capitalist intrusions as the Voice of America, the BBC (British Broadcasting Corporation), and Radio Japan. In Luoyang, on April 20, we listened to: a Voice of America news broadcast, Radio Japan, a broadcast in Russian, the BBC, the Voice of Vietnam (Democratic Republic of Vietnam), and several Chinese stations. A little over a week later, in Shi-jia-zhuang, we again listened to the Voice of America, catching a jazz hour playing Cannonball Adderley and then

---

* See Julian Schuman, "Serving the Revolution with Words," and his article "Reference News and Watergate," in *Ta Kung Pao* (English edition), June 28, 1973, p. 14.

VOA news of the Vietnam war, the Apollo 16 recovery, and the death of Nkrumah.

Radios were household items in China, common in all city and rural homes we visited. In fact, radio was the backbone of the Chinese mass media. Most radios we saw had both long- and short-wave bands, since the Chinese broadcast to many parts of their own country on short-wave frequencies. We inspected radios for sale in several stores and found that most were triple band: one long- and two short-wave. Radios that brought in stations from all over the world were as common in China as AM-FM receivers are in the United States.

Our own experience leads us to regard with the utmost skepticism any assertion that the Chinese jam incoming radio signals from capitalist countries, whether in English or Chinese. Other reports confirm this.* Zheng, for example, told us he occasionally listened to the Voice of America to try and improve his knowledge of colloquial English.

Books and Libraries

We visited several bookstores and libraries. A Xian bookstore we wandered into unannounced had a large stock of works of Marx, Engels, Lenin, Stalin, and Mao. Mao's four-volume *Selected Works* cost 2 yuan (less than $1). The store also carried pamphlet selections from these books, and we picked up a Chinese-English dual-language "pony" of Mao's "Three Constantly Read Articles" for 7 fen. It was meant for students learning English and had explanatory notes in Chinese at the bottom of each page.** The store also had a large section devoted to music and culture, with scores and picture

---

* Ibid.

** English was a popular foreign language in China; some reports estimate that as many as 50 million Chinese are learning English through radio broadcast lessons, popular English primers, and classroom lessons.

books from revolutionary Peking operas and contemporary literature covering a wide range of areas. There were some books about Vietnam, including one of letters from Vietnamese to Chinese friends. We saw no books from foreign publishers.

Xinhua bookstore in Peking had a larger variety. We particularly remember long counters stacked high with colorful children's books. Other book islands were filled with scientific and technical works, such as biophysics and biochemistry. There was a section with books in the languages of national minorities, and several texts for learning national minority languages. Lu Hsun's writings were available, as well as contemporary short stories of many varieties.* The second floor had a large department selling brightly colored posters and maps. The bookstore had two sections and was open twenty-four hours a day.

Another store we visited specialized in books published in foreign languages. In addition to foreign language editions (English, French, Spanish, etc.) of a whole range of political, historical, and cultural works published in China, the store carried books from Vietnam, Albania, and some older books from the Soviet Union. We also saw bins of used books inside some department stores. Many of the books were foreign-published texts, usually scientific.

Our bookstore visits were much too cursory to determine what's available to someone who is "book hunting." It was clear the most widely distributed and readily available books were political (the works of Marx, Engels, Lenin, Stalin, and Mao), cultural (new operas and ballets), and contemporary (often short stories with political messages). By all appearances such literature was quite popular and read extensively.

We got much more of a sense of the range of material available in the libraries we visited. The Peking University library was open to the public. The seventy-six-year-old university had built up quite a library over the years, now total-

---

* Lu Hsun (1881-1936) was one of the most gifted writers of modern China. He is revered in China today as a progressive social critic and revolutionary.

ling over 2.4 million volumes. We visited one four-story building of the library. The ground floor was a reading room. Stacks on the second floor were devoted mostly to old historical Chinese literature, some dating back several hundred years. Here we saw an ancient book on acupuncture displayed alongside a new manual on the same topic prepared during the Cultural Revolution. The new manual, we were told, had been prepared using the old book as a guide: it was an example of taking what was good from the old and combining it with the new. We also saw centuries-old art books next to new paintings which employed old techniques but used contemporary themes.

Zhou Pei-yuan, an elderly professor and one of our hosts, pulled us over to a glass case to look at some ancient scrolls. "These were originally found in Shanxi," he informed us, "but in 1942 the Japanese attacked a temple where they were stored. The Eighth Route Army defended the temple and eight soldiers died in the battle. This shows how the Army defended the culture of our country. After Liberation, 2,000 scrolls were brought to the Peking Library. A few are here at the University for display. We also have several thousand old wood-block printed books. And you can see here some examples of newly revived techniques of multicolored wood-block printing."

On the next floor we strolled through stacks of books in foreign languages: French, Spanish, and mostly English. Many books were old, probably acquired before Liberation, but others were new, crisp and shiny, contemporary Western publications. We poked about here and there, finding the works of Mark Twain, Hemingway, Washington Irving, James Fenimore Cooper, G. D. H. Cole, Howard Fast, e. e. cummings, Stephen Vincent Benet, H. G. Wells, and even the *New York Times Index* and *Reader's Guide to Periodical Literature*. A batch of contemporary Western social scientists were represented by some books acquired since the Cultural Revolution, including books by Harold Lasswell, publications by the Council on Foreign Relations, and reports by Protestant churches of Asian missionary activities, current and historical.

The library at the Central Institute for Nationalities in Peking had about 500,000 volumes, about 10 percent in languages of the minorities. Several of the national minorities had no written form of their language before Liberation, and we saw books which employed recently developed romanized alphabets. A periodical reading room had newspapers and magazines in five languages: Korean, Tibetan, Mongolian, Kazakh, and Uighur. Uighur newspapers were available in both the traditional Arabic script and in a recently developed romanized alphabet.

We jotted down at random authors and titles we recognized as we walked through the stacks. A section of cultural materials had books in Chinese, Russian, German, English, and national minority languages. Here we saw a book on French Impressionist painters in German; two huge, very beautiful volumes on Chinese porcelain arts with color plates; several song books from the Soviet Union of traditional Russian songs, published in 1952; a book of Chinese songs published in English in 1939 in Shanghai; books from German publishers about Mozart, Haydn, and other European composers, including music and scores; and a volume on Mexican painting, published in the West. There was also, of course, a wide variety of material on Chinese art and music in the collection.

In a different part of the library we found a section of American literature which had been translated into Chinese. The books had been published, for the most part, in the late 1950s. A few titles represented: John Steinbeck, *The Grapes of Wrath*; W. E. B. DuBois, *The Souls of Black Folk*; Mark Twain, *Huckleberry Finn* and *Pudd'nhead Wilson*; Shirley Graham DuBois, *Once There Was a Slave*; Theodore Dreiser, *The Financier*; and the short stories of O. Henry and Washington Irving.

"Did the library lose any books or materials during the Cultural Revolution?" we asked, mentioning that the Western press had carried many reports about old and foreign materials being burned. "Not a volume was removed or damaged during the Cultural Revolution," a member of the institute's Revolutionary Committee told us. He added that materials they considered politically bad had been left on the shelves because people can learn from negative examples, and because many books had a mixed value; some may have had a wrong analysis but included useful facts.

The Walls and Streets Speak

Wall newspapers and blackboard or bulletin board displays were common throughout China. Indeed, the walls were "read" in China, qualifying as a unique part of the nation's media. The famous *dazibao*, literally meaning "big-character posters," were an open, effective avenue of expression. Anyone could post a *dazibao*, saying anything he or she wished. *Dazibao* were apt to be pasted on any available wall space, but sometimes space had been specially constructed: long rows of sturdy wooden bulletin boards lined both sides of walkways in many factories and schools.

Dazibao played an important role. The posters were respected. If others disagreed they might paste up dozens of answers but the original remained.* *Dazibao* with special political importance were sometimes reproduced and publicized widely in the newspapers and on the radio.

The frequency of the "*dazibao* press" had obviously tapered off since the days of the Cultural Revolution. We saw many faded and weather-beaten posters, wallpapers, and old *dazibao*, remnants of greater levels of activity in previous years.

Many of us in the West first heard about *dazibao* during the Cultural Revolution. One of its first rounds was initiated by a nationally publicized *dazibao* posted by some young instructors at Peking University. The practice was actually quite old and could take several forms. Sometimes *dazibao* were only short slogans or exhortations; sometimes they were individual or group criticisms of leaders; at other times they were quite long and detailed, actually small articles on politi-

---

* This was not always true of struggles during the heat of the Cultural Revolution.

cal and theoretical subjects. They were thus one way people could dissent, be listened to, and try to convince others of their viewpoint.

There were also street demonstrations in China. To be sure, they were within the context of China's socialist consensus and the "dictatorship of the proletariat"; there were no groups of ex-landlords picketing the headquarters of the Chinese Communist Party demanding the return of their former holdings. But, probably due to the picture given us by the Western press, we tend to think political rallies, demonstrations, and parades in China are simply events where the Party mobilizes faceless masses to mechanically shout slogans. The truth is that both organized rallies and dissenting demonstrations have taken place.

The Cultural Revolution was a period when political demonstrations, protest rallies, marches, parades, and the like took place almost daily. Small newspapers were published by the dozens; countless mimeographed broadsheets were handed out. Materials and facilities for these activities were made available free, including paper, ink, brushes, posters, printing presses, halls for meetings, and public address and sound systems. Demonstrations were certainly not choreographed shows, but genuine, complex political struggles. There is no reason to believe these materials and facilities are any less available to demonstrators now than during the intense periods of the Cultural Revolution.

The Chinese attitude toward "criticism and self-criticism" gave such things as *dazibao* and demonstrations a special meaning. Criticism and self-criticism has been used, and sometimes misused, for decades within the Chinese Communist Party. It was now practiced throughout Chinese society as a whole. Leaders and officials expect criticism; rank and file were encouraged to raise criticisms. The purpose of criticism was not to embarrass, disgrace, or compete with others; it was to help others improve, to learn from mistakes, to "cure the illness and save the patient." Thus, when *dazibao* were put up, they were not usually regarded as threats to jobs or as personal affronts. Criticism, as part of the system, was considered healthy, normal, and the way things should function.

What Do You Want to Be?

What about job choice and the freedom to pursue career ambitions in China? In our country we usually associate these with individual freedom, personal fulfillment, and upward mobility. In China we often asked young people what they wanted to be, what they planned to do when they finished school. Their answers were almost always the same:

"I'll work where the Party sends me!"

"I'll serve the people wherever I'm needed."

"The Party and state can decide best where I'm needed, and I'll go there."

Westerners are sometimes horrified by such statements. Where is the freedom to choose one's job? What has China's socialism done to ambition and initiative? Were these young people perhaps afraid to state their real desires publicly?

The last question is easy to answer: They meant what they said. They weren't parroting a Party line for our benefit. As socialists we were able to talk to them in their own terms, and we found the question of jobs was only one of many areas where they put their socialist principles into practice.

Young people in China believed they should serve the people and put group interests first. They rejected the individualist ideas of building a career or seeking wealth, status, or fame. They argued as follows:

If you set your heart on becoming a doctor, for example, this might ignore the needs of other people. It could be very individualistic. Suppose your community already had enough doctors. What if engineers, mechanics, teachers, or simply more agricultural laborers were needed? If people thought only of themselves, the collective needs would not be met and everyone, in the end, would suffer. Furthermore, in a socialist society shouldn't the collective body, the group, be involved in deciding who would be the best person to go to

school and become an engineer or doctor? They agreed that
some people were better students than others. But that was
simply another reason for group involvement in job decisions.
The group could judge best who was capable of integrating
special learning with the day-to-day needs of workers and
peasants.

Young people in China, however, did admit to expressing
preferences regarding their occupations. Some people, they
acknowledged, were more skilled or talented in particular
areas, and people usually worked better in positions that interested them. Thus they combined "personal choice" with
the "needs of the state." Everyone prospered, they said,
when individuals worked at jobs that suited both individual
talents, skills, and personal preferences and the needs of society as a whole. Preferences, when expressed, were typically put in general terms rather than as individual, careerist
goals. For example, two recent visitors reported on their conversations with young people. Children of workers usually
wanted to become skilled workers; children of peasants
wished to become members of the Communist Youth League
in their production brigade; and children of intellectuals were
often torn between the traditional ethic of becoming a
scholar and the new socialist values of serving the people.*

Undoubtedly instances occurred where individuals were assigned to work they disliked. A woman in Tangshan gave us a
personal example. She told us her son had not liked his job
assignment. "In 1964, when my second son was to go to the
countryside, he did not want to go.** I didn't like the idea

* Binneg Y. Lao and Ping Sheng, "China—Impressions," 1973, unpublished manuscript.

** Assigning city youth to periods of work in the countryside has
been done for political as well as manpower reasons. Educated youth
brought skills and talents to the countryside; they also learned firsthand the conditions of rural China, where the majority of the people
live. Thus, contradictions between city and country could be eased and
a more harmonious development of the whole society would hopefully
result. Two educated youths who had settled in the countryside were
elected to the Tenth Central Committee of the Communist Party of
China in 1973.

either. But we studied *Serve the People* and I thought: If these young people don't answer the call of the Party, who will? The Party has emancipated us, we should follow its call. But my son wanted to stay in the city with our family. I was a cadre of the Street Committee. I told him he had to help set an example so we could mobilize the masses. After he had been in the countryside five years he went into the army. He wrote me a letter and asked if I thought it was all right to join. I wrote him back and said if the Party called him to go then he should go. I supported his action."

This was one of several examples we heard, all with happy endings. But occasionally young people have refused to go along with particular job assignments. When this happened teachers, cadres, and fellow students tried to persuade them. Education about socialist values, accompanied by a fair amount of group pressure, were the tools employed. If this failed the individual was not forced into a job. Most likely he or she remained at home, dependent upon family and relatives for a livelihood.* Such holdouts, although considered selfish and lacking in socialist consciousness, were not punished or imprisoned. Socialist consciousness, the Chinese believe, is developed through day-to-day work and political struggle, not through coercion.

But who did the assigning? We heard of no special groups set up for this. When people spoke of the "Party" or the "state" assigning jobs, they meant the Party Committees, the Revolutionary Committees, and other leading bodies in their factories, schools, or communes. These were the leadership groups they had helped select; committees which included shop partners and neighbors, and whose leadership was both trusted and regularly criticized.

We took up this question while visiting the Peking No. 26 Middle School. The five-year school was divided into two sections: three years of junior and two years of senior level.

---

* Lao and Sheng mention this. Neale Hunter, in *Shanghai Journal* (Boston: Beacon Press, 1969), describes a Shanghai university graduate who refused two different posts commensurate with his training. He simply remained at home.

Not all students completed all five years; more than half the junior middle graduates went directly to work in factories or in the countryside.

We asked a group of teachers and students how they decided who went on to senior middle school. One of the faculty, a member of the school's Revolutionary Committee, replied: "We decide according to the needs of the state." The school, he explained, worked in conjunction with government planning agencies to coordinate job assignments with the manpower needs of various factories and communes. "The students also choose which they want to do," the teacher continued. "The final decision is according to the conditions of each student: how their study is, what their physical condition is, their political progress, and their own choice. The choice and suggestions of the parents are also considered. Some parents want their children to go on in school, some want them to work. We weigh these factors in making a decision. Before the final decision is made we have a discussion among the students and they make their own recommendations. They discuss each other morally, intellectually, and physically. Last year about 30 percent of the junior middle school students went on to senior middle school or to a teachers' school."

Who took the next step in higher education—attending a university or an equivalent-level technical school—was determined somewhat differently. All senior middle-school graduates were expected to go into productive work. After two or three years in a factory, on a commune, or in the army, young people from all backgrounds could apply to go to college. Their applications were first considered by their coworkers; and if they felt they were qualified, the application was then sent to the university for review by teachers, students, and workers there.

Cadres at several factories told us that job assignments within the plant were usually based upon production needs. Special skills or technical training were taken into consideration and individuals could state their preferences. But if someone wanted to be a grinder and the factory already had enough grinders, then that person would be assigned to other work. If cooks were needed, they might become cooks. It depended upon the needs of the whole factory.

One of our guides put this whole question in perspective for us. "You Americans are really funny on this question," Jia Ai-mei laughed good-naturedly. "You're so concerned about 'freedom of choice' of jobs here in China. But what kind of freedom to choose jobs do you really have in your own country?"

She grinned and pointed at Stu, who happened to be wearing a jacket with the United Auto Workers union symbol. "What if you want to work for Ford Motor Company and Ford doesn't want to hire you? What kind of choice is that?"

Good question. We knew from direct experience that choice sometimes meant standing in unemployment lines.

In talking to people in our own country about the question of job choice in China, we have often been asked hypothetical questions: What if a person just wants to sit around and write poetry, can they do that? What if a person really is intent upon becoming a neurosurgeon? Isn't talent stifled and wasted by assigning jobs?

Our friend Jia couldn't conceive of many young people in China so bent upon individualist careers that they would ignore collective needs and socialist principles. She also knew that in the old society the choice of writing poetry or going to school simply hadn't existed for the vast majority of the people; it had been the privilege of the rich few. Thus she didn't speculate about hypothetical undiscovered poets or frustrated surgeons. She dealt with the realities of her society, past and present.

Cops and Guns

Another common question about democracy and freedom in China concerns the police and army. Is China, in effect, a police state?

In the West, socialist countries are often pictured as drab, gray, and humorless places where an Orwellian Big Brother is always watching over your shoulder. Regarding China, we believe such a picture belongs where it came from: back on the fiction shelf.

For example, in terms of outward appearance, the United States is much more of a "police state" than China. We saw nothing in China comparable to the fleets of riot-equipped police cars and not-so-friendly, leather-jacketed shotgun-toting cops which are part of our everyday life in Detroit. The idea of armed security guards in stores, such as we see every time we enter a drug store, supermarket, or public building here in our home town, was difficult for the Chinese to comprehend.

There were Chinese traffic cops, uniformed but unarmed, who directed traffic and enforced regulations. At first we confused their green uniforms with the similar green uniform worn by the People's Liberation Army. Evidently it also confused the Chinese, for on May Day 1972 the traffic police donned distinctive new white jackets and caps.

The only armed guards we saw in China were army and militia sentries on duty at public buildings or other important structures, such as the bridge across the Yangzi River at Wuhan.

It was common to see people in army uniform, unarmed, almost anywhere: in factories, in stores, in parks and zoos, on the streets. The army was integrated into everyday life in a way that was unfamiliar to us, but was nothing new for them. From its origin as a guerrilla army and its growth and survival as "fish in the ocean," the PLA has developed close and friendly relations with the population. It has a remarkably high reputation. We saw this whenever we visited a family with a son or daughter in the army. Most likely a picture of the soldier would be prominently displayed; mothers, fathers, grandmothers, relatives and neighbors were all proud of having kin and friends in the army. Many more young people volunteer for the PLA than are accepted, and being selected was regarded as a high honor. The presence of army personnel in all walks of everyday life produced no military atmosphere.

Democracy in China

Indeed, it was almost the opposite; it broke down barriers and differences between the army and the rest of the population.

The spit-and-polish formal style we usually associate with the military was absent in China. In its place was a relaxed and cordial relationship, almost to the point of mutual adulation, between soldiers and civilians.

The population of China was armed. Most people were taught military skills; schools, factories, and communes all had militia and self-defense units. The army was certainly not trying to keep its skills, or even arms and materials, to itself. Small-gauge shotguns and rifles, available for sporting and hunting, were sold in regular department stores. One Sunday afternoon we saw bird hunters, rifles slung across their backs, cycling along country roads on the outskirts of Guangzhou.

Freedom Is . . .

Whether you agree or disagree with their conclusions, the people of China believe they are free. They believe they enjoy a type of democracy and freedom which protects their fundamental rights.

In terms of international relations, they believe China is running its own affairs for the first time in over a century. In terms of internal affairs, they believe the people of China are controlling their own lives for the first time in history.

Are they brainwashed? Fooled? Intimidated?

We returned home with the inescapable conclusion that they believed these things because their new system has delivered. The average person, the peasant and the worker, has for the first time in memory, been able to:

—eat, not starve
—build a home, not wander about in poverty
—wear decent clothes, not rags
—enjoy family life, not sell children into brothels and slavery
—read, not depend on rich scholars for knowledge

—voice their opinions, not lose their heads for speaking out
—and build the kind of society these basics imply

They had paid for these changes with their blood. However we may judge it, they were determined to protect and preserve their new order.

They did not define their democracy and freedom in abstract, intellectual terms. They simply looked at their own lives, past and present.

7
Philosophy Is No Mystery

Liberate philosophy from the confines of the philosophers' lecture rooms and textbooks, and turn it into a sharp weapon in the hands of the masses.

—Mao Tse-tung

New China was a vast school, a Big Red Schoolhouse with an enrollment of millions. Its classrooms were factories, communes, homes, and neighborhoods. Its faculty and students were workers and peasants; indeed, everyone was a student, everyone was a teacher.

Analysis, discussion, and practical work were the order of the day. Rote memorization was out. "We no longer use the 'force feeding' method of teaching," Lao Liu once commented to us during discussions in Peking. "That may be all right for raising ducks but not for learning!"*

Study was part of everyday life. When the shift ended at the Tianjin No. 1 Machinery Factory workers gathered in groups, poring over technical and political materials. Peasants on a production brigade near Tianjin met several evenings a week, discussing agricultural problems and political philosophy. Retired folks in Peking studied together, searching for ways to make life better in their neighborhoods.

* The delicious and famous roast Peking Duck is prepared from specially force-fed birds.

256   Huan-Ying: Workers' China

It seemed that any group in China that did one activity together also found time to study together. China was reading, arguing, lecturing, listening, and learning. People used books, magazines, and newspapers. They exchanged practical experiences. They raised theoretical and philosophical problems, and they studied Marxism-Leninism and the writings of Mao Tse-tung.

Myth . . .

The phenomenon of mass study, especially the study of Mao Tse-tung's writings, has alternately amused, bewildered, and frightened Western observers. Peasants claimed that Mao's thought was the force which produced greater rice yields and fatter pigs. Reporters laughed. Respected Chinese scientists insisted that Mao's thought was their guide as they successfully reattached severed fingers and developed synthetic insulin. Reporters were puzzled. Millions all over China studied the "Little Red Book"* and labelled Mao's ideas "Mao Tse-tung Thought." Reporters cried in fright: "Dogma!" "Conformity!" "Manipulation!" "Thought control!"

J. Edward Murray is one example. Visiting China in the fall of 1972, Murray heard scores of people speak about Chairman Mao and Mao's ideas. He considered these "standard Maoist replies" and "programmed response." He heard them so often, he reported, that:

> You begin to feel that the programming has produced actual belief. The people seem to believe what they are telling you about Maoism.
>
> Mao's China, in other words, is one more totalitarianism . . . using modern propaganda methods to control and manipulate the thinking and action of 850 million people.
>
> The Mao line is the only one allowed in China. When it

---

* Its proper title is *Quotations from Chairman Mao Tse-tung.*

switches or swerves, turns on the gas or steps on the brake, these millions obey.*

Conrad, a syndicated cartoonist of the *Los Angeles Times*, fleshed out this image in a cartoon published during the time of Nixon's visit to China. Conrad drew a crowd of identically dressed, somber-looking Chinese men walking to and fro, each with his head buried in a little book. In the foreground one man, holding a book labelled *The Thoughts of Chairman Mao*, delivers the punch line: "He must be dead . . . my mind just went blank!"

There are some quite plausible explanations why most Western reporters are unable to comprehend, even minimally, the role of philosophy and study in new China. First, many are simply antagonistic to *what* is being studied. For example, Murray found it incredible that people "seem" to believe Mao's ideas. As socialists we found it quite reasonable for Chinese socialists to actually believe in their own ideology. Perhaps if Murray had talked to people who were reading John Locke, Abraham Lincoln, or Walter Lippmann, he would have found it easier to accept the idea that they believed in their stated philosophical principles.

A second difficulty for many Western reporters stems from the assumption that workers and peasants are incapable of serious philosophical and ideological study. If someone's image of laboring people is that of Archie Bunker or of mindless peasants who only want a daily bowl of rice, then they'll have deep difficulty understanding what's going on in China.

Finally, some people hold that ideology, particularly socialist ideology, is really a rhetorical cover-up for the cruder realities of power politics. They create a barrier between themselves and those who really do study, analyze, and then apply socialist ideology. Thus it seems many ob-

---

* All quotes are from Murray's article, "Why 850 Million People Obey Mao," *Detroit Free Press*, October 29, 1972, p. B-1. To be fair to Murray, we should point out the thrust of his article was how he found this "totalitarianism" of China a "strange contradiction" to its "exciting new morality" of "self-sacrifice and service to others."

servers of China grasp at labels of "dogma" or "thought control" to explain what they either disagree with or cannot comprehend, or both.

... and Reality

We talked to a lot of Chinese people about their study. Many gave similar answers to our questions. Many quoted Mao. Does this mean they were mouthing dogma? Were their minds simply wastelands filled with quotations from the omnipresent Chairman?

We answer with a resounding *NO!*

Their answers typically proceeded from the general to the specific.* Once we got beyond generalizations, after we dug beneath the surface of formalities, we learned that the people we met did not use Mao's thought as ritualistic aphorisms. They were not cynical about their socialist ideology. Many were seriously, and successfully, applying complex philosophic principles to their daily life. In fact, prior to and during the Cultural Revolution, many had fought to get Mao's writings published and more widely circulated. They studied Marxist-Leninist philosophy because they found it useful. They considered their study a first step across the bridge linking theory and practice, a way of putting socialist philosophy at their service.

Many people frankly admitted that during the Cultural Revolution dogmatism and formalism cropped up and that both still remained dangers. But why, our hosts reasoned, should that fact discredit Mao's thought? Philosophy should be analyzed and measured against the yardstick of use, rele-

---

* This tendency to first generalize and then mention specifics is probably another reason for the confusion and inability of Western reporters to deal adequately with the role of study in China. If they did not, or could not, probe deeper than the first step, all they heard were generalizations which, by their nature, tend to sound "standard" and "programmed." We found an honest interest in pursuing the topic resulted in going beyond the general, with fruitful results.

vancy, and application. And Mao's writings easily passed that test.

"We feel that in production we should study Mao Tse-tung Thought," Sun Yu-sui, a turner in the Shenyang No. 1 Machinery Factory explained. "Through study we learn to overcome difficulties in doing technical innovations. We study in our spare time; every evening we study for one-and-a-half hours.

"Workers who study well give lectures to others; technicians teach technical theories; old workers teach techniques they have learned through practical experience.

"Study helps guide our work and our practice," Sun concluded.

The same cooperative spirit flourished in Luoyang, where workers at the tractor plant explained:

"We study Marxism-Leninism and Mao Tse-tung Thought in order to integrate it with practice. Study teaches us to follow the policy of self-reliance.

"For example, in the early days of this factory there was a lot of waste. But after study we corrected our practice and now we save about six tons of material a year. We carry on study to solve the problems of the day."

In Tianjin, workers at the Xin Gang Harbor declared:

"Our study is closely linked with practical work. Before we start any task, we study articles together; we must study hard to learn how to guarantee high quality and make technical innovations to increase our mechanization. We study hard because we know that only since Liberation have we had the chance to study. We all study together and this helps us make greater contributions to development."

In the countryside, peasants on a production brigade near Tianjin told us: "Through study, the members of the commune build up a sense of responsibility to the collective. For example, there are some veteran workers in our brigade who have no children of their own. But young people, after study, decided to take water and wood from their own families to these old people, to make sure that all were taken care of.

"All the members of our commune study conscientiously

and the brigade gives guidance in study. For example, the barefoot doctors in our 'red doctors medical station' have studied 'In Memory of Norman Bethune.' They try to learn from his spirit. One of them is the mother of three children, but when she is called, even if it is the middle of the night, she goes immediately. She will leave her children, if she must, for she feels she should also serve her comrades.

"After we study, our outlook changes, and production increases as well."

Lively discussions were typical of most places we visited. But there were exceptions. Not everyone we met was bubbling over with enthusiastic accounts of study.

"Can you tell us how study has helped in your work?" we asked our hosts at the Tangshan Rolling Stock Plant. Awkward silence. Cadres and workers glanced back and forth, searching for an answer. Finally a young man on the Revolutionary Committee seized the time.

"Our study is not very good," he began. It was the most penetrating of all his remarks. "Formerly the workers didn't study very much, but now we are studying. We have read 'In Memory of Norman Bethune.' Dr. Bethune, you know, came from a great distance, over many seas, to help the Chinese people in their struggle."

He recited a few of the better known passages from Mao's famous eulogy to the revolutionary Canadian martyr, but we never learned how this information was relevant to their factory; we never got beyond the first step of generalizations.

Peasants and cadres at the Lo Kang People's Commune near Guangzhou also had a very unusual response to our inquiries about study. We raised the question toward the end of our visit, when we gathered in a meeting room beside the commune's food processing plant. "Could you tell us about study programs in the commune?" we ventured.

Our hosts urged us to please eat more of the candied fruits and preserved olives spread about on the table.

"Has study been of any practical value to you in your day-to-day life?" we persisted.

Our hosts laughed, and apologized that the fresh lichees

they offered were not of the best quality. It was a bit too early in the season for the really good ones!

We tried a slightly different approach: "Is there anyone here who can give us a personal example of their study?"

One of the commune cadres finally spoke up: "The production team is our basic unit for study. We have study six times a month in the evening."

He then gave an example of a woman in the commune who had been assigned to raise pigs. The gist of his comments was that through Mao's writings she had solved problems on her job and overcome shortcomings.

The example itself wasn't unreasonable. But it rang hollow compared to other discussions. No one in the room (there were ten or twelve present) could, or would, give a personal example of study. They seemed uninterested in the topic and quickly steered the conversation toward questions of production, to facts and figures about rice and fruit which they clearly separated from overtly ideological questions.

Study Methods

China's Big Red Schoolhouse held both regular classes, extension courses, and individual self-study. Many study groups had regular schedules, following six-month or year-long plans for study. But special classes, on-the-spot study sessions, were called when specific problems arose. We frequently saw benches and tables grouped together in corners of factory workshops, the "classrooms" for workers' study. Most often these factory classrooms included blackboards, but they were not blank slate surfaces. Most were filled with information and news in bulletin-board type display. Some had quite elaborate art work and drawings done in pastel chalks. Topics ranged from internal workshop issues to international affairs.

"Learn from Taching" was the theme of one blackboard newspaper in the Zhengzhou No. 3 Textile Mill.* One of the

* Taching is an oilfield that was developed from barren land in just three years. Just as Tachai is a model for agriculture, Taching was hailed

factory's worker-artists had sketched several workers, books in hand, standing in front of the Taching Oil Refinery. There were columns of information about the achievements of Taching and a quote from Mao's call to the whole country to follow the example of the Taching oil workers.

Workers in the Zhengzhou Textile Machinery Manufacturing Factory had received a letter from an intellectual who had recently spent a period of time working in their plant. The letter had been carefully copied on a blackboard in his former workshop. Additional blackboards carried news of other workshops, mentioned achievements of different sections of the factory, and posted public announcements.

We visited the Shenyang Transformer Factory just one day after they had hosted a visit of Cambodia's Prince Sihanouk. Blackboards throughout the factory were filled with information about Cambodia. Workers had obviously "boned up" in preparation for his visit. Some displays included multi-colored maps of Cambodia; others had short histories of Cambodia and of all Indochina. Slogans of solidarity hung on the walls and across aisles.

May Day in China is an occasion for both celebration and education, something we learned during a visit to a small district-run factory in Peking. Workshops were grouped around a small courtyard where two large blackboards had been erected. Each blackboard had a little roof to protect the chalk displays from rain and winter weather. It was May 5th and both were still filled with information about May Day. There was an explanation about the May Day holiday, "International Labor Day," describing it as an occasion to display working-class solidarity the world over. Another section outlined the origin of the May Day holiday from labor struggles in the United States, specifically an 1886 strike in Chicago.*

---

by Mao Tse-tung as a "red banner" for industry, a model of successful hard struggle and self-reliance.

   * Hundreds of thousands of workers across the United States rallied and struck on May 1, 1886, demanding the working day be reduced to eight hours. Because of police attacks a protest demonstration was

Study Materials: Positive and Negative

> *It is only through repeated education by positive and negative examples, and by making comparisons and contrasts, that revolutionary parties and revolutionary people can temper themselves, reach maturity and gain assurance of victory. Those who belittle the role of teachers by negative example are not thoroughgoing dialectical materialists.*
>
> —Mao Tse-tung, 1967

What did people study?

Answers almost always included the Marxist-Leninist classics, the works of Mao, and some contemporary areas of study, like "Learn from Tachai" and "Learn from Taching." This was no surprise to us. We had expected that workers and peasants in socialist China would be studying Marxism-Leninism. These were, to the Chinese, "positive" study materials.

But "negative examples" were also used in study. Newspaper or magazine articles about problems at particular communes or factories were study material. History, and mistakes made during the revolutionary struggle, were examined. Sometimes examples were taken from the foreign press.

Perhaps the most graphic instance we encountered of learning from negative example was at Peking University. We rounded a corner in the university library and stopped abruptly in front of a bookcase crammed with contemporary American political science works. Harold Lasswell and the Council on Foreign Relations beamed out at us from the shelves. Several of the books had been published in 1970 or 1971, and were obviously acquired since the Cultural Revolution.

---

called for Haymarket Square in Chicago on May 4. Police dispersed that rally, too, but someone—there is evidence it was a hired provocateur—threw a bomb into their ranks and several were killed. Several Chicago labor leaders were railroaded through the courts; four were hanged. Since then May Day demonstrations have served to mark international working-class solidarity. The holiday is celebrated officially in socialist countries and is observed by strikes and demonstrations in most of the world. It is probably least observed in the United States, the country of its origin.

"Where did you get these books?" we asked, a bit surprised. "And why did you buy them? After all, these writers are openly opposed to socialism. Their analysis is the opposite of yours."

Our hosts laughed and explained that several of the books had been obtained from British publishers. Others had been purchased in Hong Kong bookstores, although at inflated prices. "These writers have two things in their books," one student commented. "Fact and analysis. We use the facts; we discard their analysis."

"Our students learn which ideas are wrong by reading them," a young faculty member added. "You can only know how to combat wrong ideas if you actually read them. Chairman Mao teaches us that we can learn even from reactionaries. If we shut ourselves up in a room, then how can we help the world revolution? In order to criticize a viewpoint we must first know what it is. Mao has said that if we ignore these 'teachers by negative example' then we are not acting as true Marxist-Leninists. Our students are armed with Marxism-Leninism. They can learn to tell right from wrong. In this way they will do their work well after graduation."

Another teacher, a Red Guard during the Cultural Revolution, commented: "At the beginning of the revolution in education some of us were afraid of these types of books. Some wanted to get rid of them. But this was due to ultra-left influence. We discussed it and decided that we should use these materials. We follow the idea: 'Study things past to serve present-day use; make things foreign serve China.'"

Study in China was used in several different ways. Although examples often fall into more than one area, we have broken them down into five topics. We would like to give some concrete examples of each.

World Outlook: Promoting Socialist Values

> *Some loads are light, some heavy. Some people prefer the light to the heavy; they pick the light and leave the heavy to others. That is not a good attitude. Some comrades are different; they leave ease and comfort to others and carry the heavy loads themselves; they are the first to bear hardships, the last to enjoy comforts. They are good comrades. We should all learn from their communist spirit.*
>
> —Mao Tse-tung, 1945

The Chinese were building a socialist society, a society which relies on group, not individual, endeavor. The old individualistic concept of "every man for himself" should give way, they believed, to class solidarity, to the collectivist "all for one and one for all." This change from one "world outlook" to another is a long, difficult process. In the old society individualistic attitudes were necessary for survival. But in socialist China individualism undermined efforts to advance together, collectively.

Textile workers in Zhengzhou gave us an example. A young woman in their factory had been skipping night shift work. She preferred to be with her family and left the necessary but unpleasant task of night shift for others to do. Workers said this was a problem of her world outlook, or class orientation. The problem was solved, they said, through study and group discussion.

Zen Jiu-lan, a young worker in the Shenyang Transformer Factory, told us about a similar problem in her world outlook:

"When I first came to the factory, my work wasn't very good," she began. "Sometimes I ran into difficulties. We worked on large units, and it was very hard labor. At the end of the day I was very tired. I wanted to have an easier job.

"But I studied with my work group. We read 'Serve the People' and 'The Foolish Old Man Who Removed the Mountains.' I came to see that my job was part of the revolution, and I was determined then to fear no sacrifice. My consciousness was raised. Now I try my best to overfulfill my job. Now I am more used to my job and I don't get so tired.

"And relations among the workers in my workshop are also improved," she added with a smile.

Zen explained that taking it easy meant someone else would have to work harder. If she avoided a hard job she put more work on the shoulders of fellow workers, of class brothers and sisters. She pointed out that study had helped her build an understanding of group needs, something essential if their collective society was to function equitably.

The Individual's Role in Society

Chinese study groups dealt with other aspects of class orientation, or class consciousness. One frequently mentioned to us manifested itself in what we might call a type of job dissatisfaction.

Some people sincerely wanted to work for the common good, but they didn't like their particular jobs. They felt they could contribute more to socialism, they could serve others better, in a different, more skilled job which, they believed, used their talents better.

Dao Su-lun, a young cook at the East Is Red Auto Factory, gave us one example:

"I graduated middle school in 1966 and came to work here in February 1968," she began. "When I went to work in the kitchen I wasn't very happy. After all, I had ten years of schooling. Cooking seemed too simple, too plain. I didn't like my job. I kept hoping that I would get to change it. I wanted something with a more brilliant future. I wanted to work in the factory itself and learn techniques in the factory workshops.

"The older cooks in the kitchen knew something was bothering me, and they asked me what was wrong. When I explained, they talked to me about their sufferings in the old society. They led me in studying the 'Three Constantly Read Articles,' especially 'Serve the People.' I was deeply moved by 'Serve the People,' especially by Zhang Si-de's boundless loyalty to the people.* This was why he was able to do his job well and why he would do even very simple jobs.

"I compared my thinking with Zhang Si-de's. I looked down on my job; he did not. This showed that I didn't really mean to serve the people wholeheartedly.

"So I took Zhang Si-de as a model. I discovered that real happiness is to serve the people. Although the job as a cook is a common job, it is also a job that is part of the revolution. In my job I can give good food to the workers in the shop. They can then produce more, and thus we all serve the revolution in China and the revolution in the whole world."

Dao's example raises questions: Was group study simply used to soothe ruffled feathers? Was it a sop to keep her content and in place? A pacifier to get her to accept a menial task?

We don't think so. Dao and others we met took their socialist principles seriously. They truly felt all jobs should be considered important; no honest labor should be looked down upon. Every job had a "brilliant future" since all were a necessary part of building their new socialist society. The key to Dao's situation was this: though Dao looked down on her work, no one else did. The other cooks were proud of their contribution to society. The problem was not Dao's job; it was her attitude toward work. Even in pursuit of the noble goal of "serving the people" she had been primarily concerned about her status, her career. Study with fellow workers had helped her change some of those outdated attitudes.

We believe Dao Su-lun had also romanticized working in a

---

* Zhang Si-de was a soldier who had taken part in the Long March and who was later assigned to make charcoal in a Liberated Area in Shanxi Province. On September 5, 1944, he was killed when a charcoal kiln collapsed. A memorial meeting was held and Mao delivered the now-famous speech "Serve the People." Mao emphasized that Zhang Si-de had died in the service of the people and thus was a model for all to follow.

factory.* If she had gone to work on the shop floor, but kept her old attitudes, she still would have become bored and dissatisfied. This is exactly what happened to another young worker we met at the Shenyang Transformer Factory:

"I first came to this factory in 1969, after graduating from middle school. At that time my only thought was to get reeducation from the older workers. Like the other new workers, I was in high spirits but I didn't have much practical experience. I wanted to produce as much as possible. I started work doing grinding and at first I was happy with my job. It was something new to learn.

"But in a few months I had totally mastered the job and it became routine. After a while, doing the same grinding every hour every day, I started to think that this work was too ordinary. I wanted a more skilled job.

"I studied 'Serve the People' and Zhang Si-de was an example for me. He considered his job as part of the revolution. Then I read 'In Memory of Norman Bethune.' There, Chairman Mao says that everyone is capable of having Comrade Bethune's spirit.

"I learned that every unit I make is a part of a transformer and these transformers are sent all over China and the rest of the world, too. I make my contribution by making my small pieces.

"In the past three years I have learned much from the older workers' attitude and spirit of work. Now I understand what I am working for, and I'm satisfied with my work."

A young woman at the No. 3 Textile Mill in Zhengzhou summed up her experience:

* We found a number of cases where "educated youth" had romanticized factory work. Socialist principles exalted labor and laboring people. But some youths tended to look at factory work in a naive, idealized way. Their eagerness and desire to become workers clouded day-to-day realities of hard and oftentimes boring work, and laid the basis for disillusionment. This, by the way, is not unique to China. We are familiar with the syndrome because it has also afflicted many student radicals in the United States.

"I worked in the preparation department of this mill; I'm a middle school graduate and came to work here in 1968. At first, I didn't like my job because I had done so much study; I looked down on my work. I thought that with all my years in school, I should do better work than this. I thought I could contribute more elsewhere. So my work was not very good; I didn't work very well.

"Some of the older workers here in the factory talked with me and studied with me. They reminded me of my class background, how my parents had been poor peasants who had gone begging in the streets. They talked of their own past lives, how men and women had worked twelve hours a day and more, and how they had had to sell their sons and daughters.

"The older workers said, 'There are millions of jobs in our country, but all of them serve the revolution. All of them should be done well.' They said it was our international duty to work hard and to help others.

"They set an example for me in their own lives. They came and helped me with my washing and mending. We all studied together, and they took an interest in my education. I was deeply moved by their actions and this class education. I was determined then to do my job well, and I changed in my work.

"In December 1969 I joined the Communist Party," she concluded. Other workers proudly noted that she was also a representative on the factory's Revolutionary Committee. They added that she had been very active as a Red Guard during the Cultural Revolution.

We were impressed by the self-confidence and pride of the young workers who told these stories. Theirs was not a selfish pride about individual successes, but something that came from viewing themselves as a vital link in a collective chain. Their fellow workers clearly respected them for their change. Philosophical and political study had helped them understand their role in society, why they were working, and what they worked for.

Technical Innovations: The Creativity of the Masses

How can the study of philosophy promote technical innovations? Mao's writings and other Marxist-Leninist works do not give blueprints or designs. They do not deal with technical aspects of the hard sciences. Then why, in China, are thousands of technical and scientific advances credited to the thought of Mao Tse-tung? Is it formality, a political icing on a more practical, scientific cake? No. We concluded that it's not the icing, but rather the yeast. Study of Mao's works, and other socialist writings, had literally given rise to tens of thousands of technical innovations, ranging from cleaner pig sties to computer-controlled lathes.

"Through the study of Chairman Mao's works we learn to solve practical problems," Song Hun-jun, an old worker at the Dong Feng Watch Factory, explained. "We have studied 'On Practice'; this teaches us to rely on our own efforts. Practical experience is very important and Mao stresses self-reliance.

"We try to link the philosophic with the practical; we are determined to develop industry by our own efforts."

During our visit to the Red Flag Embroidery Factory in Tianjin we saw a new innovation: a unique three-headed sewing machine. One woman ran the machine; she operated the head in the middle and every stitch she made was duplicated by identical heads on the right and left. It was a simple, logical idea and had greatly eased the burdensome, repetitive task of mass-producing embroidery. But this innovation, we learned, came through struggle. Its creation was closely tied to workers' study. As a young worker in the factory explained:

"This three-headed sewing machine was developed only through repeated struggle against erroneous ideas. When it was first suggested many workers said that it should never be done. But others of us felt our productivity was not high enough to meet the needs of revolution and it was important to develop such a machine. We followed Chairman Mao's teaching that the Chinese people can catch up with the rest of the world.*

"We began experimenting, but we soon faced problems. We studied Chairman Mao's teaching that 'the emergence of any new thing has to follow many twists and turns. It won't do to have clear sailing; if we did, we wouldn't be tempered.'** We said to ourselves, 'If we want to make revolution, we must march forward against difficulties. We know there are tigers in the mountains, but we insist on going to the mountains.'

"So we persisted in our experiments. We learned from Mao's spirit, through his writings, and we all worked enthusiastically. At first the three pieces the machine produced were not all the same; some had defects. To solve this problem we followed Mao's teaching that we should look for the primary contradiction in the machine.† After we found the

---

* "Not only can the Chinese people live without begging alms from the imperialists, they will live a better life than in the imperialist countries." (Mao Tse-tung, "Report to the Second Plenary Session of the Seventh Central Committee of the Communist Party of China," in *Selected Works*, Vol. IV, p. 374) The people we talked to did not believe China had yet caught up in terms of wealth and technical development. But they believed they could in the future because for the first time in their history they had a social and economic system capable of such growth.

** "There are still many obstacles and difficulties along the road of revolution.... There are no straight roads in the world; we must be prepared to follow a road which twists and turns and not try to get things on the cheap." (Mao Tse-tung, "On the Chungking Negotiations," in *Selected Works*, Vol. IV, pp. 59-60)

"New things always have to experience difficulties and setbacks as they grow. It is sheer fantasy to imagine that the cause of socialism is all plain sailing and easy success, without difficulties and setbacks or the exertion of tremendous efforts." (Mao Tse-tung, "On the Correct Handling of Contradictions Among the People," in *Selected Readings*, p. 452)

† "If in any process there are a number of contradictions, one of them must be the principal contradiction playing the leading and decisive role, while the rest occupy a secondary and subordinate position.

principal contradiction, we could make the machine more precise, and we were successful in developing and perfecting it.

"This machine raised our productivity more than two times. But after it was produced, we again held discussions. Some of us asked why we had not seen the problem earlier. Others asked why some had been defeated and felt we could never solve the problems. We thought this showed there were times when we had not been truly dedicated to serving the people. At some points we had lacked faith in the masses. So we studied Mao's teaching that correct ideas come from the people, and we learned the importance of social practice."*

A worker turned engineer at the Shenyang Transformer Factory summed up how study had helped in his work:

"We follow the principle of self-reliance. Chairman Mao teaches us that we can't stop learning new things, we must never stop developing.

"After study, we have carried out many technical innovations. We have tried and succeeded in building a new type of transformer without oil boxes. This was possible only with the help of older workers who had much practical experience. This has reduced the weight of the transformer by 40 percent.

"We study Marxism-Leninism Mao Tse-tung Thought to develop the spirit of 'dare to think, dare to do.' "

Therefore, in studying any complex process in which there are two or more contradictions, we must devote every effort to finding its principal contradiction. Once this principal contradiction is grasped, all problems can be readily solved." (Mao Tse-tung, "On Contradictions," in *Selected Works*, Vol. I, p. 332)

* "Where do correct ideas come from? Do they drop from the skies? Are they innate in the mind? No. They come from social practice, and from it alone." (Mao Tse-tung, "Where Do Correct Ideas Come From?" in *Selected Readings*, p. 502)

Solving Problems

Of course it is necessary to read books, but by itself it does not solve problems. One must study the actual situation, examine practical experiences and concrete material. . . .
—Mao Tse-tung, 1957

Disputes, problems, different opinions, and disagreements were as much a part of life in China as almost any other country. It was not one big happy family; it was a country in struggle.

Philosophic ideas had helped resolve problems at the Pottery Research Institute in Tangshan. Hao Qing-zhai, Chairman of their Revolutionary Committee, explained:

"In the past, we sometimes had problems. When a question came up, different people would have different opinions, but we didn't know how to handle our differences. We had lots of arguments; we never could reach unity. So we studied 'On Contradiction' and we came to see that it is natural to have differences of opinion. That's normal; in fact, it's a good thing and we shouldn't be afraid of it.*

"After we studied 'On Contradiction' we changed our approach. Now, whenever an important question comes up we call a mass meeting. We try to involve as many people as possible in the discussion. Everyone talks and there are always lots of different opinions and lots of disagreements. We understand that we can learn from each other. We work out our differences through discussion and we now can get unity on the questions we face."

Joint study, the simple act of regularly sitting down together, provided a forum where problems could be raised and investigated. The Marxist-Leninist writings studied encouraged the ability to identify contradictions and to learn how to handle them.

* "Every difference in men's concepts should be regarded as reflecting an objective contradiction. Objective contradictions are reflected in subjective thinking, and this process constitutes the contradictory movement of concepts, pushes forward the development of thought, and ceaselessly solves problems in man's thinking." (Mao Tse-tung, "On Contradiction," *Selected Works*, Vol. I, p. 317)

Affairs of State

You should pay attention to state affairs and carry the great proletarian cultural revolution through to the end.
—Mao Tse-tung, 1966

Study helped people learn about national and world affairs. Here, too, the emphasis was on uniting theory and practice. Materials were studied to understand contemporary events and thus to set priorities in actual work.

A veteran woman cadre at the Tangshan Rolling Stock Plant told us of her study of *The Communist Manifesto*:

"Before the Cultural Revolution, we studied theory but we didn't always combine theory and practice. I had studied *The Communist Manifesto* before Liberation. Then, I had one understanding of it. I knew we had to make revolution. After Liberation, I studied it again and expanded my understanding. I began to learn something about state power. But during the Cultural Revolution I studied it again and then I realized that even after the proletariat controls the power of the state, we must still struggle against old ideas and private ideology. We must learn to carry the revolution through to the end and we must remold our outlook, even after we have state power."

Students at Peking University said they had turned to Lenin's writings on imperialism and national liberation when they investigated the conflict between India and Pakistan.

"We arm ourselves with a Marxist-Leninist viewpoint and the viewpoint of Chairman Mao when we study," one student explained. "Our emphasis is on the current movements in the world today. For example, we studied the conflict on the subcontinent. It was very complicated.

"We studied Lenin's points on national self-determination. The Soviet Union says they supported the 'right of self-determination' for Bengalis. But we think their point is ridiculous. We must first view the situation in relation to imperialism. After study we understood the fallacies of the USSR argument on 'self-determination,' and we understood how their position actually benefited the two super-powers, the U.S. and the USSR.

"What happened there [East Pakistan, now Bangladesh] was not determined by themselves [Bengalis], but by other countries.

"We understand we must oppose Soviet expansion and support Pakistan against expansion and aggression."

Several people we met mentioned having studied Mao's "On the Chungking Negotiations" when they discussed Nixon's visit to China.* They said the situation was now different, but strategic principles mentioned in the Chungking essay were useful in evaluating what China's attitude toward the United States should be.

We were given another example of applying study to current affairs in Hong Kong. There we met Mr. Lai, who worked with the China Travel Service branch in Hong Kong. He chatted with us one evening, talking about his work in Hong Kong and how the Hong Kong branch of CTS had dealt in the past with requests of Americans to visit China.

"For years," he began, "we knew the United States was our enemy and no Americans could come to China. Lots of people [Americans] came into our office, asking to go to China, but we always said no. And sometimes we didn't say it very politely," he chuckled.

"We didn't really like having Americans come in, and we especially disliked those young people with hair down to here," he pointed to his shoulders and grimaced, "where you couldn't tell if it was boy or girl.

"But then Edgar Snow came and talked with Chairman Mao. We all read that talk and studied it, and we realized that Americans would soon be visiting China. We knew that they should come in theory, but it was hard to put that into practice.

"When the American ping-pong team was invited, most of us didn't think they would accept. But they did come and I went to the airport to meet them. I still had to swallow hard

* "On the Chungking Negotiations" was written by Mao in 1945 to explain why the Communist Party was willing to sit down and negotiate with Chiang Kai-shek at that time.

when I greeted them. There was a lump in my throat, and it was very hard to be friendly. But now, after a year, things are very different. There are many more Americans coming to visit, many more. And we understand the question better now. We have kept up with our study."

It was hard to believe that Mr. Lai could have been anything but friendly. He was an honest, outgoing, jovial middle-aged man who had lived in Hong Kong since his youth. Although the employees of the Hong Kong CTS branch lived in an environment vastly different from workers in the People's Republic, they, too, took time to study, trying to combine their theory and practice.

8
Principles of Chinese Socialism

The motor-force of new China was socialist theory, Marxism-Leninism. China's practical application of that theory represented five decades of revolutionary experience, and over the years several shorthand political slogans have emerged, capsulizing fundamental philosophic and political principles of the new society. Six particularly impressed us: (1) Politics in Command; (2) Serve the People; (3) Rely on the Masses; (4) The Yenan Spirit of Self-Reliance and Hard Struggle; (5) Combine the Old and New; and (6) Criticism and Self-Criticism.

What did these principles mean in everyday life? We learned about them through visits, conversations, and also through direct personal struggles.

Politics in Command

Only by giving prominence to proletarian politics, ... putting politics in command of technique ... can we deal with various complicated situations, overcome all sorts of difficulties, and successfully fulfill our tasks.

—*Hsueh Hsiang-tung*[*]

---

[*] Hsueh Hsiang-tung, "Dialectics Applied in Driving Safely," in *Selected Essays on the Study of Philosophy by Workers, Peasants, and Soldiers* (Peking, 1971), pp. 49-50.

Politics in command? To most people in our country "politics" is a dirty word. Politicians are liars, scoundrels and fat cats living off our tax money. Politics means smoke-filled rooms and cigar-chewing bosses or, more recently, slickly packaged Madison Avenue candidates. Politics is a game, a competitive sport where winners divide the spoils and everyone is out for his or her own "piece of the pie."

Politics meant something quite different to the Chinese. Politics meant, first of all, "proletarian politics"; that is, understanding society in class terms. To "put politics in command" meant putting collective interests first, placing individual or self-interests second. It also meant politics should command technique, not technique determine policy. Political perspective was considered fundamental.

"Not to have a correct political point of view is like having no soul," Mao has argued.* New China, in this sense, has been struggling to become a country of eight hundred million souls.

For example, workers at the Wuhan Sewing Machine Factory put "politics in command" when determining wages. They explicitly excluded skill as a criterion for higher wages. For them, politics in command meant emphasizing socialist, collective consciousness and group cooperation.

An older woman at a district-run factory in Peking talked about how she had overcome difficulties when her factory began producing more complicated equipment. Her role as a workshop leader was an inspiring example of workers putting politics in command.

"When we decided to manufacture electronic lathes, I became the leader of the workshop that was to do electric wiring. But I had very little schooling; very few of us had much education at all. I was no technician. I couldn't even read blueprints. I just couldn't see where to start in learning to do wiring.

"I went to the Party Branch in our factory and they en-

---

* Mao Tse-tung, "On the Correct Handling of Contradictions Among the People," 1957, in *Selected Readings*, p. 459.

couraged me. They suggested that I study Chairman Mao's article 'On Practice.' When I read it, I learned that skills do not come by nature. Every skill is learned through practice. No one is born a technician. My comrades encouraged me. They said: 'Remember, illiterate workers have built high buildings in Peking!' " She gestured toward the window, much as her fellow workers had probably done.

"I got a little more confidence and tried to do the work. It was hard for me to copy the blueprints. Some of the workers in my section were middle school graduates. They used a compass to make circles, but I had never even seen such a thing before. I watched what they did and figured out my own methods. I got a round box and used that to draw circles. These workers encouraged me; they said my circles looked even better than theirs. But they used symbols on the blueprints that I didn't know, like A, B, C. So I made symbols of my own; A was like a ladder with something on it; B was like a 3 with a line next to it; C was half a pancake. I made my own copy of the blueprint.

"No one else could read my blueprints, but they worked for me!" she chuckled.

"But I also had problems. One man in our group had been to school and was an electrical worker. At first he looked down on me. He said the wiring could only be done by a trained electrician. He told me I should study the blueprint more, and I shouldn't try doing any wiring. He said I would only make mistakes.

"But the more I studied the blueprint, the more confused I got. I thought of what I had read in 'On Practice.' I thought that if I started to do the wiring I could learn as I worked. I went to the Party Branch and told them what I wanted to do. They supported me. They encouraged me to go ahead, and they told the electrical worker he shouldn't make fun of me. Then I tried to wire up my first panel. When I got it done everything was right except for one small wire. So I took it to the electrical worker and asked him to show me what was missing. He learned then not to make fun of me and he began to respect my spirit.

"Now I can do all the wiring on the panels. There are many other veteran workers like me who have never been to school. We sometimes find it difficult to learn new techniques. But we give priority to practice, and we learn from each other."

Her story was actually a graphic account of several socialist principles. Her concrete application of philosophic principles was a model of combining theory with practice. The encouragement and advice given by fellow workers, including those in the local Party Branch, indicated the positive power of collective support.

But perhaps most important, this incident illustrated what it meant to "put politics in command." The electrician, technically qualified, had not been chosen as workshop leader. The older, less educated woman was selected for political reasons: her class perspective, her ability to work with others, her determination to tackle and surmount difficulties. Putting politics in command had improved the collective, made it a more cohesive workshop, and ultimately upgraded the technique of individuals and the whole work group.

Politics in command had other meanings. We learned something about the importance of keeping politics in command from personal experiences.

Yu was a young, outgoing student type and a translator for CITS in Tianjin. He was also rather brash, overbearing, and condescending toward workers and peasants.

Yu was well-meaning; he was very proud of his ability to speak English. He seized every opportunity to learn new English words, plying us for the names of musical instruments during cultural performances and asking about machinery and technical terms in factories. But he carried this too far, frequently ignoring others. Yu's task, his political responsibility, was to facilitate the discussion between us and local workers and peasants. But thinking only of himself, Yu sometimes turned visits into an English dialogue, leaving people we were visiting out in the cold. More than once we urged Yu to wait until the visit was over to raise detailed linguistic questions. This helped a little.

The problem of Yu's attitude came to a head during our visit to a production brigade near Tianjin. From the moment of arrival it was clear Yu didn't mix well with the countryside.

We stopped to talk with an elderly couple, Wang Zhou-pin and Zhan Zhe-fen, in their home. Wang greeted us warmly and we chatted about their family and the local brigade. We then asked Wang, as we did almost everyone we met, to tell us about his philosophic and political study. Yu translated our question, beginning to giggle. We looked at each other blankly, not understanding what was so funny. Then Wang replied and Yu burst out laughing. He turned, and between gasps of laughter, informed us:

"It's so funny! You're asking him about study, but he's illiterate! He can't even read!"

We were stunned. We didn't find it funny at all. Neither did Wang, who sank back in his chair, obviously embarrassed by Yu's open ridicule. We knew it was appropriate to ask Wang about study, even if he was illiterate. Just a few days earlier in Peking we had met a sixty-five-year-old grandmother, also illiterate, who was a leader in her local study group. But because of Yu's insensitivity it became impossible to discuss the question with Wang. We're sure Wang did study; in fact he made some hesitant remarks to that effect after Yu's outburst. But the damage had been done. We tried to apologize for Yu's behavior, but depending upon Yu for the translation made it an awkward, if not futile, effort. We reluctantly took our leave.

Yu's behavior raised questions in our own minds. Why should he find it funny that some elderly people were illiterate? Didn't he understand that oppression and poverty in the old society had prevented many people from learning to read? Didn't he realize that in new China even illiterate people studied? If Yu had put "politics in command" he'd have understood the legacy of past oppression and what the new society was doing about it. If he had put politics in command he would have respected, not ridiculed, Wang.

We encountered similar problems a week later in Peking. Fu Bing-zhan accompanied us on a visit to Foreign Languages Printing House. Like Yu the week before, Fu became so intent on expanding his English vocabulary that he ignored his job as translator. He started answering our questions himself, not even bothering to translate them into Chinese so our factory hosts could offer their opinions. This was more than annoying or impolite, for Fu also gave answers we knew were wrong. Workers and cadres wanted to talk with us, and we with them, but we were all somewhat stymied by Fu's self-interest.

Late that afternoon we gathered in a factory meeting room for further questions and discussion. We asked about the Cultural Revolution, and several workers eagerly responded. Two men, both vice-chairmen of the plant's Revolutionary Committee, talked at great length about changes in administration, the expansion of technical innovations, and the importance of Mao's ideological leadership. Then a woman worker joined us. She got no further than a sentence or two when Fu abruptly cut her off. He turned to us and explained: "I told her she was being repetitive and that you have many questions and not much time. She shouldn't repeat what others have said!"

We sat there, quietly furious. We encouraged the woman to continue, assuring Fu we were, indeed, interested in what she had to say. But it was too late; she added a few more words and stopped, obviously intimidated by the situation.

We later criticized Fu, arguing that his basic error had been failure to put "politics in command." He had thought he knew better than the factory workers what was important. But why shouldn't workers speak for themselves? If workers repeated each other or evaded questions we also learned from that. It did not help, we argued, for Fu to attempt to orchestrate discussions. If he had put politics in command, he would have let the workers speak for themselves, and he would have been confident they could do so! There was an additional factor, we continued. He had felt it appropriate to interrupt when a woman was speaking but had let two men speak at length uninterrupted. What kind of politics on women's equality did this imply?

Our experiences with Zheng as translator were in sharp contrast to the episodes with Yu and Fu. Zheng never tired of letting others speak for themselves. He was dedicated to helping us learn from the people of his country and this was, after all, the basic purpose of our trip. Zheng's command of English was not as polished as either Yu's or Fu's, but we had better discussions with workers and peasants when he translated. He did not look down on others who had less education than he; he did not assume he could give better answers. His ability to put political concerns first more than compensated for his lesser technique. Conversely, Yu and Fu had a greater grasp of technique, but this became meaningless when they failed to consider the overall political situation.

When we raised criticisms of Fu and Yu, they agreed such problems came from thinking of self, and of technique, first. They forgot the political role a translator plays. Fu admitted that while "politics in command" was an admirable principle, it was a constant struggle to put into practice. We were to learn that through direct experience. During our trip some things came to light which challenged our own ability to "put politics in command." Let us give one example where we had to struggle against putting "self" rather than "politics" in command:

We were occasionally asked to sing, most typically after a workers' group had performed for us. This was a cultural expression of friendship, a mutual and reciprocal gesture, evidently traditional in China. Janet has always loved music. Stu, however, can hardly keep a tune and trembles at the thought of singing in front of others. He managed to stumble along on the chorus of a song or two for workers at the Wuhan Sewing Machine Factory and at the Nanniwan May 7th Cadre School. But a real trauma came at the Central Institute for Nationalities in Peking.

We attended an informal cultural performance at the Institute. Students of different national minorities had put together a collection of songs and dances for a visiting delegation of Third World activists from the United States. We were invited to sit in. But the informal evening turned out to be a bit more formal than we had expected. The performance was in the Institute's auditorium, which must have held close to one thousand, and it was packed when we arrived!

Jia Ai-mei came with us to translate. She read off items from the evening's printed program while we found our seats, and Stu paled when she hit item No. 7: "Performance by Two American Friends." Us!

It had been one thing to sing in truly informal situations, for small groups of workers. But now we were being asked to get up on stage in front of almost one thousand people. Stu began to think only of how he could get out of performing. Jia noticed Stu was rattled and quickly assured him we could bow out of a public performance if we wished. She offered to explain to our hosts at the Institute. She pointed out the program was intended to express international solidarity, and no one wished to make us uncomfortable. Anyway, she added, other guests in the audience were going to perform.

Stu was ready to accept Jia's gracious escape hatch. But Janet wouldn't agree. She urged Stu to sing. The evening was to promote friendship, and if we didn't take part, she argued, we would sabotage that goal. After all, why didn't Stu want to perform? He was afraid he would sound bad; he was embarrassed he couldn't sing well. He was putting "self" in command. He was thinking only of his feelings. But did the audience really care what he sounded like? Singing was just a symbol. The important thing was to take part and do our best, even if it was off-key. If we refused to perform, there were one thousand Chinese people in the audience who wouldn't understand why. All they would know was we had declined to demonstrate our friendship.

Janet's prodding took effect, and Stu agreed to put "politics in command." He sang. Actually it was less painful than anticipated. We sang "Solidarity Forever" with little trouble and then launched into the "Internationale." The audience recognized the first few bars and took to their feet, singing in Chinese. The auditorium rang as we all sang the same song, each in our own language. It was a thrilling feeling, and we practically floated back to our seats.

The slogan "politics in command" also had deep implications for the whole direction of China's economy:
How should production be motivated in a socialist society?
How should personal income be determined?
Are wages and material incentives politically consistent with China's socialist goals?
The role of material incentives under socialism has long been a topic of controversy. Analysts of all stripes and colors have offered opinions and profundities on the question for decades. One current school of thought—represented internationally by leading Russian economists and in China by the Liu Shao-chi line—argues that bonuses, material rewards, private plots of land, profit-motivated administration of factories, and other types of monetary incentives are a necessary and appropriate part of a socialist economy. Many Western commentators, particularly those ideologically antagonistic to socialism, gleefully pounce on such admissions of "capitalist" methods and declare that this reveals nothing less than the utopian futility of socialism itself.

We heard a third position argued in China: material incentives were indeed capitalist forms and basically antagonistic to socialist principles. Moreover, it was argued, in the present stage of China's socialist development they were actual roadblocks to increased production and economic growth. This conclusion, we learned, had not sprung forth from a desire for ideological purity. It was not a rhetorical facade covering up harsher economic realities. It came from the shop floor, from practice.

During the Cultural Revolution the question of material incentives was debated at length, in a mass way. Literally millions of workers and peasants took part and, judging from the people we met, they arrived at a general consensus on the subject: politics, not profit—the collective, not the individual—should be in command.

Su Chuan-chen, an electrician at Foreign Languages Printing House, summed it up best:

"Material incentives were like poison in our minds."

This "poison" had taken several forms during the 1950s and 1960s, varying between countryside and city and from factory to factory. Its common feature was tying personal income directly to job production and personal performance.

Material incentives had meant specific bonuses and extra income beyond regular wages. Incentives were given selectively. Bonuses, intended to stimulate production, had been given for such things as quantity and quality of work, overproduction, attendance, and type of job. Bonus systems had sometimes been elaborate and extensive. One Peking factory reported their old system had included twenty-eight different types of bonuses, including one for "comfort" for unlucky workers who did not qualify in other categories! Some factories had determined how much and what was to be produced solely by the yardstick of revenue; this, too, was considered another form of material incentive. Piecework systems of pay of any sort, whether individual or by the workshop or factory, were also regarded as material incentives.

In the countryside, material incentives had often taken the form of extending private plots of land, encouraging individual and family handicrafts, and promoting private trade to sell and distribute goods from these sources. Sometimes the work-point system in production brigades and production teams had been used as additional material incentives.*

But why were material incentives considered so poisonous? What grievances did Chinese workers and cadres raise in their

---

* Collective ownership in the communes was by its structure closer to material incentives than the state-owned industrial sector of the economy. Personal income on communes was tied to productivity in a direct way; wages in state-owned factories could be removed from such a direct link to productivity. The Chinese spoke of state ownership as a

condemnation of material incentives? We listened to many opinions and examples.

Zei Zao-huai, a cadre at the Tianjin No. 1 Machinery Factory, explained how profits had been placed before social needs:

"Before the Cultural Revolution we put profits first and used material incentives. We made small-sized products because they gave quick profits and speedy turnover of funds. But our country needed large equipment. Under the influence of Liu Shao-chi's line our whole factory made only 87 large-sized lathes between 1952 and 1966. The workers criticized this during the Cultural Revolution and in 1971 alone we made 120 of these large lathes."

Workers at the Luoyang Heavy Equipment Manufacturing Factory blamed material incentives for poor quality. "Before the Cultural Revolution we had material incentives here. For example, the more units you produced the more money you got. This hurt quality." They added that this, in turn, often created tensions between workers and cadres.

Piecework systems, we were told, caused contradictions and disputes among workers because piecework favored young workers whose strength and good health allowed them to work faster and longer. Resentment between generations was often one result.

Material incentives could even promote false status differences. A repairman in the Zhengzhou No. 3 Textile Mill recalled:

"Our department repairs machines. Because of material incentives we did not serve the needs of other departments as well as we could. We thought only of getting money. Other departments began to call us 'a department of gentlemen.' This changed during the Cultural Revolution."

Special bonuses—for attendance, overproduction, quality of work, etc.—had sometimes been distributed by decisions

---

higher form of socialism than collective ownership. This ideological judgment was consistent with the relative ability of these two forms of ownership to transcend material incentives as a means of organizing production.

of workshop groups. While this might be appealingly democratic in form, in reality such practice promoted discord and competition. A woman in the spinning department at the Zhengzhou No. 3 Textile Mill explained:

"Before the Cultural Revolution we had a brief three-minute meeting at the end of every month. We graded workers for bonuses. There were only three grades: good, middle, or backward. Many workers resented this and the system divided us. Those in the higher grade looked down on those in the lower grade. This made workers think only of the money they could get.

"Mass criticism ended this system, and we now follow the policy of putting politics forward."

Su Zhuan-zhen, the electrician at Foreign Languages Printing House who called material incentives "poison in our minds," described his department:

"I am an electrician. To get bonuses, electricians were classified with grades at the end of each month. This caused quarrels. There were awards for many things, for example, overproduction. But some jobs were easier than others and workers rushed to the easy jobs. They quarreled over which job they would get. This was harmful to the progress of the workers.

"The true nature of the revisionist line was not just to give money but to erode the minds of the workers."

Workers in China declared material incentives had held them back. As proof they pointed to increased production since the abolition of special rewards.

Miners at the Kairan Coal Mine observed:

"This mine was like the rest of China; we, too, were influenced by Liu Shao-chi's line. We had a system of material incentives." The bonus system had been thrown out during the Cultural Revolution and now, they declared, "we produce even more than the capacity this mine was designed for. In 1971-1972 we had a 72 percent increase over 1964-1965."

Workers at the Luoyang Heavy Equipment Manufacturing Factory described a similar exhilarating effect on production:

"Since then [the Cultural Revolution] our output has

actually increased 20 to 30 percent. Workers and technicians have joined the leadership of the factory at all levels and now production plans are discussed by the masses of workers.

"Now everyone knows his or her job is part of the revolution and therefore spirit is high."

Doing away with material incentives, however, had not meant casting aside all material considerations. Regular wages continued. They were not regarded as incentives, although it was acknowledged they could become so if misused. Wage differentials, such as the eight-grade wage scale in factories, were not necessarily regarded as material incentives. Wages were simply considered social necessities. The common attitude was that wages could be removed from the realm of material incentives if handled collectively from a socialist, not a personal or selfish, perspective.

Drawing the ideological line between wages as social necessity and wages as material incentives was somewhat sticky business. The resulting struggles in China to walk that thin line were obviously not easy. After all, any wages were inconsistent with the ultimate Marxist goal of a communist society where the wage system has been abolished.

But China was a socialist, not a communist, society. And tensions of that transitional stage were evident. In more than one place we were told about workers who had sought wage upgrading for personal, material reasons. It seemed reasonable, however, to expect such incidents. As long as wage differences existed, individualist tendencies would continue to raise their heads. If some individuals with old ideas lagged behind, that did not alter the fundamental, and revolutionary, fact of millions of peasants and workers struggling together to create new attitudes toward wages and material rewards.

Abolishing material incentives did not mean that workers scorned higher income and improved, more comfortable living conditions. We did not encounter any pompous self-sacrificing or superficial rejection of material comforts. No one's income had suffered because material incentives were abolished. Money previously awarded in the form of selective bonuses was now distributed equally among all workers. Income was considered important. Families clearly paid close attention to financial concerns. But money and higher income were not, in themselves, the primary goal of work. People believed material improvements, which they desired, should come collectively, not haphazardly or for some at the expense of others.

Most Chinese we spoke to agreed that their goal was the eventual abolition of wage differences. But there were ambivalent attitudes about the present stage of wage differentials and the questions of when, how, and in what way wages should be further equalized. Some argued that increased industrialization would make this possible and arbitrary equalization before the necessary economic base was built would do more harm than good. Others felt absolute equalization could not proceed ahead of people's consciousness, and the fact was many still believed somewhat higher wages were appropriate for those with more experience or special skills. Further narrowing of wage differentials, they said, would come about when people changed their attitudes. Most people also maintained equalization should come about by raising the lower grades, not by lopping off a few at the top level.

In all our visits we encountered only one overtly material incentive pay system. This was at a volunteer embroidery group in Peking. There a group of housewives, organized through their Neighborhood Committee, did fancy embroidery, which was sold to the government for export purposes. Most often the women took the work home and did it in their spare time, although they also had a central location where they sometimes worked together. They were paid a set amount for each tablecloth, bedspread, or pillowcase completed, a straight piece-rate system. Given their particular conditions piecework seemed to make sense. They were a rudimentary, volunteer group, and individuals put in widely varying amounts of time. Their group perhaps illustrated initial steps in one typical method of economic development in

China. The appropriate question to raise is: which way will their enterprise turn as it grows and becomes a full-time economic unit? Will piecework and material incentives be phased out? Or will they continue, take root, and become permanent features? Although the struggles of the Cultural Revolution have tipped the scale heavily in the first direction, we were constantly reminded that nothing about China's future is guaranteed, its socialism included.

The fundamental question was which should take command: collective, ideological motivation, or individual, material drives? Workers answered by stating they no longer worked merely for wages or money. Today they worked for the revolution.

"During the Cultural Revolution we put politics in command and brought workers' initiative into full play. Now we know why we work: not just for ourselves, but to support peoples' struggles in other countries," declared workers at the Foreign Languages Printing House.

A Peking auto worker put it this way: "Before, we thought only of money and forgot political power. We thought only of rewards and forgot the Party's leadership." A co-worker added: "I now understand my job is part of the revolution."

In a sense the Chinese are trying to have their ideological cake and eat it, too. And to a great extent they seem to be succeeding. While doing away with most material incentives they have also experienced a tremendous increase in production. This, in turn, has laid the basis for better material conditions for everyone. Putting politics in command and freeing themselves from the "poison" in their minds has promoted collective development and individual benefits.

Thus, "politics in command" meant many things. But it always meant considering class, collective, and group interests first. Sometimes it meant overcoming personal selfishness; sometimes it meant abolishing slavishness to technique. Sometimes it meant putting socialist principles ahead of profit motives. "Politics" in China meant people, and politics in command meant putting the people's interest first.

Serve the People

"Serve the People." The phrase resounded in conversation after conversation during our stay in China.

Mao Tse-tung delivered a short speech in 1944 titled "Serve the People." During the Cultural Revolution it was studied widely, one of the "three constantly read articles." The speech was a eulogy for Zhang Si-de, a rank-and-file soldier and charcoal burner who had died in an accident. Mao emphasized how Zhang had dedicated himself to the common cause. The eulogy carried a simple, but profound, message: in the service of the people every man or woman is worthy of respect; every task, every job, however mundane, is important.

This theme runs through Mao's writings. "Our duty is to hold ourselves responsible to the people. Every word, every act and every policy must conform to the people's interests."

"All our cadres, whatever their rank, are servants of the people, and whatever we do is to serve the people."*

Such a policy grew out of decades of revolutionary struggle, from the necessity for the Party and army to build mass support by meeting people's genuine needs. Today, in an entirely different situation, in a different stage of historical development, the spirit of "serve the people" is still one of the guiding principles for China's entire population.

To "serve the people" in China was not a moralistic self-sacrifice. One did not serve the people to accumulate individual virtue or demonstrate moral superiority. From what we saw, serving the people had little in common with the concept of Christian charity. Workers and peasants in China were not serving others to reap rewards, either now or in the hereafter. Their motivation was collective; it helped others and it helped the whole society. Each served in the way best suited to their talents, skills, and abilities. Railway crews took extra care to insure that workers and peasants enjoyed safe, com-

---

* Quotes are from "The Tasks for 1945" and "The Situation and Our Policy After the Victory in the War of Resistance Against Japan," both written in 1945.

fortable, and efficient journeys. Steel workers labored to provide railroads, and all industry, with the steel vital for upkeep and growth. Peasants planted crops in rotation to supply city residents a variety of vegetables throughout the year. Factory workers reciprocated by designing and producing products specifically suited to rural conditions. All this, and more, was done in the spirit of serving the people.

Serving the people had a class content in China. The people, workers and peasants, were the source, the purpose of all struggle, all effort. Those we talked to recalled that Mao called upon "all revolutionaries . . . [to] be 'oxen' for the proletariat and the masses, bending their backs to the task until their dying day."*

The workers, peasants, cadres, and students we met were all dedicated to this principle. Why? They said everyone gained if the principle was followed.

Thus, their purpose was political; they believed their system should serve the masses. But their purpose was also practical; it encouraged positive development, positive actions.

"Serve the People." These three small words, so simple in meaning, have become the backbone of China's approach to socialism. They were an inspiration, beckoning individuals to higher purpose. They were a beacon, casting light on the correct path to follow. And they were an object of struggle, to be constantly defended, to be implemented in reality as well as rhetoric.

Rely on the Masses:
"The Real Masters of Production Are the Workers"

The masses. The people. Socialism can exist only if it is created, developed, and defended by the people. So argued our Chinese comrades.

---

* Mao Tse-tung, "Talks at the Yenan Forum on Literature and Art," 1942.

Rely on the masses:

... Because knowledge comes from social practice. Thus, it is philosophically sensible.

... Because those who actually do the work have the greatest power and knowledge of production. Thus, it is economically sound.

... Because it reflects the very fabric of socialist ethics, of democracy and equality. Thus, it is morally imperative.

... Because people represent both the present and the future; because it is the people who determine history. Thus, it is strategically wise and historically necessary.

We discovered relying on the people was a point of political struggle in China. Differences over this socialist principle came to a head during the Cultural Revolution. The differences corresponded to sharply contrasting ways of running the society's factories, schools, and public institutions. For example, Wang Min, a leading cadre at the Shenyang No. 1 Machinery Manufacturing Factory, explained whether or not to "rely on the masses" had been a point of much contention in his factory:

"We had a very fierce struggle here between the two lines. The cadres had been influenced by Liu Shao-chi's line. For example, the question was to run the factory relying on the masses or relying on the experts. In my own job I did not rely on the masses, so production was low compared to now. Of course, we need some experts, but there are many more workers than experts in this factory. And the real masters of production are the workers."

What did it mean to rely on the masses as opposed to the experts? Zui Zao-huai, at the Tianjin No. 1 Machinery Factory, described dramatic increases in production:

"Because of the influence of Liu Shao-chi's line it used to take a long time to do experiments in making new machines. Before we did not put workers in the forefront and it took one and a half to two years to develop new machines. Now it takes eight months to one year."

During the Cultural Revolution workers attacked the idea that experts should run the factory. They tore down a barrier to their initiative, destroying the blockade against their involvement and participation in all aspects of industry.

We in the United States should be able to understand what Chinese workers were criticizing when they spoke of "relying on experts." After all, reliance on expertise is the backbone of modern Western industrial practices: Front office executives choose the products, determine production output and then decide what machinery and personnel will be used in the production process. Next, engineers and technicians, in white-shirted comfort far from the shop floor, design products and equipment. Skilled tradesmen then install and maintain the machinery. The majority of workers, those who do the actual production, are never consulted (save for suggestion boxes with token prizes for ideas that save the company money). The production workers usually receive the lowest pay and have to cope with the poorest working conditions. Yet their direct experience and the collective nature of their work often make them the most knowledgeable about production details.

How totally different, how revolutionary, to design and produce using a combination of workers, technicians, and cadres! Chinese workers actually wanted to integrate the people and the process, to increase production, and to automate and improve product quality. They felt it was in their interests to increase production and improve technique. The results were impressive.

Thousands upon thousands of technical innovations blossomed forth in Chinese factories when class and bureaucratic barriers to workers' initiative were broken. Workers applied practical knowledge gained from years on the shop floor. Many of these technical innovations were fairly simple by modern Western standards, but tremendously important in a country still industrially impoverished. Others were quite complex and sophisticated, challenging techniques developed anywhere. Most technical innovations, Chinese workers constantly reminded us, were a result of the Cultural Revolution. They were fruits of the struggles to "rely on the masses" instead of waiting for the experts.

"The creativity of the masses is boundless," Chinese workers declared. Here are some examples to lend credence to their assertion:

We met a young man at the Wuhan Sewing Machine Factory operating a machine he had helped design and build. It made small bolts automatically from pieces of unthreaded metal rod—a job formerly done by time-consuming hand labor. We learned he, as well as others, had often stayed hours after work, without pay, to build the machine. A small colorful plaque on the brick wall behind the new machine hailed the collective effort responsible for the innovation.

Some technical innovations made work more pleasant. We visited the spinning department of the Zhengzhou No. 3 Textile Mill where a group of women workers wound cotton thread. Each woman had about a dozen whirring spools to tend. They sat on metal chairs, something like telephone operators' chairs, which were on rollers and attached to a guide rod running the length of the machine. They glided back and forth with ease, pushing the chairs along with their feet. Formerly they had worked standing up, walking, or sometimes running, back and forth between the spools. Now they could sit down. They said this did more than make things easier; production also increased as a direct result. Across an aisle we saw other women doing the same work, but standing on their feet in the old manner. The innovation evidently had not yet been introduced throughout the entire spinning department.

Innovations at the East Is Red Auto Factory in Peking were on a much grander scale. For example, their entire paint shop had recently changed from spray painting to a quicker, more efficient dip-process. Sheet-metal pieces, stamped into fenders and hoods for their jeep, were mechanically dunked into large vats of electrically charged paint. They passed through a rust-colored primer and then through an olive-green outer coat. Excess paint was washed off, collected, and re-used. The old process, spray painting by hand, had been messy, hot, and time-consuming. Now the only spray painting we saw was to touch up small spots that didn't take in the dip.

The innovation represented a joint effort of workers, cadres, and technicians. As a result working conditions were bettered, the product improved, and production increased. It was also in this factory that we saw a newly developed automatic spotwelder, similarly the product of worker, technician, and cadre cooperation.

But we discovered our own favorite technical innovation in a kitchen. We visited the dining hall of the Zhengzhou Textile Machinery Manufacturing Factory, where food is served to over 2,500 workers per meal. Cooks here had fashioned a machine, an ingenious contraption, which made the traditional Chinese *zhaozi*, a filled steamed or boiled dumpling. We watched as a huge bowl of meat and vegetable filling was dumped into a hopper at the top and then a large mound of sticky dough was fed in from the rear. With a whir and a chug the dough was flattened; filling spilled down between two octagonal rollers, and crescent shaped dumplings plopped out ready for the steamer!

Nearby we saw an automatic *"man-tou* machine." *Man-tou*, or steamed bread, was very popular in North China and, like *zhaozi*, was tediously prepared by hand. But here a machine churned away kneading dough mechanically with a large pastry hook. The mixture was then suddenly gulped up in huge amounts and spit out the other side in neat, round buns. Two people were kept busy filling the hopper and carrying buns to nearby steamers.

The contraptions were a far cry from the streamlined, shiny chrome equipment common in institutional kitchens in the United States. Perhaps their awkward appearance reflected the cooks' preoccupation with production rather than aesthetics. But only people who had spent hours upon hours making *zhaozi* and *man-tou* by hand could have conceived and constructed such things. The machines certainly saved an incredible amount of hand labor, and in a very practical everyday area. While they were hardly the backbone of China's industrial development, they did dramatize the fruits of workers' initiative and creativity, of relying on the masses.

The Yenan Spirit of Self-Reliance and Hard Struggle

The "Yenan Period," 1935-1947, was the decisive decade of the Chinese Revolution.* During those years the revolutionary forces matured and expanded, leading the patriotic war against Japanese colonialism and paving the way to topple Chiang Kai-shek's Kuomintang regime. Today Chinese workers and peasants look back to Yenan to recapture the spirit, political clarity, and determination which propelled them through such difficult, but promising, times.

We often heard people encourage each other to meet problems with the same iron will that had radiated from the caves of Yenan. Near Yenan we learned firsthand what had comprised this "Yenan spirit of self-reliance and hard struggle"—a spirit which had become an ideological principle motivating millions.

Liu Bao-zhei had helped create the Yenan spirit; he had joined the Eighth Route Army in 1937, leaving his home in Henan Province to fight the Japanese in the North. We met Liu on a state farm nestled in the Nanniwan Valley, near Yenan. His face, rough and creased, reflected many years of labor in the harsh climate of northern Shanxi Province. Liu wore a towel tied about his head in the traditional peasant fashion of the area.

"I was a member of the 359 Brigade of the Eighth Route Army." Liu spoke in a quiet, rasping voice. "In 1940 we were fighting the Japanese at the front in the North. But the rear areas, the Border Region, were under economic blockade by the Kuomintang and had great difficulties."

Liu's deep-set eyes twinkled as he recalled events of those days. "Chairman Mao asked the 359 Brigade to come back from the front to the Yenan area. We were to safeguard the rear area where the Central Committee and Chairman Mao

---

* During this period the headquarters of the Communist Party and the revolutionary government were in Yenan, in northern Shanxi Province.

were. We guarded the 'south gate' to Yenan. There were two important roads leading to Yenan, and we took care of the southern one. The 359 Brigade came to Nanniwan (about 25 miles southeast of Yenan) in 1941. There was then a mass production campaign which emphasized self-reliance and hard struggle. We had a slogan: Use our own hands to provide ample food and clothing. The Brigade had three main tasks: production, study, and fighting.

"When we first arrived in Nanniwan it was remote—there was nothing, no people, no houses, not even cave dwellings. Grass and trees covered the ground. Our first problem was housing. We settled down and started to make shelters, using small army spades to build cave dwellings. Within twelve days the housing problem was basically solved, with one cave per company."

Liu paused and took a sip of tea, glancing around the comfortable meeting room where we sat. This building, part of a state farm, and the whole village around it, had all been built since the 1940s. It struck us as unique for China, where histories of towns and villages usually covered centuries. Liu continued: "We then divided labor; some worked on cave dwellings, some cut down trees, and some made charcoal which we then took to Yenan and sold for money to get cooking oil and salt. We needed better tools for reclaiming the wasteland. We made our own tools out of waste iron and old temple bells. But these were not enough. So we made wood products and sold them in the Yenan market to get money for more tools. Thus we solved the problem of shortage of farm tools.

"At first we had to bring in food fifty kilometers and there was a problem of transporting it, particularly the grain. We needed bags to carry the grain. We had squad meetings to discuss the problem and came up with many ideas. Some used pieces of cloth and made bags. Some soldiers took off their trousers, tied the legs closed, and filled them with grain. They carried them, full of grain, around their necks. But food was still not enough, so we relied on the masses again. Some suggested we use wild vegetables to add to our food. We mixed the wild vegetables with our grain and made a porridge.

"Next the problem of clothing was faced. We used wool from sheep to solve this, but many details were problems. Each individual was given one or two catties to spin. We used simple tools, an iron bar and hook. But this yarn was good only for knitting socks, vests, and sweaters. It was not good enough for weaving and it was very scratchy!" Liu squirmed a little at the memory.

"Later a spinning wheel was rigged up with a foot pedal. Comrades who were in comparatively poor health were organized into a spinning group. They then made weaving machines themselves and made cloth. They used various types of grasses and bark to make dyes. The clothes looked all right from a distance, but actually were very coarse and roughly made."

Self-reliance meant many other things to the 359 Brigade. Liu noted, "We used ashes, made from burning grass, for soap. Table salt served as toothpaste. In the summer we used birch-bark hats to protect us from the sun. We had no paper, so we used a stick and wrote on the ground; some made notebooks of birch bark and used charcoal. We made crude pens with the shells from bullets. There were no watches in the Brigade so we went by the sun to determine the work day.

"We used two methods to promote production, the 'emulation method' and the 'charge!' method. The 'charge!' method meant different groups would all attack the same job from different sides, as if we were fighting a battle. The slogan of the 359 Brigade became: With rifle in one hand and spade in the other we defend the Central Committee. We rely on ourselves and will provide ourselves with everything. After the first year our production was enough to be self-sufficient in basic needs, including grain. We started producing a surplus in 1942, the second year. We were requested to double production and did this by the third year. In a few years flat fields were turned into paddy fields. There were many labor heroes who came forth from our production campaign.

"We also built small factories. We made textiles, matches, porcelain, soap, paper, and refined oil for gasoline. The quality of products was often not very high, but they served their purpose and helped the war effort."

We realized that Liu Bao-zhei, like so many others we talked to throughout our visits in China, had left himself out of his story. We asked what jobs he had done.

"Personally," Liu added, "I was deputy commander of a company. I engaged in land reclamation and also did fighting. But the experience of the production campaign waged by the 359 Brigade," he quickly continued, "was only one example of the whole army. The 359 Brigade had 13,000 members at the time, five regiments."

Such was the fabric of the "Yenan spirit of self-reliance and hard struggle." In the West we have a concept of people "pulling themselves up by their own bootstraps." But, as Liu Bao-zhei's examples indicate, the Chinese often had to begin by first making the bootstrap. And they did it together, collectively, pooling energy and resources. They divided labor and spread the infectious enthusiasm and determination that became known as the Yenan spirit.

We saw several impressive examples of more recent efforts during our visits: fields where every inch of earth had been carried in by hand; flowering orchards on land excavated from sandy waste; and extensive irrigation projects which brought relief to drought-stricken fields. All had been constructed by human sweat and muscle, and by the "Yenan spirit." This spirit had literally moved mountains.

Combine the Old and New: Make the Past Serve the Present

New China was creating a society unprecedented in human history. Yet, old China was a part of that process.

We learned that the vast gulf between the tradition-bound

society of Confucius and the new socialist order was being bridged through China's determination to learn from her past. Two extremes were rejected: slavishly following tradition and rashly rejecting tradition. A unity of opposites was sought: to combine the old and new, securing the benefits of both.

The people we met were proud of their heritage and of the richness and longevity of Chinese culture.

We met old China in many places. One of the most impressive was the Long-men Caves, near the ancient city of Luoyang. Here, in an area stretching along the Yi River, over two thousand caves and niches had been hewed into rocky cliffs and some ninety-seven thousand Buddhist statues fashioned. Many dated back fifteen or sixteen hundred years. Most of the stone carvings were small, but larger ones were quite spectacular, rising up to fifty-six feet in height.

The Long-men Caves were open to the public, a popular park for family and group recreation. We arrived on a Friday morning, covering the ten miles from Luoyang by car. Regular bus transportation from the city was available and cheap. Entrance to the park itself was free. Judging by the crowds this spot of ancient religious art, although a relic of the old feudal order, had found its place in the new society.

Families, many of them three generations, wandered about, poking their heads in and out of caves, and checking some of the thirty-six hundred inscriptions carved into the rocks. The inscription left in one of the larger caves informed the modern visitor that over eight hundred two thousand workers toiled some twenty-three years to create several huge and impressive stone figures.

Here and there school-age groups gathered. Trucks arrived bringing loads of workers from Luoyang factories for a day of relaxation in the new spring warmth. Some of the streams and fountains around the small but intricately designed pagodas were being put to practical use by young women shampooing their waist length hair in cold, clear water. Children roamed about nearby with shiny, wet hair, obviously fresh from their turn at the fountain washbasin.

We met and talked with a member of the staff responsible for maintaining the park. Seventeen people worked on the park staff; four or five were university graduates and trained in history. Many of the carvings had been restored, having suffered damage during pre-Liberation times. We ourselves saw careful restoration work being done on a couple of their largest and most popular statues.

Our host settled us into some comfortable wicker chairs on a small veranda overlooking the Yi River, now lined with bright-green spring foliage. We faced a large, impressive building perched on the opposite river bank. Formerly a Buddhist monastery, we learned, it was now used as a guest house. Tea was served and our host, satisfied that we were comfortable, described the park and why these feudal religious relics were treasured and preserved in new, socialist China.

"All of the carvings here are Buddhist," he began. "Buddhism came to China from India and has about two thousand years of history in our country. Buddhism was practiced both by the ruling class and by the working class, but there were differences. The ancient ruling class used it to exploit the people; laboring people used it to escape from their hard lives.

"The carvings reflect the customs of feudal society. The Buddhas show ancient clothing. There are models of architecture, musical instruments, and examples of Chinese characters from ancient dynasties. This is a good place to study art and literature. Although most was Buddhist art, we should remember that all of it was created by the Chinese people."

He repeated this point to make sure we understood. The feudal rulers had not themselves gone out to the river bank with hammer and chisel. The actual carving had been done by working people and reflected their creativity and high cultural level. Some of the carvings, he added, took decades to complete.

"Some of the caves and carvings were destroyed by natural means over the years," he continued, "but also imperialists took many things out of China, especially Americans and Japanese. We think the people of the world should see each other's art and exchange opinions, but we don't want imperialists coming in and stealing things.

"For example, experts from the United States took a lot of carvings from this area around 1937. There is a carving of the dress of an emperor—done about the year 550 A.D.—which was taken to New York. This queen's dress from the same cave is now in Kansas City. In another cave from the Tang period, about 650 A.D., the carving technique is more advanced. A large stone lion at the entrance of that cave was taken to Boston."

He paused and frowned, obviously rather indignant at what had taken place.

"One of the United States experts," he continued, "even wrote an article and claimed we Chinese didn't want our art. He said the only way to save it was to take it to the U.S. This was a lie. There is no generation that does not respect the art of its forefathers.

"Also, United States newspapers have recently said that during the Cultural Revolution all traditional art was destroyed. This too is a lie. In fact many new relics were discovered during the Cultural Revolution."

We later saw blank spaces on the cave walls where these art objects had been stolen. Only ugly gashes remained, contrasts to their finely crafted surroundings. It made us think about our many visits to American museums. How much we took for granted these displays of old Chinese art. Rarely did we question how they had been obtained, or how the Chinese felt about it.

Learning from the past often involved, to use the Chinese term, "class education." The social conditions of the old society, its class relationships, were regarded as object lessons to be applied to today's problems. Older workers and peasants took the lead in "class education," bringing to the younger generation their experiences of the 1920s, 1930s, and 1940s. Veterans reasoned: only if the younger generation fully understood conditions of the old society, and what caused such misery, would they be vigilant and prevent China from sliding back into anything like that again.

For these reasons we will never forget Tangshan.

Class education there was dramatic and powerful. It hit in the pit of the stomach, and you were never quite the same for the experience.

Tangshan workers had put together an elaborate exhibit of their own history, housed in several small buildings. It was not textbook history, but accounts of their own lives, their families, their labor, and their struggles. The story was not pleasant; oppression never is.

Here we saw the history of Tangshan in maps, photos, near life-size clay statues, documents, cartoons, and colorful posters and charts. Here we learned that coal had been the major industry in the area, that the first mine was built in 1872, and that it was built by the people of Tangshan but controlled by the British.

Here were statistics: The British spent more each day to feed a mine horse than to pay a Chinese mine worker. About 47 fen compared to 22 fen.

Here missionaries were also mentioned, because they had supported and cooperated with the wealthy and powerful foreign businessmen.

Here were lists of workers killed or injured in the mine, posted alongside details of British profits. Wages had equaled 5 percent of the mine profits. The British director had been paid 43,076 yuan a month. Chinese workers got about 15 yuan.

Here also was information about the arrival of the Japanese in 1931, and photos of furnaces used to dispose of murdered Chinese workers after Japanese troops had quelled a strike. It was noted that after the defeat of the Japanese in 1945 Chiang Kai-shek had invited the British back. And Americans, for in 1946 U.S. Navy troops had been sent in.

Mine safety? Between 1900 and 1948 some 5,397 workers were killed in the mine and about 200,000 injured. That's one worker killed approximately every three days.

Here were tableaux of clay figures, depicting working conditions as the surviving miners remembered. Workers had sold themselves as indentured laborers; if sick or injured they were fired, with no help or aid given their families. Workers were strip-searched at the gate by the Japanese troops and the tableau included the account of one worker who had forgotten to remove his hat. He was bayoneted to death.

Here was a tableau of the elevator used to take workers down into the mine shaft. There was no gate. They were crowded together, at bayonet point, to the extent that occasionally workers fell out and were crushed to death. Another tableau depicted an incident when a section of the mine flooded. The British managers removed the mine horses but boarded up the flooded shaft with several miners trapped inside. Other workers had fought to remove the boards but more than a dozen men drowned.

Here also was a room, which we had to crouch to enter, modeled to resemble the bottom of the mine. We stood, half-stooped, in this mock-up of the mine pit. Off to one side clay models showed how workers sometimes had to crawl through one-meter-high openings.

An older worker, permanently hunched over from his years in the pre-Liberation mines, talked of what he remembered. He began as we walked to a model of the dormitories he had lived in.

"Workers lived in very crowded conditions, often thirty to forty to a room [by our estimate no larger than 20' by 20']. For food we usually got what was left over from the garbage of the bosses' table. In the summer this food would often go bad before we could get to eat it, but we had to eat it anyway, for we had nothing else.

"We were treated worse than animals! The animals got better food than we did!" he shouted angrily. In a lowered voice he continued: "In the summer the dormitories were very hot; in the winter they were freezing cold. One day I came in from work. All day water had dripped on my back in the mine. I lay down on the bed, but later I couldn't get up. It was so cold I had frozen to the bed!

"If a worker became sick he would be fired." His face darkened as he told of one of his fellow miners who had been injured. "The bosses fired him and sent their lackeys to throw him out of the dormitory. Some of us fought with them, but they took the injured man out. We went looking for him, but when we found him in the streets he was already dead. A dog had eaten part of his face." He stopped, unable to continue.

"Those were the conditions I remember," he added quietly.

Here, too, we learned that conditions in the countryside were no better than in the mine. If anything, they were worse. Clay figures dramatized the story of one peasant, representing many, whose family had been forced off the land because of debts. At first the children were sold to insure survival for the rest of the family. Finally the father and oldest son went to work in the mine.

The Tangshan workers made it clear whom they held responsible for such conditions. They said imperialists had violated their country "economically, militarily, politically, and spiritually." Their exhibit included graphic cartoons portraying British capitalists with huge noses, high silk hats, and sporting the Union Jack. American G.I.'s were slouching in a jeep, drinking beer, and shooting at people. Wealthy Chinese were in long, flowing, feudal robes. A Catholic bishop held a scepter and stood on a pile of human skulls. Another symbolic bishop held a big school in one hand and forced people into it while money floated all about him.

Finally, the Tangshan workers remembered how they had fought back.

"In the past the capitalists used many methods to oppress the workers," a veteran miner explained. "They also bought some off. They paid some high wages, but they were not able to buy off the spirit of struggle among the working class."

The last room of the exhibition detailed strikes and militant struggles. Between 1882 and 1937 there were more than thirty-eight strikes at the coal mine. From 1938 to 1948 the workers' struggles were directly combined with the war against the Japanese and then against Chiang Kai-shek's Kuomintang. In 1948 Tangshan was liberated.

This exhibition, we learned, had been set up in 1969. Its aim was "to never let the people forget the past sufferings" and "to give the young generation education about revolutionary struggles." Also, the purpose was to apply "class education" to current developments. There were several signs in the exhibition referring to "the struggle between the two roads" and the "Liu Shao-chi line." Older workers knew what the "capitalist road" had meant to them. They wanted young people to understand this and to learn from the past and prevent new forms of capitalism from cropping up.

We met Yang Pu-hao in Yenan. His experience in the old society was quite different from that of the Tangshan workers. He was a peasant from the remote area of Northwest China. His was a life tied to the land, rural and impoverished. But Yang was "making the past serve the present." Today he spent much of his time speaking to young people and visitors about the old society.

Yang's early life sounded familiar, as if we'd heard it before. His mother died when he was young; his family wandered about as beggars during famine. Yang worked as a farm hand for a landlord "but we still didn't get enough to fill our bellies." His father and his one-year-old daughter died during a famine in 1931.

But if Yang's story was familiar it was only because we had already heard many accounts of other incredible suffering and misery in the old society. Indeed, it became hard to comprehend the depth and breadth of oppression in old China, so common were accounts like Yang's. But Yang, and others, spoke of their past for a purpose, not for pity. They believed there were lessons to be learned: Why had such conditions existed? What had been necessary to change them? What was necessary to prevent the return, in any form, of old ways?

Yang made a unique contribution to our own "learning

from the past." He had lived near Yenan during the years that remote mountain village served as headquarters for the revolutionary struggle. Yang met and became friends with Mao Tse-tung. He told several anecdotes about Mao in Yenan.

We guess it was no political accident that one of the stories Yang chose to tell us corresponded rather directly to current events. Meeting with Nixon in early 1972 had not been the first time Mao had sat down and talked with the enemy. Nor had the Nixon visit been the first occasion where complexities of political, military, and diplomatic struggle had confused people. Yang recalled the time Mao negotiated directly with Chiang Kai-shek in 1945:

"When Chiang Kai-shek invited Mao to go to Chungking we were all worried about Mao's safety," Yang began. Civil war in China then appeared inevitable. Chiang was obviously determined to eliminate the Communists. Yang and the people of his village knew what life was like in Kuomintang China and, by comparison, in areas liberated by the Eighth Route Army. They wanted no more of Chiang Kai-shek.

"The villagers elected me representative to go to the Central Committee in Yenan and ask them not to let Chairman Mao go to Chungking," Yang remembered. "They did not trust Chiang Kai-shek and the Kuomintang. They disagreed with the decision for Mao to travel to Chungking. They believed that would be dangerous and they feared Mao would be killed.

"They said, 'If Chiang wants to talk, let him come to Yenan.' "

Yang smiled as he talked, gesturing decisively with tough, peasant hands. He described how he had gone to Yenan and talked to members of the Party's Central Committee.

"They explained," Yang continued, "how Mao's going to Chungking was in the interests of the whole country. They said the political situation prevented Chiang Kai-shek from doing anything, that he would not dare hurt Mao for fear of becoming isolated from the whole country."

Yang didn't indicate just how satisfied the villagers were

with this reply. But Mao did go to Chungking, and the historic 1945 Chungking negotiations were held. There the Communist Party built a political basis which rallied people from all sectors of China's society to the common cause of a new, democratic China. The negotiations forced Chiang to choose between two courses of action: to cooperate honestly with democratic and economic reforms or to gamble that he could hold on to power through foreign support and military superiority. Chiang chose the latter and lost his gamble—for he never conceived that millions of people like Yang could become a political, let alone military, force.

"When we heard the news of Mao's safe return," Yang beamed, "we wanted to go right away to the Central Committee and see Mao. At midnight I gathered eggs and chickens to take with me. It was all I had that I could use for a gift. I took them to welcome Mao. I walked to the Date Garden [Mao's residence at the time], arriving there in the early morning, just at daybreak. I saw Mao riding in a jeep in the traffic. He waved at me and said we would have a chance to talk later in the day. So that day I met Mao in the Date Garden.

"I told him of our worries about his safety," Yang nodded, the white towel tied about his head in Shanxi peasant style bobbing up and down, "and how we were now very relieved. Mao explained to me why he had gone to Chungking. He said there would probably be civil war. He said it was necessary to expose the Kuomintang, that we needed to exhaust all means of peaceful resolution of China's problems. If we did this we could then unite many more if Chiang Kai-shek chose the course of war. We could isolate Chiang. Then Mao asked me about the crops. I replied that the crops were not so good that year. He said perhaps we had had a hard time and sent home to the villagers some fresh pears and fruits from trees that grew in the Date Garden."

China has not forgotten its past. The arts, crafts, skills, and technical advances of the old society were preserved, nurtured and developed in new ways, to serve the new society. But neither was the bitterness of the old society forgotten.

Lessons of the past were considered important and necessary to make clear what direction continued development should take. The underlying principle followed was from Mao: "Ancient Chinese culture should neither be totally rejected nor blindly copied but should be accepted discriminatingly so as to help the progress of China's new culture."

Criticism and Self-Criticism:
Cure the Sickness to Save the Patient

"We still have many shortcomings. Please give us your criticisms so we can improve and correct our weaknesses."

We heard this request often at workplaces, schools, and other institutions we visited. At first we tended to regard it a formality—simply politeness and modesty. But as our trip progressed we came to understand this was a serious request. Criticism and self-criticism played an important role in everyday life in China.

Almost everyone, socialist or not, believes it is a good thing to learn from mistakes. Our introduction to criticism and self-criticism had come not in China but in the United States. The concept had been part of our own political work in the progressive movement. We had seen mutual criticism and self-criticism strengthen groups to which we belonged, bringing us closer together. We had seen it check and correct individual weaknesses, both in ourselves and in others. We had seen its use improve joint ventures.

But we had also seen it misused. Criticism and self-criticism had sometimes served as a camouflage for personal attacks or as a smokescreen to direct attention away from one's own errors. Thus we had learned that if the concept were to work there must be an explicit basis of trust and unity. Constructive criticism, we had learned, must be honest and objective, not subjective. It had to be politically, not personally, motivated and should be specific, not generalized or amorphous.

"Cure the sickness to save the patient," many workers told

us, quoting Mao's admonition on how to conduct criticism.*

We found many of our opinions about criticism and self-criticism paralleled closely both theory and practice in China. But while in China we gained a much deeper understanding of the concept. We discovered some of our own weaknesses in applying criticism as a positive tool. Perhaps appropriately, this happened at Mao's birthplace, Shaoshan, in Hunan Province.

Shaoshan was beautiful, almost idyllic and serene in impact. A small village tucked away in South China's rolling mountains, Shaoshan left impressions of bright green, red, and blue: green, spring foliage; red, iron-rich soil; blue, crystal-clear sky. The contrast was sharp and most pleasant. In the United States natural beauty on this scale is usually enshrined by cramped trailer spaces, crowded tenting grounds, and littered, urbanized national parks. In Shaoshan we felt we'd arrived a few decades before such an invasion.

But Shaoshan did have many visitors. Of all places we visited in China this was most like a tourist spot. Mao's birthplace and former home were now museums seen daily by thousands. Nearby was a large, elaborate exhibit of the history of the Chinese Communist Party, detailing its decades of revolutionary struggle. Special trains and buses from nearby cities brought crowds of daily visitors to Shaoshan. Guesthouses, stocked with souvenir counters, contributed to the resort-like atmosphere.

After a thorough tour of the historical exhibits we were scheduled to spend two sessions talking to a "leading cadre" in charge of the Shaoshan museum. This discussion turned out to be the biggest bummer of our trip. But it was a learning experience for us as well.

---

* "... our aim in exposing errors and criticizing shortcomings, like that of a doctor curing a sickness, is solely to save the patient and not to doctor him to death. ... In treating an ideological or political malady, one must never be rough and rash but must adopt the approach of 'curing the sickness to save the patient.' " (Mao Tse-tung, "Rectify the Party's Style of Work," *Selected Works*, Vol. III, pp. 49-50)

We had not been clear why Zheng had suggested including the discussion in our schedule. Sure, we were interested in the Party's history. But that had been covered by the exhibit and quite competently explained by a local guide. Nevertheless, the discussion began after a late breakfast. It was our second day in Shaoshan. There was, in addition to ourselves and Zheng, the "leading cadre," the local guide who had accompanied us through the exhibits the previous day, Ge (a China International Travel Service representative from Changsha), and our auto driver who was also from nearby Changsha. The cadre, a rather suave and debonair man, first asked if we had questions about the exhibit. We raised several of historical interest covering internal political struggles in the Chinese Communist Party and its relations with the Third International during the 1920s and 1930s.

Then he began. We sat there with open mouths. After paying lip service to a "discussion" among "comrades" he rambled along for an hour and a half straight. There was no chance for questions; no opportunity for anyone else to contribute. In fact, he ignored our questions and simply gave a mechanical summary of the exhibits we had seen the previous day. His routine spiel completed, he glanced at his watch, declared we had covered enough for the morning, said we'd get back together after lunch, and breezed out of the room so quickly no one had a chance to respond.

We were steaming. After a quick huddle in our room we sought out Zheng, discovering him, Ge, the driver, and the local guide in their own intense conversation. They were probably as upset as we were.

"What went wrong this morning?" we asked Zheng. "That was a complete waste of time!" We then made several specific criticisms: (1) the cadre had monopolized the discussion; (2) he had simply repeated what we had seen in the exhibits; (3) he had asked for questions and then ignored them; (4) he had denied obvious political facts. (For example, he insisted that the struggles of the Cultural Revolution had not changed or affected any exhibits in the museum. Yet the local guide herself had noted that half the museum was constructed during or since the Cultural Revolution.)

Zheng agreed there were grounds for criticism and that something had to be done. He and the local guide agreed to talk to the cadre during lunch and find out why this had happened.

"Okay," we replied, "but we suggest the discussion for this afternoon be canceled. If it's anything like this morning it will be a waste of time. Why don't we return to Changsha early? There's a lot in the city we're interested in seeing."

"Your criticisms are correct," Zheng responded, "but how do you expect our cadre friend to change if you leave and give him no chance to improve? If you criticize you should then stay and give him a chance to correct his errors. You should be more patient."

Zheng's attitude stopped us in our tracks. We had been ready to hurl criticisms and run. But what would that have accomplished? Would that "cure the sickness to save the patient"? While we were justifiably angered by what had happened, we were wrong to want to leave. That was criticism just to make *us* feel good. If we had truly raised our criticisms in a spirit of improving the situation then we had the duty to stay and give the cadre a chance to change his ways.

So we stayed. Zheng and the others did talk to the cadre over lunch and we began the afternoon session by mutually acknowledging the morning's disaster. We had earlier raised with Zheng some possible explanations for what had happened; we now raised them directly with the cadre. It became obvious that he had simply not known answers to the questions we raised and had chosen to bluff his way through. He now admitted this and apologized.

Our afternoon session was much more frank than the morning. Nothing great came from the discussion but improvements were evident. We all learned from the experience. On our part we learned that raising criticism must be done in a positive way. It's easy to criticize, to gripe, and to point out others' weaknesses. It's something more to be constructive and handle criticism in a manner so others can, and will, respond positively.

We had other occasions to deal directly with criticism and self-criticism while in China, such as our experience dealing with male chauvinism. We emerged from these struggles with very positive feelings. Raising differences, pointing out problems, and frankly evaluating our trip did not create tensions. Such criticism was not considered impolite or forward. Rather, criticism and self-criticism, correctly handled, brought us and our Chinese hosts closer together. It built bridges of trust and friendship from which we could then proceed to tackle problems. We returned home with a practical experience that convinced us criticism and self-criticism was a tremendously valuable and overwhelmingly positive tool to be used in the construction of China's socialism.

9
National Minorities: Equality, Autonomy, and Unity

China seen from the West is one country, one people. China seen by the Chinese is one country, many peoples. They say: "China is a unified state of many nationalities."

There are fifty-five nationalities in all. The majority group, the Hans, constitute about 94 percent of the total population. The fifty-four national minorities make up the remaining 6 percent.

That small percentage belies the enormity of the "nationalities question" in China. The minority groups total more than 40 million people. Ten of the fifty-four national minorities have populations of over 1 million, making them larger in absolute numbers than a dozen members of the United Nations.* Another seven national minorities have populations of between ½ million and 1 million. At the opposite extreme, ten minority groups number less than 10,000, and one of these is under 1,000.

Due to the chauvinistic policies of the Han dynasties and the Kuomintang government, some groups were not recognized as separate nationalities until after Liberation. Indeed, many minority peoples resisted such identification, fearing it

---

* The ten are: Zhuang (7.8 million); Hui (3.9); Korean (1.3); Mongol (1.6); Manchu (2.4); Miao (2.7); Buyi (1.3); Tibetan (2.8); Uighur (3.9); and Yi (3.3). These figures are probably somewhat low, since they are from a 1957 census.

would bring further discrimination. The government of the People's Republic carried out extensive investigations during the early 1950s. Then, in accordance with each group's own wishes, separate nationalities were defined on the basis of such things as common language, culture, social structure, and in many cases, territory.

The minority groups live over widespread regions, occupying between 50 and 60 percent of the total land area of China. The greatest concentrations are in the Southwest, in the provinces of Yunnan, Sichuan, Tibet, Guangxi, Guizhou, and on the islands of Taiwan and Hainan. A second area of concentration lies in the Northwest border regions of Xinjiang, Gansu, and Inner Mongolia. Although these areas contain many of China's natural resources, they are economically the least developed regions of the country.

Historically China's national minorities fall into three broad groupings. The northwestern, or Altaic, group includes Turkic, Mongol, and Tungus peoples, who occupy traditional homelands which were incorporated into the Chinese state during the Han Dynasty (206 B.C.-220 A.D.). Second, Tibetans in the Southwest also occupy their historic homeland. Ties developed between Tibetans and Hans as early as the seventh century, and Tibet was formally incorporated into China during the Yuan (Mongol) Dynasty (1271-1386 A.D.). A third grouping includes the southern minorities, such as the Yi, Miao, Yao, and Wa. Over the centuries the Hans expanded to the south, gradually displacing these peoples to their present homes in southern uplands and southwestern border areas.*

Linguistic diversity is considerable. Many groups in the West and Northwest speak languages with alphabets derived from Arabic script. In the Southwest most of the minorities speak languages of the Sino-Tibetan family. Tibetan uses a script of Indian origin, as does Tai. Several minorities in this group developed written forms only after Liberation. A small number of people in the Southwest speak languages of the

---

* See Keith Buchanan, *The Transformation of the Chinese Earth* (New York: Praeger, 1970), Chapter 3.

Austronesian-Asiatic language family. The Hui and Manchu use Han writing (characters) and speech.

Religion has stronger roots among the national minorities than among the Hans. The traditional religion of about one-third of the total minority population was either Islam or Buddhism. Islam was the largest grouping, practiced by about ten different nationalities. Buddhism was practiced by about five groups; two of these, the Tibetans and Mongols, adhered to Lamaist Buddhism. Polytheism and other less systematized forms of religion were also widespread. During the nineteenth century small groups of Catholics and Protestants arose among a few nationalities in the Southwest.

At the time of Liberation China's economy was semi-feudal and semi-colonial. Developing capitalist relations had been hindered by more than a century of colonial exploitation by the Western powers. Most minorities, however, had not even reached this level of development. Over thirty of the minorities still had a feudal, landlord-ruled economy; elements of a capitalist economy had appeared in only a few places. The serf system still prevailed in Tibet and among the Tai of Yunnan Province. The Yi in southern Sichuan Province still had a system of outright chattel slavery. Other groups were nomadic herders or hunters; some were in various stages of primitive society. Several minorities, as noted above, had not developed a written language. In pre-Liberation days "aborigines," "tribes," and "barbarians" were common terms used to describe the minorities.

Old China's Han rulers had oppressed the nationalities, discriminating against them culturally and exploiting them economically. (Only on two occasions did minority groups hold power in China: the Mongols [Yuan Dynasty, 1271-1368] and the Manchus [Ching Dynasty, 1644-1911]; their treatment of the Hans was reciprocal.) By the time of Liberation a legacy of inequality, suspicion, and discord had been built between the Hans and the national minorities. This has changed dramatically. The policy of the People's Republic has been to promote "equality, autonomy, and unity" and "to oppose both Han chauvinism and local nationalism."

The Central Institute for Nationalities

Our interest in the present status of China's national minorities resulted in a visit to the Central Institute for Nationalities in Peking. The Institute enrolled national minority students from all parts of China—more than forty different groups were represented in the student body at the time of our visit. It is just one of eight special nationalities institutes; others are in Tibet, Qinghai, Gansu, Yunnan, Guangxi, and other autonomous areas.

A small welcoming committee greeted us upon our early morning arrival. It was a diverse group, both in appearance and nationality: Fan Fu-zhan was a Han cadre at the Institute; he was rather quiet and stayed in the background during the day. Tu Er-xun was a Uighur teacher from the far western province of Xinjiang. He wore a square black and white Uighur cap and handsome black leather riding boots. Han Zhu-song, a woman of Korean nationality, wore a high-waisted Korean dress; her outgoing and aggressive cheerfulness complemented the bright pastels of her traditional garment. Ce Dun and Mao Xin-hun, Tibetans, had both put on versions of the multicolored Tibetan patchwork apron. Mao also wore a very warm-looking Tibetan hat with a tremendously thick fur brim and ear flaps. Zhan Shou-zhai, vice-chairman of the Institute's Revolutionary Committee, and Fei Xiao-tong, a veteran professor, were both Hans. Their everyday blue cotton tunics stood out against the colorful splash and contrast of the minority costumes.

The whole group spent the day with us. They took us to visit classes, showed us their library, shared lunch in a special Islamic dining room, and discussed at length the question of national minorities in China. They first described their Institute:

"The Central Institute for Nationalities," Zhan Shou-zhai began, "is under the administration of the Committee for Affairs of Nationalities of the State Council. From the beginning of the revolution we have trained cadres from among the minorities. The first institute for minorities was set up in

Yenan [in the late 1930s] and since Liberation we have set up several others in different regions. This Central Institute was established in 1951. Our purpose is to serve the national minorities, to train cadres and other personnel for socialist construction. From 1951 to the Cultural Revolution over 9,000 students graduated from our Institute. Most went back to their regions to build socialism. In November 1971 we enrolled our first group of worker-peasant-soldier students. Now we have 691 students in three major departments.*

"The first is the Politics Department, which has two sections. One is for cadres who are already at their posts. They come here for one or two years and then return to their jobs. The other section is general political training; this is for educated youths who have worked and done labor for at least two years. We aim to train cadres for the basic level.

"The second department is Languages. Presently we are teaching Tibetan, Mongolian, Uighur, and Kazakh. Others will soon be started. We teach the Han language to national minority students and also the languages of other minorities. There are forty-one Han students here studying national minority languages. One of our goals is to train cadres as interpreters and translators.

"The third department is Culture. Here again we have two sections, music and dance. We will add a section on fine arts. We also have a Research Department. We study the history of the minorities and the policies toward them in the past. Presently we have 465 teachers; 137 are from national minorities, and we are trying to increase their numbers. Some students will stay on after they finish their courses and become teachers."

After this introduction our first stop was an extensive ex-

---

* Like other educational institutions the Central Institute was closed for a period during the Cultural Revolution. Also, similar to other institutions, the Institute now sought to serve more genuinely the class interests of workers and peasants—thus the emphasis on new "worker-peasant-soldier" students. By the fall of 1972 the Institute had enrolled an additional 1,100 students from sixteen provinces, municipalities, and autonomous regions, consisting of forty-six different nationalities.

hibition in one of the Institute's main buildings. The exhibition emphasized that China's various nationalities had coexisted since ancient times and had created China's overall history and culture. Here we were joined by a young man of, we believe, the Miao nationality. He wore a distinctive turban-like headpiece and a loose blouse, the traditional style for his people. He accompanied us through the exhibition, patiently and thoroughly explaining displays and answering our questions.

"Before Liberation," he began, "all minorities were oppressed, as were Hans, by the 'three big mountains' of feudalism, capitalism, and imperialism. In addition, minorities were oppressed by their own ruling class and also as national minorities."

He turned and led us to some displays about living conditions among the minorities before Liberation. They were appalling.

The Yi nationality of southern Sichuan Province was one example. Many of the Yi nationality had been held in chattel slavery, bought and sold as property. The Yi had been divided into four groups: the Black Yi, the slavemasters, accounted for 5 percent of the Yi population and owned more than 70 percent of the land, livestock, and farm tools. They considered themselves nobles and were hereditary rulers. Another group, the *chuno*, owned some land but had to work without pay, like serfs, for the nobles a certain number of days each year. The other two groups, the majority of the population, were slaves with neither property nor personal freedom. The only difference between these two groups was the particular way in which they were bound to the nobles. Two high-priced male slaves, we learned, had equaled the price of a cow or ox. Five women slaves equaled one horse. Old photographs in the exhibition showed Yi slaves, many disfigured from torture and overwork, chained to their tasks in the fields.

The Tai nationality in Southwestern China had formerly practiced a type of serfdom where labor was divided by villages. Whole settlements were responsible to feudal lords for various tasks. For example, one village wove cloth; another looked after the children of the noble's family; yet another arranged elaborate funerals and took care of the cemetery. The entire livelihood of the feudal rulers was thus provided by the serf villages. This heavy burden was enforced by terror and torture. Photos in the display were not pretty. They revealed serfs with hands or noses chopped off, mouths gouged and gored. There were also photos of the old Tai rulers posing with British officers and Indian mercenary soldiers, their allies in maintaining power during the late nineteenth and early twentieth centuries.

Tibet was another example. Tibet formerly had a system of serfdom. Much of the population was bound to the land and toiled endlessly for feudal landowners. Lamaist Buddhism had been tightly woven into Tibet's social structure, and its religious superstitions were supportive of the feudal economic and political arrangements. Here in the exhibit were old photographs of Tibetan officials using serfs, not horses or donkeys, as beasts of burden to carry them across the rugged terrain piggy-back style. Tibetan serfs had been used to lay foundations during the construction of Lamaist temples. But they were not just laborers; some were killed and their bodies, literally, became part of the structure.

Tibetan serfs suffered severe penalties for disobedience. The beautiful and mysterious Potala Palace in Lhasa is one of the world's most famous landmarks. But the beauty of Tibet's temples and palaces, we learned, concealed within a "hell-on-earth." Behind the walls were hideous jails and torture chambers. We saw small display models of water-filled dungeons and of caves filled with scorpions where unlucky serfs, chained to the wall, were killed by repeated stings. Glass cases nearby contained various weapons and tools of torture.

The Tibetan nobles had been particularly fond of gouging out eyes and had refined their technique to a fairly sophisticated "art." A heavy concave stone (one was in the display case) was placed on the victim's head. The weight made the eyes protrude and they could then be gouged easily. Sharp tools for this purpose were also in the case. Bleeding had been cauterized with boiling oil. Next to these particular implements was a photo of a former serf who was now a member of the Revolutionary Committee of Tibet. While a serf he had been blinded in this manner.

Runaway serfs sometimes had tendons in their legs severed, crippling them for life. Amputation was another favorite of the feudal rulers. But the most grisly display was a glass case which contained several bowls made from human skulls, a horn made from human bones, a drum made from human skin, and a human hand and wrist which had been dried and preserved. These had been trophies kept by the former Tibetan nobles.

Ce Dun's Story

Ce Dun, one of the Tibetan students accompanying us, personalized the general conditions characterized in these displays. Slowly and softly she spoke about her life in old Tibet.*

"I was a serf," she began. "Production and tools were very backward in Tibet, and the standard of living was very low. My parents worked for a Lamaist monastery. My father boiled water, my mother worked in the vegetable garden. Everything she grew went to the monastery; we were given only the bran [chaff] from the barley as payment. But this grain was not ground fine, it was very coarse. It was worse than what they gave to the dogs. We only had half of what we needed to eat. We had a very hard life.

"My aunt used to sell wine. Once some Lamas [priests]

* The period Ce Dun talked about included that between 1951 and 1959. Social reforms proceeded more slowly in the minority areas than in the rest of China, a result of the government's policy of regional autonomy. Thus, what are now called the "democratic reforms" in Tibet (land reform and the abolition of the serf system) were not carried out until 1959.

came to her shop and got drunk. They smashed all her wine jars. Then they seized her and took her to the monastery. They tortured her, beat her with bars with nails in them, whipped her with ropes. She was stripped and beaten almost to death. It was summer and her wounds became infected and got worms in them. We had no money for medical treatment and so my aunt died. Soon after this my mother got sick and couldn't work any longer. My older brother was forced to become a Lama.* But he fell in love with a nun. They managed to run away, but were caught and tortured. Finally he ran away again, to another part of Tibet. But life was no better there.

"Both my parents died when I was about six years old. Some neighbors took pity on me and accepted me into their household. They took care of me for two years. But when I was eight I had to start work as a slave in a businessman's house. From then on I only had rags to wear. They never gave me enough to eat. I had bugs all over my body. I was young and had to work very hard. I was tired all the time, but I couldn't go to sleep before the masters did. I had to stay up to wait on them until they went to bed. When I dozed off they would prick me with pins or put snuff in my nose, which burns the nostrils, to keep me awake. I had to get up early in the morning, start the fire, make tea, clean the floor, and take the tea to the masters before they got up.

"Once, early in the morning, it was dark and I was very sleepy. I fell down a flight of stairs when I was carrying the tea kettle and it broke. The masters said I had to pay for it. But I was a slave. I was never paid anything. I didn't have a penny. How could I ever pay? I considered my life was hopeless. I wanted Tibet to be liberated. I wanted the People's Liberation Army to come to Tibet and emancipate the millions of serfs.

"In 1956 I was carrying the businessman's child on my back. The child began to cry and I was afraid I would be tortured for this. So I ran away to a unit of the People's

---

* Serf families in old Tibet were required to give their second sons to Lamaist monasteries.

Liberation Army. I had heard they were helping the serfs. I was in rags. They gave me money for clothes and took me in. That year I joined the Communist Youth League. In 1957 I studied at the Institute for Minorities in Tibet. In 1959 I returned to my home to take part in the democratic reforms. I joined the Communist Party in 1962 and worked in my county Party Committee during the period of democratic reforms. During the Cultural Revolution I worked as deputy secretary of the Party Branch in my county. We did socialist education.

"Had it not been for the Communist Party and Chairman Mao I wouldn't have been able to come to this Institute to study. I would still be a serf. Thanks to the Party and Chairman Mao the children of emancipated serfs can now study. Today great emphasis is placed on training cadres of national minority peoples. Now in Tibet most of the cadres are Tibetan."

We asked Ce Dun about her life now. She told us she was twenty-nine, married, and the mother of four children. Her husband was also a cadre. He had remained in Tibet with the children while she was studying in Peking. "This was unheard of in the past—that a mother would have the chance to study in Peking. Recently one of my children was seriously ill. He was flown to Peking for treatment. My husband came with him. All these expenses were paid by the government. I am very happy now. In 1970 I found my older brother again. He is working as an accountant in a restaurant. He, too, has a good life now."

Ce Dun's story was not exceptional. The nightmare of past oppression had led many among the national minorities to rebel, to struggle against their wretched conditions.

"The national minorities," the guide at the exhibition emphasized, "also have a revolutionary history. Several nationalities participated in the Taiping Rebellion in the 1850s and others fought the Manchu Dynasty over the years.* Another

* The Taiping Rebellion was a mid-nineteenth-century revolutionary peasant movement against the feudal rule and national oppression of

example was a rebellion of Yi slaves in 1914-1916. But all these rebellions failed due to lack of correct leadership."

The exhibition ended with accounts of more recent developments, particularly the changes in minority areas since the Cultural Revolution. A colorful array of different costumes, dresses, and cultural and art objects was included. It was a good introduction and provided a useful basis for an all-afternoon discussion about the current status of national minorities and just what, in practice, the policy of "equality, autonomy, and unity" meant.

China's Nationalities Policy

"Equality and unity among nationalities is the basic principle for solving all matters concerning the national question," one of our hosts stressed. "After Liberation, establishing equality was of the first priority. Regional autonomy is a way of insuring equality and unity."

Zhan Shou-zhai, vice-chairman of the Institute's Revolutionary Committee, joined in: "Our Constitution [of the People's Republic] says that we should carry out autonomy in all areas where minorities are settled in concentrated ways. We have 5 autonomous regions, 29 autonomous *zhou*, and 69 autonomous counties.* A region often has several national minority groups. For example, in the Xinjiang-Uighur Autonomous Region there are thirteen different national minorities. They have, where appropriate, Kazakh autonomous *zhou* and autonomous counties. If there are several nationalities within one county, there is joint administration. In Yun-

---

the Ching (Manchu) Dynasty. Beginning in 1851, its army marched through much of central China, held Nanjing as its capital for a period, but was finally defeated in 1864.

* Regions are comparable to provinces in size; *zhou* are administrative units between the size of a region and a county. The five autonomous regions are: Tibet, Inner Mongolia, Guangxi-Zhuang Autonomous Region, Xinjiang-Uighur Autonomous Region, and the Ningxia-Hui Autonomous Region.

nan, for example, there is a county where the Tai and Jingpo live. One group lives in the mountains and the other in the valleys. They jointly govern the county."

"What does autonomy mean in practice? How is an Autonomous Region different from a province?" we asked. Professor Fei Xiao-tong, who had taught at the Institute for more than twenty years, replied: "Autonomous areas are inseparable parts of the People's Republic of China. They are like administrative units elsewhere. They are local governments and part of the apparatus of the People's Republic. The difference is they have autonomous rights in internal affairs. For example:

"They can choose their own forms of administration in accordance with the characteristics of the nationalities in their area. They can use their own written and spoken language. They can choose the language, and it is legal for all purposes.* Cadres in the autonomous areas come from the national minorities as much as possible—to the best of everyone's ability.**

"Economically, the autonomous areas receive special preference from the central government. Compared to other provinces, they pay less taxes to the state and receive more economic investments.† This is so these areas can make faster-than-average progress and catch up with the rest of the country. Finally," Fei concluded, "autonomous areas can make their own local laws with the approval of the central government."

"What kind of laws?" Janet inquired.

Several in our host group conferred. One of the students

* In the past, before Liberation, national minority languages were not recognized by the central government. All legal and educational matters were conducted in Chinese.

** Cadres from minority groups have multiplied rapidly since Liberation. For example, in the early 1950s there were only about nine hundred cadres from minorities in the Guangxi-Zhuang Autonomous Region. In 1970 there were about seventy-eight thousand. More recent press reports indicate that this trend is continuing.

† These are the collective taxes on agricultural production which communes pay to the state. There are no individual taxes.

explained that such local laws could cover questions of legal holidays, celebrations of various national festivals, and school semester schedules. Published information on this same question also mentions laws apportioning electoral representation to the National People's Congress, and local regulations "for organizing organs of self-government and tax collection."*

"In addition to autonomy," we continued, "you have mentioned opposing both Han chauvinism and local nationalism. Could you explain that?"

"Yes, we do oppose both," Professor Fei replied. "But in practice we stress opposing Han chauvinism. This is the more important because the Hans are in the great majority and because Han chauvinism was actively encouraged in the past. Discrimination by the Hans must be fought because of its historic roots. We have passed laws forbidding the use of names and terms that discriminate against minorities. For example, in the past we used a character meaning 'animal' to refer to national minority people. This has been abolished. Also, some names of localities and places were given by Hans in a chauvinistic way. Some were quite discriminatory and insulting. Before Liberation the capital of Xinjiang had been given a Han name which meant 'we have conquered this place.' Now we use the traditional Uighur name, Urumchi, which means 'beautiful place.' The old Han name for the capital of Inner Mongolia meant 'forced to surrender to Han.' It has now been changed to Huhehot.

"We have destroyed old monuments which praised the defeat of minorities by the Hans because these, too, insulted the national minorities. We also educate Han people to build unity and mutual respect. The Party and government give special attention to educating people of the Han nationality to overcome Han chauvinism."

Fei paused a moment and then proceeded to the second part of our question. "We also oppose local nationalism. By local nationalism we mean those ideas opposed to unity with other nationalities, the ideas of those who want to isolate

* See "About National Minorities in China," *China Reconstructs*, December 1972.

themselves, keep backward customs, or try to split the country."

Although opposing reactionary forms of local nationalism, the central government's attitude toward "backward customs" has actually contained a fair degree of flexibility and autonomy. The history of how Tibet's serf system was gradually transformed bears this out.

In 1951 a formal agreement was signed between the traditional rulers of Tibet and the new central government in Peking. It guaranteed regional autonomy, recognized the status of the existing political system, and held that reforms should come with local agreement, not by compulsion on the part of central authorities. Tibetan troops were reorganized into the People's Liberation Army, and other PLA units entered Tibet to take up national defense duties on the borders. Gradual reforms did take place, but in 1959 Tibet's traditional ruling groups, using U.S. and Indian weapons, attempted to reestablish their ebbing power. The nobles' rebellion was defeated and political and economic reforms were accelerated. The serf system was finally abolished and land reform completed.*

A recent Chinese statement contended: "As for undesirable customs, it is for the different nationalities to reform these of their own accord as their people raise their level of political consciousness and scientific and cultural knowledge."** Our own impressions, both from our visit and from historic analysis, are that the central government certainly sees itself, and Han cadres, helping as catalysts in the process of change. But only as catalysts: the basic thrust for change has to come from the masses of the nationalities themselves.

---

* For those interested in pursuing the question of Tibet, we suggest: *India's China War* by Neville Maxwell (New York: Doubleday-Anchor, 1972); *A Curtain of Ignorance* by Felix Greene, Chap. 13 (New York: Doubleday, 1964); *The Timely Rain* by Stuart and Roma Gelder (New York: Monthly Review Press, 1965); *Tibet,* by Alan Winnington (New York: International Publishers, 1957); and *When Serfs Stood Up in Tibet,* by Anna Louise Strong (Peking: New World Press, 1960).

** Statement in *China Reconstructs,* December 1972.

Professor Fei continued: "Historically, China has long been a unified country, unlike some other countries with national minorities. In China all nationalities were under a unified regime as early as the thirteenth century. The national minorities of China were not oppressed nations—China as a whole was an oppressed nation—oppressed by imperialism, feudalism, and capitalism. Thus the Han people, too, were oppressed. The national minorities were also oppressed by their own ruling class. Also, the Han ruling class often colluded with the minority ruling classes."

Fei's remark that national minorities in China had not been "oppressed nations" was important. It indicated a key aspect of China's national minority policy and is worth a brief digression because of its implications.

Marxist-Leninist theory (which the Chinese use) holds that "nations" are historically constituted groups of people with all the following characteristics: common language, common culture, common economic life and economic cohesion, and common territory.* Furthermore, this analysis contends, nations are specifically a historical product of the period of rising capitalism. The emerging capitalist class sought to shatter the confines of old tribal and feudal structures and to consolidate their own political power. Thus, in many places, and particularly in Western Europe and the United States, national consolidation and national independence became the political expression of capitalists seeking control over their home territories.

However, subsequent developments changed the nature of

* Important sources on the Marxist-Leninist approach to the national question include the essays of Lenin and Stalin. See Lenin (1) "Critical Remarks on the National Question"; (2) "The Right of Nations to Self-Determination"; and (3) "The Socialist Revolution and the Right of Nations to Self-Determination." Stalin, "Marxism and the National Question." These essays are available in both *Collected Works* of Lenin and of Stalin. Marx and Engels dealt with the topic most directly when analyzing the question of Irish independence (which they supported). See Marx and Engels, "Marx's Letter to Engels of November 2, 1867" and "Marx's Letter to Engels of November 30, 1867" in *Selected Correspondence of Marx and Engels* (Moscow: 1965).

national movements in other parts of the world. The growth of capitalism, and its transformation into colonialism and imperialism, meant a search for new territories and more raw materials. Colonies and client states were established. Weaker nations were subjected to national oppression and many emerging nations were held in check. A sharp difference between "oppressor" nations and "oppressed" nations became the principal feature of national movements. "Oppressed" nations, Marxist-Leninist theory contends, have the absolute right to "self-determination." This means the right to free themselves from all bonds of national oppression and to determine their own political future, up to and including the formation of a completely independent nation state.

The key to all this is that nations have the right of self-determination. In Marxist-Leninist theory, if you consider a group a nation you recognize it has the right to determine all aspects of its political existence.

"National minorities" are different from nations. The term is a bit ambiguous and has been applied to different types of groups. Members of a nation living outside their common territory are usually called national minorities. Examples would be Koreans living in China or Chinese living in Korea. Also groups with some, but not all, of the characteristics of a nation are often called national minorities. This would be the case, for example, of groups whose economic development had not reached national cohesion but who nevertheless shared a language, culture, or perhaps territory. Marxist-Leninist theory holds that national minorities should have full democratic rights and full equality but that they do not have the right of complete self-determination, i.e., to secede territorially. Forms of local autonomy within a larger unified state are considered appropriate means to guarantee the equality of national minorities.

Thus Fei's designation carried with it crucial implications regarding the questions of autonomy, equality, and the right to secession. As "nations" the minorities would have been viewed as possessing the inalienable right to secede from the Chinese state (although supporting the right to do this and advocating it as a specific program are quite different things). But viewed as national minorities, it was possible to regard these groups in terms of both autonomy and inseparability from the People's Republic.

Whether or not China's minorities have the right to self-determination (in the Marxist-Leninist sense of the term) is a question which the Chinese Communist Party has answered differently at different times. In 1931 the Communist Party-led All-China Congress of Soviets adopted a resolution which, although somewhat confusing in terminology, was nevertheless crystal-clear on the question of self-determination:

> ... The First All-China Congress of Soviets ... categorically and unconditionally recognizes the right of national minorities to self-determination. This means that in districts like Mongolia, Tibet, Sinkiang [Xinjiang], Yunnan, Kweichow [Guizhou], and others, where the majority of the population belongs to non-Chinese nationalities, the toiling masses of these nationalities shall have the right to determine for themselves whether they wish to ... create their own independent state, or whether they wish to join the Union of Soviet Republics, or form an autonomous area inside the Chinese Soviet Republic.*

In 1937 the Party's Central Committee approved a resolution drafted by Mao Tse-tung which urged Party members to "mobilize [to resist Japanese aggression] all ... minority nationalities in accordance with the principle of self-determination and autonomy."** This approach was affirmed again in 1945 when Mao said the Party recognized the right to self-determination of all the nationalities in China.†

By 1947, however, changes in Party policy became apparent. An army manifesto drafted by Mao Tse-tung stated their policy would be to "Recognize the right to equality and

---

* *Fundamental Laws of the Chinese Soviet Republic* (New York: International Publishers, 1934), cited in Moseley, ed., *The Party and the National Question in China* (Cambridge, Mass.: MIT Press, 1966).

** "For the Mobilization of All the Nation's Forces for Victory in the War of Resistance," *Selected Works*, Vol. II, p. 26.

† "On Coalition Government," *Selected Works*, Vol. III, pp. 255-56.

autonomy of the minority nationalities within the borders of China."* No mention was made of self-determination. In 1949 the new Constitution of the People's Republic held that: "The People's Republic of China is a unified, multinational state.... Regional autonomy applies in areas entirely or largely inhabited by national minorities. National autonomous areas are inalienable parts of the People's Republic of China."**

Professor Fei was quite frank in noting that the Party had changed its position on the nationalities question after the defeat of the Japanese in 1945. It was felt that the accumulation of centuries of forcible encroachment by foreign imperialists, plus the specific political conditions of China at the time, had brought about an intimate and indestructible identification among the nationalities. Thus all nationalities joined together to form an indivisible state: the People's Republic of China.

Fei's remarks contained what must have been some of the major considerations at that time. "Remember," he emphasized, "national struggles are in the end class struggles. The oppression of the national minorities was really by ruling classes, not by the Han people."

"Have there been separatist movements among China's national minorities?" we inquired. "What were they like?"

"Historically, separatist movements appeared among national minorities for two reasons," Fei responded. "First, many were provoked by the imperialists and, second, many genuinely wanted to be free of Han oppression. But, as I've said, that was oppression of the Han ruling class, not all the Han people. Many minorities wanted to end oppression but did not necessarily seek independence. Separatism wasn't really a big question and has become even less so since the oppression by the Han ruling class has ended. In recent years

* "Manifesto of the Chinese People's Liberation Army," *Selected Works*, Vol. IV, p. 150.
** "Constitution of the People's Republic of China," in *Documents of the First Session of the First National People's Congress* (Peking: 1955), cited in Moseley, *The Party and the National Question*.

the only separatist movements among China's national minority people have been a few in the old ruling classes who wanted to split from the People's Republic. This is what happened, for example, in Tibet in 1959."

"Has China," we asked, "handled the nationalities question in the same way Russia did after the 1917 revolution?"*

"No," Fei quickly replied, "our historical situation is different from that of Russia. We have a much longer history of unified government than Russia. There the Tsarist type of oppression of nations, the larger size of the nationalities population, and the more recent history of the Russian empire made for a different situation. Thus federated republics, as in the Soviet Union, were not set up in China. Actually, Marx was not for a federated republic system, but Russia had special conditions and Lenin recognized this."

Fei concluded, "In China, after Liberation, the equality of national minorities was the first priority. The question we faced was how to realize equality among minorities who in the past had been oppressed within a unified country. Thus we had the goals of both equality and unity. Regional autonomy was used as the means to insure both."

"We understand religion was particularly strong among many national minorities," we asked, "particularly Islam and Buddhism. How has the religion question been dealt with in the autonomous areas?"

Ce Dun, the Tibetan student, responded. "Let's take the example of Lamas in Tibet. Before Liberation, people were literally forced to become Lamas. A serf family had to give their second son to a monastery. Today there are only a few old Lamas left. Nobody wants to be one. There is freedom of religion and also freedom to have no religion."

Another student added: "We are Marxist-Leninist and therefore atheists. But religion is an ideological problem and

---

* The Soviet Union, where less than half the population was Russian at the time of the 1917 revolution, was called by Lenin a "Prisonhouse of nations." The USSR was formed as a federation of separate national republics, each with the right of secession. The republics were regarded as nations which had formerly been oppressed by the Tsarist empire.

cannot be solved by force. It can only be solved by education. For example, different local laws in autonomous areas and different holidays for the schools, for religious purposes, are respected."

Tu Er-xun, a Uighur teacher, reminded us: "The dining room where we ate lunch together is a special Islamic dining room. The Islamic kitchen here at the Institute does not serve pork."

"But this is an Institute for cadre training," we responded. "Does that mean you have students here who are still religious?"

"We do not know of any students in the Institute who are religious," Tu chuckled. "We have our kitchen now because of custom and taste."*

We then asked about population trends in minority areas. Were Hans moving into these areas, bringing their culture with them?

"Before Liberation," Zhan Shou-zhai replied, "the populations of the national minorities, especially among the Mongolians and Tibetans, were generally decreasing due to the severe oppression they suffered. There was much disease and very high infant mortality. Since Liberation, the populations of the minorities have been increasing. In Mongolia, for example, the population increased between 20 and 30 percent in the first ten years. The government generally encourages increased population in national minority areas.**

"Only a small number of Hans have migrated to the minority areas. Some were there already, before Liberation, and more recently some technicians have been sent to the border areas. There has been very little moving out of the autonomous areas by national minority people. Only a few cadres have left, for political reasons dealing with their jobs."

Our visit to the Central Institute for Nationalities only

---

* We also encountered a similar Islamic dining room at the Foreign Languages Printing House in Peking.

** In the Han areas, on the other hand, government policy is to encourage birth control.

gave us a small taste of the diversity to be found among China's national minorities. But the cultures of national minorities, despite their small numbers, were visible throughout China. Virtually every cultural performance we saw included their songs and dances; some of the most popular were from Tibet and Mongolia. Music from all regions, often with new Han words, was common on records and in performances. Songs heard over loudspeakers on our long train rides often included tunes from or about national minorities. We saw Han schoolchildren and nursery toddlers, dressed in colorful nationality costumes, learning the dances of various nationalities. Huge murals on walls and billboards often depicted minorities. One common mural was of Chairman Mao surrounded by representatives of the different national minorities, each clad in distinctive national dress. In Guangzhou we attended a performance by a cultural group from Hainan Island. The touring performers included both Hans and national minorities. The minorities were an integral part of the program, representing part of the total cultural life of Hainan Island. They were not presented as some sort of quaint or exotic addition to Han culture.

Equality and autonomy, diversity and unity. These were the goals which China's many different peoples sought in their common effort to construct a new society.

10
The Struggle Between Two Lines

"The struggle between two lines—the class struggle—continues."

For us this oft-mentioned statement represents the most distinctive and important principle of Chinese socialism. The Chinese see their revolutionary history, both before and since Liberation, as a continuing "struggle between two lines," between the socialist world outlook, the proletarian way of doing things, and the capitalist, or bourgeois, world view. The Chinese say the competition between these two perspectives is a feature of the current historical era and is found in both capitalist and socialist societies.

New Forms

"You say the class struggle takes on new forms under socialism," we once inquired. "What are some of these new forms?"

We raised the question during a discussion with some cadres from China International Travel Service in Peking. The group included Zheng and Fu Bing-zhan, both translators; Liu Yu-kun, the older cadre we affectionately called Lao Liu; and Zhao Ri-chen and Xi Jin-huan, two younger cadres from the Peking office of CITS.

Lao Liu spoke up: "Our country is now under a proletarian dictatorship. The forms of class struggle are different than in capitalist countries. Under capitalism the fronts are clear. Here the bourgeoisie and landlords cannot openly call on the people to overthrow the proletarian dictatorship. So they try to undermine it by finding agents in the Communist Party. They try to sabotage it. On the one hand, they try to make the people outside the Party decadent, to poison their minds, to make them leave the revolutionary ranks. As Mao said, they use 'sugar-coated bullets.'* They also try to worm their way into the Party, to disguise themselves as revolutionaries. Thus the forms of class struggle are mainly manifested inside the Party by the struggle between two lines."

"It is more difficult to maintain proletarian dictatorship than to seize state power in the first place," declared Xi, who picked up the conversation where Lao Liu left off. "There are two ways used by the bourgeoisie to overthrow the proletarian dictatorship. First, the proletarian dictatorship can be overthrown by reactionary armed forces. That happened in 1871 when the Paris Commune was destroyed. That was visible overthrow. The imperialists also tried to kill the new Soviet Republic after it was founded in 1917. Another example was the reactionary action in Hungary in 1956. The second form is difficult to see. It is gradual evolution. Marx and Engels foresaw this problem. Lenin also saw the problem of a 'newly born bourgeoisie,' but he died in 1924, very early.

"Stalin tried to strengthen the proletarian dictatorship in the Soviet Union. But he made errors. After changing the ownership of production, he declared [in 1936] that classes no longer existed. But shortly before his death he realized that these problems still existed. He wrote about them in

---

* In 1949 Mao warned that the bourgeoisie, with their military defeat, would change tactics and use "sugar-coated bullets" and flattery to regain power. ("Report to the Second Plenary Session of the Seventh Central Committee of the Communist Party of China," in *Selected Works*, Vol. IV, p. 374)

'Economic Problems of the Soviet Union' [in 1952].* But he, too, died shortly thereafter.

"Thus the first proletarian party and the first socialist country," Xi asserted, "changed their color. And the bourgeoisie around the world saw this. For example, John Foster Dulles talked of his hope for the second and third generations of Chinese turning from socialism.

"Mao has said the period of socialism is a long period, that we still have classes and class struggle. Our main danger lies in the capitalist roaders. Because of this, Chairman Mao personally initiated the Cultural Revolution."

Lao Liu leaned forward and added: "The struggle against the bourgeois line includes the struggle against both 'Left' and Right opportunism."

"Left" and Right

"Left" and Right opportunism? The terms are not commonly used in the United States and have little political meaning for most Americans. However, in the Chinese context they are terms descriptive of the twists and turns of China's political struggles.

Opportunism means taking advantage of circumstances with little regard for principles. In socialist politics it is a term used to indicate errors or mistakes, whether conscious or unconscious. Put most briefly, "Left" errors, or ultra-leftism, occur during the revolutionary struggle for socialism when one tries to "go too fast." Right errors stem from "going too slow." The key to going fast or slow is one's relation to the people, to the masses. Mao put it this way:

> If we tried to go on the offensive when the masses are not yet awakened, that would be adventurism [a form of "Left" oppor-

---

* This essay has recently been reprinted and circulated in an English edition by Foreign Languages Printing House in Peking.

tunism]. ... If we did not advance when the masses demand advance, that would be Right opportunism.*

Recklessness, adventurism, or overconfidence—these are types of "Left" errors. Reformism, capitulation to the enemy, or avoiding the class struggle—these are types of Right errors. Since both kinds of mistakes harm the struggle for socialism, both are considered as serving the interests of the capitalist class. Therefore, "Left" errors are said to be Left, i.e., socialist, in appearance only.** They are Right, i.e., capitalist, in essence.

Many Marxists label Right errors revisionist, that is, revising the principles of socialism and class struggle to the point of abandoning them. "Left" errors are often considered anarchist, meaning opposing the socialist state as well as the capitalist state. But "Left" errors are, in the end, also revisionist since they, too, abandon the class struggle for socialism.

We found Lao Liu's remarks about "Left" and Right opportunism most revealing. He had pointed out that the "struggle between two lines" was not between the "Left" and the Right. It was, rather, between the socialist and the capitalist roads. And the capitalist road included both "Left" and Right deviations.

This meant several things. It meant that Lao Liu, like all the other Chinese we talked with, did not consider the Cultural Revolution a personal power struggle between Mao Tse-tung and Liu Shao-chi, or any other individuals. Nor did he consider it, as have many Western commentators, a struggle between "reds" and "experts"; or between "idealists" and "pragmatists"; or between "rebels" and "loyalists." Rather, he regarded it as an ideological battle between two different class perspectives. As such it became quite complicated. Two ideological camps developed, with Mao Tse-tung and Liu

---

* "Talk to Shansi-Suiyuan Daily Editorial Staff," Mao Tse-tung, *Selected Works*, Vol. IV, p. 243.

** Thus the common practice of putting Left in quotation marks when referring to "Left" opportunism. Ultra-left is another term used to designate the same type of mistakes.

Shao-chi as their chief representatives; but they were representatives of two contending political lines, not simply personal competitors for power. Furthermore, Lin Piao was regarded as another representative of the bourgeois camp, not the proponent of a third perspective.

The principal emphasis in the early stages of the Cultural Revolution had been against Right errors. But, it was pointed out to us, cadres who made Right errors had sometimes swung wildly from one extreme to the other. Liu Shao-chi, for example, while Right opportunist in most periods, on some occasions had adopted ultra-left postures. It was argued that in his case this was probably a deliberate smokescreen. Ultra-leftism provided Liu Shao-chi with a facade of socialist rhetoric while serving the ultimate interests of his Right opportunist politics. In addition, other forms of "Left" opportunism emerged during later stages of the Cultural Revolution. Some of these "Left" errors were a direct result of the struggle against Right opportunism. Intense political struggles can produce overreactions and, as the Chinese put it, one tendency obscures the other. For a time conditions were such that, as Chou En-lai said at the Tenth Party Congress, "The struggle against Liu Shao-chi's revisionism covered Lin Piao's revisionism."

The *People's Daily* of October 14, 1972, aptly described this relationship between Right and "Left" opportunism:

> Liu Shao-chi and his company pushed the Right opportunist line, assuming the airs of bureaucratic overlords and vigorously demanding special privileges. They opposed ... ideological and political work. They advocated that "rules and regulations are omnipotent" ... *Such a right opportunist line provided the best breeding ground for the growth of anarchism.*
>
> ... swindlers like Liu Shao-chi [i.e., Lin Piao, et al.], knowing that the masses resented Right opportunism, cunningly incited ultra-"left" trends of thought, ... advocating ... "rules and regulations are useless," clamouring for "smashing everything" ... Their purpose was to ... destroy socialist labour discipline and to bring about the disintegration of socialist production. ...*

* Translated in *China Quarterly*, January-March 1973, p. 193. Our emphasis.

If all this sounds confusing, you're right. It is.

There are ways, however, to unravel even the most complex events. We returned home convinced that analyzing China in light of the "two-line struggle" was key to understanding the new society. We could not point to any one thing and say: "There's the class struggle!" But it was there.

We encountered shining examples of socialist cooperation, outstanding accomplishments due to collective efforts, but we also discovered problems, areas where old attitudes, old and new contradictions, restrained socialist development. We met people who truly personified socialist ethics, who served the people well. But we also met people who seemed out of place in a socialist environment, whose self-centered, aggressive egos would have been much more at home in Western intellectual circles.

How are these contrasts to be explained? What do they mean?

Let us give some examples which, we hope, can bring life to the concept of the two-line struggle. Our visit to the Dong Feng (East Wind) Watch Factory in Tianjin is a good place to start.

The East Wind: It Doesn't Always Prevail

It was a bright, windy May morning. Yu, a local Tianjin guide and translator, pointed out sights as we drove through the city.

"There's the school Chou En-lai once attended," he puffed proudly. A few blocks later he chuckled, "And there's the middle school I once attended! It's near the river where I went swimming."

Yu had stayed up late the previous night preparing for our tour of the watch factory. He now produced a carefully compiled list of technical terms, noted first in Chinese and then in English. With him we pooled our layman's ignorance of such things as mainspring, watch stem, dial, movement, and the like.

The watch factory reposed impressively on the edge of town. It was a solid four-story brick building with long wings reaching forth from its grandiose main entrance. The structure literally towered over surrounding suburban farmland. When our car pulled up to the front door we decided the monstrous building *had* to have been erected under Russian influence. We fought our way inside against heavy gusts of spring wind. The cadre in charge of a small welcoming committee by-passed the customary brief introduction and immediately suggested we tour the workshops.

It was like touring a Detroit factory. The cadre whisked us through workshop after workshop, stopping neither to describe the work being done nor to introduce us to workers. Other members of the welcoming committee fell into line behind, a silent trailing entourage. The whole atmosphere was a stark contrast to other factories we'd visited. Workers ignored us. In other factories they had been enthusiastic, eagerly describing their jobs. Here no one spoke unless directly approached, and even their answers, when given, were short and abrupt. Heads and hands remained glued to production.

We stopped, and Stu, hoping to start a conversation, asked a question of a woman placing dials on wristwatches. Yu translated the question a couple of times and got no response, not even a nod or gesture. Total rebuke. Yu, a bit embarrassed, mumbled an improvised answer himself and quickly ushered us on to another work area. We noticed that workers treated the leading cadre the same way they treated us. They spoke only when he asked them direct questions and then gave quick, brief answers. We began to suspect the rather grim atmosphere reflected more the relationship between workers and cadres than attitudes to foreign visitors.

The whirlwind tour of workshops ended and we retired to a small meeting room for discussion. Three or four veteran workers were present but the cadre who had sailed us through the workshops monopolized the conversation. A pattern began to develop. Political attitudes emerged which called to mind the struggle between two lines.

This had been the first wristwatch factory in China. It now manufactured several models of a fairly high-quality 19-jewel watch. Most of the equipment and lathes, not surprisingly, were of Swiss manufacture. Chinese workers, however, were now making their own duplicates of the Swiss originals. Their plant had grown from a humble beginning of four watch repairmen in 1954 to its present 1,600 workers, with a production of 2,500 wristwatches a day.

"Our factory was formally established in 1958, under the guidance of the Great Leap Forward," the cadre host began. "But owing to the Liu Shao-chi line the factory was run by experts. Experts from the Soviet Union were invited. At first we were happy, for they brought blueprints, plans, and experience. But they forced us to copy their models and manufacture watches just like those in the Soviet Union."

He interrupted his narrative to open an oblong black box. Inside were six or seven wristwatches, a material history of the factory's production. One was the 1955 model of the Chinese repairmen, simple and practical, rather undistinguished. The second was the Russian model, fat and heavy—so sturdy it felt as if a tank could roll over it without doing damage. People in the room giggled while comparing the Russian-inspired piece to the attractive slim models they presently manufactured. Russian style, or lack of it, was clearly not up to Chinese aesthetic tastes.

"The Soviet experts issued various orders for us to follow," the cadre reminisced. "For example, we had been using pear wood, common in China, for grinding. They said what we were doing was all wrong, that we should only use wood from a certain kind of tree. But that tree grew only in the Soviet Union. After a long search we did find one small piece of this wood in a forestry research institute in Hebei Province. But of course we could never have regular supplies of it.

"In 1960 Khrushchev withdrew the experts and they took away their blueprints and data. In those days workers had not been allowed to touch the precision grinders, and when anything went wrong we had to call the Soviet experts to repair them. When the experts left, no one knew how to repair the machines. We had trouble adjusting. But in 1963 we began production again; so it was only after the Soviet experts left that we really began producing watches on our own."

The conversation continued along this vein, almost entirely technical. It was clear great strides had been made. They had, indeed, overcome many technical difficulties. But we were struck by the lack of broader ideological concerns. Here the Cultural Revolution was discussed only in terms of increased production. Nothing was said about socialist consciousness, class struggle, material incentives, or internationalism and solidarity with Third World struggles. The Cultural Revolution was discussed as if it were something of the distant past, something over and done with. Bulletin boards with educational materials, so common in other factories, were conspicuous by their absence. Here we saw only a few posters about production improvements and displays hailing the achievements of some model workers.

The factory had both strengths and weaknesses. Its obvious strengths were in technical areas; weaknesses appeared to be in politics, in ideology. Through self-reliance they now produced high-quality wristwatches. But there seemed to be poor relations between workers and cadres; this implied a weakness in workers' participation in leadership. It is possible the sudden need to develop their own technical skills, following the pullout of the Soviet experts, had brought about an understandable emphasis on technique. The politics of workers' control, of the mass line, however, apparently had been slighted.

In the terminology of the two-line struggle this example was generally symptomatic of Right opportunism. But as we've already noted, the struggle between the two lines also involves "Left" errors. Our visit to Peking University provided us with some concrete information about ultra-leftism in practice.

A Period of Factionalism

Some of the earliest struggles of the Cultural Revolution were waged at Peking University. In May 1966 a group of young instructors put up a big-character poster criticizing the university's leadership, charging it with revisionism and taking the capitalist road. The struggles that ensued were complex, but by June 1967 the old "capitalist roaders" had been thoroughly exposed and discredited. A university "Cultural Revolution Committee" was formed to replace the old authorities. Then a new period of struggle broke out, a period of factionalism and internal squabbling between different revolutionary groups. "Left" errors became a problem. We listened to Wei Kuang-wu, a former Red Guard and participant in those struggles, describe this period:

"Two factions developed with different opinions about the Cultural Revolution Committee, the temporary leading body at the university. Some thought the new committee was itself revisionist or reactionary, some thought not. It had been elected by the students and teachers but there were no workers or soldiers on it. It was composed only of intellectuals.

"At the beginning of the Cultural Revolution it did some good work. It led students to repudiate Lu Ping [the old President of Peking University] and to carry on revolution and go to the countryside and other parts of the country. Those things were correct. But because the members were intellectuals, their world outlook was not completely remolded. They also made mistakes.

"Some considered the power given by the teachers and students as their own personal power. They didn't listen to criticism, but only listened to praise. They said all criticism was a 'reverse current,' and they called their critics reactionaries. They didn't follow Chairman Mao's teaching to 'draw a clear line between the contradictions among ourselves and the contradictions with the enemy.' Since they wouldn't take any criticism from the masses, dissatisfaction set in.

"Two groups developed. One believed the Committee had adopted a new revisionist line. They wanted to repudiate the

Committee. The other group said it had made mistakes and should be criticized but not repudiated. The Committee itself did not learn from the previous year's experience of the Cultural Revolution and stood only by the side of the group which supported it. This sharpened the differences between the two factions. Most students and teachers had not yet thoroughly remolded their political consciousness. We weren't modest; we never doubted that we were correct. Our partial achievements meant puffed heads. We didn't think it was necessary to criticize ourselves. We thought we were the most important people. We thought 'without us, the world will not turn.' Class enemies were able to take advantage of this situation to get us to fight each other.

"Class enemies spread the 'only I am correct' type of thinking. They led people to think 'only I am revolutionary,' 'only I am leftist.' Each group insisted on its own viewpoint and the class enemies fanned the fire. Some class enemies told the two groups that their differences were 'fundamental,' and that they could not make compromises with each other. By June 1967 the two groups were totally separated. The group which supported the Cultural Revolution Committee called itself the Commune of New Peking University and the other called itself Jinggang Mountain Corps at Peking University. Based on their original different viewpoints, the two groups began to adopt differences on other matters.

"For example, at this time many of the cadres at the university had stopped working altogether, and the two groups differed on how to deal with cadre problems. There were differences on who was a 'bad' and who was a 'good' cadre.

"They called each other names, like 'revisionists' or 'reactionaries.' But in fact most were revolutionary comrades. They attacked each other as class enemies and did not use a proletarian viewpoint to judge things. They judged things only in terms of their group, their factional perspective.

"Both groups actually were composed of revolutionary people, but at this point the class enemies began to say 'history is written by strong men' and 'we should use arms.'

Fanned by class enemies, the struggle broke out into fighting in March 1968. This lasted only a short period, but it led the revolution astray.

"Bricks, stones, and sticks were used at first and then broadswords and spears. Each side occupied some dormitories for its own use. We neglected the most important task, to repudiate the capitalist roaders. Some class brothers were wounded during the fighting, so workers and peasants were against us for fighting.

"Many of us knew this was not following Chairman Mao's teaching, but we couldn't change the situation. Many people left Peking University when fighting broke out and went to factories and the countryside. Some went home. The number of people at the University fell to between 100 and 200, although both sides claimed a following of 4,000. The leaders of the groups became 'generals without an army.'

"At this time Chairman Mao had made a nationwide call for workers to take leadership in everything. In August 1968 a Workers' and People's Liberation Army Propaganda Team came to Peking University."

Here the veteran Red Guard paused and asked a member of that team to continue. The team was still at the university, a permanent part of its leadership. Chang Chuang-you, a worker from Xinhua Printing House, had been with the Team when it arrived at Peking University. He continued the story: "The first thing we did was to propagate Chairman Mao's teachings. Debate by reasoning was used, not force. We asked the groups to pull down their fortresses and go to the classrooms to unite together. Soon we had unity, but only in organization. The groups were not united ideologically until later. We organized Mao Tse-tung Thought study classes for the students and teachers. We gave them class education by asking old workers and peasants to come and tell them of the bitter life in the old society. In this way we led students to see their fighting only benefited the class enemies. The workers and soldiers had individual heart-to-heart talks with students and gave them more class education.

"About one-third of the teachers and students were activists and they were the first ones to understand the need for unity. We held meetings in their departments where they spoke out and influenced the others. Thus the whole university was pushed forward.

"We had three principles in our work. First, no matter what group you are in, if you follow the teachings of Chairman Mao we will support you. Second, wrong ideas and wrong actions are dealt with in study sessions and meetings to help people see their mistakes. Third, we will wage mass movements to criticize or remove from leadership those deliberately opposing Mao's teachings. There were very few in this third group, and even here those who admitted their mistakes and corrected themselves still had a way out.

"When the masses of students and teachers came to understand the need for unity, the handful of class enemies was isolated. Repudiating them was also a class education for the masses.

"It took between four and six months to achieve ideological unity. At first there were some who spoke of unity at meetings but acted differently. As Chairman Mao said, 'They shook hands over the table; they kicked each other underneath.'

"The Workers' and PLA Team was able to accomplish this only because we applied the teachings of Marxism-Leninism and Mao Tse-tung Thought, not because we were heroes. In this group talking to you today are people who were in different factions during the Cultural Revolution."

Another ex-student summed up this experience: "We now know if we depend only on intellectuals we cannot manage our affairs well. We know the working class must exercise leadership in everything. The process of eliminating factionalism is a process of remolding one's world outlook. Factionalism and sectarianism are aspects of bourgeois individualism. At the beginning of the Cultural Revolution the bourgeois world outlook still influenced us. We sought careers and fame. We were narrow-minded. As Chairman Mao said, we had lost our heads; we were swollen from head to foot. We learned that class enemies can instigate factionalism when we make these mistakes.

"The working class should also learn from the struggle. Teachers and students should follow the leadership of the working class. And most important, we should follow the teachings of Chairman Mao."

"Left" in Form

"Left" mistakes during the Cultural Revolution had been particularly strong in student circles, but they were by no means limited to students and intellectuals. Some of the Party's top leadership, as the case of Lin Piao indicates, succumbed to the revolutionary-sounding sirens of ultra-leftism. Exactly what happened during the heat of the Cultural Revolution's fierce struggles is still not completely known. We claim no inside track or secret information in this regard. However, it is clear, as more and more information emerges from investigations about the Cultural Revolution, that an identifiable ultra-leftist trend was ascendant in certain places at certain times.

Our own conversations, plus more recent data, make possible a composite picture of the ultra-leftist tendency.* The struggle between the two lines lurched "leftward" under the influence of those who espoused the following:

(1) *Overthrow all.* The purpose of the Cultural Revolution, as seen by Mao and his supporters in the Party's Central Committee, was to uproot the "handful" of "Party persons

---

* Our compilation of ultra-left characteristics in this form is not intended to imply that we believe this was the program of any one particular group or faction. These are general characteristics. How unified the ultra-left was during the Cultural Revolution is highly questionable and also difficult to judge since two of its main characteristics were factionalism and intrigue. Another complicating factor was overlapping with Right opportunist tendencies.

in power taking the capitalist road." The principal Party document outlining the goals of the Cultural Revolution, the August 1966 "Decision of the Central Committee of the Chinese Communist Party Concerning the Great Proletarian Cultural Revolution," explicitly called for the retention of most (95 percent) of the cadres. Ultra-left groups, however, called for, and in some cases carried through, the overturning of 90 percent or more of the cadres.

Some went even further. They claimed China was a capitalist state, ruled by a "Red capitalist class" headed by Chou En-lai. They called for complete overthrow of all state and Party structures and the smashing of the People's Liberation Army, which they regarded as a tool of the decaying "Red capitalists." They argued China needed a "real" revolution to "negate the past seventeen years."*

Pursuing the vision of the 1871 Paris Commune, ultra-leftists called for the redistribution of property and power, and the establishment of a new society in a "People's Commune of China."** Their vision of the "Commune" was at best vague. But they left no doubt about their opposition to the new "three-in-one" Revolutionary Committees which were formed throughout China to seize power from those "taking the capitalist road." Early in 1967 Mao had called for

---

* An example of this ultra-left perspective can be found in "Whither China," a document published in several Chinese regional newspapers in early 1968. It was written by an ultra-left group in Hunan Province, called Sheng-wu-lian. The group was said to have had close ties to the notorious "May 16th Group." In March 1968 Sheng-wu-lian was denounced by top Party leaders, including Chiang Ching, as a group manipulated by "hooligans and counterrevolutionaries." "Whither China" was translated into English by U.S. government-related monitoring services in Hong Kong. It appeared in the "Survey of China Mainland Press," No. 4190 and also Union Research Service Nos. 19-20, 1968.

** This should not be confused with the people's communes established in the countryside in the late 1950s and now the basic form of collective agriculture. The ultra-leftists meant something quite different.

the establishment of these Revolutionary Committees "where power needs to be seized," stating they were "a provisional organ of power that is revolutionary and representative and has proletarian authority."* In opposition to this the ultra-leftists called the Revolutionary Committees "bourgeois reformism." They considered the "three-in-one" combination tantamount to reinstating the same bureaucrats toppled as "capitalist roaders."

The "overthrow all" mentality of the ultra-leftists led them to attempt to seize power from many newly established Revolutionary Committees. Repeated struggles ensued in schools, factories, and communes as one group overthrew another and vied for power. All claimed to be the "true" revolutionaries. The situation often became quite confusing. Some newly established Revolutionary Committees were not genuine, as the ultra-leftists claimed. In fact, some had been fashioned by "capitalist roaders" in an attempt to hang on to power by deception. Thus careful analysis was needed to distinguish lap-dog committees from genuine Revolutionary Committees. But ultra-leftists demanded across-the-board opposition to all Revolutionary Committees, and to 90 percent or more of the cadres.

The ultra-left did not stop at attempts to seize power at the local levels. By late 1967 a national-level ultra-left conspiracy, known as the "May 16th Group," was uncovered. May 16th leaders, whose goal was nothing less than overthrowing Mao's leadership and seizing overall state power, recruited conspirators from various ultra-left student and worker factions. They directed their main opposition at Chou En-lai. The People's Liberation Army (PLA) was another principal target. In some provinces they seized PLA arms depots and launched armed struggles.

The May 16th Group included top Party leaders like Wang Li, Kuang Feng (Guang Feng), and Ch'i Pen-yu (Qi Ben-yu), all original members of the Party's Cultural Revolution Com-

---

* See Chapter 2 for a brief description of the Revolutionary Committees.

mittee.* Also implicated were several top military leaders: Yang Ch'eng-wu (Yang Cheng-wu), Hsiao Hua (Xiao Hua), Yu Li-hsin (Yu Li-xin), and Fu Ch'ung-pi (Fu Chung-bi). May 16th conspirators, it is today asserted, even included Lin Piao and Chen Po-ta, members of the Political Bureau of the Central Committee.

The style of the May 16th Group was ultra-leftist. However, some May 16th leaders (Yang Ch'eng-wu, Yu Li-hsin, and Fu Ch'ung-pi) have also been cited as leaders of an earlier Right opportunist movement. That movement, called the "February Adverse Current," had specifically sought to stem the growing criticism of Liu Shao-chi. Wang Li, another leader of the May 16th Group, further illustrates how Right and "Left" sometimes overlapped. Recent investigations have revealed that Wang Li actually had direct ties with Liu Shao-chi.** But if some of these leaders were involved in both rightist and ultra-leftist tendencies, it would not necessarily have indicated a change of politics. It would simply have been a switch of tactics.

(2) *"I am the core—only we are revolutionary."* Ultra-left groups tended toward sectarianism and factionalism. They believed themselves the only "pure" revolutionaries. This led to treating friends as enemies. They considered almost everyone not in their particular group as "class enemies."

Editorials in the Chinese press have criticized this attitude and called it the "mountain stronghold mentality." This rather colorful term originated in the days of guerrilla warfare, when revolutionaries were holed up in scattered mountain bases and a similar tendency to form cliques arose.

The "mountain stronghold mentality" usually divorced ultra-left groups from the masses of workers and peasants they claimed to lead. This, in turn, produced a type of built-in elitism in their approach to political change. The people, they argued, did not yet realize that their true interests lay in

---

* A special committee set up by the Party's Central Committee to lead the Cultural Revolution.
** See Hinton, *Turning Point in China*, p. 75.

ultra-left programs. For example, the people didn't "understand" and thus naively supported three-in-one Revolutionary Committees as the means to seize power from "capitalist roaders." But, ultra-leftists claimed, their group (or groups) knew the "truth" and thus it became incumbent upon them to lead the way, to take "vanguard" actions. One result of this was that in the hands of ultra-leftists Mao's concept of the mass line ("from the masses, to the masses") became: "in place of the masses."

(3) *Mao is a genius.* The ultra-leftists were the loudest and most strident of those appearing to support Mao. There is no question that Mao's writings were a sharp and effective tool in the struggle against the policies advocated by Liu Shao-chi and other "capitalist roaders." However, ultra-leftists took a "more Mao than thou" attitude. They stripped Mao's works of substance and turned them into dogma and formalism. Mao's concept of "politics in command," so useful in rooting out individualism and subjectiveness, was transformed into reciting slogans and waving the "Red Book." Dogma replaced substance; formalism replaced practice. Mao, against his wishes, was exalted by statues and praised as "our great teacher, great leader, great supreme commander and great helmsman!" Mao badges proliferated and grew, some to the extent they had to be worn on chains around the neck.

Ultra-leftists proclaimed Mao was a "genius." Lin Piao declared that Mao was the greatest genius ever, the likes of which emerged only once every several thousand years in China and once every several hundred years in the entire world. "Everything he says is truth, and every phrase he utters is worth ten thousand phrases," Lin Piao said.*

Furthermore, the ultra-left argued, the philosophical works of Marx, Engels, Lenin, and Stalin, were now out of date. One needed only to read Mao. "The writings of Marx and

* Quoted in "Remarks Transmitted by Hsia Hua," 1966, in *Chinese Law and Government*, Vol. VI, No. 1, Spring 1973, p. 53.

The ultra-left significance of Lin Piao's remarks is clear because of hindsight. Public criticism in China's press has now attributed the "genius" theory to Lin Piao and subjected that theory to scathing attack.

Lenin are too numerous . . . are too far removed from us. In the classical works of Marxism-Leninism, we must devote 99 percent of our efforts to the study of Chairman Mao's works," Lin Piao opined in the fall of 1966. "Chairman Mao stands much higher than Marx, Engels, Lenin or Stalin."* The study of socialist principles became, under the influence of ultra-leftists, a formalistic, ritualistic "movement for the study and living application of Mao Tse-tung Thought."

Why did the ultra-leftists, who in substance opposed Mao's policies and leadership, take such a pro-Mao stance? There appear to be several reasons.

First: it would be politically foolish, considering the contours of China's politics, for anyone to oppose Mao openly. There *is* a genuine and deep respect for Mao on the part of China's masses, a love developed over five decades of struggle and change. Thus any group bent on overthrowing Mao's leadership, from either the Left or Right, finds it opportune to cloak itself in Mao's mantle. The Chinese say such opportunists "wave the red flag to oppose the red flag."

Second: consider this question. How can Mao's political power be sapped if his prestige is too great to challenge directly? One method would be to elevate Mao to a pedestal. Turn him into a figurehead. Make Mao superhuman. Create a demigod whose image becomes so inflated and unreal it isolates him from real power.

Third: there were probably many among the ultra-left rank and file who actually believed they were the true supporters of Mao's policies. But their dogmatic approach to politics blinded them to reality. We believe this quite possible. "Dogma is more useless than cow dung," Mao himself once observed. We couldn't agree more. We know from our own political experience that once bitten by the dogma-bug many well-intended activists can ignore obvious contradictions between their own ideology and their practice.

---

* "Instructions on Raising the Study of Chairman Mao's Writings to a New Stage," ibid., pp. 30-31.

The ultra-left distortion of Mao's thought into dogmatism and formalism had several concrete effects. It swung the political pendulum from the rigidity of Liu Shao-chi's "capitalist road" policies to rigidity in the other direction. Before the Cultural Revolution many factories had been run by experts. "Technique" was in command and workers' initiative stifled. For the most part this has been changed, but only after many workers also learned firsthand of ultra-left "solutions." In some factories ultra-leftists eliminated entirely all "bourgeois" posts of technicians and engineers. Those who had formerly held such jobs were sent into the shops for fulltime production work. Ultra-leftists chastised veteran workers for including technical and mechanical materials in study sessions with younger workers. They argued: only ideology was important; only Mao's works should be studied. Nothing else mattered. "Politics in command" became "all politics and no technique." The results were, predictably, a drop in production and confusion within the factories. The ultra-left "solution" proved to be no better in achieving socialist goals (workers' control with increased production) than had the Right opportunist policies of the Liu Shao-chi line.

We learned of similar experiences in other fields. Prior to the Cultural Revolution, teachers of English (as a foreign language) often used Dickens and Shakespeare as texts—hardly materials useful to training competent, modern-day translators! But during the Cultural Revolution ultra-leftists demanded that only English translations of the "Quotations from Chairman Mao Tse-tung" be used. Again, hardly adequate material to teach vocabulary, grammar, or colloquial usage of English!

(4) *Export the revolution.* Ultra-leftists tended toward a militant-sounding international policy. They continually and stridently proclaimed support for all struggles against U.S. imperialism. They predicted the complete collapse of the world capitalist system in the near future. Their internationalist practice, however, substituted revolutionary bravado and bluster for concrete support of peoples' struggles throughout the world. Their interpretation of proletarian

internationalism called for the export of their own particular brand of "revolutionary struggle" regardless of the situation or conditions in other countries.* In fact their posture leaned toward national chauvinism.

China's ultra-leftists were impressed by the high tide of national liberation struggles throughout the Third World in the late 1960s. And justifiably so. They hailed these struggles and the growing peoples' movements within the capitalist countries as indications of the imminent downfall of United States imperialism. This, in itself, did not distinguish the ultra-leftists from others in China, although the ultras probably tended to foresee a much more immediate and rapid collapse of world capitalism.

The ultra-left, however, proclaimed that people throughout the world would win liberation only when they, too, followed Mao Tse-tung Thought. Lin Piao, for example, asserted that grasping "Mao Tse-tung Thought—Marxism-Leninism at its highest in the present era" was necessary: (a) for "oppressed nations" to "be able to win liberation"; (b) for socialist countries "to prevent the restoration of capitalism"; (c) for countries "where political power has been usurped by revisionists . . . to overthrow the rule of revisionism and re-establish the dictatorship of the proletariat"; and (d) for the "people of all countries" to shatter the "entire old world." He added that dissemination of Mao Tse-tung Thought throughout the world was one of "the glorious tasks entrusted to the people of our country by history" and "our incumbent internationalist duty."**

* Marxist-Leninist theory holds that proletarian internationalism, class solidarity which cuts across national boundaries, is fundamental to the cause of the working class and its allies. Thus it is the duty of all revolutionaries to support the struggles of their class brothers and sisters in other countries. But this does not alter the fact, the Chinese argue, that genuine revolutions must be made by each people in their own country. No one, not even those from socialist countries, can make someone else's revolution.

** Quotations are from Lin Piao's "Speech at the Peking Rally Celebrating the Fiftieth Anniversary of the October Revolution," on November 6, 1967; in *Important Documents of the Great Proletarian Cultural Revolution in China* (Peking: Foreign Languages Press, 1970).

Contrast this to the attitude of Mao and his supporters. They definitely regarded Mao's writings as important and decisive in China's struggles. They considered them the "concrete application" of Marxism-Leninism to the specific conditions of China. They believed Mao had "inherited, defended, and developed" Marxism-Leninism. They felt there were general and theoretical truths to be found in Mao's works, and they felt revolutionaries everywhere should study and learn from each other. But they did not build up Mao's writings as grandiose cure-alls for the world's problems. They did not claim: "Mao Tse-tung Thought marks a completely new stage in the development of Marxism-Leninism ... at the highest level."* To the contrary, they argued Marxism-Leninism should be applied to the specific conditions of each country —as Mao had done for China.

One of the consequences of the ultra-left international perspective was a self-selected position of holding all the answers for everyone. *They* were the purveyors of revolutionary wisdom for the world's oppressed people. *They* were the revolutionary leaders. Actually, this posture was simply the transfer to the international scene of their "I am the core" type thinking. But here it acquired characteristics in addition to its obvious arrogance. Speaking of "the glorious tasks entrusted to the people of our country by history" sounds like a rationale for big nation chauvinism—ominously so in a country with centuries of traditional condescension toward "foreign devils."

In fact, some extremely nationalistic and anti-foreign attitudes emerged during the Cultural Revolution. Foreigners resident in China sometimes became targets of ultra-left groups (although a few foreigners actually became ultra-leftists themselves). Some foreigners were hounded out of the country; a few were unjustly jailed. Families of mixed marriages suffered discrimination during what is now called a period of "anti-foreignism."

On March 8, 1973 (International Women's Day), Premier

---

* Lin Piao, August 18, 1966, ibid.

Chou En-lai met with foreigners living and working in China. The Premier condemned Chinese chauvinism, racism, and exclusiveness in the treatment of foreigners. He apologized for injustices during the period of "anti-foreignism." He said that Mao had recently observed there was a Chinese tendency to be conservative and cliquish in contact with foreigners. But in new China, he concluded, a new spirit should prevail which kept the whole world in view and truly upheld the principle of proletarian internationalism.

The "internationalism" of China's ultra-leftists found concrete expression during the fall of 1967. In August of that year ultra-leftists seized the Foreign Ministry. Chen Yi, then Foreign Minister, was accused of following a foreign policy of "three surrenders and one extinction": surrender to United States imperialism, surrender to Soviet revisionism, surrender to domestic reaction, and extinguishing the flames of worldwide revolution. Yao Teng-shan, former Chargé d'Affaires in Indonesia, was installed in Chen Yi's place. Diplomatic files were seized and some secret documents were publicized through wall posters. Chou En-lai argued that Chen Yi should be criticized but not overthrown. Chou was himself held captive in his office for a few days during the same month. Yao, along with Wang Li, a member of the Party's Cultural Revolution Committee and a May 16th conspirator, implemented their version of a "revolutionary" foreign policy. According to William Hinton:

> They proceeded to send directives all over the world that in effect amounted to the export of the Cultural Revolution. Their goal was to turn overseas embassies and consulates into active centers for political agitation against the host governments. Under Wang Li's influence Chinese sailors in Italian ports fought physically with native longshoremen who would not wear Mao buttons. At home, in Peking, British diplomats were beaten up and the British Chancery was burned out in retaliation for the arrest of Chinese newsmen in Hongkong.*

---

* Hinton, *Turning Point in China*, pp. 74-75.

It took about two weeks for cadres responsible to Premier Chou En-lai to regain control of the Foreign Ministry. Chen Yi, however, was never reinstated as Foreign Minister and the post remained vacant until early 1972.

These and other incidents precipitated the closing of several foreign embassies and consulates in China. Some foreign diplomats, harassed and bewildered, headed for home.

There were several other manifestations of ultra-left foreign policy during this period. Foreign ships were boarded and their cargoes seized. Chinese diplomats fought British bobbies in the streets of London. Editorials and statements appeared in the Chinese press which opposed any Vietnamese-United States negotiations; other articles focused on armed revolutionary struggles against Ne Win in Burma and Sihanouk in Cambodia.* The Democratic People's Republic of Korea (North Korea), one of China's ideological allies in the struggle against revisionism, was criticized for not being "revolutionary" enough. Korea responded with carefully worded suggestions of Chinese dogmatism. Some ultra-leftists held it was "revolutionary" to sever diplomatic relations with other countries. And finally, despite profuse vocal support for the Vietnamese, ultra-leftists closed railway lines and seized shipments of arms and ammunition bound for Vietnam, keeping the armaments for their own use.

(5) *Problems are solved by force.* The decision of the Central Committee guiding the Cultural Revolution had been quite clear on the question of force: "When there is debate, it should be conducted by reasoning, not by coercion or force." Cadres and others who had made mistakes were to be dealt with by "curing the sickness to save the patient." The formula of "unity-criticism-unity" was to be applied to all except a handful of class enemies.

Ultra-leftists, however, argued that "history is written by strong men." Some leaned on Marxist theory to justify their use of violence. Since the Cultural Revolution was that of

---

* This was before the coup, probably engineered by the CIA, which toppled Sihanouk's Cambodian government in 1970. See Sihanouk's book, *My War with the C.I.A.* (New York: Pantheon, 1972).

one class overthrowing another, they reasoned, armed struggle was historically inevitable and necessary. After all, they continued, the historic mission of the proletariat was the violent overthrow of the capitalist class. A new, Red capitalist class, they claimed, was ruling China and, of course, they represented the proletariat.

Thus ultra-leftists seized People's Liberation Army (PLA) arms depots and shipments of arms headed for Vietnam. In the fall of 1967 they promoted a gun-seizing movement under the slogan "Arm the Left," and then launched what they called "local revolutionary wars." Ultra-leftists controlled various cities for short periods of time, labeling such takeovers "a state of armed mass dictatorship." The Party's Central Committee responded. They issued an order in September 1967 which forbade the seizure of arms from the PLA and instructed the PLA, until then under strict orders never to use force, to resist gun-seizure with force if necessary. During the same month Chiang Ching made an important speech criticizing ultra-leftism. She specifically denounced the May 16th Group and condemned arms seizures and the attacks on army units by ultra-left groups.

It's not known to what extent armed conflicts actually took place, but reports of serious incidents came from Fushun and Shenyang in the Northeast, to Wuhan in Central China, to Wuzhou in the Southwest. Fatalities due to factional fighting undoubtedly ran into the hundreds, possibly more. Most of the serious fighting apparently took place in late 1967 and in 1968.

Undue use of force against friends (as opposed to class enemies) is a characteristic of ultra-leftists the world over. Of course, ultra-leftists have no monopoly on the glorification of violence: consider the example of fascism. But ultra-leftists do tend toward a lot of boasting and posturing about the use of force. They often invoke visions of armed struggle not to solve problems but rather to impress others that they are, indeed, really "revolutionary." We have encountered these tendencies among ex-Red Guards we met in China as well as among student revolutionaries in the United States.

(6) *Smash all that is old.* Instead of "combining the old and new,"* the ultra-leftists took a dim view of anything from the old society. There were struggles during the Cultural Revolution, sometimes quite fierce, to save historic and cultural relics from destruction by ultra-leftists. Should Buddhist pagodas, temples, and ancient libraries close or remain open? Should old books and materials be removed from libraries? These questions were often raised, appropriately, in the course of struggles against Right errors, against unquestioned acceptance of the old culture. Then ultra-left responses became a new problem. Excesses were apparently committed; but some Red Guard units, we were told, had protected historic and cultural relics from other, ultra-left, Red Guard groups bent on blindly destroying "everything old."

Where "Left" and Right Meet

How can the super-revolutionaries—the ones most against revisionism, most against capitalist roaders—be "Right in essence"? Isn't it going a bit far to lump ultra-leftists and Rightists together in the same "capitalist road"?

Let's examine the facts. Look at the Chinese Cultural Revolution. In practice the ultra-leftists and Rightists shared several important perspectives.

A significant convergence of interests took place after the initial ousting of the "handful of capitalist roaders in power." Now both ultra-leftists and Liu Shao-chi supporters, some who had just been toppled from office, called for the "overthrow of all." The bureaucrats, of course, were trying to maneuver their way back into power. And when ultra-leftists proposed the wholesale overthrow of those who still held positions of authority, the Right opportunists recognized an open avenue of operation. Is it any wonder investigations later revealed that Liu Shao-chi supporters consciously joined

---

* See Chapter 8.

ultra-left groups, pushing hard for the "overthrow all" policy?

More specifically, both the ultra-left and the Liu Shao-chi supporters opposed the creation of genuine three-in-one Revolutionary Committees. The ultra-left, under the banner of super-socialism, denounced these new organs of power as "bourgeois." The capitalist roaders, on the other hand, fought to maintain (or regain) power in the structures they had traditionally controlled. They opposed Revolutionary Committees as "anti-Party" and "renegade" cliques. Both tendencies were threatened by the truly revolutionary coalition of workers or peasants, cadres, and representatives from the People's Liberation Army. Neither could effectively control such a coalition and thus both attempted to distort the formation of three-in-one combinations.

One of the reasons both the ultra-leftists and the Rightists opposed the three-in-one Revolutionary Committees was the involvement of the People's Liberation Army. The PLA, an integral part of all three-in-one committees, was a stronghold for Mao's political line. It was probably the most stable institution during the whole Cultural Revolution. Rightists correctly understood PLA involvement meant exposure of, and opposition to, their policies. Ultra-leftists considered the PLA a conservative influence, a tool of the "Red capitalists." Thus both actively opposed PLA political intervention in schools, factories, and communes. Both saw it to their advantage to promote splits and discord within the PLA, to undermine the coherence and influence of the PLA. Ultra-leftists spearheaded attempts to disrupt the PLA internally, under the slogan "pull out the minority in the army." But who would appreciate this more than the Rightists, watching one of their principal opponents being torn asunder? It's reasonable to speculate they did more than simply sit back and applaud.

Both ultra-leftists and Rightists used Mao as a smokescreen for their real politics. This was more true of the ultra-left, but the Rightists have shown they, too, could cloak themselves in Mao's mantle when advantageous. Undoubtedly the rank-and-file in both tendencies presumed they were the true followers of Mao's line. It's difficult to believe, however, the top leaders and ideological heavies in either camp had any illusions about following Mao's politics. They knew what it was they opposed, and Mao's cloak of respectability was usually shed when they were pushed to the wall. Liu Shao-chi and his supporters had often vocalized respect for Mao's leadership; but they also prevented publication and circulation of Mao's works. The May 16th Group, and later Lin Piao, eulogized Mao to the extreme. But both chose to scheme for power rather than implement Mao's "mass line" and support the new Revolutionary Committees.

"Left" and Right met in other, more literal ways, too. Perhaps one of the most telling indications of the basic perspectives of the ultra-leftists is to look where some of these super-militants are today. A few of the young people caught up in the whirl of ultra-leftism fled to Hong Kong when their fantasies crumbled around them. Their comments now reveal what had really been at the root of their revolutionary posturing. Consider these excerpts from an interview, in Hong Kong, with a former Red Guard:

> The Cultural Revolution interrupted our education, and afterwards we not only had to leave school but leave our city home to labour for a lifetime in the village, one boy remarked to me plaintively. *"But you were a committed Red Guard once. Weren't you still serving society in a revolutionary way in the countryside?"* He laughed bitterly. "How could I serve society in the village? Do you really think the peasants were more progressive than I? What did they know of Mao's works or of armed struggle in the Cultural Revolution? No, the Government used us. I wanted to continue my study and then apply my knowledge in a factory."
>
> The most militant of the Red Guards seemed, in the end, to be the most disillusioned and psychologically disoriented. Some had hoped to use the Cultural Revolution as a channel for upward mobility . . .*

---

* "Innocents in Limbo," by David Raddock, *Far Eastern Economic Review*, April 29, 1972, p. 19. Emphasis in original.

You be the judge: do these comments reflect socialist ethics or do they reflect individualism and career-seeking?

Some of these former super-revolutionaries now sit and brood about Mao being an "Uncle Tom." Others have found routes to personal success by selling colorful, questionable "memoirs" to Kuomintang and American publishers.* One former Red Guard, billing himself as "Mao's bodyguard," recently toured the United States under the sponsorship of a reactionary U.S. student group.

The militant ultra-left and the bureaucratic Right both, in the end, placed themselves above the people. The Rightists were a bit more open about it; they argued it was necessary for managers and experts to run things. They said this was simply realistic. Practical. Ultra-leftists, on the other hand, championed mass participation in the running of society while actually tearing down all forms of authority. Both fabricated justifications for acting in place of the masses. One considered the people technically ignorant, backward, and uneducated. The other believed people were misled, naive, and had not yet realized what were their "true" interests. The inevitable conclusion, for both, was that those "qualified" or those who "understood" should wield power. Take your pick. But what, in the end, is the difference? How close are either to the goals of socialist democracy and the application of Mao's concept of the "mass line"?

One final point about the unity of "Left" and Right. Perhaps one reason most of us don't really conceive of ultra-leftists and Rightists snuggling up together is an assumption we make about China's politics. Western analysts usually describe Chinese politics as being on a continuum, with a "Left," Right, and Center. Or of Radicals, Pragmatists, and an "in-between" group which is slightly radical and somewhat pragmatic. The scenario generally has Mao or Chou En-lai sitting in the middle, shrewdly playing the two extremes

---

* See, for example, Ivan and Miriam London, *The Revenge of Heaven: Journal of a Young Chinese* (New York: Putnam, 1972), based on interviews with Ken Ling (pseudonym).

off against each other. The "Left" and Right are the farthest apart and the most antagonistic to each other.

The first problem with this model is that it simply doesn't describe reality. In real life there are too many exceptions to its rigid categorization. Those who persist in viewing China's politics in this manner inevitably end up as contortionists, twisting facts and stubbing toes. But more fundamentally, this perspective fails to take into account the motivating factor of political struggle in China: the competition between values of the old, individualist society versus values of the new, cooperative society.

The machinations of China's Right and "Left" tendencies become more comprehensible when they are viewed as part of the ideological "struggle between two lines." Envision two ideological camps. They are in fundamental opposition to each other. One camp champions socialist, cooperative, and collective ideals. The other, consciously *and* unconsciously, promotes bourgeois, individualist, and competitive ethics. Both have internal tensions in addition to external competition with each other. As objective conditions change, so do the tactics of the camps. Sometimes the correct policy for the socialist camp is to push hard, rapidly. Sometimes the correct policy is to slow down, to collect and regroup forces. Sometimes, even, the correct policy is to make a temporary retreat. Moreover, the wrong policy at the wrong time can land someone, unsuspectingly, in the other camp. What distinguishes any political action is not whether it is militant or mundane, not whether it supports change or prevents change, and not whether it is "radical" or "pragmatic." The test is whether or not it promotes socialism. In practice both the ultra-left and the Right opportunist tendencies hinder socialist development. They are both based on individualist, elitist, and competitive ethics. Thus both are rooted, in spite of rhetoric, in the bourgeois camp. Switching from one bourgeois tendency to another does not necessitate a fundamental change of world outlook, and is actually a much shorter journey than jumping from one ideological camp to the other.

Politics, someone might quip, makes strange bedfellows.

We suggest this is not the case in China. Ultra-leftists and Rightists are not strange bedfellows. They're natural, and often willing, partners.

Lin Piao: The Two-Line Struggle Continues

The Lin Piao affair, which reached its climax when Lin attempted an armed coup d'état in mid-September 1971, is still shrouded with mystery for most Westerners. For two years the Western press carried rumors and sensational, highly questionable "inside scoops" about the fate of Lin Piao. Chinese authorities officially announced details of the affair to the rest of the world in August 1973. Their account did not elaborate details and many questions about specifics still remain. However, certain events appear to be clear: Lin Piao, and a few supporters, planned to seize power from the Chinese Communist Party Central Committee through an armed coup. Their plans included the assassination of Mao Tse-tung and other leaders. But the assassination attempt failed and the coup aborted before it really got off the ground. On the night of September 12, 1971, Lin and a few of his chief conspirators fled the country by jet. The plane, however, crashed in Mongolia and all aboard perished.

Our purpose here is not to mull over details of the incident.* It is likely more details will gradually become known as the Chinese themselves release more information from their investigations.

We feel it is more important to know what the Lin Piao affair meant. Why did it happen? What did Lin Piao represent politically?

We visited China six or seven months after the incident. It

---

* Probably the most detailed and authoritative account of Lin's plot is in an article by Wilfred Burchett. It was published in two places: "Lin Piao's Plot: The Full Story," *Far Eastern Economic Review,* August 20, 1973, p. 22; and "Behind Lin Piao's Flight from China," in *The Guardian* (New York), August 29, 1973, p. 20.

was a time when the Western press carried only speculation and rumors about Lin Piao and the Chinese press carried nothing which mentioned Lin Piao by name. It became evident to us, however, that the question of Lin Piao's political role was being discussed internally, among the Chinese themselves. But they would not talk to foreigners about the subject.

"Can you tell us about Lin Piao?" we asked Lao Liu and Xi Jin-huan during our conversations in Peking. "What is fact and what is rumor?"

Xi smiled and folded his hands:

"We have nothing to say in this area. If you read *Hongqi* and *Peking Review* you can see the struggle between two lines continues in China."*

That was it. Next question, please.

Subsequent events confirm our belief that the Chinese were discussing this topic among themselves at the time of our visit. We respect their massive ability to get their house in order without outside interference. Their unity and cohesion are impressive. Westerners tend to think if something is not reported in our press, or at least in the Chinese press which U.S. agencies monitor, then the Chinese people do not know about it. We assume the Chinese people have not been "informed" by their government. Such assumptions are highly unwarranted; they ignore basic aspects of China's new society, such as the communication role of the Chinese Communist Party and of the mass organizations at workplaces, schools, and in the neighborhoods.

Let us give another example of something not publicly announced but apparently well known by people throughout China. When we visited Changsha in May 1972, people talked with us about the discovery of a two-thousand-year-old Han tomb. It was an open topic of conversation, but to our knowledge had not yet been reported in the press. Evidently

* *Hongqi* (Red Flag) is the theoretical journal of the Chinese Communist Party. *Peking Review* is a weekly foreign-language periodical from Peking. It often reprints important articles from the regular Chinese press.

analysis and preparation of this rare archeological find were being completed before the official announcement. The find was announced in the Chinese media in August 1972. Reports were then published abroad. *Newsweek*, for example, declared in its August 14, 1972, issue that the tomb was "unearthed in the region of Changsha *last week.*" Of course, this matter, unlike the Lin Piao affair, was openly discussed with foreign visitors. The point is that the Han tomb and its contents were known throughout China even though it had not yet been publicly announced in the press, either Chinese or Western.

By the end of 1972 the Lin Piao affair was a topic of open discussion with visiting foreigners. The Chinese did not mull over sordid details of the September incident. Rather, they dealt with the Lin Piao affair politically. Workers and peasants described the influence of ultra-left policies in factories, communes, and schools. They reported that Lin Piao's brand of ultra-leftism had been the subject of mass struggles. It had affected the daily life of millions. Workers reported that through many struggles they came to learn what the ultra-left line was, to understand its dangers, and thus to expose and defeat it. At the beginning, they said, it had not been clear where the ultra-left line originated or that Lin Piao represented its top leadership. Lin's abortive coup, moreover, happened *after* the ultra-left line had been thoroughly discredited through mass political struggle. The coup, evidently, was the last desperate act of a politically defeated man.

How had that political struggle unfolded? And what were the issues? It's possible, with hindsight, to go back and see that ideological battle as it raged in the pages of the Chinese press. From the beginning of the Cultural Revolution to the present, Lin Piao's political career passed through six distinct periods. These periods form a process of political struggle—a struggle in which Lin Piao's brand of politics germinated, sprouted, blossomed, and then was rudely uprooted when masses of rank-and-file workers and peasants recognized it to be a "poisonous weed."

(1) *Lin Piao the public ally.* The first period of Lin Piao's

contemporary political career stretched from the beginning of the Cultural Revolution (1965-1966) until April 1969, the time of the Ninth National Congress of the Communist Party. This was a time of Lin Piao's rising prominence; he adroitly rode the waves of the Cultural Revolution to new heights of personal prestige.

Throughout this period Lin Piao was publicly identified as one of Mao's closest allies in the struggle against Liu Shao-chi's type of revisionism. The Chinese now claim personal ambition was the reason Lin Piao so zealously pursued Liu Shao-chi. It is now argued that Lin was more interested in eliminating an important rival for power than in exposing Liu Shao-chi's politics. Lin's participation in the May 16th Group conspiracy (1967)—if the charges of his involvement are true—would certainly justify such a conclusion.

It is definitely clear that during this period Lin was a principal promoter of the Mao cult. Lin declared in 1966 that Mao was a "genius" and that history was propelled by "geniuses" and "heroes." It was Lin Piao who announced that Mao Tse-tung Thought was "even more superior ... more developed" than Marxism-Leninism, who scoffed at the works of Marx, Engels, Lenin, and Stalin as hopelessly out of date, and who encouraged formalism and ritualism in the study of Mao's writings. It was Lin who dubbed Mao "our great teacher, great leader, great supreme commander, and great helmsman," a formalistic salutation (called the "four greats") which Mao personally squelched.

Lin also made speeches attacking the idea of peace talks about Vietnam as "swindles for the purpose of stamping out the raging flames of the Vietnamese people's national revolutionary war."* He argued the world had entered an entirely new historical era "in which imperialism is heading for total collapse and socialism is advancing to worldwide victory." In this era, he proclaimed, one of the "glorious tasks entrusted

---

* Lin Piao, speech on October 1, 1966, in *Important Documents*, p. 269.

to the people of our country by history" was to "grasp ... Mao Tse-tung Thought and disseminate it still more widely throughout the world."*

This was the heyday of the ultra-left. It was a time of turmoil and struggle, a time when true politics were not always immediately clear. It was also Lin Piao's heyday. Lin's rise to power coincided with the declining influence of Liu Shao-chi and his supporters. Selected as sole vice-chairman of the Central Committee in August 1966, Lin was given special attention in the press and labeled Mao's "close comrade-in-arms." Lin's rising star reached its zenith in April 1969, when he was officially designated Mao's successor in the Party Constitution adopted at the Ninth Party Congress.

(2) *Lin Piao the political opponent.* But Lin Piao's zenith also marked the beginning of his slide into infamy. The next period, from April 1969 until August 1970, was a period of developing political struggle between Lin Piao and the majority of the Central Committee who aligned themselves with Mao Tse-tung.

The Chinese now assert that Lin Piao prepared a draft Central Committee Report for the Ninth Party Congress (April 1969) which was rejected in total by the majority of the Central Committee. Lin felt that the Cultural Revolution was over. The "bourgeois headquarters" of Liu Shao-chi had been smashed, Lin argued, and all political enemies of socialism had been completely routed. The main task now was to concentrate on economic production. Lin's Draft Report (prepared in conjunction with Chen Po-ta) was rejected as being nothing less than a warmed-over version of Liu Shao-chi's "theory of productive forces." Liu's theory held that the socialist revolution was completed in China, the class struggle was basically over, and thus people should leave political struggle behind and now immerse themselves in production. Liu Shao-chi had grounded this theory on the premise that, using Marxist terminology, the principal contra-

* Lin Piao, speech in November 1967, in ibid., p. 306.

diction in China was no longer between the bourgeoisie and proletariat, but rather "between the advanced socialist system and the backward productive forces." Lin Piao, it is now argued, had adopted the same perspective in his Draft Report.

Lin did eventually deliver the Central Committee's Report at the Ninth Congress. The report he read, however, was not based on his original draft. Indeed, studying the final report confirms the claim that it was much more Mao's than Lin's. Mao's perspective that the class struggle continues under socialism was completely upheld. Liu Shao-chi's revisionism was roundly denounced. There were a few spots, however, which sounded like the Lin Piao of the Cultural Revolution: the characterization of the historical era and the international situation, and also the formalism concerning Mao and Mao Tse-tung Thought. But perhaps most significantly the Report, while hailing the victory over Liu Shao-chi's revisionism, explicitly stated that "Left" and Right tendencies still existed within the Party and predicted more "two-line" struggles in the future.

Although Lin's draft was rejected he obviously still wielded considerable power. Enough power, in fact, to get himself appointed Mao's "successor" at this same Party Congress. The developing struggle with Lin had not yet burst into open confrontation. Lin enjoyed tremendous public prestige and was now saluted as Mao's "close comrade-in-arms *and successor.*"

This was a period when Lin Piao played the role of a political opponent, but evidently within the Party's framework. The political debate developed in a style consistent with Chinese inner-party struggle. Individual protagonists were not named in the press; polemics emphasized concepts and theories, not personalities. This is typical of the early rounds of political struggle in China. Generally, individuals are criticized by name only after repeated unsuccessful attempts to convince them to correct their errors. Thus, as the Cultural Revolution unfolded in 1966 the Central Committee cautioned against "criticism of anyone by name in the press" unless careful discussion was carried out and appropriate Party Committees approved the action. This reticence to criticize by name has resulted in a frequent use of political euphemisms. For example, Liu Shao-chi was not criticized by name in the Chinese press until quite late in the Cultural Revolution. But for a considerable period he was obviously the person referred to as "China's Khrushchev." Once Liu Shao-chi was openly criticized, however, his name became a handle to use in political criticism of others. This practice might seem elaborate and ritualistic, since it does not really obscure who is being criticized. However, it does allow struggles to emphasize political points instead of personalities. We would guess that cadres who were the unnamed subjects of such criticism found it easier to reform than if they had been personal targets.

During the months immediately following the Ninth Party Congress the "theory of productive forces" was attacked in the press. It was made abundantly clear "the pernicious influence of the 'theory of productive forces' . . . has not yet been eliminated."* Other philosophical articles fired broadsides against remnants of Confucian ideology, emphasizing that class struggle continued in China and that defeated class ideologies would pop up again and again in new forms.

Ultra-left tendencies also continued to appear in the press. A "Mass Movement to Study and Apply Mao Tse-tung Thought in a Living Way" was promoted, significantly omitting any mention of the study of Marx, Engels, Lenin, or Stalin. The formulation of "Marxisim-Leninism–Mao Tse-tung Thought" of Cultural Revolution days became, in many quarters, simply "Mao Tse-tung Thought." The 1970 "New Year's Editorial," a major political statement prepared jointly by the *People's Daily*, *Red Flag*, and *Liberation Daily*, characterized world affairs and China's international role with rhetoric reminiscent of a Lin Piao speech.

The political struggle became sharper in the late summer of 1970. In mid-July an article in the *People's Daily* explicitly

* *Peking Review*, No. 38, September 19, 1969.

raised the question of inner-Party struggle, suggested how it should be conducted, and warned against sectarianism, selfishness, and arrogance. It urged serious study of the fundamentals of Marxist-Leninist ideology to ward off remaining "influences of the ideology of 'Left' and Right opportunism." It concluded that the Party must "give the comrades who have committed errors ample opportunity to wake up."*

Evidently Lin Piao didn't wake up. He continued to dream of personal power and in late August 1970, transformed his political struggles into a sharp inner-Party factional fight.

(3) *Lin Piao the factionalist.* The third stage of Lin's contemporary career began at a Plenum of the Central Committee in August 1970. This period lasted until February 1971, and was a time of intense factional struggle within the Party. Lin and his supporters still held considerable power and influence. Battlelines were drawn. Struggles were not just polemics—state power was at stake.

Lin Piao made an open move for more personal power at the August Plenum. Chen Po-ta, under cover of debate about a new state constitution, led a small group of Lin's supporters who tried to designate Lin as state chairman. (Liu Shao-chi had formerly held the position.) The move evidently caught most of the Central Committee by surprise, but the maneuver was rebuffed. It did crystallize matters. From that point forward the struggle with Lin was considered a "struggle between two headquarters."

Lin came out swinging. Polemics sharpened. Mao's cloak of respectability was still Lin's best cover, and he used it extensively. "Mao Tse-tung Thought" was promoted to the specific exclusion of Marxism-Leninism; formalism in study and ritualism in practice persisted. Some examples:

> Carrying red banners ... students held high their red-covered copies of *Quotations from Chairman Mao Tse-tung* as they greeted the morning sun rising from the east. Looking up at the

---

* *Peking Review,* no. 33, August 14, 1970.

brilliant portrait of our great leader Chairman Mao, they made a solemn pledge in the square: "Chairman Mao, dear Chairman Mao!"...*

or:

Long Live Chairman Mao! ... is the strongest utterance of our era.**

Ultra-left formalism was also pushed in organized ways. For example, a province-wide "Congress of Activists on the Living Study and Application of Mao Tse-tung Thought" was held in Henan. References to Mao as a "genius" persisted.

Lin also promoted himself directly. One might even suspect a conscious public relations campaign. Lin's distinguished military career was trumpeted loudly, emphasizing that he had been *commander* at several crucial battles during the long years of revolutionary struggle. Some points were exaggerated. "Great" and "creative" quotations from "Vice-Chairman Lin" were sprinkled throughout the press, and revolutionaries were now urged to rally around Mao as leader *and* "Vice-Chairman Lin as deputy leader."

Debates raged on the economic front. In December 1970, a group in the Ministry of Commerce argued that commerce, "the exchange of commodities," was *the* economic base of worker-peasant cooperation during the period of socialism. They wanted increased commodity production "not for profit but for the peasants," saying that "socialist commerce is commerce of a new type."† Such policies—which pushed commodity production while ignoring the question of capital accumulation—have since come under heavy criticism and are attributed to Lin Piao's camp.

Mao's camp promoted the study of his writings within a more general campaign to study Marxism. They spoke about distinguishing true Marxists from phoney Marxists, and reminded people that the two-line struggle continued. They

---

* *Peking Review*, No. 40, September 30, 1970.
** *Peking Review*, No. 43, October 23, 1970.

† "Orientation of China's Socialist Commerce," *Peking Review*, No. 50, December 11, 1970.

criticized ideas about the "dying out of class struggle" and analyzed, from a Marxist point of view, new manifestations of the idealist (as opposed to materialist) approach to politics.

During this period Mao himself (in a talk with Edgar Snow) publicly criticized the personality cult and how it had gone too far.

During this period, also, some very practical measures were taken to break up Lin Piao's factional power base. A campaign was launched within the Party to criticize materials Chen Po-ta had presented to the August Plenum, and in December 1970, a special enlarged Politbureau conference was held to deal head-on with Lin's factionalism. The Peking Military Region and work groups in the Party's Military Affairs Commission, spots where Lin had support, were reorganized in ways to break up factional concentrations.

The January 1971 "New Year's Editorial" of *People's Daily*, *Red Flag*, and *Liberation Daily* seems to symbolize the state of affairs at that time. It reads like a political compromise, almost as if alternate paragraphs were written by the two contending groups. There are aspects of ultra-left formalism about Mao and Mao Tse-tung Thought. But the piece also calls for study of basic Marxist-Leninist philosophy in order "to distinguish between genuine and phoney Marxism." Quoting Mao, the editorial urges "the whole nation should learn from the People's Liberation Army" and, in a fashion promoted by ultra-leftists, omits Mao's conclusion that "the People's Liberation Army should learn from the people of the whole country." On the other hand, the editorial specifically criticizes "arrogance and rashness," and urges people to be alert in distinguishing contradictions among the people from contradictions with class enemies.

The tide of these struggles, however, turned against Lin Piao. By February 1971, it became clear Lin's faction had failed in its bid for power. But now they were more than just a minority political tendency within the Party. They were not the "loyal opposition." They were now a bitter, discredited faction which had unsuccessfully tried to maneuver and buffalo its way into power.

(4) *Lin Piao the conspirator.* The fourth stage of Lin Piao's declining political career covers the period when he was consciously planning a military coup: from February 1971 until his death in September 1971. Lin's move from factionalist to conspirator coincided, probably not coincidentally, with serious erosion of his political influence. He had lost the political battle. For example, Lin's faction had apparently lost access to the nation's major media by the time their coup, "Project 571," was planned in February and March 1971.

"Project 571" was Lin's plot for the complete seizure of state power through a military coup d'état. The plan called for assassination of Mao and other top leaders, establishment of Lin's military authority in several major cities, and creation of a rival Central Committee. It also reportedly counted on military backing from the Soviet Union.

Although a secret conspirator, Lin still benefited from China's customary practice of displaying public unity among national leaders. Personally Lin still received favorable press, and during this period he continued to function in his posts of Vice-Chairman of the Central Committee and Minister of Defense.

Lin's political line, however, came under increasingly heavy attack. Public polemics sharpened and the political direction of the attacks became more and more evident. (However, we cannot judge just how clear it was to the public at that time whether Lin Piao personally stood behind the political tendencies being criticized.)

The movement to study fundamentals of Marxist-Leninist theory was accelerated, with the stated purpose of enabling everyone to distinguish between genuine and "sham" Marxists. The cult around Mao and his writings began to disappear. Claims that Mao Tse-tung Thought was the "highest development" of Marxist theory were dropped. Articles emphasized that Mao's thought represented the concrete "application" of Marxism-Leninism to China's particular situation. Party unity was stressed. Warnings against "splitting," "careerists," and "schemers" were issued. Political statements which had previously denounced "Liu Shao-chi's revisionism" now added "other political swindlers" to the revisionist category. Polemics emphasized that all political enemies were not of a "monolithic bloc." Industry and agriculture were encouraged to practice economy, to prevent waste, and to implement the principles of self-reliance. And finally, a devastating broadside was launched against the "genius" and "hero" theories of history and the whole philosophical perspective they represented.

One of the more important public documents of the period was published in July 1971. Prepared on the occasion of the fiftieth anniversary of the Chinese Communist Party, the statement detailed eight points "the whole Party should pay attention to and study." Every single point had relevance to the struggle against Lin's faction: (1) Marxist theory was again emphasized. (2) Current inner-Party struggle was acknowledged, but members were urged to follow the principle of "unity-criticism-unity." (3) Special warnings against arrogance and "careerists" were issued. (4) It was pointed out that in the struggle against one incorrect political tendency, another erroneous tendency might be obscured. (5) Everyone was urged to "adhere to the mass line"; "pseudo-Marxists" who kept "aloof" from the masses were denounced. (6) The principles of Party democratic centralism were reiterated and the creation of "many centers" within the Party was condemned. (7) There was a significant emphasis that the army must follow Party leadership. (8) And, finally, application of the principle of proletarian internationalism was encouraged but with special recognition that both "Left" and Right errors should be avoided.

Lin's judgment was now that his only hope for power was through a military coup. And in September 1971, that's what he tried.

But the coup failed. Lin Piao died in mid-September when he fled China and his plane crashed in Mongolia. However, Lin's politics, and in an ideological sense his political career, did not perish in that crash.

(5) *Lin Piao the "political swindler."* There was a period

following Lin's abortive coup, from September 1971 to August 1973, when China asked itself what had happened. What had Lin Piao represented politically? Lin was not mentioned by name in the media during this period; but there was little doubt he was chief among the "other political swindlers" now cited in ideological polemics.

This was a period of heavy political analysis, of study, and of assessment to discover the ideological roots of Lin's conspiracy. Massive political introspection was carried out through a "movement for criticizing revisionism and rectifying the style of work." Watchwords for this campaign were the "three do's and three don't's": "Practice Marxism, and not revisionism; unite, and don't split; be open and aboveboard, and don't intrigue and conspire."

During this period the ideological exposure of Lin's political line continued and deepened. Critical analysis expanded to include several new areas. Now frequent mention was made of "careerists . . . having illicit relations with foreign countries." The People's Liberation Army was urged to "learn from the people of the whole country." Cadres were reminded to be modest, prudent, and to follow the principle of "plain living." Lin Piao was now criticized, without specific mention of his name, for wavering during earlier periods of history, particularly in 1927-1930. Economic theories which had emphasized distribution and commerce, to the exclusion of accumulation, were now specifically labeled revisionist. The concept of "millions of proletarian successors" was introduced and criticism of "careerists" included accusations that they had used Confucianist, not Marxist, ideology.

China's proclamations about world affairs changed in tone. As always, importance was placed on upholding the principle of proletarian internationalism and supporting national liberation movements. But now it was emphasized that the general principles of Marxism-Leninism had to be "integrated with the practice of one's own country," and that self-reliance was indispensable for the people of each country to obtain independence and maintain sovereignty. (Lin Piao, remember, had talked about China's "glorious" task to disseminate Mao Tse-tung Thought in order for others to make revolution.)

A comparison of these different approaches to world affairs is instructive. For example, the 1970 and 1972 "New Year's Editorials" both talk about China's role in the world, and both even make use of the same quotation from Mao. But they reach significantly different conclusions. In 1970, when Lin Piao was still high in the saddle, it was proclaimed:

> Chairman Mao teaches us: CHINA OUGHT TO HAVE MADE A GREATER CONTRIBUTION TO HUMANITY. Under the leadership of the great leader Chairman Mao, our great Party, great people, great country, and great army can surely fulfill the glorious mission assigned us by history and will never fail to live up to the hope placed on us by the people of the world...

Compare that with the 1972 message:

> Our achievements are inseparable from the support of the proletariat and revolutionary people the world over. We must ... firmly support ... oppressed people and oppressed nations throughout the world.... we should remain modest and prudent, guard against arrogance and impetuosity, study and work harder and strive to MAKE A GREATER CONTRIBUTION TO HUMANITY by winning new victories.

And, in 1973, Wang Hung-wen spoke about international relations in these terms:

> ... we must persist in the principle of NEVER SEEK HEGEMONY ... we must never be conceited, not even after a hundred years, and never be cocky, not even after the twenty-first century. At home, too, we must oppose every manifestation of 'great-power' chauvinism... *

---

* Quotes are from the joint "New Year Editorial" (*People's Daily, Red Flag,* and *Liberation Daily*) of 1970 and 1972. Wang Hung-wen's remarks are from his "Report on the Revision of the Party Constitution" at the Tenth National Party Congress, August 24, 1973. See: *Documents of the Tenth National Congress of the Chinese Communist Party* (Peking, 1973).

By mid-1972 Chinese leaders were talking openly about Lin Piao with foreign visitors. However, Lin was still not criticized by name in China's public media. This did not happen until the Tenth National Party Congress in August 1973.

(6) *Lin Piao the traitor.* China's internal analysis of the Lin Piao affair culminated with the Tenth National Party Congress in late August 1973. There Lin Piao was finally denounced openly, by name. And what a denunciation! In shrill rhetoric typical of Chinese politics, Lin was labeled a "bourgeois careerist, conspirator, double-dealer, renegade and traitor."

Chou En-lai delivered a report to the Tenth Party Congress which summarized the charges against Lin Piao. Chou reviewed events at the previous (1969) Ninth Party Congress and said that Lin had then supported a new form of Liu Shao-chi's political line. Chou also outlined Lin's attempts to seize power by scheming in August 1970, and by armed coup in September 1971. Chou contended that Lin's ambition grew over the years with his rise in position and that "he wanted to have everything under his command."

Chou also charged that for a period of time Lin had impaired the Party's traditional work style of "seeking truth from facts," "following the mass line," and of "modesty, prudence and hard work." Lin and "his handful of sworn followers," Chou asserted, eulogized Mao to the extreme, "never opened their mouths without shouting 'Long Live!'," and "spoke nice things to your face but stabbed you in the back."

Chou claimed that inside China Lin's faction represented the political interests of the "landlord and bourgeois classes" and internationally they "wanted to capitulate to Soviet revisionist social-imperialism and ally themselves with imperialism." Lin, Chou said, was a "super-spy."

Historically, Chou asserted, Lin Piao had engaged in "machinations within our Party" for decades, always committing "Right opportunist errors" and invariably playing "double-faced tricks."

Chou also refuted Lin's political line, stating: "We are still in the era of imperialism and the proletarian revolution" and "the fundamental principles of Leninism are not outdated." Finally, Chou urged Party members to study Marx, Engels, Lenin, and Stalin, as well as the work of Mao Tse-tung, and called for the training of "millions of successors."

Wang Hung-wen delivered a report to the Tenth Party Congress about revision of the Party Constitution. The paragraph concerning Lin Piao as Mao's "successor" was dropped; Wang stated frankly this deletion was "the inevitable result of Lin Piao's betrayal of the Party and the country and his own final rejection of the Party and the people."

There were other significant revisions in the Party Constitution. Formalism concerning Mao and Mao Tse-tung Thought was largely eliminated, along with the ultra-left characterization of the present era as one "in which imperialism is heading for total collapse and socialism is advancing to worldwide victory." New additions to the 1973 Constitution emphasized democracy within the Party ranks. One notable addition stated: "It is absolutely impermissible to suppress criticism and to retaliate."

The Tenth Party Congress represented a political summation of Lin's past political role. Since then some of the charges against Lin have been expanded or amplified. For example, Lin has been accused of promoting anti-trade union policies under the slogan "for workers, to work well means politics." This, critics charge, meant Lin wanted workers to bury themselves in details of production and not participate in politics. Furthermore, Lin is accused of opposing educated youth going to the countryside, having called the practice "reform through forced labour." More details have been added to claims that Lin "schemed within the Party for decades" and took a "Right opportunist" turn at every important point in the Party's history. It has also been argued that Lin slandered the socialist achievements of the Chinese people by "raining curses" from a "reactionary stand" and describing "the excellent situation at home as being quite hopeless."

In China, Lin Piao has become an infamous political symbol. His political career lives on; it will continue as a teacher by "negative example." Lin Piao's career will illustrate for decades to come different forms that the struggle between the two lines can take. It will represent the constant political danger, and the ultimate futility, of making "Left" and Right errors.

It is instructive to look at how the Chinese have dealt with the whole Lin Piao affair. Such degeneration on the part of one of their oldest and most respected leaders certainly had to send political shockwaves through the whole society. How could such a thing have happened? China's millions sought answers to this question through a multistaged process. First, they launched a period of investigation and internal discussion, aimed at finding out exactly *what* had happened and what it represented politically. Following this, they evaluated the political message of this investigation, analyzing and criticizing the specific political form Lin Piao had taken (ultra-leftism). As their analysis progressed they came more and more to emphasize the Right "essence" of Lin Piao's ultra-left form. This, in turn, led them to look for the roots of Lin Piao's policies, to unearth the underlying philsophical concepts. And here the ghost of Confucius appeared. Lin Piao, the Chinese discovered, had adhered closely to many ancient Confucian principles, concealing reactionary feudal concepts within his revolutionary-sounding thetoric. Thus, the campaign to "Criticize Lin Piao and Confucius" blossomed forth, representing a logical continuation of the society-wide effort to understand the meaning, the form, and the *roots* of the Lin Piao affair.

More Cultural Revolutions?

Will such upheavals as the Cultural Revolution and the Lin Piao affair happen again?

Certainly.

At the time of the Ninth Party Congress in 1969 it was pointed out "there still exists . . . interference from the 'Left' or the Right." Few of us then realized the degree of truth to that statement. Now, after the Lin Piao affair has run its course, we know the comment was more a description than a prophesy.

At the time of the Tenth Party Congress in 1973 it was stated "such struggles will occur ten, twenty, or thirty times. Lin Piaos will appear again . . ." We believe it. If you look you can see important political struggles going on in China right now. Today. And tomorrow.

The Chinese perceive these struggles as an inevitable reflection of the competition between their old and new societies. Or, as they would put it, the inevitable reflection of the continuing class struggle, the "struggle between the two lines."

They are preparing themselves for future battles. A significant movement to study the philosophical works of Marx, Engels, Lenin, and Stalin, as well as Mao, has spread across China since the Lin Piao affair. Workers and peasants are biting into such heavy theoretical writings as Marx's "Critique of the Gotha Program," Engels' "Anti-Dühring," and Lenin's "Materialism and Empirio-Criticism." They are determined, they state, to equip themselves to distinguish genuine from sham Marxism.

They argue that the roots of the bourgeois line, of both Right and "Left" errors, lie in the philosophical perspective known as idealism. They say idealism is a philosophy which deduces reality from abstract concepts. It is opposed to materialism, which understands reality from experience, from practice. In the struggle for socialism errors arise when one loses sight of reality—when abstract desires take command of practice. If theory is deduced from the abstract, from what one *thinks* instead of what *is*, then Marxism becomes a sham. It is transformed into metaphysics which bears little resemblance to genuine materialism.

"Where do correct ideas come from?" Mao asks. "Do they drop from the skies?"

No, he answers: The Marxist perspective is materialist and knowledge comes from practice. Understanding this, the Chinese argue, is key to understanding the struggle between the two lines. This is how to distinguish both "Left" and Right deviations from the correct road to socialism. This is how to be prepared for the inevitable political struggles of the future.

11
Of China and Mao Tse-tung

The air-conditioned railroad coach provided welcome relief from South China's sticky heat. It was also our return link to Hong Kong. The landscape outside was as it had been when we entered China, fertile and lush. And we were again preoccupied as green-brown patches flashed past the train window. In contrast to our lively discussion when we made this trip coming north, we now sat quietly, mulling over events of the previous seven weeks. Zheng smiled at us from across the aisle. He playfully teased three lively little girls, the young daughters of Italian diplomats, who darted, giggling, up and down the car.

Again and again our thoughts turned to the one aspect of China which has impressed virtually every Western visitor: the presence of Mao everywhere, in pictures, statues, wall posters, quotations, music, and badges and lapel pins worn by people the country over. This "personality cult," as some have called it, had provoked several questions on our part. We recalled a conversation in Peking.

"Each class must have its own Party and leaders," Xi Jin-huan had asserted. "My own feeling is that there is not a personality cult regarding Chairman Mao. People who say there is a personality cult don't know much about China."

Xi, and Lao Liu, both argued Mao's leadership was inseparable from the new China. Any question of personality cult had to be considered in light of Mao's actual political role over the years. They pointed out history shows that when Mao's leadership was followed the revolutionary struggle advanced. When Mao was ignored it suffered setbacks. They ticked off four decades of examples, beginning in the late 1920s and continuing up to the present. Mao's leadership, they contended, had been responsible for the vast improvement in the lives of millions brought by Liberation. Thus Mao's crucial role in the success of China's revolution was the base for the genuine love and respect for him we saw throughout China. People put up pictures of Mao, sang songs of praise, and erected statues because *they* wanted to, not because Mao promoted a cult of personality.

We thought back to our many visits. Most vivid, perhaps, had been the peasant near Xian who thrust his notebook under our noses to prove he could now read and write. "This is from Chairman Mao!" he had declared almost defiantly, tears running down his face.

It is not relevant whether Western dilettantes scoff at this declaration. The point is that masses of Chinese people *do* feel this way. Before they had starved; now they eat. Before they were illiterate; now they read. Thus, much of what some call a personality cult is the outward manifestation of a genuine and materially based love for Mao Tse-tung.

There are additional factors to be weighed in the personality cult question. During the Cultural Revolution Mao's writings, and his quotations, took on specific political meaning. Promoting Mao Tse-tung Thought was less the adoration of a man than it was one form of struggle for a political line. "Before the Cultural Revolution," Lao Liu remarked, "we couldn't propagate Mao Tse-tung Thought due to the influence of the Liu Shao-chi revisionist line. So now we give Mao's thought prominence. Specific forms were used at specific periods of time."

Mao as the political figure, as the representative of a political position: that was another meaning behind the songs, signs, statues, posters, and lapel pins. Lao Liu also noted: "The Party has said it is not appropriate to stress the role of the individual. For example, a Party resolution just before

Liberation forbade streets to be named after leaders. No birthdays of leaders were to be celebrated. None are. No cities or streets are named for Mao."*

Although the 1949 resolution forbade celebration of leaders' birthdays, there seems to have been a bit of fudging in that regard. Calendars circulated during the Cultural Revolution by Guozi Shudian (China Publications Center) noted: "December 26, 1893, is the birthdate of our great leader Chairman Mao" and printed the date in red, a contrast to the everyday black numerals. This special treatment, however, was conspicuously absent in 1973 and 1974 calendars.

The historical and political context established, Lao Liu and Xi then dealt with the negative side of the question. They acknowledged that politics had sometimes slipped into adoration, respect into worship.

"Much propaganda has gone beyond Mao's wishes," Xi asserted. He asked if we had read Mao's 1971 interview with Edgar Snow.** Xi reminded us that Mao had told Snow that the personality cult, while meeting particular political needs at one time, had been overdone. Mao specifically ridiculed the "four greats" and the proliferation of pictures and plaster statues. Snow also mentioned that the only Chinese officials he met during this 1971 trip who did not wear Mao badges were the secretary and translator sitting in on this direct interview with Mao.

We heard another story about Mao badges. Mao, upon entering the Great Hall of the People at the Ninth Party Congress in 1969, confronted a sea of Mao buttons and lapel pins. It is reported that Mao declared he wanted his "air-

---

* Lao Liu was referring to a 1949 Central Committee resolution adopted at Mao's own suggestion. It is interesting to compare this with practices in the Soviet Union during the corresponding period after the success of their revolution. There several cities and districts were named after living revolutionaries, particularly Stalin.

** Snow interviewed Mao in December 1971. The interview was published in the United States in *Life*, April 30, 1972, and later in Snow's last book, *The Long Revolution*. We were told that a Chinese-language version of the book was also circulated throughout China.

planes back." Evidently he felt the metal used on the thousands of lapel pins could have been put to more practical use.*

Although we saw Mao badges worn throughout China, we also saw many unadorned lapels. Badges and pins could be purchased in stores alongside Mao's pictures, woven silk portraits, and other memorabilia. Several people told us they wore the badges to show their respect and love for Mao. But, they added, displaying a badge no longer played the specific political role it once had. There was no longer any social pressure to have lapels politically decorated.

Another aspect of the question of whether there is a Mao Tse-tung personality cult is its cultural context. In our opinion this is of considerable import. We doubt any individual will ever be publicly admired in the United States the way Mao is in China—even in the unlikely event someone equals Mao's degree of popularity. The United States does not have a three-thousand-year legacy of emperor worship. China does. For example, Edgar Snow was once told that in the early 1950s it had been necessary to post guards in front of the main reviewing stands during National Day celebrations. The guards, he learned, were there to stop peasants from prostrating themselves before the new leaders in the traditional head-to-ground kow-tow.**

Mao's role in the course of China's history and his impact upon the lives of millions are probably unparalleled anywhere, anytime. Teacher, guerrilla, military commander, philosopher, theorist, writer, strategist, political and party leader: Mao has been all. Indeed, as Xi and Lao Liu asserted, his role has been inseparable from new China.

Yet the Chinese also consider Mao a product of that which he helped create. He represents a unique synthesis of their aspirations, their determination to shake off centuries of

---

* This story has apparently made the rounds among various visitors to China. Han Suyin has included it in her latest book, *The Morning Deluge* (Boston: Little Brown, 1972), p. 383.

** Snow, *The Long Revolution*, p. 69.

oppression and poverty. Those things which shaped China also shaped Mao. Mao was midwife to new China; but China also begat Mao.

The East is Red.

So runs a line of one of China's most famous revolutionary songs. It continues:

Rises the sun,
China has brought forth a Mao Tse-tung.

China, its people, its culture, rose to meet the circumstances of its historic situation. China, its people, its culture, brought forth a leader. As much as new China reflects Mao's unique role, so does Mao belong to new China.

On the Guangzhou-Hong Kong train we recalled other personal glimpses of that vast totality known as China. A kaleidoscope of images rolled past:

• We remembered the evening in the Guangzhou park when Zheng tried unsuccessfully to talk with a little girl. His northern speech and her southern dialect had been so different neither could understand the other.

• We chuckled again at An Wei's humor. A local guide in Yenan, An Wei delighted in telling jokes. A favorite involved an imaginary meeting between Chou En-lai and Khrushchev, when the latter had been Soviet Premier. Khrushchev, it seemed, tried to ridicule Chou's class background. "We two have only one thing in common," Mr. K. declared. "We are both Premiers of our respective countries. But we are actually quite different because I come from a working-class background and you come from a bourgeois background." Chou reportedly rejoined: "No, Khrushchev, you're wrong. We have one more thing in common. We're both traitors to our class!"

• There had been the sales clerks turned construction workers in Tianjin's largest department store. We had watched them working on a multistoried addition to their building. This was their application of the principle of self-reliance.

• There were also the many foreign visitors we met

throughout China: Italians, Norwegians, Palestinians, Mexicans, Australians, Vietnamese, Canadians, Africans from several countries, Japanese, Koreans, Cubans, Yugoslavs, Ceylonese (Sri Lanka), and fellow Americans.

• We will never forget the workers at a textile printing and dyeing factory who gave us a unique keepsake. We told them many Westerners claimed all Chinese wore drab blue or gray clothing. They laughed uproariously and then presented us with cotton fabric sample books illustrating dozens of patterns and designs. "Take these home," they offered good-naturedly. "Show the American people what is worn in China!"

There was also much we had missed. Our book reflects these omissions. Any visitor to China returns somewhat in the position of the proverbial blind men describing the elephant. Our primary interests—workplaces and ideology—determined what we emphasized in our visits. We felt they struck to the heart of the society. But we could not take in everything. For example, we have not reported on the astounding technical and social advances made in the health care and medical fields. Similarly, we have slighted the People's Liberation Army, undoubtedly one of the most important institutions in China. Other important topics not included are: the neighborhood and street committees (organizations important in the daily life of all city residents); overall aspects of economic planning and production in China's socialist economy; or the whole area of China's foreign policy, a topic understandably on the minds of many Americans today.

We knew our visit was really ending when the train arrived at the familiar surroundings of the Shumchum border station—familiar because we had entered China here. But now everything seemed to be in reverse. Zheng accompanied us as we passed quickly and summarily through customs. Before we were really aware of it we'd walked the length of the long reception building and faced the covered bridge to Hong Kong.

Parting with Zheng was genuinely difficult. We now discovered how deep a comradeship we'd developed. He embraced both of us and we turned and walked away, sad and silent, afraid to turn around because we were fighting back tears. When we did look back Zheng waved a final good-bye and raised his fist in salute. We returned the signal and walked across that narrow stream which now was the widest river in the world.

Coming back did make it seem a different world, but one that was all too familiar. We were immediately surrounded by hawkers selling pop, candy, and trinkets at inflated prices. They were followed by child beggars who made a pretense of selling ragged copies of yesterday's newspapers they had obviously scavenged. The papers carried news of a public campaign under way in Hong Kong against bribing officials. "It is a crime to offer or accept a bribe" was the slogan. Another story, titled "Girl Saved from Brothel by Soap Box," told of "a pretty teenaged girl" who escaped kidnappers by throwing a soap box out a window to attract help. The kidnappers had held her captive, raped her, and planned to sell her to a brothel.

Welcome home.

Since our return to the United States we have spoken to many people about China. We find Americans are very curious. There is genuine interest in discovering what is actually happening in new China. We believe the recent increased contacts between the peoples of our two countries—our trip is but one small example—have contributed positively toward mutual friendship. For twenty years United States government Cold War policy has kept the Chinese and American peoples apart. Incredible distortions about People's China have been a regular part of our mass media. But America, by necessity, is now removing its blinders, opening its eyes. And it is discovering a China that has been there all along.

In our opinion there are still many popular misconceptions about China. Some old stereotypes are being destroyed, such as charges that the Chinese people are starving or that they are herded into concentration camps. But others remain and new myths are being constructed—such as assertions that the

Chinese people have no freedom; that they are regimented; that they cannot disagree with their government; and that they live drab, dull lives.

But why is there such interest in a nation half a world away?

The answer is China's socialism. China attracts the attention of the world precisely because it is building a bold new socialist society. The rest of the world cannot look the other way, whatever its opinion. Some, the beneficiaries of our status quo, see China as a challenge, a threat. Others, looking at our problems, view China as an inspiration, an example, a hope. Of course China is neither evil incarnate nor a panacea. China is complex, varied, and diverse. New China has both strengths and weaknesses. The tremendous strides taken during the past twenty years speak for themselves. But China's most distinguishing feature—its most fundamental and revolutionary feat—is its continuing struggle to construct a society based on people, not profit; a society motivated by cooperation, not competition. In today's world this not only attracts attention. It commands attention.

Appendix

Part I: Romanization

There are several different and complex systems for transliterating Chinese sounds into romanized letters and words. We have chosen to use the system devised by the Chinese themselves, called "pin yin," or the Chinese Phonetic Alphabet.

The basic alphabet is as follows:*

pin yin	key	pin yin	key
b	*b*ed (voiceless)	t	*t*ea
c	ha*ts*	w	*w*ay
d	*d*ay (voiceless)	x	*sh*ip
f	*f*an	y	*y*ou
g	*g*ay (voiceless)	z	rea*ds* (voiceless)
h	*h*ard	ch	chur*ch*
j	*j*eer	sh	*sh*irt
k	*k*eep	zh	ju*dge*
l	*l*aw		
m	*m*an	a	f*a*ther
n	*n*o	e	h*er* (British)
p	*p*eak	i	s*ee*

* This table is taken from one printed in *China Reconstructs*, July 1972.

395

q	*ch*eer	o	*saw*
r	lei*s*ure	u	r*u*de
s	*s*ound	ü	German ü (*i* pronounced with lips rounded)

If you wish to investigate further, we suggest:

(1) *Elementary Chinese*, Parts I and II, published in Peking as a text for English-speaking students to learn Chinese. It is available with tapes and may be ordered from: China Books and Periodicals, 2929 Twenty-fourth St., San Francisco, California 94110.

(2) A brief layman's explanation of the pin yin system may be found in the introduction to *China! Inside the People's Republic*, by the Committee of Concerned Asian Scholars (Bantam Books).

(3) Pin yin is used in the Chinese language series by John DeFrancis, *Beginning Chinese* (and related readers), published by Yale University Press, New Haven, Connecticut.

(4) Finally, there is a good Chinese-to-English dictionary available which explains and employs the pin yin system. It is *A Modern Chinese-English Dictionary for Students*, by C. C. Huang, published by the Center for East Asian Studies, University of Kansas, Lawrence, Kansas.

Pin yin is probably the most consistent and least confusing of the various systems for romanization of Chinese sounds. It is a system which the Chinese have developed and is the one they now use for most translation work. However, because other romanization systems had been used for many years, there are several names and terms which are not generally transliterated into pin yin, even by the Chinese. For example, Mao Tse-tung in pin yin is correctly transliterated as Mao Ze-dong. To avoid confusion we have used the older romanization for the following well-known names:

Form used:	*pin yin:*	*Form used:*	*pin yin:*
Mao Tse-tung	Mao Ze-dong	Peking	Beijing
Chou En-lai	Zhou En-lai	Yenan	Yan-an

Liu Shao-chi	Liu Shao-qi
Lin Piao	Lin Biao
Chiang Kai-shek	Jiang Jie-shi
Kuomintang	Guomindang
Chungking	Chongqing
Tachai	Dazhai
Taching	Dajing

In other cases where there might be confusion we have indicated transliterations in both pin yin and the older romanization system.

Part II: A Table of Typical Prices

The following list shows typical prices for consumer goods which we found in stores throughout China. All prices are given in the Chinese yuan. One yuan equals 100 fen. In terms of exchange, 1 yuan equals approximately $ .50 U.S.

The average monthly salary for Chinese workers was about 50 to 60 yuan. Spendable income for peasants in communes was generally a bit less. Families usually had two or three wage-earners in the household. Rent typically equaled about 5 percent of a family's total income, and health and education were 1 percent or less. There were no personal income taxes.

Food	Yuan
rice, per jin	.18
flour, per jin	.18
wheat, per jin	.15
fresh pork, per jin	.90
eggs, per jin	.90
cooked boneless ham, per jin	1.40
fresh vegetables, per jin	.08-.20
apples (varies by season, April price), per jin	.38-.47
assorted sausages, meats, per jin	.85-2.00
loose tea, per jin	6.00
canned pears, per can	.75
tomato paste, 20 oz. can	1.43
shrimp chips, box	.68
raisin and nut pastry, each	.10-.15
20 large sugar cookies	3.00
assorted cookies, each	.08
ice cream on a stick	.05-.15
mild wine (about 1 liter)	1.75
60 proof wine (about 1 liter)	3.98
hard candy, per jin	1.30-1.50

Dining Hall Prices

steamed bread, large piece	.03
flat bread	.01
vegetables, per bowl	.02–.03
soup	.08
fried cakes	.05
cooked chicken, per jin	1.00
cup tea	.01
simple restaurant meal	.10–.15

Clothing

leather shoes	6.00–9.00
ballet shoes	4.00
fur-lined boots	9.00–21.00
rubber thongs	2.71
plastic sandals	3.00
tennis shoes	4.00–5.00
sneakers	3.00–4.00
suede "desert boots"	14.00–16.00
sweater type jacket	4.58–6.00
knit sweater	16.67–20.00
gym shorts	1.60
man's undershirt	2.70
socks	.90–1.00
woman's short-sleeve blouse	3.50–9.00
woman's heavy long-sleeve shirt	4.50–7.00
woman's slacks	4.99
woman's silk & nylon jacket	16.90
man's wool slacks	25.00
man's cotton slacks	5.48
man's cotton jacket	6.62
straw hats	.60–1.20
cotton cloth, per meter	.41
corduroy cloth, per meter	1.24
rent sewing machine, per hour	.04
(pattern cutting & marking service available for a few fen)	
fur coat (fox)	400.00–500.00
jacket (cat hair)	70.00

Household Items

thermos bottle	4.00–6.00
replacement filler	1.00
painted enamel cups	1.04
tea box (storage)	2.48
27-piece porcelain tea set	32.00
large dresser	46.00
wood wardrobe	62.50
alarm clock	16.30
colored sheets	6.00–11.00
towels	.64–1.00
heavy wool blanket	53.00
artificial silk quilt cover	9.43
wall hanging (carpet size)	7.50
fluorescent lamp	12.76
sewing machine, footpedal	116.00–120.00
3-band table radio	120.00–150.00
portable 3-band radio	111.00
long-wave portable radio	50.00
toothpaste	.09

Children

glass baby bottle	.38
infant's shoes	.38–1.00
stuffed toys	.40–.60
small dolls	.84
wind-up toy motorcycle	2.24
toy truck	1.86
child's cap	.60–.90

Recreation

small plastic records, each	.30
4 or 5 record set, Peking Opera	12.00
soccer ball	5.70–10.80
basketball	11.00, 20.00–21.60
ping-pong paddle	1.68
pi-ba (large stringed instrument)	82.30
er-hu (2-stringed fiddle)	22.00
hu-chin (smaller fiddle)	2.50
theater tickets	.20–.40
use of baths at hot springs, 40 minutes	.20–.40
admission to Wuhan's East Lake Park	.05
admission to Guangzhou's Cultural Park	day .03
	night .08
large tape recorder	680.00
television	400.00

Transportation

bicycle	135.00
Wuhan (to and from work):	
1 month bus ticket	1.50
1 month trolley ticket	1.00
3 month train ticket	.50

Other

camera (44mm lens, rangefinder)	120.00
film, 12 exposures, including developing	2.00–3.00
notebooks and notepads	.10–.40
watches, good quality	100.00–200.00
metal watch band	2.76
leather watch band	1.15
magnifying eyeglasses	3.00
sunglasses	2.27–3.00
large set of calipers	20.00
calculator machine	558.00
bamboo umbrellas	2.00
cloth umbrellas	2.00–9.00
megaphone (bullhorn)	113.00
haircut	.30–.50
cigarettes, pack	.16–.50
small hand-carved vase	1.68
large vase (art object)	870.00
small jade carvings (rings)	1.00

1 jin equals 1.1 lbs

Part III:
Notes on Members of the
Tenth Central Committee of the Chinese Communist Party

The following in no way represents an all-inclusive listing of China's top leaders. There are many significant leaders outside the Party's Central Committee, such as government ministers, leaders of the National People's Congress, and leaders in the trade union, women's federation, and other mass organizations. The members of the Central Committee noted here have been selected with the sole intention of illustrating the various ages and backgrounds represented on the Central Committee.

Full Members:

(The first four, plus Chou En-lai, comprise the five vice-chairmen of the Tenth Central Committee. Mao Tse-tung is the Chairman.)

Kang Sheng is a veteran revolutionary whose activities date back to Shanghai in the mid-1920s. He has often been active in cultural matters, has held many Party posts over the years, and was an active supporter of Mao in the Cultural Revolution.

Li Teh-sheng (Li De-sheng)* is a veteran army commander and a Party cadre. He has been in charge of the army's General Political Department.

Yeh Chien-ying (Ye Jian-ying), also an old revolutionary, joined the Chinese Communist Party in 1924 and was a commander in the Red Army by 1928. A veteran of the Long March, Yeh has served in top military and Party posts.

Wang Hung-wen (Wang Hong-wen), in his mid-thirties, is the youngest of the fine vice-chairmen of the Tenth Central Committee. Wang, a demobilized PLA soldier, served as a local-level cadre in Shanghai's No. 17 Cotton Mill before the Cultural Revolution. He rose to leadership during the Cultural Revolution as one of the first organizers of Shanghai's Workers' Headquarters, the group which toppled the Liu Shao-chi authorities in the city. Wang was a member of the Ninth Central Committee (1969) and was selected as a vice-chairman at the Tenth.

Chang Chun-chiao (Zhang Chung-qiao) was elected as Secretary-General of the Presidium of the Tenth National Party Congress in 1973. Chang, formerly a Party leader in Shanghai, also rose to national prominence during the Cultural Revolution as one of the principal leaders of the Shanghai Workers' Headquarters. He served both on the Ninth and Tenth Central Committees.

---

* Names are spelled here as they appeared in English-language documents from China; pin yin romanization follows in parentheses where it is different. Although pin yin is being adopted as the official system of romanization, the Chinese still use the older Wade-Giles romanization system for many names.

Tsai Chang (Cai Chang) is a leading woman cadre of the older generation, active since student days in the 1920s. She is one of the few women veterans of the Long March and was Chairman of the All-China Women's Federation in 1949. She was an active supporter of Mao's forces during the Cultural Revolution.

Teng Ying-chao (Deng Ying-chao) is also a veteran woman leader. She was active in the May 4th Movement in 1919, joined the Communist Party in its early days, and made the trek of the Long March. She has been a top leader in the Women's Federation, and was the first elected to the Central Committee in 1928.

Chiang Ching (Jiang Qing) is one of the principal advocates of the new revolutionary theater and opera. She had gone to Yenan in the mid-1930s as a young actress, and there met and married Mao Tse-tung. She has been active in cultural affairs through the years but rose to prominence and national leadership during the Cultural Revolution. She was first elected to the Central Committee in 1969.

Lu Yu-lan is a young (born in 1940) peasant leader. She was elected head of a cooperative at the age of fifteen and led struggles to build cooperatives and people's communes. She has also been active in training women revolutionary cadres.

Chu Teh (Zhu De) is one of the oldest veterans of China's revolutionary struggles. Military commander of the Red Army when it was formed in the late 1920s, Chu fought alongside Mao for decades. He is a member of the Political Bureau of the Tenth Central Committee.

Yao Wen-yuan is another young leader who has emerged from the Cultural Revolution. A Shanghai journalist, Yao authored an essay criticizing cultural trends in late 1965. It was one of the first salvos of the Cultural Revolution. Yao is a member of the Political Bureau of the Tenth Central Committee.

Keng Chi-chang (Geng Qi-chang) was a Henan regional cadre who in 1958 had been attacked by Liu Shao-chi forces as a "Right deviationist" because of his opposition to policies which were wrecking the newly established people's communes. He became an active leader in the Cultural Revolution and was elected to both the Ninth and Tenth Central Committees.

Chi Teng-kui (Ji Deng-kui), also from Henan, is well known for playing a leading role in the Cultural Revolution there.

Chen Yung-kuei (Zhen Yong-gui), a former poor peasant and former Party Secretary of the Tachai Brigade, had fought against Liu Shao-chi agricultural policies for over a decade. He was elected to the Political Bureau of the Tenth Central Committee.

Wang Kuo-fan (Wang Guo-fan) was an organizer of a "beggars' cooperative" during the early 1950s. He served on both the Ninth and Tenth Central Committees.

Wei Feng-ying was a beggar before Liberation and later became an outstanding worker in a Shenyang factory. She was a leading rebel during the Cultural Revolution and became a member of Shenyang's Revolutionary Committee. She is a punching machine operator.

Li Su-wen is a grocer's assistant from Shenyang. She has won national recognition for her dedication and service to the people.

Tang Chi-shan (Tang Qi-shan) was, in 1969, the Chairman of the Peking Red Guard Congress. He has served on both the Ninth and Tenth Central Committees.

Wei Kuo-ching (Wei Guo-qing) is a leader of the Zhuang minority and a political leader in the Guangxi-Zhuang Autonomous Region.

Wu Kuei-hsien (Wu Gui-xian) is a woman textile worker from Xian. A member of the Ninth Central Committee, she became an alternate member of the Political Bureau of the Tenth Central Committee.

Saifudan is head of the Xinjiang Autonomous Region's Revolutionary Committee and Party Secretary for that region. A member of the Ninth and Tenth Central Committees, he was also selected as an alternate member of the Political Bureau at the Tenth.

Ni Chih-fu (Ni Zhi-fu) is a Peking worker, a drilling

machine operator turned engineer. He has designed a new type of high-speed, top-quality and long-service drill bit. He is active in trade union activities and has published articles on the study of philosophy.

Hsing Yen-tzu (Xing Yan-zi), in her early thirties, is an educated youth who has settled in the countryside; she is a full member of the Tenth Central Committee. Her father had become deputy head of a Tianjin factory, but at the age of eighteen, Hsing returned to her home village. She became a local leader and was active in the Cultural Revolution.

Pa Sang (Ba Sang) is from Tibet. She is a graduate of the Institute for Nationalities in Tibet and is Secretary of the Party Committee of the Tibet Autonomous Region.

Chuang Tse-tung (Chuang Ze-dong) is one of the outstanding table-tennis players in the world. His sports activities took on diplomatic overtones in the era of ping-pong diplomacy. He has headed traveling Chinese table-tennis delegations, including the one which visited the United States in 1972.

Huang Hua traces his revolutionary activity back to student days in the 1930s. He has spent much of his life in diplomatic service and most recently has been one of China's main spokesmen at the United Nations.

Chiao Kuan-hua (Qiao Guan-hua) has a background of extensive experience in diplomatic affairs. He was one of China's spokesmen at United Nations discussions during the Korean War in the early 1950s. He is now Deputy Foreign Minister and in 1971 became head of the Chinese delegation to the United Nations.

Huang Chen (Huang Zhen) is a veteran peasant revolutionary. A Central Committee member of both the Ninth and Tenth Central Committees, he has also recently served as head of the Chinese Liaison Office in Washington, D.C.

Kuo Mo-jo (Guo Mo-ruo) is one of China's oldest and most respected intellectuals. Over eighty years old, Kuo has a distinguished history of literary and historical criticism and was active in the Cultural Revolution.

Chi Peng-fei (Ji Peng-fei) became China's Foreign Minister in early 1972. He had earlier served as acting Foreign Minister for a period following Chen Yi's suspension from that office during the Cultural Revolution.

Teng Hsiao-ping (Deng Xiao-ping) and *Tan Chen-lin* (Tan Zhen-lin) are both veteran Party leaders. They were both criticized as "capitalist roaders" during the Cultural Revolution and were excluded from the Ninth (1969) Central Committee. Both have recently returned to public political activity and were elected to the Tenth Central Committee.

Ulanfu (Wulanfu), a Party leader in Inner Mongolia, was also criticized heavily during the Cultural Revolution. His selection to the Tenth Central Committee marked a return to public political leadership.

Li Chiang (Li Qiang), a member of both the Ninth and Tenth Central Committees, recently took charge of the Foreign Trade Ministry. He has an extensive background in the foreign trade field, was a radio and telecommunications specialist, and during the 1960s was active in trade relations with Eastern Europe and North Korea and North Vietnam.

Alternate Members:

Tang Wen-sheng is in her early thirties. Known in the West as Nancy Tang, she is one of the principal English translators who accompany Mao and Chou En-lai during diplomatic meetings. She was selected as an alternate Central Committee member at the Tenth Party Congress.

Yang Kuei (Yang Gui) is a young cadre from Linxian County, Henan Province, site of the famous Red Flag Canal. He is an alternate member of the Tenth Central Committee.

Chu Ke-chia (Zhu Ke-jia) is an educated youth who has settled in the countryside.

Ta Lo (Da Lou; also transliterated as Ta Leh) is a graduate of the Central Institute for Nationalities. He was an alternate member of the Ninth Central Committee, as well as the Tenth, and also serves as a Deputy Secretary of the Qinghai Provincial Committee of the Communist Party.

Ma Ming became an alternate member of the Tenth Central Committee. He is the leader of a well-known work team at the Longyen Iron Mine in Hebei Province.